# THE LOEB CLASSICAL LIBRARY

FOUNDED BY JAMES LOEB

EDITED BY

## G. P. GOOLD

PREVIOUS EDITORS

# EURIPIDES

# III

LCL 9

# EURIPIDES

## SUPPLIANT WOMEN
## ELECTRA · HERACLES

EDITED AND TRANSLATED BY

DAVID KOVACS

HARVARD UNIVERSITY PRESS
CAMBRIDGE, MASSACHUSETTS
LONDON, ENGLAND
1998

*Library of Congress Cataloging-in-Publication Data*

Euripides.
  Suppliant women; Electra; Heracles / Euripides; edited
and translated by David Kovacs.
    p.  cm.—(The Loeb classical library; L9)
  Greek and English.
  Includes bibliographical references and index.
  ISBN 0-674-99566-X (alk. paper)
  1. Euripides—Translations into English. 2. Greek drama
(Tragedy)—Translations into English. 3. Mythology,
Greek—Drama. I. Kovacs, David. II. Title. III. Series: Loeb
classical library; 9.
PA3975.A2    1998
882'.01—dc21                              97-36082

# CONTENTS

For Ellen

# PREFACE

This volume, like its two predecessors, presents a new Greek text as well as a new translation. For an explanation of my editorial principles and of the simplified system for reporting manuscript readings, see the general introduction in Volume One. I have discussed in my *Euripidea Altera* (Leiden, 1996) some of the readings and conjectures adopted here. Readers unfamiliar with the conventions of classical editing should note that text (whether Greek or English) enclosed between square brackets is deemed to be spurious. Angle brackets mark words or lines thought to have been accidentally omitted by copyists. As in previous volumes, where I have marked a lacuna of a line or more I have usually filled in, purely by way of illustration, what the sense seems to require. Unattributed supplements are my own.

The translation contains one new departure from the practice of previous volumes: the treatment of lyric verse, those parts of the plays that were sung in the original performance. I have marked passages as lyric by translating them line-for-line to match the Greek in contrast to the prose typography I use for spoken verse.

I have received help of various kinds that I am delighted to acknowledge here. A grant from the Division of Research of the National Endowment for the Humanities, an independent federal agency, enabled me to devote half of my time in the two academic years 1990-92 to this volume and its predecessor. In 1996-97 I received a second such grant to work on this volume and its successor. I am grateful to the Endowment for its support of my work. I was also elected, for that year, to a Visiting Fellowship at Balliol College, Oxford. My thanks to the Master and Fellows for their splendid hospitality. An exchange program between the University of Virginia and the Terza Univerisità di Roma enabled me to check manuscript readings in the Vatican Library.

Several people discussed textual problems with me or criticized my translation. I have had profitable discussions with Martin West, James Diggle, Charles Willink, Jasper Griffin, and Chris Collard. George Goold's criticisms and queries have been invaluable, and he, Philippa Goold, and Margaretta Fulton have all improved the English translation. Finally, my wife supplied advice and encouragement at crucial points.

This volume carries a proud father's dedication to his daughter, to whose growing love of the theater he hopes it will contribute.

David Kovacs

University of Virginia

# SUPPLIANT WOMEN

# ABBREVIATIONS

# INTRODUCTION

*Suppliant Women*, like *Children of Heracles*, mirrors the political realities of its day. It belongs to the late 420s B.C., perhaps being produced in 423, and is full of reflection on democracy and autocracy, the rule of law, and the undesirability—or necessity—of going to war. The action centers on the right of the dead to a proper burial, an issue that was a live one in the aftermath of the battle of Delium (424), when the victorious Boeotians refused the defeated Athenians permission to take up their dead. Contemporary theological reflection also comes to the fore in a debate about whether the gods govern the world with man's interest in mind and man has only himself to blame for trouble, or whether there is an element of tragedy in human life because of divine malice or indifference.

A fragment of ancient literary criticism, preserved in our only manuscript, says "The play is an encomium of Athens." It is true that in Attic tragedy Athens and Athenians are almost always sympathetically portrayed. But patriotic fervor alone does not explain why this play has been constructed as it has. The theological issues seem to make the largest and most encompassing frame for what is here, though it must be admitted that it is hard to be sure how the first audience reacted to some speeches or scenes and what contribution they make to the whole. The following

3

is a tentative attempt to describe the action and issues of the play.

In all versions of the legend of Thebes' dynasty the two sons of Oedipus, Eteocles and Polynices, kill each other in battle as the result of their father's curse that they would "divide their inheritance with the sword." Polynices, in exile in Argos, appeals for help against his brother and together with six Argive champions mounts the expedition of the Seven Against Thebes. The attackers are defeated, and Creon, the new king of Thebes, refuses to grant them burial.

In our play Adrastus, king of Argos, and the mothers and sons of the Seven have come to Eleusis in Attica to appeal to the Athenians for help in burying their dead. They first approach Aethra, Theseus' mother, who is in Eleusis to sacrifice to the two goddesses of Eleusis, Demeter and Kore (Persephone). But then Theseus, king of Athens, arrives, and Adrastus addresses him. At first he refuses to help: Adrastus, he has learned, ignored warnings against the expedition from god and seer alike. Theseus does not want to involve himself in the affairs of such an imprudent person. He sets forth a view of the world in which the gods give mortal men everything they need to deliver their life from brutishness—including divination in regard to the uncertain future—and any tragedy in mortal life is the fault of men themselves. Theseus' views are up-to-date (this optimistic view of human life here has affinities with the late-fifth-century Sophists). But it is out of character, in an Athenian myth, for Athenians to refuse a request for help.

Aethra causes him to change his mind. After noting that it is unconventional for women to be in the public eye by giving advice, she points out that if Theseus takes up the

Argive cause he will be bringing about what the gods approve, winning credit for restoring the common laws of Hellas, and continuing the city's policy of studied vigor and activism. (With this view, that Athens flourishes by pushing herself forward even into matters that might be thought not to concern her, cf. Thucydides 1.70.) Theseus is persuaded and goes off to win the people's assent to this expedition: for although Athens is ruled by the people, Theseus is the man who gave the people their power, and he still retains much influence. Euripides' audience might have thought of Pericles, who had helped to make Athens more democratic but who seemed to enjoy an almost monarchical power and prestige, as Thucydides points out (2.65).

The next scene pits Theseus against a Theban herald, who has come to tell Athens to refuse Adrastus' request and to expel him from Attica before sundown. Before delivering his message he casts aspersions on democratic government, saying that its leaders are upstart knaves who impose upon a farmer citizenry who have no leisure to learn the art of government. Theseus replies by extolling the rule of law and the equality of citizens. He then tells the Herald that Athens will not take orders from foreign powers and that unless Thebes allows burial, he will come and bury them by force. He exits to join the army.

After a choral ode in which the mothers express their doubts about the justice of the gods, a messenger speech of unusual length and detail announces the result of the expedition. Creon and the Thebans, after once more refusing burial, have been defeated by the bravery and sagacity of Theseus. Theseus further distinguishes himself by his restraint in refusing to harm the defeated city once

5

he has recovered the dead and by his tender care for the bodies of the seven champions and their soldiers.

Theseus' heroism on behalf of the laws of the gods has been rewarded by success. But the rest of the play seems designed to show that the world, in spite of the occasional correspondence between deserts and reward, is full of tragic suffering. The Chorus respond to the news of their sons' imminent burial not with joy but with renewed grief. Their grieving is redoubled when the cortege arrives bearing the bodies of their sons, and Adrastus joins the Chorus in a long duet of lamentation.

Theseus asks Adrastus for an oration over the fallen, an explanation of their great courage. It was the custom at Athens for a public oration to be made each year over those who died for the city in war. Here Adrastus, in myth a speaker notable for his eloquence, is given the role that fell to Pericles and others in historical times. He describes the way of life adopted by the five men he praises, a life of modesty, poverty, and physical austerity. Training like this, he says, taught them to be brave. (Only Capaneus, Eteoclus, Hippomedon, Parthenopaeus, and Tydeus are eulogized by Adrastus. Amphiaraus' body is not available since both he and his chariot were swallowed up in the earth. Polynices himself was presumably buried in Theban soil.) The speech chimes in well with the democratic belief that virtue can be acquired by education and counters the aristocratic belief in the necessity of noble birth. After this speech Theseus announces that he is making a separate pyre for Capaneus, who as a victim of Zeus's lightning is holy; the others are to be cremated together.

Capaneus' pyre is the focus of the next scene. Evadne, Capaneus' widow, appears suddenly above the *skene* and announces that she intends to join her husband in death by leaping onto his pyre. Her father Iphis comes on the scene looking for her, discovers her intention, and tries to dissuade her. But she is bent on making a glorious end for herself and surpassing all other women in wifely devotion. She leaps to her death, and Iphis is left to lament the loss of his daughter as well as of his son, who was one of the Seven. The Chorus again blame the ruinous fate of Oedipus for causing suffering in Argos.

The strains of tragedy continue when the sons of the Argive heroes, who form a second chorus, appear bearing urns containing their fathers' ashes. In the course of their antiphonal lament with the mothers they announce their intention of sacking Thebes once they grow to manhood. Though this will involve still more suffering, Thebes is, as we learn, fated to fall to the sons of the Seven.

Then Theseus addresses Adrastus and the mothers: he is giving them the ashes but asks them to remember for all time the gratitude they owe Athens. Just as they are making their final farewells, Athena appears aloft. She tells Theseus to exact an oath that Argos will never invade Attica and will help to prevent invasion by others. The terms of the oath are to be inscribed on a bronze tripod and dedicated in Delphi. As for the sons of the Seven, Athena predicts that they will one day take Thebes and win glory.

To find the whole to which these parts contribute is not at all easy. Most of the play's episodes, however, ring changes on the themes of heroism and the tragic view of life. Theseus in his first speech to Adrastus attempts to show that tragedy is avoidable. His mother corrects him and demonstrates that he must take up Adrastus' cause and heroically shoulder his burden. The debate with the herald

7

pits arguments of prudence from despotic Thebes against the noble altruism of democratic Athens, whose leader is willing to risk his life on behalf of Panhellenic law and the law of the gods. Athenian success in recovering the dead does not, however, change the basically tragic nature of human life, and the mothers' laments, the deaths of Evadne and Iphis, and the cries for vengeance of the sons show a world in which fate and the gods often bring misery on humankind. In almost the last words of the play, Athena promises the sons of the Seven that they will provide generations to come with a theme for song, one of the few consolations left to unhappy mortals whose lives have been crossed by inscrutable destiny.

One conundrum deserves mention here. The Chorus represents the mothers of the Argive heroes. They are described as seven in number (lines 12-13 by implication, 100-2, 963-5), but a tragic chorus in Euripides' time consisted of fifteen. There are also several references to "servants" or "attendants," probably of the mothers. Boeckh and Hermann suggested that seven mothers plus seven attendants made up a chorus of fourteen, an unlikely arrangement. Wilamowitz, though he remarks that the Athenian theatergoer did not expect realism as his modern counterpart does (since the chorus of Aeschylus' *Suppliants* had to represent the fifty daughters of Danaus), posits a chorus of mothers (presumably seven) and a chorus of attendants (presumably eight), who combine after line 286 and thereafter all represent the mothers. The situation is further complicated by the use of a second chorus of Sons of the Seven, which ought to be of the same size as the chorus of mothers. The solution adopted in this edition is that of Collard, who accepts Wilamowitz' admonition against literal-mindedness and draws the most natural conclusion, namely that a chorus of fifteen is being used to represent the collective notion of the mothers of the fallen. The chorus of sons would then also be fifteen. The attendants are referred to in the third person in the lines Wilamowitz assigns to them, and it is likely that they are stage extras rather than a separate chorus. I have called them attendants of the mothers since they seem closely identified with their fortunes, but it is just possible that they are identical with the attendants of the temple mentioned in line 2.

## SELECT BIBLIOGRAPHY

### Editions

U. von Wilamowitz-Moellendorff, *Analecta Euripidea* (Berlin, 1875; rpt. Hildesheim, 1963), pp. 73-130.
—— *Griechische Tragödien Übersetzt* I[8] (Berlin, 1919), pp. 193-284.
N. Wecklein (Leipzig, 1913).
T. Nicklin (Oxford, 1936).
C. Collard (Groningen, 1975).
—— (Leipzig, 1984).

### Literary Criticism

C. Collard, "The Funeral Oration in Euripides' *Supplices,*" *BICS* 19 (1972), 39-53.
J. W. Fitton, "The Suppliant Women and the Heraclidae of Euripides," *Hermes* 89 (1961), 430-61.

R. B. Gamble, "Euripides' Suppliant Women: Decision and Ambivalence," *Hermes* 98 (1970), 385-404.

R. Goossens, *Euripide et Athènes* (Brussels, 1962), pp. 417-66.

R. Rehm, "The Staging of Suppliant Plays," *GRBS* 29 (1988), 263-307.

W. D. Smith, "Expressive Form in Euripides' *Suppliants*," *HSCP* 71 (1966), 151-70.

G. Zuntz, *The Political Plays of Euripides* (Manchester, 1955).

——— "Über Euripides' Hiketiden," *MH* 12 (1955), 20-34.

## Dramatis Personae

| | |
|---|---|
| ΑΙΘΡΑ | AETHRA, mother of Theseus |
| ΧΟΡΟΣ | CHORUS of the mothers of the Seven |
| ΘΗΣΕΥΣ | THESEUS, King of Athens |
| ΑΔΡΑΣΤΟΣ | ADRASTUS, king of Argos |
| ΚΗΡΥΞ | HERALD from Thebes |
| ΑΓΓΕΛΟΣ | MESSENGER, former servant of Capaneus |
| ΕΥΑΔΝΗ | EVADNE, wife of Capaneus, one of the Seven |
| ΙΦΙΣ | IPHIS, aged father of Evadne |
| ΠΑΙΔΕΣ | Chorus of the SONS of the Seven |
| ΑΘΗΝΑ | ATHENA |
| Nonspeaking roles: | Attendants of the mothers, Athenian herald |

## A Note on Staging

The *skene* represents the temple of Demeter and Persephone at Eleusis in Attica. In front of it is an altar. Eisodos A leads to places in Eleusis and Athens, Eisodos B to Thebes and Argos.

11

# ΙΚΕΤΙΔΕΣ

ΑΙΘΡΑ

Δήμητερ ἑστιοῦχ᾽ Ἐλευσῖνος χθονὸς
τῆσδ᾽, οἵ τε ναοὺς ἔχετε πρόσπολοι θεᾶς,
εὐδαιμονεῖν με Θησέα τε παῖδ᾽ ἐμὸν
πόλιν τ᾽ Ἀθηνῶν τήν τε Πιτθέως χθόνα,
5 ἐν ᾗ με θρέψας ὀλβίοις ἐν δώμασιν
Αἴθραν πατὴρ δίδωσι τῷ Πανδίονος
Αἰγεῖ δάμαρτα Λοξίου μαντεύμασιν.
    ἐς τάσδε γὰρ βλέψασ᾽ ἐπηυξάμην τάδε
γραῦς, αἳ λιποῦσαι δώματ᾽ Ἀργείας χθονὸς
10 ἱκτῆρι θαλλῷ προσπίτνουσ᾽ ἐμὸν γόνυ,
πάθος παθοῦσαι δεινόν· ἀμφὶ γὰρ πύλας
Κάδμου θανόντων ἑπτὰ γενναίων τέκνων
ἄπαιδές εἰσιν, οὕς ποτ᾽ Ἀργείων ἄναξ

2 αἵ Willink

---

[1] Trozen, in the Peloponnesus. Pittheus was its king.

[2] In the usual version of the myth of Theseus' parentage, Aegeus begets Theseus by a casual encounter with Aethra in Trozen. Theseus, when grown to manhood, makes his way to Athens and is united with his father, but Aethra remains in Trozen. Here she is made the wife of Aegeus—the marriage sanctioned

# SUPPLIANT WOMEN

*When the action of the play begins,* AETHRA *is at an altar in front of the temple of Demeter, surrounded by the* CHORUS, *representing the mothers of the Seven against Thebes, who sit holding suppliant branches. On either side of the Chorus are their attendants. At the door of the temple lies the prostrate* ADRASTUS *surrounded by young boys, the Sons of the Seven, who later form a second chorus.*

#### AETHRA

Demeter, guardian of this land of Eleusis, and you servants of the goddess who keep her temple, I pray for prosperity for myself, my son Theseus, the city of Athens and Pittheus' land![1] It was in Trozen that Pittheus, my father, raised me, Aethra, in a prosperous house and gave me as wife to Pandion's son Aegeus at the behest of Apollo's oracles.[2]

I make this prayer as I look upon these old women. They have left their homes in Argos and are falling with suppliant branches at my knees because of their terrible sufferings. They have lost their children: their seven noble sons perished before Cadmus' gates,[3] men once led by

by Apollo—and occupies a position of importance in the Athenian state.    [3] Thebes is called "city of Cadmus" and the Thebans "Cadmeans" throughout this play.

Ἄδραστος ἤγαγ᾽, Οἰδίπου παγκληρίας
15 μέρος κατασχεῖν φυγάδι Πολυνείκει θέλων
γαμβρῷ. νεκροὺς δὲ τοὺς ὀλωλότας δορὶ
θάψαι θέλουσι τῶνδε μητέρες χθονί,
εἴργουσι δ᾽ οἱ κρατοῦντες οὐδ᾽ ἀναίρεσιν
δοῦναι θέλουσι, νόμιμ᾽ ἀτίζοντες θεῶν.
20      κοινὸν δὲ φόρτον ταῖσδ᾽ ἔχων χρείας ἐμῆς
Ἄδραστος ὄμμα δάκρυσιν τέγγων ὅδε
κεῖται, τό τ᾽ ἔγχος τήν τε δυστυχεστάτην
στένων στρατείαν ἣν ἔπεμψεν ἐκ δόμων·
ὅς μ᾽ ἐξοτρύνει παῖδ᾽ ἐμὸν πεῖσαι λιταῖς
25 νεκρῶν κομιστὴν ἢ λόγοισιν ἢ δορὸς
ῥώμῃ γενέσθαι καὶ τάφου μεταίτιον,
κοινὸν τόδ᾽ ἔργον προστιθεὶς ἐμῷ τέκνῳ
πόλει τ᾽ Ἀθηνῶν. τυγχάνω δ᾽ ὑπὲρ χθονὸς
ἀρότου προθύουσ᾽, ἐκ δόμων ἐλθοῦσ᾽ ἐμῶν
30 πρὸς τόνδε σηκόν, ἔνθα πρῶτα φαίνεται
φρίξας ὑπὲρ γῆς τῆσδε κάρπιμος στάχυς.
δεσμὸν δ᾽ ἄδεσμον τόνδ᾽ ἔχουσα φυλλάδος
μένω πρὸς ἁγναῖς ἐσχάραις δυοῖν θεαῖν
Κόρης τε καὶ Δήμητρος, οἰκτίρουσα μὲν
35 πολιὰς ἄπαιδας τάσδε μητέρας τέκνων,
σέβουσα δ᾽ ἱερὰ στέμματ᾽. οἴχεται δέ μοι

---

27 κοινὸν Stahl: μόνον L

---

4 Oedipus, angry with his two sons Eteocles and Polynices,
laid a curse upon them that they would divide their inheritance
with a sword. In most versions of the story, after the brothers had

14

Adrastus, king of Argos, when he tried to secure for his son-in-law, the exiled Polynices, his portion of the heritage of Oedipus.[4] The spear laid these men low, and their mothers want to bury them. But those in power prevent them: flouting the gods' ordinances they refuse them permission to take up their dead.

Sharing the burden of these women's appeal to me is Adrastus here. His face is wet with tears as he lies upon the ground, lamenting the ill-fated expedition he led from home. He urges me to supplicate my son and persuade him to recover the dead, either by parley or by might of spear, and be the cause of their winning a burial, laying this task in common upon my son and the city of Athens. I happen to be offering sacrifice for the plowing of the earth and have left my house and come to this sanctuary, where the stalk of grain first appeared bristling over our land.[5] Since I feel the constraint of these suppliant branches—which bind without any chain—I stay here at the sacred hearths of the two goddesses, Kore and Demeter, in pity for these gray-headed mothers bereft of their sons and in reverence

made an agreement that each should rule a year in turn, with the other leaving the country, Eteocles refused to give up the throne when his year was over. Polynices sought help from Adrastus, whose daughter he had married, and an Argive army tried to put him on the throne. But Eteocles and Polynices, facing each other at one of the seven gates, each received a mortal wound at the other's hand, and the attack on Thebes failed.

[5] The festival of the Proerosia was celebrated before the fall planting. The Athenians at about the time of this play greatly expanded the festival by requiring their allies and inviting others to contribute a percentage of their produce to the goddesses at Eleusis.

κῆρυξ πρὸς ἄστυ δεῦρο Θησέα καλῶν,
ὡς ἢ τὸ τούτων λυπρὸν ἐξέλῃ χθονὸς
ἢ τάσδ' ἀνάγκας ἱκεσίους λύσῃ, θεοὺς
40 ὅσιόν τι δράσας· πάντα γὰρ δι' ἀρσένων
γυναιξὶ πράσσειν εἰκὸς αἵτινες σοφαί.

ΧΟΡΟΣ

στρ. α

ἱκετεύω σε, γεραιά, γεραιῶν ἐκ στομάτων πρὸς
γόνυ πίπτουσα τὸ σόν·
†ἄνομοι τέκνα λῦσαι φθιμένων νεκύων† οἳ
45 καταλείπουσι μέλη
θανάτῳ λυσιμελεῖ θηρσὶν ὀρείοισι βοράν·

ἀντ. α

ἐσιδοῦσ' οἰκτρὰ μὲν ὄσσων δάκρυ' ἀμφὶ
βλεφάροις, ῥυ-
50 σὰ δὲ σαρκῶν πολιᾶν
καταδρύμματα χειρῶν· τί γάρ; ἃ φθιμένους παῖ-
δας ἐμοὺς οὔτε δόμοις
προθέμαν οὔτε τάφων χώματα γαίας ἐσορῶ.

στρ. β

55 ἔτεκες καὶ σύ ποτ', ὦ πότνια, κοῦρον φίλα ποιη-
σαμένα λέκτρα πόσει σῷ· μετά νυν
δὸς ἐμοὶ σᾶς διανοίας, μετάδος δ' ὅσσον ἐπαλγῶ
μελέα ⟨'γὼ⟩ φθιμένων οὓς ἔτεκον·

---

44 ἀνόμους καταπαῦσαι Campbell, tum fort. νεκύων φθι-
μένων (Italie) cl. 52: possis etiam ἀνόμων ἄπο λῦσαι / νέκυας
φθιμένων    59 ⟨'γὼ⟩ Kirchhoff

for their suppliant wreaths. I have sent a herald to the city
to summon Theseus here so that either he will remove
from the land the distress they cause or discharge his duty
to the suppliants by doing an act of piety toward the gods.
It is proper for women, if they are wise, to do everything
through their men.

### CHORUS

I beseech you, aged lady, from aged lips,
falling at your knees:
stop the lawless men[6] who are leaving the bodies of the
  slain
in limb-loosening death
as food for mountain beasts!

Look at the pitiable tears upon our cheeks
and the gashes our hands have torn
in our old and wrinkled flesh! How can we do otherwise?
  Our dead sons
we could not lay out in the house for burial or see a mound
of earth raised over their tombs.

You too once bore, my lady, a son, making your bed pleas-
  ing
to your husband. So grant me
a portion of your kind regard, grant it, in pity for the grief
  that I, unlucky one,
feel for my son's death.

---

[6] I translate Campbell's attractive but uncertain conjecture.
The rest of the line is likewise uncertain.

17

60 παράπεισον δὲ σόν, ὤ, λίσσομαι, ἐλθεῖν τέκνον
    Ἰσμη-
    νὸν ἐμάν τ᾽ ἐς χέρα θεῖναι νεκύων
    θαλερῶν σώματ᾽ ἀλαίνοντ᾽ ἄταφα.

ἀντ. β

    ὁσίως οὔχ, ὑπ᾽ ἀνάγκας δὲ προπίπτουσα προσαι-
      τοῦσ᾽
    ἔμολον δεξιπύρους θεῶν θυμέλας·
65 ἔχομεν δ᾽ ἔνδικα, καὶ σοί τι πάρεστι σθένος ὥστ᾽
    εὐ-
    τεκνίᾳ δυστυχίαν τὰν παρ᾽ ἐμοὶ
    καθελεῖν· οἰκτρὰ δὲ πάσχουσ᾽ ἱκετεύω σὸν ἐμοὶ παῖ-
    δα ταλαίνᾳ 'ν χερὶ θεῖναι νέκυν, ἀμ-
70 φιβαλεῖν λυγρὰ μέλη παιδὸς ἐμοῦ.

στρ. γ

    ἀγὼν ὅδ᾽ ἄλλος ἔρχεται
    γόων γόοις διάδοχος· ἀ-
    χοῦσι ⟨δὲ⟩ προσπόλων χέρες.
    ἴτ᾽ ὦ ξυνῳδοὶ κακοῖς,
    ἴτ᾽ ὦ ξυναλγηδόνες
75 χορὸν τὸν Ἅιδας σέβει·
    διὰ παρῆδος ὄνυχι λευ-
    κὸν αἱματοῦτε χρῶτα φόνιον· ⟨αἰαῖ.⟩

    60 λίσσομαι Stinton: λισσόμ᾽ Tr    62 σώματ᾽ ἀλαίνοντ᾽
ἄταφα Murray: σώματα λάινον τάφον L
    68 σὸν ἐμοὶ Musgrave: τὸν ἐμὸν L
    69 ταλαίνᾳ 'ν Wilamowitz: τάλαιν᾽ ἐν L
    71 γόοις Valckenaer: γόων L    72 ⟨δὲ⟩ Willink

Prevail on your son, I beg you, to go to the Ismenus River[7]
and put into my hands the bodies
of the young dead who are unburied.

It was not in pious worship but under compulsion, falling
   in entreaty,
that I came to the goddesses' fire-receiving altars.
But my plea is just, and you have some power to relieve
my misfortune by the noble son
you bore. Because of my pitiable sufferings I entreat your
   son
to put in my luckless hands my dead child so that I may
   embrace
his heart-grieving limbs.

*The attendants beat their breasts and scratch their cheeks
in gestures of mourning.*

See, others in emulation
take up the lament with lament of their own,
and attendants' hands resound on their breasts.
Take up, O fellow singers with misfortune,
fellow mourners,
the dance Hades honors!
Across your cheek with your nails
bloody your white skin! ‹Ah me!›

---

[7] One of the rivers of Boeotia, running through the city of
Thebes. Ismenus is properly spelled Hismenus and Ismene (An-
tigone's sister) Hismene (see Mastronarde on *Phoenissae* 101), but
I have kept the customary English spelling.

---

77 ‹αἰαῖ› post Wilamowitz (ἒ ἔ) Diggle

τὰ γὰρ φθιτῶν τοῖς ὁρῶσι κόσμος.

ἀντ. γ

ἄπληστος ἅδε μ᾽ ἐξάγει
χάρις γόων πολύπονος, ὡς
80 ἀλιβάτου ⟨τις⟩ ἐκ πέτρας
ὑγρὰ ῥέουσα σταγὼν
ἄπαυστος αἰεὶ †γόων†.
τὸ γὰρ θανόντων τέκνων
ἐπίπονόν τι κατὰ γυναῖ-
85 κας ἐς γόους πάθος πέφυκεν· αἰαῖ.
θανοῦσα τῶνδ᾽ ἀλγέων λαθοίμαν.

ΘΗΣΕΥΣ

τίνων γόους ἤκουσα καὶ στέρνων κτύπον
νεκρῶν τε θρήνους, τῶνδ᾽ ἀνακτόρων ἄπο
ἠχοῦς ἰούσης; ὡς φόβος μ᾽ ἀναπτεροῖ
90 μή μοί τι μήτηρ, ἣν μεταστείχω ποδὶ
χρονίαν ἀποῦσαν ἐκ δόμων, ἔχῃ νέον.
 ἔα·
τί χρῆμα; καινὰς ἐσβολὰς ὁρῶ λόγων,
μητέρα γεραιὰν βωμίαν ἐφημένην
ξένας θ᾽ ὁμοῦ γυναῖκας οὐχ ἕνα ῥυθμὸν
95 κακῶν ἐχούσας· ἔκ τε γὰρ γερασμίων
ὄσσων ἐλαύνουσ᾽ οἰκτρὸν ἐς γαῖαν δάκρυ,
κουραί τε καὶ πεπλώματ᾽ οὐ θεωρικά.
τί ταῦτα, μῆτερ; σὸν τὸ μηνύειν ἐμοί,
ἡμῶν δ᾽ ἀκούειν· προσδοκῶ τι γὰρ νέον.

<hr>

80 ἀλιβάτου τις ἐκ Willink: ἐξ ἀλιβάτου πέτρας L

The rites we owe the dead adorn the living.

Insatiable pleasure in tears, unstinting of labor,
brings forth my utterance,
like some stream of water pouring
from a steep cliff
in never-ceasing flow!
For when their children die,
the grief in women's hearts is ever involved
in the toil of lamentation. Ah me!
In death may I forget these woes!

*Enter* THESEUS *with retinue by Eisodos A.*

THESEUS
Whose is the wailing, the beating of breasts, and the keen-
ing for the dead that I have heard? The sound has come
from this temple. How fearful I am that my mother may
have met with some mischance! She has been long away
from the house, and I have come to find her.

But what is this? Here are strange things to speak of,
my aged mother sitting at the altar, and foreign women
with her in many attitudes of misery. From their aged eyes
they shed pitiable tears on the ground, and the cut of their
hair and the garments they wear are not fit for a festival.
What does this mean, mother? It is your task to tell me and
mine to listen. I expect bad news.

---

⁸² δρόσων Camper: ῥοὰν Eden
⁸⁵ πάθος πέφυκεν Zuntz: πέφυκε πάθος L
⁸⁷ γόους Elmsley: γόων L    ⁹⁴ ξένας Elmsley: -ους L
⁹⁷ τε Markland: δὲ L

21

ΑΙΘΡΑ

100 ὦ παῖ, γυναῖκες αἵδε μητέρες τέκνων
τῶν κατθανόντων ἀμφὶ Καδμείας πύλας
ἑπτὰ στρατηγῶν· ἱκεσίοις δὲ σὺν κλάδοις
φρουροῦσί μ᾽, ὡς δέδορκας, ἐν κύκλῳ, τέκνον.

ΘΗΣΕΥΣ

τίς δ᾽ ὁ στενάζων οἰκτρὸν ἐν πύλαις ὅδε;

ΑΙΘΡΑ

105 Ἄδραστος, ὡς λέγουσιν, Ἀργείων ἄναξ.

ΘΗΣΕΥΣ

οἱ δ᾽ ἀμφὶ τόνδε παῖδες; ἦ τούτων τέκνα;

ΑΙΘΡΑ

οὔκ, ἀλλὰ νεκρῶν τῶν ὀλωλότων κόροι.

ΘΗΣΕΥΣ

τί γὰρ πρὸς ἡμᾶς ἦλθον ἱκεσίᾳ χερί;

ΑΙΘΡΑ

οἶδ᾽· ἀλλὰ τῶνδε μῦθος οὑντεῦθεν, τέκνον.

ΘΗΣΕΥΣ

110 σὲ τὸν κατήρη χλανιδίοις ἀνιστορῶ.
λέγ᾽ ἐκκαλύψας κρᾶτα καὶ πάρες γόον·
πέρας γὰρ οὐδὲν μὴ διὰ γλώσσης ἰόν.

ΑΔΡΑΣΤΟΣ

ὦ καλλίνικε γῆς Ἀθηναίων ἄναξ,
Θησεῦ, σὸς ἱκέτης καὶ πόλεως ἥκω σέθεν.

# SUPPLIANT WOMEN

#### AETHRA

My son, these women are the mothers of sons, the seven
generals who died before Cadmus' gates. They keep watch,
encircling me, as you see, with their suppliant boughs.

#### THESEUS

But who is this man who weeps so pitiably in the doorway?

#### AETHRA

Adrastus, they say, king of the Argives.

#### THESEUS

And the boys round about him? Are they these women's
sons?

#### AETHRA

No, they are the sons of the slain warriors.

#### THESEUS

Well, why have they come to supplicate us?

#### AETHRA

I know why, but from this point on it is their turn to speak,
my son.

#### THESEUS

You there, with your head wrapped in your garments, my
question is for you! Uncover your head, leave off your
weeping, and speak! Nothing is ever achieved unless it is
spoken.

#### ADRASTUS

Theseus, king of Athens, glorious in victory, I have come
as suppliant to you and your city!

ΘΗΣΕΥΣ

115 τί χρῆμα θηρῶν καὶ τίνος χρείαν ἔχων;

ΑΔΡΑΣΤΟΣ

οἶσθ᾽ ἣν στρατείαν ἐστράτευσ᾽ ὀλεθρίαν;

ΘΗΣΕΥΣ

οὐ γάρ τι σιγῇ διεπέρασας Ἑλλάδα.

ΑΔΡΑΣΤΟΣ

ἐνταῦθ᾽ ἀπώλεσ᾽ ἄνδρας Ἀργείων ἄκρους.

ΘΗΣΕΥΣ

τοιαῦθ᾽ ὁ τλήμων πόλεμος ἐξεργάζεται.

ΑΔΡΑΣΤΟΣ

120 τούτους θανόντας ἦλθον ἐξαιτῶν πόλιν.

ΘΗΣΕΥΣ

κήρυξιν Ἑρμοῦ πίσυνος, ὡς θάψῃς νεκρούς;

ΑΔΡΑΣΤΟΣ

κἄπειτά γ᾽ οἱ κτανόντες οὐκ ἐῶσί με.

ΘΗΣΕΥΣ

τί γὰρ λέγουσιν, ὅσια χρῄζοντος σέθεν;

ΑΔΡΑΣΤΟΣ

τί δ᾽; εὐτυχοῦντες οὐκ ἐπίστανται φέρειν.

ΘΗΣΕΥΣ

125 ξύμβουλον οὖν μ᾽ ἐπῆλθες; ἢ τίνος χάριν;

ΑΔΡΑΣΤΟΣ

κομίσαι σε, Θησεῦ, παῖδας Ἀργείων θέλων.

THESEUS

What are you seeking? What is it you need?

ADRASTUS

Do you know the disastrous expedition I led?

THESEUS

Yes: not in silence did you pass through Hellas.

ADRASTUS

On this expedition I lost the finest men of Argos.

THESEUS

That is what cruel-hearted war does.

ADRASTUS

I went to ask the return of their bodies from Thebes.

THESEUS

Relying on Hermes' heralds,[8] so that you might bury the dead?

ADRASTUS

Yes, and the slayers forbade me.

THESEUS

What did they say? Your request was a pious one.

ADRASTUS

Say? Their prosperity proved too much for them to bear.

THESEUS

Have you come to me for advice? Or for what?

ADRASTUS

I want you, Theseus, to recover Argos' sons.

---

[8] Hermes was patron of heralds, who carried messages between armies and peoples at war.

ΘΗΣΕΥΣ

τὸ δ' Ἄργος ὑμῖν ποῦ 'στιν; ἢ κόμποι μάτην;

ΑΔΡΑΣΤΟΣ

σφαλέντες οἰχόμεσθα. πρὸς σὲ δ' ἥκομεν.

ΘΗΣΕΥΣ

ἰδίᾳ δοκῆσάν σοι τόδ' ἢ πάσῃ πόλει;

ΑΔΡΑΣΤΟΣ

130   πάντες σ' ἱκνοῦνται Δαναΐδαι θάψαι νεκρούς.

ΘΗΣΕΥΣ

ἐκ τοῦ δ' ἐλαύνεις ἑπτὰ πρὸς Θήβας λόχους;

ΑΔΡΑΣΤΟΣ

δισσοῖσι γαμβροῖς τήνδε πορσύνων χάριν.

ΘΗΣΕΥΣ

τῷ δ' ἐξέδωκας παῖδας Ἀργείων σέθεν;

ΑΔΡΑΣΤΟΣ

οὐκ ἐγγενῆ συνῆψα κηδείαν δόμοις.

ΘΗΣΕΥΣ

135   ἀλλὰ ξένοις ἔδωκας Ἀργείας κόρας;

ΑΔΡΑΣΤΟΣ

Τυδεῖ <γε> Πολυνείκει τε τῷ Θηβαιγενεῖ.

ΘΗΣΕΥΣ

τίν' εἰς ἔρωτα τῆσδε κηδείας μολών;

ΑΔΡΑΣΤΟΣ

Φοίβου μ' ὑπῆλθε δυστόπαστ' αἰνίγματα.

THESEUS

But where is your Argos? Is it merely an idle boast?

ADRASTUS

We have fallen and are in ruins. We have come to you.

THESEUS

Was it you alone or the whole city that decided this?

ADRASTUS

All the offspring of Danaus beg you to bury our dead.

THESEUS

But why did you march seven companies against Thebes?

ADRASTUS

I did this as a favor to my two sons-in-law.

THESEUS

To which of the Argives did you give your daughters?

ADRASTUS

It was no native marriage tie that I made for my house.

THESEUS

So you gave Argive girls to foreign husbands?

ADRASTUS

⟨Yes,⟩ to Tydeus and to Theban-born Polynices.

THESEUS

What made you desire such a marriage?

ADRASTUS

I was beguiled by Apollo's dark oracles.

---

131 λόχους Pierson: ὄχους L    136 ⟨γε⟩ Hermann
136–7 suspectos habebat Wecklein

27

ΘΗΣΕΥΣ
τί δ᾽ εἶπ᾽ Ἀπόλλων παρθένοις κραίνων γάμον;

ΑΔΡΑΣΤΟΣ
140  κάπρῳ με δοῦναι καὶ λέοντι παῖδ᾽ ἐμώ.

ΘΗΣΕΥΣ
σὺ δ᾽ ἐξελίσσεις πῶς θεοῦ θεσπίσματα;

ΑΔΡΑΣΤΟΣ
ἐλθόντε φυγάδε νυκτὸς εἰς ἐμὰς πύλας . . .

ΘΗΣΕΥΣ
τίς καὶ τίς; εἰπέ· δύο γὰρ ἐξαυδᾷς ἅμα.

ΑΔΡΑΣΤΟΣ
. . . Τυδεὺς μάχην ξυνῆψε Πολυνείκης θ᾽ ἅμα.

ΘΗΣΕΥΣ
145  ἦ τοῖσδ᾽ ἔδωκας θηρσὶν ὡς κόρας σέθεν;

ΑΔΡΑΣΤΟΣ
μάχην γε δισσοῖν κνωδάλοιν ἀπεικάσας.

ΘΗΣΕΥΣ
ἦλθον δὲ δὴ πῶς πατρίδος ἐκλιπόνθ᾽ ὅρους;

ΑΔΡΑΣΤΟΣ
Τυδεὺς μὲν αἷμα συγγενὲς φεύγων χθονός.

ΘΗΣΕΥΣ
ὁ δ᾽ Οἰδίπου ⟨παῖς⟩ τίνι τρόπῳ Θήβας λιπών;

ΑΔΡΑΣΤΟΣ
150  ἀραῖς πατρῴαις, μὴ κασίγνητον κτάνοι.

THESEUS
What did Apollo say to ordain marriage for the maidens?

ADRASTUS
"Your daughters to a boar and lion marry."

THESEUS
And how did you interpret the god's oracle?

ADRASTUS
Two exiles came to my door by night . . .

THESEUS
You tell me two at once. What men are they?

ADRASTUS
. . . and fought each other, Tydeus and Polynices.

THESEUS
You gave your daughters to these men, thinking they were
beasts?

ADRASTUS
Yes: I thought they battled like two wild animals.

THESEUS
Why did they leave their own countries?

ADRASTUS
Tydeus was in exile for shedding kindred blood.

THESEUS
And the ‹son› of Oedipus, why did he leave Thebes?

ADRASTUS
Because of his father's curse, to avoid killing his brother.

---

149 ‹παῖς› Erfurdt, Porson

ΘΗΣΕΥΣ
σοφήν γ' ἔλεξας τήνδ' ἑκούσιον φυγήν.

ΑΔΡΑΣΤΟΣ
ἀλλ' οἱ μένοντες τοὺς ἀπόντας ἠδίκουν.

ΘΗΣΕΥΣ
οὔ πού σφ' ἀδελφὸς χρημάτων νοσφίζεται;

ΑΔΡΑΣΤΟΣ
ταῦτ' ἐκδικάζων ἦλθον· εἶτ' ἀπωλόμην.

ΘΗΣΕΥΣ
155 μάντεις δ' ἐπῆλθες ἐμπύρων τ' εἶδες φλόγα;

ΑΔΡΑΣΤΟΣ
οἴμοι· διώκεις μ' ᾗ μάλιστ' ἐγὼ 'σφάλην.

ΘΗΣΕΥΣ
οὐκ ἦλθες, ὡς ἔοικεν, εὐνοίᾳ θεῶν.

ΑΔΡΑΣΤΟΣ
τὸ δὲ πλέον, ἦλθον Ἀμφιάρεώ γε πρὸς βίαν.

ΘΗΣΕΥΣ
οὕτω τὸ θεῖον ῥᾳδίως ἀπεστράφης;

ΑΔΡΑΣΤΟΣ
160 νέων γὰρ ἀνδρῶν θόρυβος ἐξέπλησσέ με.

ΘΗΣΕΥΣ
εὐψυχίαν ἔσπευσας ἀντ' εὐβουλίας.

154 ταῦτ' ἐκδικάζων Hermann, Lenting: ταυτὶ δικάζων L
158 τὸ Musgrave: τί L
159 ἀπεστράφης Reiske: σ' ἀπεστράφη L

THESEUS

A wise act, this voluntary exile!

ADRASTUS

But those who stayed behind wronged those who left.

THESEUS

Surely his brother did not rob him of his property?

ADRASTUS

It was this crime I came to punish. And there I was destroyed.

THESEUS

Did you consult seers and examine the flames of burnt offerings?

ADRASTUS

Ah! You press me hard just where my failure is greatest!

THESEUS

It appears you went to war without the gods' good will.

ADRASTUS

And what is more I went against the wish of Amphiaraus.[9]

THESEUS

Did you so lightly turn aside from divine guidance?

ADRASTUS

Yes: the shouting of young men put me out of my wits.

THESEUS

It was bravery rather than prudence that you pursued.

---

[9] A seer and the only pious man among the Seven, Amphiaraus was forced by his wife to take part in the expedition.

# EURIPIDES

ΑΔΡΑΣΤΟΣ

ὃ δή γε πολλοὺς ὤλεσε στρατηλάτας.

ἀλλ᾽, ὦ καθ᾽ Ἑλλάδ᾽ ἀλκιμώτατον κάρα,
ἄναξ Ἀθηνῶν, ἐν μὲν αἰσχύναις ἔχω
165 πίτνων πρὸς οὖδας γόνυ σὸν ἀμπίσχειν χερί
[πολιὸς ἀνὴρ τύραννος εὐδαίμων πάρος]·
ὅμως δ᾽ ἀνάγκη συμφοραῖς εἴκειν ἐμαῖς.
σῶσον νεκρούς μοι τἀμά τ᾽ οἰκτίρας κακὰ
καὶ τῶν θανόντων τάσδε μητέρας τέκνων,
170 αἷς γῆρας ἥκει πολιὸν εἰς ἀπαιδίαν,
ἐλθεῖν δ᾽ ἔτλησαν δεῦρο καὶ ξένον πόδα
θεῖναι μόλις γεραιὰ κινοῦσαι μέλη,
πρεσβεύματ᾽ οὐ Δήμητρος ἐς μυστήρια
ἀλλ᾽ ὡς νεκροὺς θάψωσιν, ἃς αὐτὰς ἐχρῆν
175 κείνων ταφείσας χερσὶν ὡραίων τυχεῖν.
σοφὸν δὲ πενίαν τ᾽ εἰσορᾶν τὸν ὄλβιον,
[πένητά τ᾽ ἐς τοὺς πλουσίους ἀποβλέπειν
ζηλοῦνθ᾽, ἵν᾽ αὐτὸν χρημάτων ἔρως ἔχῃ,]
τά τ᾽ οἰκτρὰ τοὺς μὴ δυστυχεῖς δεδορκέναι.
⟨ἀλλ᾽ οὐ δέδοικα τἀμὰ δυστυχήματα
μή μ᾽ οὐκ ἐάσῃ τῷδε πρὸς χάριν λέγειν
πείθειν θ᾽ ἃ χρῄζω; τόν τε γὰρ πειστήριον
εἶναι θέλοντα φαιδρόνουν εἶναι χρεών,⟩
180 τόν θ᾽ ὑμνοποιὸν αὐτὸς ἂν τίκτῃ μέλη
χαίροντα τίκτειν· ἢν δὲ μὴ πάσχῃ τόδε,

---

<sup>162</sup> fort. δὴ ᾽μὲ πολλούς τ᾽    v. del. Dindorf
<sup>166</sup> del. Dindorf    <sup>174</sup> ἃς versio Melanchthonis et Xylandri:
ὡς L    <sup>177–8</sup> del. Bothe

32

**ADRASTUS**

Yes, the very thing that destroys many generals.

But, O most valiant warrior in Greece, king of Athens, though I consider it disgraceful to fall upon the ground and cover your knees with my hands, [since I am an old king who was once prosperous,] yet I must yield to my misfortunes. (*He kneels before Theseus.*) Bring the dead safely back, I pray, take pity on my troubles and on these mothers whose sons have been slain! Gray old age has come upon them in childlessness, and they have taken it upon themselves to come and plant their foreign steps here, though they can barely move their aged limbs. This is no sacred embassy to Demeter's mysteries: they have come to bury their dead sons, though it is by these sons' hands that they themselves ought to be buried and receive a funeral. It is a wise thing for the rich man to look on poverty [and the poor man to turn his gaze on the rich in envy, so that desire for money may seize him,] and for those who are not unfortunate to look at what is pitiable.

⟨But am I not afraid that the ruin of my fortunes will prevent me from pleasing this man by my speech and gaining what I want? The speaker who wants to be persuasive must be cheerful,⟩[10] just as the poet must compose in joy the songs he composes. If that is not the case with him, he

[10] Unless 180–3 are an alien addition whose presence here is wholly mysterious, we must place a lacuna before 180 of indeterminate length whose content may have been something like what is given above.

---

179 δεδορκέναι Tyrwhitt: δεδοικέναι L     post h. v. lac. indic. Matthiae     180 αὐτὸν Scaliger

33

οὔτοι δύναιτ᾽ ἂν οἴκοθέν γ᾽ ἀτώμενος
τέρπειν ἂν ἄλλους· οὐδὲ γὰρ δίκην ἔχει.

   τάχ᾽ οὖν ἂν εἴποις· Πελοπίαν παρεὶς χθόνα
185  πῶς ταῖς Ἀθήναις τόνδε προστάσσεις πόνον;
ἐγὼ δίκαιός εἰμ᾽ ἀφηγεῖσθαι τάδε.
Σπάρτη μὲν ὠμὴ καὶ πεποίκιλται τρόπους,
τὰ δ᾽ ἄλλα μικρὰ κἀσθενῆ· πόλις δὲ σὴ
μόνη δύναιτ᾽ ἂν τόνδ᾽ ὑποστῆναι πόνον·
190  τά τ᾽ οἰκτρὰ γὰρ δέδορκε καὶ νεανίαν
ἔχει σε ποιμέν᾽ ἐσθλόν· οὗ χρείᾳ πόλεις
πολλαὶ διώλοντ᾽, ἐνδεεῖς στρατηλάτου.

ΧΟΡΟΣ

κἀγὼ τὸν αὐτὸν τῷδέ σοι λόγον λέγω,
Θησεῦ, δι᾽ οἴκτου τὰς ἐμὰς λαβεῖν τύχας.

ΘΗΣΕΥΣ

195  ἄλλοισι δὴ ᾽πόνησ᾽ ἁμιλληθεὶς λόγῳ
τοιῷδ᾽. ἔλεξε γάρ τις ὡς τὰ χείρονα
πλείω βροτοῖσίν ἐστι τῶν ἀμεινόνων.
ἐγὼ δὲ τούτοις ἀντίαν γνώμην ἔχω,
πλείω τὰ χρηστὰ τῶν κακῶν εἶναι βροτοῖς.
200  εἰ μὴ γὰρ ἦν τόδ᾽, οὐκ ἂν ἦμεν ἐν φάει.
αἰνῶ δ᾽ ὃς ἡμῖν βίοτον ἐκ πεφυρμένου
καὶ θηριώδους θεῶν διεσταθμήσατο,
πρῶτον μὲν ἐνθεὶς σύνεσιν, εἶτα δ᾽ ἄγγελον
γλῶσσαν λόγων δούς, ὥστε γιγνώσκειν ὄπα,
205  τροφήν τε καρποῦ τῇ τροφῇ τ᾽ ἀπ᾽ οὐρανοῦ
σταγόνας ὑδρηλὰς ὡς τά τ᾽ ἐκ γαίας τρέφῃ

cannot give pleasure to others if he himself is suffering: that is not the way of things.

Perhaps you might object, "Why do you pass over the Peloponnesus and lay this task on Athens?" It is my duty to explain this. Sparta is savage and devious in its ways, and the other states are small and weak. It is your city alone that could undertake this labor. It looks on what is pitiable and it has in you a good leader who is vigorous. For want of such a general many cities have perished.

CHORUS LEADER
I make the same plea as he, Theseus: pity my misfortunes!

THESEUS
I once had a debate with other men, and my argument was of this nature. Someone said that mortals have more of bad than of good. But I hold the opposite view, that mortals enjoy more good things than bad. If it were not so, we would not be looking on the light of day. I praise the god who set our life in order, rescuing it from its confused and brutish state. First he put reason in us, then he gave us a tongue to utter words, so that we can understand speech, gave us too the fruit of the ground as nourishment and with it the rain from heaven, so that it might nourish what grows in the earth and quench our bellies' thirst. Furthermore he

---

187 ὠμὴ Canter: ἡ 'μὴ L
190 νεανιῶν Markland
190-2 del. Dindorf
206 τ' Markland: γ' L

# EURIPIDES

ἄρδῃ τε νηδύν· πρὸς δὲ τοῖσι χείματος
προβλήματ᾽ αἰθόν ⟨τ᾽⟩ ἐξαμύνασθαι θεοῦ
πόντου τε ναυστολήμαθ᾽, ὡς διαλλαγὰς
210 ἔχοιμεν ἀλλήλοισιν ὧν πένοιτο γῆ.
ἃ δ᾽ ἔστ᾽ ἄσημα κοὐ σαφῶς γιγνώσκομεν,
ἐς πῦρ βλέποντες καὶ κατὰ σπλάγχνων πτυχὰς
μάντεις προσημαίνουσιν οἰωνῶν τ᾽ ἄπο.
ἆρ᾽ οὐ τρυφῶμεν, θεοῦ κατασκευὴν βίῳ
215 δόντος τοιαύτην, οἷσιν οὐκ ἀρκεῖ τάδε;
ἀλλ᾽ ἡ φρόνησις τοῦ θεοῦ μεῖζον σθένειν
ζητεῖ, τὸ γαῦρον δ᾽ ἐν φρεσὶν κεκτημένοι
δοκοῦμεν εἶναι δαιμόνων σοφώτεροι.

ἧς καὶ σὺ φαίνῃ δεκάδος οὐ σοφῆς γεγώς,
220 ὅστις κόρας μὲν θεσφάτοις Φοίβου ζυγεὶς
ξένοισιν ὧδ᾽ ἔδωκας ὡς δόντων θεῶν,
[λαμπρὸν δὲ θολερῷ δῶμα συμμείξας τὸ σὸν
ἤλκωσας οἴκους· χρὴ γὰρ οὔτε σώματα
ἄδικα δικαίοις τὸν σοφὸν συμμειγνύναι
225 εὐδαιμονοῦντας τ᾽ ἐς δόμους κτᾶσθαι φίλους.
κοινὰς γὰρ ὁ θεὸς τὰς τύχας ἡγούμενος
τοῖς τοῦ νοσοῦντος πήμασιν διώλεσεν
τὸν οὐ νοσοῦντα κοὐδὲν ἠδικηκότα,]
ἐς δὲ στρατείαν πάντας Ἀργείους ἄγων,
230 μάντεων λεγόντων θέσφατ᾽ εἶτ᾽ ἀτιμάσας,
βίᾳ παρελθὼν θεοὺς ἀπώλεσας πόλιν.
[νέοις παραχθεὶς οἵτινες τιμώμενοι
χαίρουσι πολέμους τ᾽ αὐξάνουσ᾽ ἄνευ δίκης,
φθείροντες ἀστούς, ὁ μὲν ὅπως στρατηλατῇ,

36

gave us protection against the winter cold <and> a way to
ward off the sun god's blazing heat, and the means to sail
the sea so that each land might trade with others for the
things it lacks. Matters that are unclear and of which we
have no reliable knowledge are foretold to us by seers who
examine fire, the folds of entrails, or the flight of birds. The
god has made provision like this for our life: are we not
being hard to please if this is not enough for us? But arro-
gance tries to be mightier than the god. With our vainglo-
rious minds we think we are wiser than the powers divine.

   You too clearly belong to this foolish band. You gave
your daughters under compulsion of Phoebus' oracles to
foreigners on the understanding that the gods had be-
stowed them; [but by mixing your bright house with mud
you ruined it. The wise man should not mingle unjust bod-
ies with just: he ought to win prosperous friends for his
house. Considering their lots to be cast together the gods
destroy the healthy and innocent with the troubles of the
diseased;] yet when you were leading all the Argives on an
expedition, when seers were uttering prophesies, you set
them at nought, forcibly transgressed the will of the gods,
and destroyed your city. [You were led astray by young men
who enjoy being honored and who multiply wars without
justice to the hurt of the citizens. One wants to be gen-

---

208 ⟨τ'⟩ Faber, Milton     219 σοφῆς Markland: σοφὸς L
221 δόντων Scaliger: ζώντων L     222-8 del. Lueders
223 χρὴ Hartung: χρῆν L     225 τ' Markland: δ' L
228 οὐ νοσοῦντα Lambinus: συννοσοῦντα L
230 del. Wilamowitz
232–45 suspectos hab. Wecklein (238-45 del. Th. Miller)

235 ὁ δ' ὡς ὑβρίζῃ δύναμιν ἐς χεῖρας λαβών,
ἄλλος δὲ κέρδους οὕνεκ', οὐκ ἀποσκοπῶν
τὸ πλῆθος εἴ τι βλάπτεται πάσχον τάδε.
τρεῖς γὰρ πολιτῶν μερίδες· οἱ μὲν ὄλβιοι
ἀνωφελεῖς τε πλειόνων τ' ἐρῶσ' ἀεί·
240 οἱ δ' οὐκ ἔχοντες καὶ σπανίζοντες βίου
δεινοί, νέμοντες τῷ φθόνῳ πλέον μέρος,
ἐς τοὺς <τ'> ἔχοντας κέντρ' ἀφιᾶσιν κακά,
γλώσσαις πονηρῶν προστατῶν φηλούμενοι·
τριῶν δὲ μοιρῶν ἡ 'ν μέσῳ σῴζει πόλεις,
245 κόσμον φυλάσσουσ' ὅντιν' ἂν τάξῃ πόλις.]
κἄπειτ' ἐγὼ σοὶ σύμμαχος γενήσομαι;
τί πρὸς πολίτας τοὺς ἐμοὺς λέγων καλόν;
χαίρων ἴθ'· εἰ γὰρ μὴ βεβούλευσαι καλῶς
αὐτός, πιέζειν σὴν τύχην ἡμᾶς τί δεῖ;

ΧΟΡΟΣ

250 ἥμαρτεν· ἐν νέοισι δ' ἀνθρώπων τόδε
ἔνεστι· συγγνώμην δὲ τῷδ' ἔχειν χρεών.
[ἀλλ' ὡς ἰατρὸν τῶνδ', ἄναξ, ἀφίγμεθα.]

ΑΔΡΑΣΤΟΣ

οὔτοι δικαστήν σ' εἱλόμην ἐμῶν κακῶν
οὐδ', εἴ τι πράξας μὴ καλῶς εὑρίσκομαι,
255 τούτων κολαστὴν κἀπιτιμητήν, ἄναξ,
ἀλλ' ὡς ὀναίμην. εἰ δὲ μὴ βούλῃ τάδε,
στέργειν ἀνάγκη τοῖσι σοῖς· τί γὰρ πάθω;
ἄγ', ὦ γεραιαί, στείχετε, γλαυκὴν χλόην
αὐτοῦ λιποῦσαι φυλλάδος καταστεφῆ,

eral, another to get power into his hands and commit wanton abuse, another wants wealth and does not consider whether the majority is at all harmed by being so treated. There are three classes of citizens: the rich are useless and always lusting for more; the poor, who lack their their daily bread, are dangerous, for they assign too great a place to envy ‹and› hurl their stings at the rich, being deceived by the tongues of wicked leaders; of the three classes the one in the middle preserves states by keeping to the discipline that the city establishes.] And after this shall I become *your* ally? What creditable explanation can I offer my citizens? Farewell, go your way! If you yourself have acted rashly, why should your misfortune press upon us?

### CHORUS LEADER

He has made a mistake. But this is natural in young men, and you should forgive him. [But to a healer of these things, my lord, we have come.]

### ADRASTUS

I did not choose you, sir, to be the judge of my troubles or the punisher and rebuker of any discreditable deeds I am found to have committed, but to win benefit. If you refuse me this, I must put up with your decision: what else can I do?

Come, aged ladies, leave your gray-green branches

---

242 ‹τ'› Kirchhoff     248 ἴθ'· εἰ γὰρ μὴ edd. post Matthiae et Hermann: ἴθι· μὴ γὰρ L

249 σὴν . . . τί δεῖ Hermann: τὴν . . . λίαν L

252 del. Matthiae

259 καταστεφῆ Scaliger: καταστροφῆ L

260 θεούς τε καὶ γῆν τήν τε πυρφόρον θεὰν
Δήμητρα θέμεναι μάρτυρ' ἡλίου τε φῶς
ὡς οὐδὲν ἡμῖν ἤρκεσαν λιταὶ θεῶν.
  ⟨καίτοι τί πάσχω; χεῖρα σὴν ἱκνούμενος
ἀπεῖπον, ἓν μέγιστον διολέσας ἔπος;
ἡ γὰρ τεκοῦσά σ' ἐστὶ Πιτθέως κόρη,⟩
ὃς Πέλοπος ἦν παῖς, Πελοπίας δ' ἡμεῖς χθονὸς
ταὐτὸν πατρῷον αἷμα σοὶ κεκτήμεθα.
265 τί δρᾷς; προδώσεις ταῦτα κἀκβαλεῖς χθονὸς
γραῦς οὐ τυχούσας οὐδὲν ὧν αὐτὰς ἐχρῆν;
μὴ δῆτ'· ἔχει γὰρ καταφυγὴν θὴρ μὲν πέτραν,
δοῦλος δὲ βωμοὺς θεῶν, πόλις δὲ πρὸς πόλιν
ἔπτηξε χειμασθεῖσα· τῶν γὰρ ἐν βροτοῖς
270 οὐκ ἔστιν οὐδὲν διὰ τέλους εὐδαιμονοῦν.

ΧΟΡΟΣ

βᾶθι, τάλαιν', ἱερῶν δαπέδων ἀπὸ Περσεφονείας,
βᾶθι καὶ ἀντίασον γονάτων ἐπὶ χεῖρα βαλοῦσα,
τέκνων τεθνεώτων κομίσαι δέμας, ὦ μελέα 'γώ,
οὓς ὑπὸ Καδμείοισιν ἀπώλεσα τείχεσι κούρους.
275 [ἰώ μοι· λάβετε φέρετε πέμπετε †κρίνετε†
ταλαίνας χέρας γεραιάς.]
πρός ⟨σε⟩ γενειάδος, ὦ φίλος ⟨ὦ φίλος⟩,
ὦ δοκιμώτατος Ἑλλάδι ⟨γαίᾳ⟩,

262 post h. v. lac. indic. Melanchthon-Xylander
273 τεθνεώτων Reiske: τε θνατῶν L       274 Καδμείοισιν
ἀπώλεσα τείχεσι Hermann: τ- Κ- ἀ- L       275–6 del. Dindorf
277 ⟨σε⟩ Markland       ⟨ὦ φίλος⟩ Willink       ⟨γαίᾳ⟩ Willink

decked with foliage here and go, calling the gods, the earth,
Demeter the torchbearer, and the light of the sun to wit-
ness that your petitions in the gods' name have been un-
availing.

⟨But what is wrong with me? Have I given up suppli-
cating your hand and forgotten my single strongest argu-
ment? Your mother was the daughter of Pittheus,⟩ who
was the son of Pelops, and we of Pelops' land have the same
ancestral blood in our veins as you. What are you doing?
Will you abandon this tie and expel from the land old
women who have received nothing of what is owed them?
No! The beast has the cliff as its refuge, the slave the gods'
altars, and one city when storm-beaten takes refuge with
another. Where mortal fortunes are concerned, nothing
remains prosperous to the end.

*The Chorus leave their suppliant boughs in a circle around
Aethra and group themselves in supplication around The-
seus.*

CHORUS

Go then, unfortunate women, from the sacred precinct of
    Persephone!
Go, grasp his knees in supplication, and entreat him
to recover the bodies of your fallen sons, O unhappy me,
sons we have lost under the walls of Cadmus' city.
[Ah me! Take, bear, send, lift
the old and wretched hands.]
By your beard, dear friend, ⟨dear friend,⟩
most glorious man in the eyes of Hellas' ⟨land⟩,

41

ἄντομαι ἀμφιπίτνουσα τὸ σὸν γόνυ
καὶ χέρα δειλαία, οἴκτισαι ⟨οἴκτισαι⟩
280 ἀμφὶ τέκνων μ' ἱκέτιν καὶ ἀλάταν
οἰκτρὸν ἰήλεμον οἰκτρὸν ἱεῖσαν.
μηδ' ἀτάφους, τέκνον, ἐν Κάδμου χθονὶ χάρματα
θηρῶν
παῖδας ἐν ἡλικίᾳ τᾷ σᾷ κατίδῃς, ἱκετεύω.
βλέψον ἐμῶν βλεφάρων ἔπι δάκρυον, ἃ περὶ σοῖσι
285 γούνασιν ὧδε πίτνω τέκνοις τάφον ἐξανύσασθαι.

ΘΗΣΕΥΣ

μῆτερ, τί κλαίεις λέπτ' ἐπ' ὀμμάτων φάρη
βαλοῦσα τῶν σῶν; ἆρα δυστήνους γόους
κλυοῦσα τῶνδε; κἀμὲ γὰρ διῆλθέ τι.
ἔπαιρε λευκὸν κρᾶτα, μὴ δακρυρρόει
290 σεμναῖσι Δῃοῦς ἐσχάραις παρημένη.

ΑΙΘΡΑ

αἰαῖ.

ΘΗΣΕΥΣ

τὰ τούτων οὐχὶ σοὶ στενακτέον.

ΑΙΘΡΑ

ὦ τλήμονες γυναῖκες.

ΘΗΣΕΥΣ

οὐ σὺ τῶνδ' ἔφυς.

279 δειλαία Hermann: -αν L    ⟨οἴκτισαι⟩ Musgrave
280 ἱκέτιν Markland: -ταν L    καὶ Stinton ap. Collard: ἤ
τιν' L

I beg you, clasping your knees
and hand in my misery: pity, <O pity> me,
the suppliant and wanderer on my sons' behalf,
as I utter a pitiable, pitiable cry!
Do not, my son, stand by in your youthful vigor
and let my sons lie unburied in Cadmus' land to delight the
    wild beasts, I implore you!
Look at the tears on my cheeks! See how I fall
at your knees entreating you to win burial for my sons!

*Aethra covers her face with the folds of her robe and weeps
aloud.*

THESEUS

Mother, why are you weeping, holding your fine-spun gar-
ments before your eyes? Is it because you hear the un-
happy wailing of these women? In some measure it has
affected me also. Raise up your white head, do not shed
tears as you sit by the holy altar of Deo.[11]

AETHRA

Ah me!

THESEUS

You must not groan at these women's fate.

AETHRA

O luckless women!

THESEUS

You are not one of their number.

[11] Another name for Demeter.

---

282 Κάδμου χθονὶ Wilamowitz: χ- K- L        κύρματα Wake-
field

# EURIPIDES

ΑΙΘΡΑ

εἴπω τι, τέκνον, σοί τε καὶ πόλει καλόν;

ΘΗΣΕΥΣ

ὡς πολλά γ᾽ ἐστὶ κἀπὸ θηλειῶν σοφά.

ΑΙΘΡΑ

295 ἀλλ᾽ εἰς ὄκνον μοι μῦθος ὃν κεύθω φέρει.

ΘΗΣΕΥΣ

αἰσχρόν γ᾽ ἔλεξας, χρήστ᾽ ἔπη κρύπτειν φίλους.

ΑΙΘΡΑ

οὔτοι σιωπῶσ᾽ εἶτα μέμψομαί ποτε
τὴν νῦν σιωπὴν ὡς ἐσιγήθη κακῶς,
οὐδ᾽, ὡς ἀχρεῖον τὰς γυναῖκας εὖ λέγειν
300 δείσασ᾽ ἀφήσω τῷ φόβῳ τοὐμὸν καλόν.
ἐγὼ δέ σ᾽, ὦ παῖ, πρῶτα μὲν τὰ τῶν θεῶν
σκοπεῖν κελεύω μὴ σφαλῇς ἀτιμάσας.
[σφαλῇς γὰρ ἐν τούτῳ μόνῳ, τἄλλ᾽ εὖ φρονῶν.]
πρὸς τοῖσδε δ᾽, εἰ μὲν μὴ ἀδικουμένοις ἐχρῆν
305 τολμηρὸν εἶναι, κάρτ᾽ ἂν εἶχον ἡσύχως.
†νυνὶ δὲ σοί τε τοῦτο τὴν τιμὴν φέρει†
κἀμοὶ παραινεῖν οὐ φόβον φέρει, τέκνον,
ἄνδρας βιαίους καὶ κατείργοντας νεκροὺς
τάφου τε μοῖραν καὶ κτερισμάτων λαχεῖν
310 ἐς τήνδ᾽ ἀνάγκην σῇ καταστῆσαι χερί,

---

296 ἔπη κρύπτειν Hermann: ἐπικρύπτειν L      φίλους
Barnes: -οις L    299 post h. v. lac. fort. indicanda, e.g. ⟨δοκοῦν
ἅπασι, μή μ᾽ ἐπαινέσῃ πόλις⟩

AETHRA

Shall I say something, my son, that brings honor to you and to the city?

THESEUS

Yes, for much wise advice can be heard even from women.

AETHRA

But the suggestion I have in my heart causes me to hesitate.

THESEUS

For shame—keeping good words from your near and dear!

AETHRA

I shall not hold my peace and then at some later time reproach myself for my present silence, nor, since it is a useless thing for women to be eloquent, shall I, out of fear, let go of the noble task that is mine.

I urge you first of all, my son, to consider the will of the gods lest you meet with disaster by neglecting it. [You fail in this one thing, being sensible in all else.] In addition, if you were not called to be courageous on behalf of the wronged, I would hold my peace. As matters stand, my son, this course of action brings you honor, and I feel no fear in recommending it, urging you to use force to compel men who are violent and deprive the dead of due burial to grant

---

νόμιμά τε πάσης συγχέοντας Ἑλλάδος
παῦσαι· τὸ γάρ τοι συνέχον ἀνθρώπων πόλεις
τοῦτ᾽ ἔσθ᾽, ὅταν τις τοὺς νόμους σῴζῃ καλῶς.
ἐρεῖ δὲ δή τις ὡς ἀνανδρίᾳ χερῶν,
315 πόλει παρόν σοι στέφανον εὐκλείας λαβεῖν,
δείσας ἀπέστης, καὶ συὸς μὲν ἀγρίου
ἀγῶνος ᾔψω φαῦλον ἀθλήσας πόνον,
οὗ δ᾽ ἐς κράνος βλέψαντα καὶ λόγχης ἀκμὴν
χρῆν ἐκπονῆσαι δειλὸς ὢν ἐφηυρέθης.
320 μὴ δῆτ᾽ ἐμός γ᾽ ὤν, ὦ τέκνον, δράσῃς τάδε.
ὁρᾷς; ἄβουλος ὡς κεκερτομημένη
τοῖς κερτομοῦσι γοργὸν ὄμμ᾽ ἀναβλέπει
σὴ πατρίς· ἐν γὰρ τοῖς πόνοισιν αὔξεται.
αἱ δ᾽ ἥσυχοι σκοτεινὰ πράσσουσαι πόλεις
325 σκοτεινὰ καὶ βλέπουσιν εὐλαβούμεναι.
οὐκ εἶ νεκροῖσι καὶ γυναιξὶν ἀθλίαις
προσωφελήσων, ὦ τέκνον, κεχρημέναις;
ὡς οὔτε ταρβῶ σὺν δίκῃ σ᾽ ὁρμώμενον
Κάδμου θ᾽ ὁρῶσα λαὸν εὖ πεπραγότα
330 ἔτ᾽ αὐτὸν ἄλλα βλήματ᾽ ἐν κύβοις βαλεῖν
πέποιθ᾽· ὁ γὰρ θεὸς πάντ᾽ ἀναστρέφει πάλιν.

ΧΟΡΟΣ

ὦ φιλτάτη μοι, τῷδέ τ᾽ εἴρηκας καλῶς
κἀμοί· διπλοῦν δὲ χάρμα γίγνεται τόδε.

ΘΗΣΕΥΣ

ἐμοὶ λόγοι μέν, μῆτερ, οἱ λελεγμένοι
335 ὀρθῶς ἔχουσ᾽ ἐς τόνδε, κἀπεφηνάμην

it, preventing them from violating what all Greece holds
lawful. It is the decent observance of the laws that holds
together all human communities.

Furthermore someone will say that you timidly stood
aside out of physical cowardice, although you could have
won for the city a crown of glory. They will say that you
struggled against a wild boar, a trivial labor, but where you
ought to have struggled through in the face of enemy hel-
mets and spear points, you showed yourself a coward. You
are my child, son—do not act thus! Don't you see? Your
country, when it is taunted with rashness, turns its fierce
visage against its taunters. It flourishes in strenuous action.
Cities that keep quiet and do no deeds of glory have no
glory in their glances but only caution.[12]

Go, my son, and help the dead and these unhappy
women in their hour of need! I have no fear for you. You
are setting out in a just cause, and I am confident, as I see
the people of Cadmus prospering, that their future dice
casts will be different. Heaven overturns all things.

CHORUS LEADER

O dearest of women to me, your words were nobly spoken
both in his eyes and in mine! This is a double joy!

THESEUS

Mother, the words I spoke to this man were the truth: I

[12] Athens had a reputation among the Greeks for vigorous
(and meddlesome) activism. Compare the remarks of the Corin-
thian ambassadors at Thucydides 1.70.

---

322 γοργὸν ὄμμ' Wecklein: γοργόν' ὧς L
330 ἄλλα βλήματ' αὐτὸν Broadhead

γνώμην ὑφ' οἵων ἐσφάλη βουλευμάτων·
ὁρῶ δὲ κἀγὼ ταῦθ' ἅπερ με νουθετεῖς,
ὡς τοῖς ἐμοῖσιν οὐχὶ πρόσφορον τρόποις
φεύγειν τὰ δεινά. πολλὰ γὰρ δράσας καλὰ
340 ἔθος τόδ' εἰς Ἕλληνας ἐξεδειξάμην,
ἀεὶ κολαστὴς τῶν κακῶν καθεστάναι.
οὔκουν ἀπαυδᾶν δυνατόν ἐστί μοι πόνους.
τί γάρ μ' ἐροῦσιν οἵ γε δυσμενεῖς βροτῶν,
ὅθ' ἡ τεκοῦσα χὐπερορρωδοῦσ' ἐμοῦ
345 πρώτη κελεύεις τόνδ' ὑποστῆναι πόνον;
    δράσω τάδ'· εἶμι καὶ νεκροὺς ἐκλύσομαι
λόγοισι πείθων· εἰ δὲ μή, βίᾳ δορὸς
ἤδη τότ' ἔσται κοὐχὶ σὺν φθόνῳ θεῶν.
δόξαι δὲ χρῄζω καὶ πόλει πάσῃ τόδε,
350 δόξει δ' ἐμοῦ θέλοντος· ἀλλὰ τοῦ λόγου
προσδοὺς ἔχοιμ' ἂν δῆμον εὐμενέστερον.
καὶ γὰρ κατέστησ' αὐτὸν ἐς μοναρχίαν
ἐλευθερώσας τήνδ' ἰσόψηφον πόλιν.
λαβὼν δ' Ἄδραστον δεῖγμα τῶν ἐμῶν λόγων
355 ἐς πλῆθος ἀστῶν εἶμι· καὶ πείσας τάδε,
λεκτοὺς ἀθροίσας δεῦρ' Ἀθηναίων κόρους
ἥξω· παρ' ὅπλοις θ' ἥμενος πέμψω λόγους
Κρέοντι νεκρῶν σώματ' ἐξαιτούμενος.
    ἀλλ', ὦ γεραιαί, σέμν' ἀφαιρεῖτε στέφη
360 μητρός, πρὸς οἴκους ὥς νιν Αἰγέως ἄγω,
φίλην προσάψας χεῖρα· τοῖς τεκοῦσι γὰρ

340 ἐξεδειξάμην Hermann: -λεξάμην L

48

spoke my mind about the counsels that ruined him. Yet I can also see what you say to me, that it is not like me to run from danger. By many glorious deeds I have demonstrated to the Greeks that my custom is always to be a punisher of the wicked. So I cannot refuse hard tasks. What will my enemies say about me when you, who bore me and would naturally be worried about me, are the first to urge me to undertake this toil?

Here is what I shall do: I shall go and win release of the bodies, persuading the Thebans with my words. If that fails, then it shall be done by force, and the gods will not begrudge it. I want the city too to ratify this decision, and ratify it they will since that is what I wish. But if I add my reasons I will have more of the people's good will. And in fact I have made the people sovereign by freeing this city and giving them equal votes. I shall take Adrastus along as the proof of what I am saying and appear before the citizen assembly. When I have won them over on this point, I shall gather a picked band of Athenian youth and return here. Sitting in encampment I shall send a message to Creon, asking for the bodies of the dead.

So, aged women, remove your suppliant boughs from my mother so that I may bring her to Aegeus' house,[13] taking her beloved hand in mine. That son is a poor wretch

---

[13] I.e. his own house: Aegeus, now dead, was Theseus' father.

---

347 πείθων Nauck: πείσων L
348 τότ᾽ Diggle: τόδ᾽ L
350 τοῦ] fort. τοι
352 αὐτὸς Kirchhoff
355 ἀστῶν Elmsley: αὐτῶν L

δύστηνος ὅστις μὴ ἀντιδουλεύει τέκνων
κάλλιστον ἔρανον· δοὺς γὰρ ἀντιλάζυται
παίδων παρ' αὑτοῦ τοιάδ' ἂν τοκεῦσι δῷ.

ΧΟΡΟΣ

στρ. α

365 ἱππόβοτον Ἄργος, ὦ πάτριον ἐμὸν πέδον,
†ἐκλύετε τάδ', ἐκλύετε†
ἄνακτος ὅσια περὶ θεοὺς
καὶ μεγάλα Πελασγίᾳ
καὶ κατ' Ἄργος;

ἀντ. α

εἰ γὰρ ἐπὶ τέρμα καὶ τὸ πλέον ἐμῶν κακῶν
370 †ἱκόμενος ἔτι ματέρος
ἄγαλμα† φόνιον ἐξέλοι,
γᾶν δὲ φίλιον Ἰνάχου
θεῖτ' ὀνήσας.

στρ. β

καλὸν δ' ἄγαλμα πόλεσιν εὐ-
σεβὴς πόνος χάριν τ' ἔχει
τὰν ἐς αἰεί.
τί μοι πόλις κρανεῖ ποτ'; ἆ-
375 ρα φίλιά μοι
τεμοῦσι καὶ τέκνοις ταφὰς
ληψόμεσθα;

366 ἐκλύετ' ‹ἔπεα› τάδ', ἐκλύετ' ‹ὦ› Willink
368 fort. κατ' ἄνδρας, tum γᾷ pro καὶ Willink

50

who does not serve his parents, making his noble contribution to the feast. When he has made it, he receives back from his own children services like those he gave his parents.

*The Chorus pick up their suppliant boughs. Exit* THESEUS *with retinue,* AETHRA, *and* ADRASTUS *by Eisodos* A.

CHORUS
Horse-pasturing Argos, ground my fathers trod,
have you heard, have you heard
from the king these words god-fearing
and great in the eyes of Pelasgia and Argos?

May he go to the utmost end of my troubles and beyond,
rescue a mother's
blood-stained darling,
and make a friend of the land of Inachus[14]
by doing her good!

Pious toil is a glorious adornment
to cities, and it wins gratitude
for all time.
What will the city decide to do for me?
Will they make a treaty
of friendship with me, and will we win
burial for our sons?

---

[14] The chief river of Argos.

---

370–1 ἱκόμενος ἔτι ματέρος ἄγαλ- / μα ⟨λῦμα⟩ φόνιον Willink
376 τεμοῦσι Willink: τεμεῖ L

ἀντ. β

ἄμυνε ματρί, πόλις, ἄμυ-
νε, Παλλάδος, νόμους βροτῶν
μὴ μιαίνειν.
σύ τοι σέβεις δίκαν, τὸ δ' ἧσ-
σον ἀδικίᾳ
380   νέμεις ἀεί τε δυστυχῆ
πάντα ῥύῃ.

ΘΗΣΕΥΣ

τέχνην μὲν αἰεὶ τήνδ' ἔχων ὑπηρετεῖς
πόλει τε κἀμοὶ διαφέρων κηρύγματα·
ἐλθὼν δ' ὑπέρ τ' Ἀσωπὸν Ἰσμηνοῦ θ' ὕδωρ
σεμνῷ τυράννῳ φράζε Καδμείων τάδε·
385   Θησεύς σ' ἀπαιτεῖ πρὸς χάριν θάψαι νεκρούς,
συγγείτον' οἰκῶν γαῖαν, ἀξιῶν τυχεῖν,
φίλον τε θέσθαι πάντ' Ἐρεχθειδῶν λεών.
κἂν μὲν θέλωσιν, αἰνέσας παλίσσυτος
στεῖχ'· ἢν δ' ἀπιστῶσ', οἵδε δεύτεροι λόγοι,
390   κῶμον δέχεσθαι τὸν ἐμὸν ἀσπιδηφόρον.
στρατὸς δὲ θάσσει κἀξετάζεται παρὼν
Καλλίχορον ἀμφὶ σεμνὸν εὐτρεπὴς ὅδε.
καὶ μὴν ἑκοῦσά γ' ἀσμένη τ' ἐδέξατο
πόλις πόνον τόνδ', ὡς θέλοντά μ' ᾔσθετο.

380 τε Willink: τὸν L
388 αἰνέσας Cobet: αἰνέσαι L
393 γ' Hermann: τ' L

52

O city of Pallas, protect, protect
a mother: see that the laws
of mortals are not defiled!
You honor justice, paying
no honor to injustice,
and always rescue
all that is unfortunate.

*Enter* THESEUS *with retinue,* ADRASTUS, *and an Athenian
herald by Eisodos A.*

### THESEUS
As on all other occasions you have served the city and me
by this art you practice of carrying proclamations, so now
cross the Asopus and the waters of the Ismenus and tell
the haughty king of the Cadmeans the following: "Theseus
asks you as a favor to bury the dead; he is your neigh-
bor and thinks it right that his request be granted; do this
and you will make the whole host of the Erechtheids your
friends." If they consent, thank them and hurry back home.
But if they refuse to listen, then give them a second mes-
sage: they should expect revelers of mine at their door,
revelers who carry shields. Our army here sits in readiness
and is being reviewed around the holy spring of Callicho-
rus.[15] The city gladly and willingly took up this task when
they heard that I wished them to do so.

*Enter a Theban* HERALD *by Eisodos B.*

[15] A sacred spring at Eleusis, famous in the legend of Deme-
ter.

395 ἔα· λόγων τίς ἐμποδὼν ὅδ' ἔρχεται;
Καδμεῖος, ὡς ἔοικεν οὐ σάφ' εἰδότι,
κῆρυξ. ἐπίσχες, ἤν σ' ἀπαλλάξῃ πόνου
μολὼν ὕπαντα τοῖς ἐμοῖς βουλεύμασιν.

ΚΗΡΥΞ

τίς γῆς τύραννος; πρὸς τίν' ἀγγεῖλαί με χρὴ
400 λόγους Κρέοντος, ὃς κρατεῖ Κάδμου χθονὸς
Ἐτεοκλέους θανόντος ἀμφ' ἑπταστόμους
πύλας ἀδελφῇ χειρὶ Πολυνείκους ὕπο;

ΘΗΣΕΥΣ

πρῶτον μὲν ἤρξω τοῦ λόγου ψευδῶς, ξένε,
ζητῶν τύραννον ἐνθάδ'· οὐ γὰρ ἄρχεται
405 ἑνὸς πρὸς ἀνδρὸς ἀλλ' ἐλευθέρα πόλις.
δῆμος δ' ἀνάσσει διαδοχαῖσιν ἐν μέρει
ἐνιαυσίαισιν, οὐχὶ τῷ πλούτῳ διδοὺς
τὸ πλεῖστον, ἀλλὰ χὠ πένης ἔχων ἴσον.

ΚΗΡΥΞ

ἓν μὲν τόδ' ἡμῖν ὥσπερ ἐν πεσσοῖς δίδως
410 κρεῖσσον· πόλις γὰρ ἧς ἐγὼ πάρειμ' ἄπο
ἑνὸς πρὸς ἀνδρός, οὐκ ὄχλῳ, κρατύνεται·
οὐδ' ἔστιν αὐτὴν ὅστις ἐκχαυνῶν λόγοις
πρὸς κέρδος ἴδιον ἄλλοτ' ἄλλοσε στρέφει.
[ὁ δ' αὐτίχ' ἡδὺς καὶ διδοὺς πολλὴν χάριν
415 ἐσαῦθις ἔβλαψ', εἶτα διαβολαῖς νέαις
κλέψας τὰ πρόσθε σφάλματ' ἐξέδυ δίκης.]
ἄλλως τε πῶς ἂν μὴ διορθεύων λόγους
ὀρθῶς δύναιτ' ἂν δῆμος εὐθύνειν πόλιν;

But what is this? Who is this coming to stand in the way of my message? I cannot tell for sure, but he seems to be a Cadmean herald. Wait a minute to see whether he will save you effort by coming to meet my intentions.

HERALD

Who is the land's master? To whom shall I bring a message from Creon, who controls Cadmus' land since Eteocles was killed near the seven gates in fraternal bloodshed by Polynices?

THESEUS

To begin with, stranger, you started your speech on a false note by asking for the master here. The city is not ruled by a single man but is free. The people rule, and offices are held by yearly turns: they do not assign the highest honors to the rich, but the poor also have an equal share.

HERALD

Your words put me one point ahead, as in a game of draughts. The city I have come from is ruled by one man and not by a rabble. There is no one to fool the city with flattering speech and lead it this way and that to suit his own advantage. [At first he is welcome and gives much pleasure, but later he causes harm, and then, by the further expedient of slander, he conceals his earlier misdeeds and slips out of the reach of justice.] And anyway how can the common people, if they cannot even make a speech properly, know the right way to guide a city? It is time, not

---

402 ἀδελφῇ Camper: -φοῦ L     ὕπο] θ' ὁμοῦ Camper
408 ἴσον σθένει Herwerden: sed fort. delendi 406-8
414-6 del. Kovacs     414 ὁ] τὸ Wilamowitz

ὁ γὰρ χρόνος μάθησιν ἀντὶ τοῦ τάχους
420 κρείσσω δίδωσι. γαπόνος δ' ἀνὴρ πένης,
εἰ καὶ γένοιτο μὴ ἀμαθής, ἔργων ὕπο
οὐκ ἂν δύναιτο πρὸς τὰ κοίν' ἀποβλέπειν.
ἦ δὴ νοσῶδες τοῦτο τοῖς ἀμείνοσιν,
ὅταν πονηρὸς ἀξίωμ' ἀνὴρ ἔχῃ
425 γλώσσῃ κατασχὼν δῆμον, οὐδὲν ὢν τὸ πρίν.

ΘΗΣΕΥΣ

κομψός γ' ὁ κῆρυξ καὶ παρεργάτης λόγων.
ἐπεὶ δ' ἀγῶνα καὶ σὺ τόνδ' ἠγωνίσω,
ἄκου'· ἅμιλλαν γὰρ σὺ προύθηκας λόγων.
οὐδὲν τυράννου δυσμενέστερον πόλει,
430 ὅπου τὸ μὲν πρώτιστον οὐκ εἰσὶν νόμοι
κοινοί, κρατεῖ δ' εἷς τὸν νόμον κεκτημένος
αὐτὸς παρ' αὑτῷ· καὶ τόδ' οὐκέτ' ἔστ' ἴσον.
γεγραμμένων δὲ τῶν νόμων ὅ τ' ἀσθενὴς
ὁ πλούσιός τε τὴν δίκην ἴσην ἔχει,
435 [ἔστιν δ' ἐνισπεῖν τοῖσιν ἀσθενεστέροις
τὸν εὐτυχοῦντα ταῦθ', ὅταν κλύῃ κακῶς,]
νικᾷ δ' ὁ μείων τὸν μέγαν δίκαι' ἔχων.
τοὐλεύθερον δ' ἐκεῖνο· Τίς θέλει πόλει
χρηστόν τι βούλευμ' ἐς μέσον φέρειν ἔχων;
440 καὶ ταῦθ' ὁ χρῄζων λαμπρός ἐσθ', ὁ δ' οὐ θέλων
σιγᾷ. τί τούτων ἔστ' ἰσαίτερον πόλει;
[καὶ μὴν ὅπου γε δῆμος αὐθέντης χθονός,
ὑποῦσιν ἀστοῖς ἥδεται νεανίαις·
ἀνὴρ δὲ βασιλεὺς ἐχθρὸν ἡγεῖται τόδε,

haste, that gives superior learning. Now the poor farmer, even if he is no fool, has no chance, because of his labor, to attend to the city's business. What is more, the better sort find it a sorry business when a man of low birth, a former nonentity, achieves prominence by entrancing the common people with his glib tongue.

#### THESEUS

This herald is a clever talker and loves to speak elaborately on what is no part of his errand! Well, since you have begun this contest, hear me out: for it was you who proposed this debate.

There is nothing more hostile to a city than a tyrant. In the first place, there are no common laws in such a city, and one man, keeping the law in his own hands, holds sway. This is unjust. When the laws are written, both the powerless and the rich have equal access to justice, [and it is possible for the weaker man to address the same words to the fortunate man whenever he is badly spoken of,] and the little man, if he has right on his side, defeats the big man. Freedom consists in this: "Who has a good proposal and wants to set it before the city?" He who wants to enjoys fame, while he who does not holds his peace. What is fairer for a city than this?

[Wherever the people rule the land, they take pleasure in the young citizens that are its strength. But a king thinks this hateful, and he kills the nobles ⟨and⟩ all he

---

421 μὴ ἀμαθής Lobeck: κἀμαθής L      fort. ἔργων ⟨θ᾽⟩
423-5 del. Kirchhoff: ἢ δὴ hic tantum apud Eur.
432 ἔστ᾽ ἴσον Tyrwhitt: ἐστί σοι L      435-6 del. Nauck
440 δ᾽ οὐ Hartung: μὴ L      442-55 del. Kovacs

57

445 καὶ τοὺς ἀρίστους οὓς <τ᾿> ἂν ἡγῆται φρονεῖν
κτείνει, δεδοικὼς τῆς τυραννίδος πέρι.
πῶς οὖν ἔτ᾿ ἂν γένοιτ᾿ ἂν ἰσχυρὰ πόλις
ὅταν τις ὡς λειμῶνος ἠρινοῦ στάχυν
τόλμας ἀφαιρῇ κἀπολωτίζῃ νέων;
450 κτᾶσθαι δὲ πλοῦτον καὶ βίον τί δεῖ τέκνοις
ὡς τῷ τυράννῳ πλείον᾿ ἐκμοχθῇ βίον;
ἢ παρθενεύειν παῖδας ἐν δόμοις καλῶς,
τερπνὰς τυράννοις ἡδονάς, ὅταν θέλῃ,
δάκρυα δ᾿ ἑτοιμάζουσι; μὴ ζῴην ἔτι
455 εἰ τἀμὰ τέκνα πρὸς βίαν νυμφεύσεται.]
    καὶ ταῦτα μὲν δὴ πρὸς τὰ σ᾿ ἐξηκόντισα.
ἥκεις δὲ δὴ τί τῆσδε γῆς κεχρημένος;
κλαίων γ᾿ ἂν ἦλθες, εἴ σε μὴ ᾿πεμψεν πόλις,
περισσὰ φωνῶν· τὸν γὰρ ἄγγελον χρεὼν
460 λέξανθ᾿ ὅσ᾿ ἂν τάξῃ τις ὡς τάχος πάλιν
χωρεῖν. τὸ λοιπὸν δ᾿ εἰς ἐμὴν πόλιν Κρέων
ἧσσον λάλον σου πεμπέτω τιν᾿ ἄγγελον.

ΧΟΡΟΣ

φεῦ φεῦ· κακοῖσιν ὡς ὅταν δαίμων διδῷ
καλῶς, ὑβρίζουσ᾿ ὡς ἀεὶ πράξοντες εὖ.

ΚΗΡΥΞ

465 λέγοιμ᾿ ἂν ἤδη. τῶν μὲν ἠγωνισμένων

---

445 <τ᾿> Markland    449 νέων Kirchhoff: νέους L: quo accepto τομαῖς pro τόλμας Nauck
455 νυμφεύσεται Hermann: -εύεται L
458 γ᾿ Lenting: δ᾿ L    460 πάλιν Reiske: πόλει L

regards as proud, fearing for his power. How then could a
city be strong in the future when someone culls and cuts
away the boldest of the young as one does the towering
stalk in a springtime meadow?[16] And why should one ac-
quire wealth and a livelihood for one's children merely to
produce greater livelihood for the tyrant? And why gently
raise girls in the house only to be a sweet pleasure for the
ruler when he wants them and a source of tears for those
who raised them? Better to die than see one's children
forcibly molested!]

This is the answer I have launched in reply to your
words. But what is your errand, what do you want from this
land? If your city had not sent you, we would have made
you regret coming here and talking so much. A messenger
should say what he has been told to say and then depart at
once. Henceforth let Creon send to my city a messenger
less talkative than you!

CHORUS LEADER
Ah, how true it is that when fortune favors the base, they
behave insolently, thinking they will be prosperous for
ever!

HERALD
Now I shall speak. As regards our debate, you hold to your

16 Perhaps an allusion to the story, told in Herodotus 5.92, that
when a messenger was sent by Periander, tyrant of Corinth, to
Thrasybulus, tyrant of Miletus, to ask how to make his reign se-
cure, Thrasybulus proceeded to lop the tallest of the ears of
wheat, hinting that Periander should kill those ablest to oppose
him.

σοὶ μὲν δοκείτω ταῦτ', ἐμοὶ δὲ τἀντία.
ἐγὼ δ' ἀπαυδῶ πᾶς τε Καδμεῖος λεὼς
Ἄδραστον ἐς γῆν τήνδε μὴ παριέναι·
εἰ δ' ἔστιν ἐν γῇ, πρὶν θεοῦ δῦναι σέλας
470  λύσαντα σεμνὰ στεμμάτων μυστήρια
τῆσδ' ἐξελαύνειν, μηδ' ἀναιρεῖσθαι νεκροὺς
βίᾳ, προσῆκοντ' οὐδὲν Ἀργείων πόλει.
κἂν μὲν πίθῃ μοι, κυμάτων ἄτερ πόλιν
σὴν ναυστολήσεις· εἰ δὲ μή, πολὺς κλύδων
475  ἡμῖν τε καὶ σοὶ συμμάχοις τ' ἔσται δορός.
    σκέψαι δέ, καὶ μὴ τοῖς ἐμοῖς θυμούμενος
λόγοισιν, ὡς δὴ πόλιν ἐλευθέραν ἔχων,
σφριγῶντ' ἀμείψῃ μῦθον ἐκ βραχιόνων.
ἐλπὶς γάρ ἐστ' ἄπιστον, ἢ πολλὰς πόλεις
480  συνῆψ' ἄγουσα θυμὸν εἰς ὑπερβολάς.
ὅταν γὰρ ἔλθῃ πόλεμος ἐς ψῆφον λεώ,
οὐδεὶς ἐφ' αὑτοῦ θάνατον ἐκλογίζεται,
τὸ δυστυχὲς δὲ τοῦτ' ἐς ἄλλον ἐκτρέπει.
εἰ δ' ἦν παρ' ὄμμα θάνατος ἐν ψήφου φορᾷ,
485  οὐκ ἄν ποθ' Ἑλλὰς δοριμανὴς ἀπώλλυτο.
    καίτοι δυοῖν γε πάντες ἄνθρωποι λόγοιν
τὸν κρείσσον' ἴσμεν, καὶ τὰ χρηστὰ καὶ κακά,
ὅσῳ τε πολέμου κρεῖσσον εἰρήνη βροτοῖς·
ἣ πρῶτα μὲν Μούσαισι προσφιλεστάτη,
490  Ποιναῖσι δ' ἐχθρά, τέρπεται τ' εὐπαιδίᾳ,
χαίρει δὲ πλούτῳ. ταῦτ' ἀφέντες οἱ κακοὶ
πολέμους ἀναιρούμεσθα καὶ τὸν ἥσσονα
δουλούμεθ', ἄνδρες ἄνδρα καὶ πόλις πόλιν.

opinions and I shall hold to the opposite. But I and all the people of Cadmus' city forbid you to admit Adrastus into your land. If he is already here, break the sacred spell of suppliant boughs and drive him from this land before the sun god's light goes down. Do not attempt to take up the dead by force, since you have no connection to the city of Argos. If you do as I say, you will steer your city out of the waves. If you do not, both we and you and your allies will have heavy seas.

Think this over, and do not, from anger at my words, make some boastful answer on slender grounds, claiming that you live in a free city. Hope is a thing not to be trusted, and it has set cities at war with each other by kindling anger to excess. When a war comes to be voted on by the people, no one reckons on his own death: others, he thinks, will suffer that misfortune. If death stood before his eyes as he cast his vote, Hellas would not be perishing from spear madness.

Yet all men know which of two speeches is better, what is good and what is bad, and how much better for mortals is peace than war. Peace is beloved by the Muses and hated by the Avenging Spirits, she delights in lovely children and glories in wealth. We worthless mortals let these good things go, starting wars and enslaving the weaker party, men enslaving men and cities cities.

---

466 τἀντία Porson, Hermann: τἀναντία L
469 γῇ Reiske: τῇ L    471 τῆσδ'] γῆς Jacobs
479 ἐστ' ἄπιστον Fix: ἔστι κάκιστον L
482 ἐφ' Fritzsche: ἔθ' L
487 καὶ καλά Reiske: χοἱ κακοί West

σὺ δ' ἄνδρας ἐχθροὺς καὶ θανόντας ὠφελεῖς,
495 θάπτων κομίζων θ' ὕβρις οὓς ἀπώλεσεν;
οὔ τἄρ' ἔτ' ὀρθῶς Καπανέως κεραύνιον
δέμας καπνοῦται, κλιμάκων ὀρθοστάτας
ὃς προσβαλὼν πύλαισιν ὤμοσεν πόλιν
πέρσειν θεοῦ θέλοντος ἤν τε μὴ θέλῃ,
500 οὐδ' ἥρπασεν χάρυβδις οἰωνοσκόπον
τέθριππον ἅρμα περιβαλοῦσα χάσματι,
ἄλλοι τε κεῖνται πρὸς πύλαις λοχαγέται
πέτροις καταξανθέντες ὀστέων ῥαφάς.
ἢ νῦν φρονεῖν ἄμεινον ἐξαύχει Διὸς
505 ἢ θεοὺς δικαίως τοὺς κακοὺς ἀπολλύναι.
    φιλεῖν μὲν οὖν χρὴ τοὺς σοφοὺς πρῶτον τέκνα,
ἔπειτα τοκέας πατρίδα θ', ἣν αὔξειν χρεὼν
καὶ μὴ κατᾶξαι. σφαλερὸν ἡγεμὼν θρασὺς
νέος τε ναύτης· ἥσυχος καιρῷ σοφός.
510 καὶ τοῦτό μοι τἀνδρεῖον, ἡ προμηθία.

⟨ΧΟΡΟΣ⟩
ἐξαρκέσας ἦν Ζεὺς ὁ τιμωρούμενος,
ὑμᾶς δ' ὑβρίζειν οὐκ ἐχρῆν τοιάνδ' ὕβριν.

ΑΔΡΑΣΤΟΣ
ὦ παγκάκιστε . . .

ΘΗΣΕΥΣ
        σίγ', Ἄδραστ', ἔχε στόμα,

494 ἐχθροὺς θεοῖς Markland
496 οὔ τἄρ' Markland: οὔτ' ἂν L

62

Will you help men who were hostile and have been killed? Will you give burial to those who were destroyed by their own insolence? It was wrong, then, that Capaneus' body was turned to smoke by the thunderbolt, he who put his ladders against the gates and swore that he would sack the city whether the gods wanted him to or not! It was wrong that a chasm swallowed up the seer, engulfing his four-horse chariot in its gaping hole, and that the other captains lie near the gates, their skulls smashed by boulders! Therefore either confidently claim that you are wiser than Zeus or admit that the gods are right to destroy the wicked.

Wise men should love their children first, then their parents, then their country, which they should make great and not destroy. A brash leader, like a young sailor, is prone to error. The man inactive in season is wise. In my view, bravery really amounts to discretion.

⟨CHORUS LEADER⟩

Zeus who punished them was enough, and you ought not to have committed such an outrage.

ADRASTUS

Unspeakable villain . . .

THESEUS

Hold your tongue, Adrastus: do not shove your reply in

---

497 ὀρθοστάτας Nauck: -τάτων L
498 ὅς Nauck: ἃς L      505 δικαίου Markland
509 νέος Orelli: νεώς L: λεώς Diggle      ἥσυχος ⟨δὲ καὶ πόλιν / καὶ ναῦν ἔσωσε χρώμενος⟩ καιρῷ σοφῶς Hartung
510 τοι Hermann      511n ⟨Χο.⟩ Elmsley

καὶ μὴ 'πίπροσθεν τῶν ἐμῶν τοὺς σοὺς λόγους
515 θῆς· οὐ γὰρ ἥκει πρὸς σὲ κηρύσσων ὅδε
ἀλλ' ὡς ἔμ'· ἡμᾶς κἀποκρίνασθαι χρεών.
   καὶ πρῶτα μέν σε πρὸς τὰ πρῶτ' ἀμείψομαι.
οὐκ οἶδ' ἐγὼ Κρέοντα δεσπόζοντ' ἐμοῦ
οὐδὲ σθένοντα μεῖζον, ὥστ' ἀναγκάσαι
520 δρᾶν τὰς Ἀθήνας ταῦτ'· ἄνω γὰρ ἂν ῥέοι
τὰ πράγμαθ', οὕτως εἰ 'πιταξόμεσθα δή.
πόλεμον δὲ τοῦτον οὐκ ἐγὼ καθίσταμαι,
ὃς οὐδὲ σὺν τοῖσδ' ἦλθον ἐς Κάδμου χθόνα,
νεκροὺς δὲ τοὺς θανόντας, οὐ βλάπτων πόλιν
525 οὐδ' ἀνδροκμῆτας προσφέρων ἀγωνίας,
θάψαι δικαιῶ, τὸν Πανελλήνων νόμον
σῴζων. τί τούτων ἐστὶν οὐ καλῶς ἔχον;
εἰ γάρ τι καὶ πεπόνθατ' Ἀργείων ὕπο,
τεθνᾶσιν, ἠμύνασθε πολεμίους καλῶς,
530 αἰσχρῶς δ' ἐκείνοις, χἠ δίκη διοίχεται.
ἐάσατ' ἤδη γῇ καλυφθῆναι νεκρούς,
ὅθεν δ' ἕκαστον ἐς τὸ φῶς ἀφίκετο
ἐνταῦθ' ἀπελθεῖν, πνεῦμα μὲν πρὸς αἰθέρα,
τὸ σῶμα δ' ἐς γῆν· οὔτι γὰρ κεκτήμεθα
535 ἡμέτερον αὐτὸ πλὴν ἐνοικῆσαι βίον,
κἄπειτα τὴν θρέψασαν αὐτὸ δεῖ λαβεῖν.
   δοκεῖς κακουργεῖν Ἄργος οὐ θάπτων νεκρούς;
ἥκιστα· πάσης Ἑλλάδος κοινὸν τόδε,
εἰ τοὺς θανόντας νοσφίσας ὧν χρῆν λαχεῖν
540 ἀτάφους τις ἕξει· δειλίαν γὰρ ἐσφέρει
τοῖς ἀλκίμοισιν οὗτος ἢν τεθῇ νόμος.

64

ahead of mine! This man's message is not to you but to me, and it is I who must answer.

I shall address your first point first. I am not aware that Creon is my master or mightier than I, or that he can force Athens to carry out these commands of his. Things will be completely topsy-turvy if we allow ourselves to be dictated to in this way. As for this war, it was not I who began it: I did not come to the land of Cadmus with these Argives but am merely asking you, without harming your city or bringing man-wearying war against it, to allow the burial of the dead, maintaining the custom of all the Greeks. What is improper in this? Whatever you have suffered at the hands of the Argives, they are dead: you have fought off the enemy to your glory and their shame. Justice has run its course. Now let the dead be buried in the earth, and let each element return to the place from whence it came into the light of day, the spirit to the upper air, the body to the earth. We do not possess our bodies as our own: we live our lives in them, and thereafter the earth, our nourisher, must take them back.

Do you think it is Argos you harm by not burying the dead? You are wrong: all Hellas is concerned if the dead are deprived of their due and kept unburied. If your action becomes customary, it will turn brave men into cowards.

---

523–4 fort. ὃς οὔτε (Kirchhoff) ... νεκρούς τε (Paley)
532 ἑκάτερον Paley    φῶς Porson: σῶμ' L
539 νοσφίσας Markland: -ίσεις L

κἀμοὶ μὲν ἦλθες δείν' ἀπειλήσων ἔπη,
νεκροὺς δὲ ταρβεῖτ' εἰ κρυφήσονται χθονί;
τί μὴ γένηται; μὴ κατασκάψωσι γῆν
545 ταφέντες ὑμῶν; ἢ τέκν' ἐν μυχοῖς χθονὸς
φύσωσιν, ἐξ ὧν εἰσί τις τιμωρία;
σκαιόν γε τἀνάλωμα τῆς γλώσσης τόδε,
φόβους πονηροὺς καὶ κενοὺς δεδοικέναι.
[ἀλλ', ὦ μάταιοι, γνῶτε τἀνθρώπων κακά·
550 παλαίσμαθ' ἡμῶν ὁ βίος· εὐτυχοῦσι δὲ
οἱ μὲν τάχ', οἱ δ' ἐσαῦθις, οἱ δ' ἤδη βροτῶν,
τρυφᾷ δ' ὁ δαίμων· πρός τε γὰρ τοῦ δυστυχοῦς,
ὡς εὐτυχήσῃ, τίμιος γεραίρεται,
ὅ τ' ὄλβιός νιν πνεῦμα δειμαίνων λιπεῖν
555 ὑψηλὸν αἴρει. γνόντας οὖν χρεὼν τάδε
ἀδικουμένους τε μέτρια μὴ θυμῷ φέρειν
ἀδικεῖν τε τοιαῦθ' οἷα μὴ βλάψει πόλιν.]
πῶς οὖν ἂν εἴη; τοὺς ὀλωλότας νεκροὺς
θάψαι δόθ' ἡμῖν τοῖς θέλουσιν εὐσεβεῖν.
560 ἢ δῆλα τἀνθένδ'· εἶμι καὶ θάψω βίᾳ.
οὐ γάρ ποτ' εἰς Ἕλληνας ἐξοισθήσεται
ὡς εἰς ἔμ' ἐλθὼν καὶ πόλιν Πανδίονος
νόμος παλαιὸς δαιμόνων διεφθάρη.

ΧΟΡΟΣ

θάρσει· τὸ γάρ τοι τῆς Δίκης σῴζων φάος
565 πολλοὺς ὑπεκφύγοις ἂν ἀνθρώπων ψόγους.

---

543 κρυφήσονται Elmsley: κρυβ- L
545 μυχοῖς Markland: -ῷ L      547 γνώμης Markland

To me you have come uttering dreadful threats: are you nevertheless afraid of the dead if they are hidden in the earth? What are you afraid may happen? That they will overthrow your land from the grave? Or that in the depths of the earth they will beget children who will avenge them? It is a foolish waste of breath to give voice to fears that are base and idle.

[Foolish mortals, learn of mankind's woes! Our life is a struggle. Some had good fortune once, some will in the future, some have it now. But it is the deity who enjoys himself. The poor man praises and honors him in the hope of prospering, and the rich man exalts him for fear that he will be lose his favoring breeze. Knowing this, we should not get angry if moderate wrong is done to us, and we should do such wrongs as will not harm the city.]

Well, what will it be? We want to act piously: grant us permission to bury the dead. Otherwise, what comes next is plain: I will come and bury them by force. The news shall never be brought to the Greeks that the ancient law of the gods, coming before me and the city of Pandion, was there annulled.

#### CHORUS LEADER

Be of good cheer! If you keep the light of Lady Justice from being extinguished, you will escape much censure by mortals.

---

549–57 del. Kovacs (post 179 collocavit Murray)
551 τόθ' Markland        554 τ' Markland: δ' L
557 βλάψει Matthiae: -ψαι L        πάλιν Canter
559 δόθ' Kirchhoff: δὸς L        εὐσεβεῖν Markland: εἰσιδεῖν L
565 ψόγους Hartung: λόγους L

ΚΗΡΥΞ

βούλῃ συνάψω μῦθον ἐν βραχεῖ τιθείς;

ΘΗΣΕΥΣ

λέγ᾽, εἴ τι βούλῃ· καὶ γὰρ οὐ σιγηλὸς εἶ.

ΚΗΡΥΞ

οὐκ ἄν ποτ᾽ ἐκ γῆς παῖδας Ἀργείων λάβοις.

ΘΗΣΕΥΣ

κἀμοῦ νυν ἀντάκουσον, εἰ βούλῃ, πάλιν.

ΚΗΡΥΞ

570    κλύοιμ᾽ ἄν· οὐ γὰρ ἀλλὰ δεῖ δοῦναι μέρος.

ΘΗΣΕΥΣ

θάψω νεκροὺς γῆς ἐξελὼν Ἀσωπίας.

ΚΗΡΥΞ

ἐν ἀσπίσιν σοι πρῶτα κινδυνευτέον.

ΘΗΣΕΥΣ

πολλοὺς ἔτλην δὴ χἀτέρους ἄλλους πόνους.

ΚΗΡΥΞ

ἦ πᾶσιν οὖν σ᾽ ἔφυσεν ἐξαρκεῖν πατήρ;

ΘΗΣΕΥΣ

575    ὅσοι γ᾽ ὑβρισταί· χρηστὰ δ᾽ οὐ κολάζομεν.

ΚΗΡΥΞ

πράσσειν σὺ πόλλ᾽ εἴωθας ἥ τε σὴ πόλις.

ΘΗΣΕΥΣ

τοιγὰρ πονοῦσα πολλὰ πόλλ᾽ εὐδαιμονεῖ.

566 τιθείς Diggle: σέθεν L

**HERALD**

Do you wish me to make a brief reply?

**THESEUS**

Say anything you like: you are not one to keep quiet.

**HERALD**

You will never take the sons of the Argives from our land.

**THESEUS**

Hear me then in reply, if you please.

**HERALD**

I shall: I can hardly refuse you your turn.

**THESEUS**

I shall take the dead from Asopus' land and bury them.

**HERALD**

You will first have to run risks behind your shield.

**THESEUS**

I have had other hard tasks many and various.

**HERALD**

Did your father beget you then to be a match for all comers?

**THESEUS**

Yes, all who are insolent. I do not punish what is virtuous.

**HERALD**

You and your city are always busybodies.

**THESEUS**

Her toils are great. Hence great is her good fortune.

---

573 χἀτέρους ἄλλοις Blomfield: χἀτέροις ἄλλους Diggle

ΚΗΡΥΞ

ἔλθ᾽, ὥς σε λόγχη σπαρτὸς ἐν κόνει βάλῃ.

ΘΗΣΕΥΣ

τίς δ᾽ ἐκ δράκοντος θοῦρος ἂν γένοιτ᾽ Ἄρης;

ΚΗΡΥΞ

580 γνώσῃ σὺ πάσχων· νῦν δ᾽ ἔτ᾽ εἶ νεανίας.

ΘΗΣΕΥΣ

οὔτοι μ᾽ ἐπαρεῖς ὥστε θυμοῦσθαι φρένας
τοῖς σοῖσι κόμποις· ἀλλ᾽ ἀποστέλλου χθονὸς
λόγους ματαίους οὔσπερ ἠνέγκω λαβών.
περαίνομεν γὰρ οὐδέν.

ὁρμᾶσθαι χρεὼν
585 πάντ᾽ ἄνδρ᾽ ὁπλίτην, ἁρμάτων τ᾽ ἐπεμβάτην
μοναμπύκων τε φάλαρα †κινεῖσθαι στόμα†
ἀφρῷ καταστάζοντα Καδμείαν χθόνα.
χωρήσομαι γὰρ ἑπτὰ πρὸς Κάδμου πύλας
590 αὐτὸς σίδηρον ὀξὺν ἐν χεροῖν ἔχων
589 αὐτός τε κῆρυξ. σοὶ δὲ προστάσσω μένειν,
Ἄδραστε, κἀμοὶ μὴ ἀναμείγνυσθαι τύχας
τὰς σάς. ἐγὼ γὰρ δαίμονος τοὐμοῦ μέτα
στρατηλατήσω καινὸς ἐν καινῷ δορί.
ἓν δεῖ μόνον μοι, τοὺς θεοὺς ἔχειν ὅσοι
595 δίκην σέβονται· ταῦτα γὰρ ξυνόνθ᾽ ὁμοῦ
νίκην δίδωσιν. ἀρετὴ δ᾽ οὐδὲν φέρει
βροτοῖσιν, ἢν μὴ τὸν θεὸν χρῄζοντ᾽ ἔχῃ.

578 κόνει βάλῃ Kirchhoff: πόλει λάβῃ L    581 ἐπαρεῖς
Cobet: ἐπαίρεις L    θυμοῦσθαι Musgrave: θυμῶσαι L

**HERALD**

Come and let the Sown Men's spear[17] hurl you into the dust!

**THESEUS**

What sort of martial fury can come from a dragon?

**HERALD**

You'll learn by painful experience. You are still young.

**THESEUS**

You will not stir me up to anger with your boastful talk. Leave the country, and take with you the foolish words you brought here! We are accomplishing nothing.

*Exit HERALD by Eisodos B.*

(*to his retinue*) All hoplites must march, and all riders of chariots and of single horses must set their cheekpieces, dripping with foam, in motion onward to the land of Cadmus! I shall proceed to Cadmus' seven gates: I myself shall wield a whetted sword and I myself shall be my herald. Adrastus, I order you to stay behind: do not mingle your fortunes with mine. I shall lead the expedition accompanied by my own destiny, a fresh general with a fresh fighting force. I need only one thing more, to have as my allies the gods who reverence justice. The presence of these things together gives victory. Valor accomplishes nothing for mortals unless it has the gods on its side.

[17] Referring to the legend that the original population of Thebes sprang up from a dragon's teeth, sown in the ground by Cadmus.

---

586 fort. κινῆσαι πρόσω     589 et 590 inter se trai. Markland
596 φέρει L^γρ marg.: λέγει L: fort. τελεῖ

ΧΟΡΟΣ

στρ. α

—ὦ μέλεαι μελέων ματέρες λοχαγῶν,
ὥς μοι ὑφ᾽ ἥπατι χλωρόν ⟨τι⟩ δεῖμα θάσσει . . .
600—τίν᾽ αὐδὰν τάνδε προσφέρεις νέαν;
—. . . στράτευμα πᾷ Παλλάδος κριθήσεται.
—διὰ δορὸς εἶπας ἢ λόγων ξυναλλαγαῖς;
—γένοιτ᾽ ἂν κέρδος· εἰ
δ᾽ ἀρειφάτῳ φόνοι μάχᾳ,
στερνότυπες ⟨εἶτ᾽⟩ ἀνὰ πτόλιν
605 κτύποι φανήσονται, τάλαι-
να τίνα λόγον, τίν᾽ ἂν τῶνδ᾽
αἰτίαν λάβοιμι;

ἀντ. α

—ἀλλὰ τὸν εὐτυχίᾳ λαμπρὸν ἄν τις αἱροῖ
μοῖρα πάλιν· τόδε μοι θάρσος ἀμφιβαίνει.
610—δικαίους δαίμονας σύ γ᾽ ἐννέπεις.
—τίνες γὰρ ἄλλοι νέμουσι συμφοράς;
—διάφορα πολλὰ θεῶν βροτοῖσιν εἰσορῶ.

599 ⟨τι⟩ Hartung    θάσσει Murray: ταράσσει L
603 ἀρειφάτῳ Willink: -τοι L
604 στερνότυπες Hartung: στερνοτυπεῖς τ᾽ L    ⟨εἶτ᾽⟩
Willink    ἀνὰ πτόλιν post Markland Murray: ἀνὰ τόπον
πάλιν L
605 τάλαινα Hermann: ὦ τ- L
608 εὐτυχίᾳ Markland: εὐτυχῇ L
609 θάρσος Heath: θράσος L

*Exit* THESEUS *with retinue and Athenian herald by Eisodos B.*

CHORUS A
O luckless mothers of luckless captains,
how pale fear sits upon my heart . . .

CHORUS B
What is this strange word you utter?

CHORUS A
. . . to learn how Pallas' army will be put to judgment!

CHORUS B
Do you mean by the spear or in exchanges of words?

CHORUS A
May the result be good! But if
slaughters occur in murderous battle
and ⟨then⟩ throughout the city is heard
the thud of hand upon breast,
what then? What accounting, what blame
will fall to unhappy me?

CHORUS B
But the man glorious in good fortune
may be destroyed in turn by fate: that is the confidence that
    surrounds me.

CHORUS A
You speak of gods who are just.

CHORUS B
Yes, for who else is it that metes out what befalls?

CHORUS A
Yet I see that the gods' ways are different from those of
    mortals.

—φόβῳ γὰρ τῷ πάρος
διόλλυσαι· δίκα δίκαν
δ᾽ ἐκάλεσε καὶ φόνος φόνον,
615 κακῶν δ᾽ ἀναψυχὰς θεοὶ
βροτοῖς νέμουσι, πάντων
τέρμ᾽ ἔχοντες αὐτοί.

στρ. β

—τὰ καλλίπυργα πεδία πῶς ἱκοίμεθ᾽ ἄν,
Καλλίχορον θεᾶς ὕδωρ λιποῦσαι;
620—ποτανὰν εἴ σέ τις θεῶν κτίσαι,
διπόταμον ἵνα πόλιν μόλοις,
εἰδείης ἂν φίλων
εἰδείης ἂν τύχας.
—τίς ποτ᾽ αἶσα, τίς ἄρα πότμος
ἐπιμένει τὸν ἄλκιμον
625 τᾶσδε γᾶς ἄνακτα;

ἀντ. β

κεκλημένους μὲν ἀνακαλούμεθ᾽ αὖ θεούς·
ἀλλὰ φόβων πίστις ἅδε πρῶτα.
ἰὼ Ζεῦ, τᾶς παλαιομάτορος
παιδογόνε πόριος Ἰνάχου,
630 πόλει μοι ξύμμαχος
γενοῦ τᾷδ᾽ εὐμενής.

621 μόλοις Wilamowitz: μόλω L
622 τύχας Heath, Tyrwhitt: ψυχάς L
623 τίς (prius) Reiske: ἔτι L

74

### CHORUS B

It is your earlier fear
that is destroying your good sense. One plea of justice,
like one murder, calls forth another,
and the gods, who hold the destiny
of all things in their own hands,
grant respite from misfortune to mortals.

### CHORUS A

O how I would like to go to the land of fair towers[18]
and leave behind the goddess' spring of Callichorus!

### CHORUS B

If some god gave you wings
to go to the city of two rivers,
you would know, you would know
how your friends are faring.

### CHORUS A

What fate, what outcome
awaits this land's
brave king?

### CHORUS

I call once more on the gods I invoked before.
Yet this is my only hope in time of fear.
O Zeus, who sired the children
of our ancestress, Inachus' heifer daughter,[19]
for my sake be this city's
stout ally!

[18] Thebes.     [19] Io, daughter the river god Inachus, was be-
loved by Zeus and became the father of the Argive royal house.
She was transformed into a heifer, either by Zeus to conceal his
amour from Hera, or by Hera as part of her revenge.

τὸ σὸν ἄγαλμα, τὸ σὸν ἵδρυμα
πόλεος ἐκκόμιζέ μοι
πρὸς πυρὰν ὑβρισθέν.

ΑΓΓΕΛΟΣ

γυναῖκες, ἥκω πόλλ᾽ ἔχων λέγειν φίλα,
635  αὐτός τε σωθείς (ᾑρέθην γὰρ ἐν μάχῃ
ἣν οἱ θανόντες ἑπτὰ δεσπόται λόχων
ἠγωνίσαντο ῥεῦμα Διρκαῖον πάρα)
νίκην τε Θησέως ἀγγελῶν. λόγου δέ σε
μακροῦ ἀπολύσω· Καπανέως γὰρ ἢ λάτρις,
640  ὃν Ζεὺς κεραυνῷ πυρπόλῳ καταιθαλοῖ.

ΧΟΡΟΣ

ὦ φίλτατ᾽, εὖ μὲν νόστον ἀγγέλλεις σέθεν
τήν τ᾽ ἀμφὶ Θησέως βάξιν· εἰ δὲ καὶ στρατὸς
σῶς ἐστ᾽ Ἀθηνῶν, πάντ᾽ ἂν ἀγγέλλοις φίλα.

ΑΓΓΕΛΟΣ

σῶς, καὶ πέπραγεν ὡς Ἄδραστος ὤφελεν
645  πρᾶξαι ξὺν Ἀργείοισιν οὓς ἀπ᾽ Ἰνάχου
στείλας ἐπεστράτευσε Καδμείων πόλιν.

ΧΟΡΟΣ

πῶς γὰρ τροπαῖα Ζηνὸς Αἰγέως τόκος
ἔστησεν οἵ τε συμμετασχόντες δορός;
λέξον· παρὼν γὰρ οὐ παρόντας εὐφρανεῖς.

632 ἐκκόμιζέ μοι Musgrave: ἐκκκομίζομαι L
636 ἣν Dobree: ἵν᾽ L    δεσπόται λόχων Musgrave: δε-
σποτῶν λόχοι L    639 ἀπολύσω Herwerden: ἀποπαύσω L
642 βάξιν Reiske: τάξιν L

The darling of your city, its stay and shield,
insulted by the Thebans,
bring him back, I pray, for burial!

*Enter* MESSENGER *by Eisodos B.*

##### MESSENGER

Women, I have come with much welcome news to report!
I was captured in the battle the seven fallen captains fought
beside the stream of Dirce, but I have come home safely
and bring you news of Theseus' victory! To save you much
talk, I was the servant of Capaneus, whom Zeus burned up
with his fiery thunderbolt.

##### CHORUS LEADER

O welcome messenger! What good news is your return
home and the report you bring about Theseus! If the Athe-
nian army is safe, your news will be wholly good.

##### MESSENGER

Yes, it is safe and is faring well: would that Adrastus had
fared so and the Argives with whom he set out from the
Inachus to the city of the Cadmeans!

##### CHORUS LEADER

How did the son of Aegeus and his fellow soldiers win the
victory?[20] Tell us: you were there and will bring joy to those
who were not.

[20] Lit. "set up Zeus's trophy." A *tropaion*, or trophy to mark a
military victory, was a marker set up in honor of Zeus Tropaios,
"Zeus god of the rout," who gave the victory.

---

644 πέπραγεν Pierson: πεπραγμέν᾽ L
645 οὓς Reiske: ὡς L    649 οὐ Wecklein: τοὺς L

ΑΓΓΕΛΟΣ

650 λαμπρὰ μὲν ἀκτὶς ἡλίου, κανὼν σαφής,
ἔβαλλε γαῖαν· ἀμφὶ δ᾽ Ἠλέκτρας πύλας
ἔστην θεατὴς πύργον εὐαγῆ λαβών.
ὁρῶ δὲ φῦλα τρία τριῶν στρατευμάτων·
τευχεσφόρον μὲν λαὸν ἐκτείνοντ᾽ ἄνω
655 Ἰσμήνιον πρὸς ὄχθον, ὡς μὲν ἦν λόγος,
αὐτόν τ᾽ ἄνακτα, παῖδα κλεινὸν Αἰγέως,
καὶ τοὺς σὺν αὐτῷ δεξιὸν τεταγμένους
κέρας, παλαιᾶς Κεκροπίας οἰκήτορας,
λαιῷ τε Πάραλον ἐστολισμένον δορὶ
660 κρήνην παρ᾽ αὐτὴν Ἄρεος· ἱππότην ⟨δ᾽⟩ ὄχλον
πρὸς κρασπέδοισι στρατοπέδου τεταγμένον,
ἴσους ἀριθμόν· ἁρμάτων δ᾽ ὀχήματα
ἔνερθε σεμνῶν μνημάτων Ἀμφίονος.
Κάδμου δὲ λαὸς ἧστο πρόσθε τειχέων,
665 νεκροὺς ὄπισθε θέμενος, ὧν ἔκειτ᾽ ἀγών,
ἱππεῦσι δ᾽ ἱππῆς ἦσαν ἀνθωπλισμένοι
τετραόροισί τ᾽ ἀντί᾽ ἅρμαθ᾽ ἅρμασιν.
κῆρυξ δὲ Θησέως εἶπεν ἐς πάντας τάδε·
Σιγᾶτε, λαοί· σῖγα, Καδμείων στίχες,
670 ἀκούσαθ᾽· ἡμεῖς ἥκομεν νεκροὺς μέτα,
θάψαι θέλοντες, τὸν Πανελλήνων νόμον
σῴζοντες, οὐδὲν δεόμενοι τεῖναι φόνον.

659 λαιῷ Diggle: αὐτὸν L, ex 656 lapsum      τε Murray: δὲ L
660 ⟨δ᾽⟩ Reiske      666 δ᾽ Hermann: θ᾽ L

78

### MESSENGER

Bright rays of the sun, sure measure of truth, were striking the earth. I stationed myself to watch at the Electran gate on a tower commanding a good view. I saw the three divisions of the army. The hoplites extended themselves upwards to a hill (Ismenus' Hill, I have heard it called). The king himself, the glorious son of Aegeus, and his own men, the ancient settlers of Cecropia,[21] formed the right wing. On the left stood Paralus,[22] equipped with a spear, right next to Ares' Spring.[23] The cavalry were stationed in two equal companies on the edges of the army, and the chariots were below the august Tomb of Amphion. The Cadmean army sat before the walls, with the corpses, the object of the fighting, behind them. Cavalry were stationed opposite cavalry, and four-horsed chariots opposite chariots. Theseus' herald spoke as follows to all: "Silence, men at arms, be still, you ranks of Cadmeans, and listen! We have come for the dead, wishing to bury them! We are upholding the law of all the Greeks! It is not our desire to shed blood!"

[21] Cecropia, from Cecrops, King of Athens, was an old name for the acropolis.

[22] The unifying of Attica under the leadership of Athens was the work of Theseus and is represented here as a recent accomplishment. Paralus, the eponymous hero of the coastal people, leads the forces of Attica, and Theseus leads the Athenian contingent.

[23] The hoplites are stationed to the south of the city between the Hill of Ismenus (SE) and the Spring of Ares (SW). The cavalry are stationed on either side of the hoplites (E and W), and the chariots occupy the area north of the city, where the tomb of Amphion is located.

κοὐδὲν Κρέων τοῖσδ᾽ ἀντεκήρυξεν λόγοις,
ἀλλ᾽ ἦστ᾽ ἐφ᾽ ὅπλοις σῖγα. ποιμένες δ᾽ ὄχων
675 τετραόρων κατῆρχον ἐντεῦθεν μάχης·
πέραν δὲ διελάσαντες ἀλλήλων ὄχους
παραιβάτας ἔστησαν ἐς τάξιν δορός.
χοὶ μὲν σιδήρῳ διεμάχονθ᾽, οἱ δ᾽ ἔστρεφον
πώλους ἐς ἀλκὴν αὖθις †ἐς παραιβάτας†.
680 ἰδὼν δὲ Φόρβας, ὃς μοναμπύκων ἄναξ
ἦν τοῖς Ἐρεχθείδαισιν, ἁρμάτων ὄχλον
οἵ τ᾽ αὖ τὸ Κάδμου διεφύλασσον ἱππικὸν
συνῆψαν ἀλκὴν κἀκράτουν ἡσσῶντό τε.
λεύσσων δὲ ταῦτα κοὐ κλύων (ἐκεῖ γὰρ ἦ
685 ἔνθ᾽ ἅρματ᾽ ἠγωνίζεθ᾽ οἵ τ᾽ ἐπεμβάται)
τἀκεῖ παρόντα πολλὰ πήματ᾽ οὐκ ἔχω
τί πρῶτον εἴπω, πότερα τὴν ἐς οὐρανὸν
κόνιν προσαντέλλουσαν, ὡς πολλὴ παρῆν,
ἢ τὰς ἄνω τε καὶ κάτω φορουμένας
⟨ὥσπερ κλύδωνας συστάσεις ἐπεμβατῶν,
εἶτ᾽ ἐμπλακέντας ἱππικαῖς ἐν ἡνίαις
ἄνδρας τραχείας πρὸς πέτρας φορουμένους⟩
690 ἱμᾶσιν, αἵματός τε φοινίου ῥοὰς
τῶν μὲν πιτνόντων, τῶν δὲ θραυσθέντων δίφρων
ἐς κρᾶτα πρὸς γῆν ἐκκυβιστώντων βίᾳ
πρὸς ἁρμάτων τ᾽ ἀγαῖσι λειπόντων βίον.
νικῶντα δ᾽ ἵπποις ὡς ὑπείδετο στρατὸν
695 Κρέων τὸν ἐνθένδ᾽, ἰτέαν λαβὼν χερὶ
696 χωρεῖ πρὶν ἐλθεῖν ξυμμάχοις δυσθυμίαν.
699 κἀς μέσον ἅπαντα συμπατάξαντες στρατὸν

Creon made no proclamation in answer to this speech
but sat near his weapons in silence. It was the drivers of
four-horse chariots who then began the battle. Driving
their chariots through each other's lines they set down their
armed passengers in battle ranks. As these men battled it
out with swords, the drivers wheeled their horses about to
come to their aid. Phorbas, leader of the Athenian cavalry,
saw the throng of chariots, and so did the marshals of the
Cadmean horse, and they joined battle, by turns victorious
and vanquished. Since I stood at the spot where both chari-
ots and cavalry were fighting, I saw first-hand the many
travails that took place there. I do not know what I should
mention first, the great clouds of dust, rising up to heaven,
or how ‹troops of cavalry, like sea waves,› swept back and
forth, ‹how men entangled in the gear of their horses were
dragged onto rough rocks› by the leather straps, how crim-
son blood flowed in rivers as some men were cut down and
others, their chariots being smashed, were hurled head-
long to earth and lost their lives in the wreckage of the
chariots.

Now when Creon saw that the army on this side was
winning with its cavalry, he took up his shield and moved
forward before his allies could be discouraged. Dashing
their whole force into the breach, the Thebans gave death

---

679 αὖ παραιβάταις Hartung
681 ὄχλονMarkland: ὄχον L
689 post h. v. lac. indic. Kirchhoff      697–8 vide post 702
699 ita Diggle: καὶ συμπατάξαντες μέσον πάντα στρατὸν L

700 ἔκτεινον ἐκτείνοντο καὶ παρηγγύων
κελευσμὸν ἀλλήλοισι σὺν πολλῇ βοῇ·
702 Θεῖν᾽, ἀντέρειδε τοῖς Ἐρεχθείδαις δόρυ.
697 καὶ μὴν τὰ Θησέως γ᾽ οὐκ ὄκνῳ διεφθάρη,
698 ἀλλ᾽ ἵετ᾽ εὐθὺς λαμπρ᾽ ἀναρπάσας ὅπλα.
703 λόχος δ᾽ ὀδόντων ὄφεος ἐξηνδρωμένος
δεινὸς παλαιστὴς ἦν· ἔκλινε γὰρ κέρας
705 τὸ λαιὸν ἡμῶν· δεξιοῦ δ᾽ ἡσσώμενον
φεύγει τὸ κείνων· ἦν δ᾽ ἀγὼν ἰσόρροπος.

κἂν τῷδε τὸν στρατηγὸν αἰνέσαι παρῆν·
οὐ γὰρ τὸ νικῶν τοῦτ᾽ ἐκέρδαινεν μόνον
ἀλλ᾽ ᾤχετ᾽ ἐς τὸ κάμνον οἰκείου στρατοῦ.
710 ἔρρηξε δ᾽ αὐδήν, ὥσθ᾽ ὑπηχῆσαι χθόνα·
Ὦ παῖδες, εἰ μὴ σχήσετε στερρὸν δόρυ
Σπαρτῶν τόδ᾽ ἀνδρῶν, οἴχεται τὰ Παλλάδος.
θάρσος δ᾽ ἐνῶρσε παντὶ Κραναϊδῶν στρατῷ.
αὐτός θ᾽ ὅπλισμα τοὐπιδαύριον λαβὼν
715 δεινῆς κορύνης διαφέρων ἐσφενδόνα
ὁμοῦ τραχήλους κἀπικειμένας κάρᾳ
κυνέας θερίζων κἀποκαυλίζων ξύλῳ.
μόλις δέ πως ἔτρεψαν ἐς φυγὴν πόδα.
ἐγὼ δ᾽ ἀνηλάλαξα κἀνωρχησάμην
720 κἄκρουσα χεῖρας. οἱ δ᾽ ἔτεινον ἐς πύλας.
βοὴ δὲ καὶ κωκυτὸς ἦν ἀνὰ πτόλιν
νέων γερόντων ἱερά τ᾽ ἐξεπίμπλασαν
φόβῳ. παρὸν δὲ τειχέων ἔσω μολεῖν
Θησεὺς ἐπέσχεν· οὐ γὰρ ὡς πέρσων πόλιν
725 μολεῖν ἔφασκεν ἀλλ᾽ ἀπαιτήσων νεκρούς.

and received it, passing the command along the ranks with great shouts: "Strike, push hard against the sons of Erechtheus!" For his part Theseus did not allow his own affairs to be ruined by hesitation: snatching up his bright armor he rushed forward. But the company of men sprung from the dragon's teeth was hard to wrestle against: they turned back our left wing, while their own left was beaten and put to flight by our right. The battle was evenly balanced.

At this point the general did a praiseworthy deed. He not only got the benefit of his victorious wing but went off toward the part of his army that was struggling. His shout burst forth so that the land echoed with it: "Either stop these Sown Men's hard spears, lads, or it's all over for Pallas Athena!" That put courage in the hearts of all the Athenian army. Then taking in his hands the Epidaurian weapon,[24] a fearful mace, he kept laying about him with it, snapping necks and harvesting helmeted heads with it. The Thebans barely managed to turn and flee. I raised a shout of joy, leapt into the air, and clapped my hands. They meanwhile were making for the gates. In the city young and old were crying and lamenting and crowding into the shrines in terror. But though he could have entered the city, Theseus halted. "I have not come," he said, "to sack the city but to ask for the dead."

[24] Theseus in his youth had killed the Epidaurian robber Periphetes, who used a club to kill his victims.

---

697-8 post 702 trai. Murray     705 δεξιοῦ Markland: -òν L
713 Κραναϊδῶν Musgrave: Δαναΐδων L
716 κἀπικειμένας Reiske: -ον L
718 ἔτρεψαν Hermann: -εν L

83

τοιόνδε τοι στρατηγὸν αἱρεῖσθαι χρεών,
ὃς ἔν τε τοῖς δεινοῖσίν ἐστιν ἄλκιμος
μισεῖ θ᾽ ὑβριστὴν λαόν, ὃς πράσσων καλῶς
ἐς ἄκρα βῆναι κλιμάκων ἐνήλατα
730 ζητῶν ἀπώλεσ᾽ ὄλβον ᾧ χρῆσθαι παρῆν.

ΧΟΡΟΣ

νῦν τήνδ᾽ ἄελπτον ἡμέραν ἰδοῦσ᾽ ἐγὼ
θεοὺς νομίζω καὶ δοκῶ τὰς συμφορὰς
ἔχειν ἐλάσσους τῶνδε τεισάντων δίκην.

ΑΔΡΑΣΤΟΣ

ὦ Ζεῦ, τί δῆτα τοὺς ταλαιπώρους βροτοὺς
735 φρονεῖν λέγουσι; σοῦ γὰρ ἐξηρτήμεθα
δρῶμέν τε τοιαῦθ᾽ ἂν σὺ τυγχάνῃς θέλων.
ἡμῖν γὰρ ἦν τό τ᾽ Ἄργος οὐχ ὑποστατὸν
αὐτοί τε πολλοὶ καὶ νέοι βραχίοσιν.
Ἐτεοκλέους δὲ σύμβασιν ποιουμένου,
740 μέτρια θέλοντος, οὐκ ἐχρῄζομεν λαβεῖν,
κἄπειτ᾽ ἀπωλόμεσθ᾽. ὁ δ᾽ αὖ τότ᾽ εὐτυχής,
λαβὼν πένης ὣς ἀρτίπλουτα χρήματα,
ὕβριζ᾽, ὑβρίζων τ᾽ αὖθις ἀνταπώλετο
Κάδμου κακόφρων λαός. ὦ κενοὶ βροτῶν,
745 οἳ τόξον ἐντείνοντες †τοῦ καιροῦ† πέρα
καὶ πρὸς δίκης γε πολλὰ πάσχοντες κακά,
φίλοις μὲν οὐ πείθεσθε, τοῖς δὲ πράγμασιν·
πόλεις τ᾽, ἔχουσαι διὰ λόγου κάμψαι κακά,
φόνῳ καθαιρεῖσθ᾽, οὐ λόγῳ, τὰ πράγματα.
750 ἀτὰρ τί ταῦτα; κεῖνο βούλομαι μαθεῖν,

This is the kind of general one should choose, a man who is brave in the hour of danger and who hates an insolent people, a people who in their prosperity tried to climb to the highest rung of the ladder, and lost the blessedness they might have enjoyed.

CHORUS LEADER

Now that I have seen this unlooked for day I believe in the gods and think that my misfortunes have grown less since these men have paid the penalty!

ADRASTUS

O Zeus, why do men say that hapless mortals have any wisdom? We are dependent upon you and do whatever is your will. Argos, we thought, was irresistible, and we ourselves were many and had young, strong arms. Eteocles proposed terms of agreement and made moderate requests, but we refused to accept them and were ruined. In its turn the foolish people of Cadmus, once so prosperous, acted insolently, like a poor man who suddenly becomes rich, and in their insolence were destroyed. O foolish mortals, who shoot beyond the mark and justly suffer much calamity, you do not learn from your friends but only from events! Cities, you could bring your misfortunes to an end by speech, but you carry out your affairs by bloodletting, not words!

But what use are these reflections? I want to know how

---

726 τοι Elmsley: τὸν L    733 ἐλάσσους Markland: ἔλασσον L: quo servato fort. σθένειν

739 δὲ Jacobs: τε L

745 εὐκαίρου vel εἰκότος Page: ὧν ἐχρῆν Kovacs

747 λόγοις Wecklein cl. Ion 649, S. Ai. 330

πῶς ἐξεσώθης· εἶτα τἄλλ᾿ ἐρήσομαι.

ΑΓΓΕΛΟΣ
ἐπεὶ ταραγμὸς πόλιν ἐκίνησεν δορός,
πύλας διῆλθον ᾗπερ εἰσῄει στρατός.

ΑΔΡΑΣΤΟΣ
ὧν δ᾿ οὕνεχ᾿ ἀγὼν ἦν νεκροὺς κομίζετε;

ΑΓΓΕΛΟΣ
755   ὅσοι γε κλεινοῖς ἕπτ᾿ ἐφέστασαν λόχοις.

ΑΔΡΑΣΤΟΣ
πῶς φής; ὁ δ᾿ ἄλλος ποῦ κεκμηκότων ὄχλος;

ΑΓΓΕΛΟΣ
τάφῳ δέδονται πρὸς Κιθαιρῶνος πτυχαῖς.

ΑΔΡΑΣΤΟΣ
τοὐκεῖθεν ἢ τοὐνθένδε; τίς δ᾿ ἔθαψέ νιν;

ΑΓΓΕΛΟΣ
Θησεύς, σκιώδης ἔνθ᾿ Ἐλευθερὶς πέτρα.

ΑΔΡΑΣΤΟΣ
760   οὓς δ᾿ οὐκ ἔθαψε ποῦ νεκροὺς ἥκεις λιπών;

ΑΓΓΕΛΟΣ
ἐγγύς· πέλας γὰρ πᾶν ὅ τι σπουδάζεται.

ΑΔΡΑΣΤΟΣ
ἦ που πικρῶς νιν θέραπες ἦγον ἐκ φόνου;

752 δορός Hermann: δορί L
755 λόχοις Reiske: δόμοις L
760 ποῦ Hermann: ποῖ L      ἥκεις Heath: ἥκει L

86

you got safely home. After that I will ask my other questions.

MESSENGER

When the tumult of war stirred up the city, I went out by the gates where the army was coming in.

ADRASTUS

The corpses for which they fought, did you bring them back?

MESSENGER

Yes, those who led the seven famous companies.

ADRASTUS

What do you mean? Where are the rest of the dead?

MESSENGER

They are buried near the glens of Cithaeron.

ADRASTUS

On the far or near side? By whom were they buried?

MESSENGER

By Theseus, near Eleutherae's shady eminence.[25]

ADRASTUS

Where have you left the bodies he did not bury?

MESSENGER

Close by: whatever we earnestly work for is near.

ADRASTUS

Was it gruesome for the servants to remove the bodies from the carnage?

[25] A small village on the Attic side of the mountain.

# EURIPIDES

ΑΓΓΕΛΟΣ

οὐδεὶς ἐπέστη τῷδε δοῦλος ὢν πόνῳ.

⟨ΑΔΡΑΣΤΟΣ

πῶς εἶπας; Αἰγέως σφ᾽ ὧδ᾽ ἐτίμησεν τέκνον;⟩

ΑΓΓΕΛΟΣ

φαίης ἂν εἰ παρῆσθ᾽ ὅτ᾽ ἠγάπα νεκρούς.

ΑΔΡΑΣΤΟΣ

765  ἔνιψεν αὐτὸς τῶν ταλαιπώρων σφαγάς;

ΑΓΓΕΛΟΣ

κἄστρωσέ γ᾽ εὐνὰς κἀκάλυψε σώματα.

ΑΔΡΑΣΤΟΣ

δεινὸν μὲν ἦν βάσταγμα κᾀσχύνην ἔχον.

ΑΓΓΕΛΟΣ

τί δ᾽ αἰσχρὸν ἀνθρώποισι τἀλλήλων κακά;

ΑΔΡΑΣΤΟΣ

οἴμοι· πόσῳ σφιν συνθανεῖν ἂν ἤθελον.

ΑΓΓΕΛΟΣ

770  ἄκραντ᾽ ὀδύρῃ ταῖσδέ τ᾽ ἐξάγεις δάκρυ.

ΑΔΡΑΣΤΟΣ

δοκῶ μέν, αὗταί γ᾽ εἰσὶν αἱ διδάσκαλοι.
ἀλλ᾽ εἶμ᾽ ἵν᾽ αἴρω χεῖρ᾽ ἀπαντήσας νεκροῖς
Ἅιδου τε μολπὰς ἐκχέω δακρυρρόους,
φίλους προσαυδῶν ὧν λελειμμένος τάλας

763 post h. v. lac. indic. Hermann
765 αὐτὸς Reiske: αὐτῶν L

88

MESSENGER

No slave was set to do this task.

‹ADRASTUS

What? Did Theseus show them so much honor?›

MESSENGER

You would have said so if you had been there when he tended them.

ADRASTUS

Did he himself wash the poor men's wounds?

MESSENGER

Yes, and he spread out biers for them and covered their bodies.

ADRASTUS

Carrying them was dreadful task, and a shameful one.

MESSENGER

Why should men consider one other's misfortunes shameful?

ADRASTUS

Ah me! How much better for me to have died with them!

MESSENGER

Your tears are useless, and you make these women weep too.

ADRASTUS

It is they, I think, who are the teachers in this.

Well I shall go to meet the dead, raise my hand in farewell to them, and offer them the tearful songs of Hades, bidding farewell to my friends. Left behind by them

---

768 κακά] fort. φέρειν     772 εἶμ᾽ ἵν᾽ Blaydes: εἶεν L

89

775 ἔρημα κλαίω· τοῦτο γὰρ μόνον βροτοῖς
οὐκ ἔστι τἀνάλωμ᾽ ἀναλωθὲν λαβεῖν,
ψυχὴν βροτείαν· χρημάτων δ᾽ εἰσὶν πόροι.

ΧΟΡΟΣ

στρ. α

τὰ μὲν εὖ, τὰ δὲ δυστυχῆ·
πόλει μὲν εὐδοξία
780 καὶ στρατηλάταις δορὸς
διπλάζεται τιμά·
ἐμοὶ δὲ παίδων μὲν εἰσιδεῖν μέλη
πικρόν, καλὸν θέαμα δ᾽ εἴπερ ὄψομαι,
τὰν ἄελπτον ἀμέραν
785 ἰδοῦσα, πάντων μέγιστον ἄλγος.

ἀντ. α

ἄγαμόν μ᾽ ἔτι δεῦρ᾽ ἀεὶ
Χρόνος παλαιὸς πατὴρ
ὤφελ᾽ ἀμερᾶν κτίσαι.
τί γάρ μ᾽ ἔδει παίδων;
790 τὸ μὲν γὰρ ἤλπιζον ἂν πεπονθέναι
πάθος περισσόν, εἰ γάμων ἀπεζύγην,
νῦν δ᾽ ὁρῶ σαφέστατον
κακὸν τέκνων φιλτάτων στέρεσθαι.

—ἀλλὰ τάδ᾽ ἤδη σώματα λεύσσω

775 ἔρημα] ἀνόνητα Wecklein
788 ἀμερᾶν Porson: ἀμέρα L
790 fort. πρὶν μὲν vel τὸ πρὶν
793 στέρεσθαι Blomfield: στερεῖσθαι Tr²: στερεῖ L

90

I, unlucky man, weep in loneliness. For mortals there is
only one thing that cannot be regained once it is spent: a
man's life. Money can be recovered.

*Exit* ADRASTUS *and* MESSENGER *by Eisodos B.*

#### CHORUS
Some things are well, others ill.
The city has won glory,
and its generals have
a double meed of honor.
But for us to look on the bodies of our sons
is painful (though it will be a fair sight if we ever behold
      it),
seeing that day we never looked for,
the greatest of all woes.

Would that old Time, father of our days,
had made me
ever unwedded to this day!
What need had I of children?
I would have thought that I had suffered
some strange fate if I had been deprived of marriage,
but now I see that the keenest
misfortune is to be bereft of my dear children.

*Enter* ADRASTUS *and* THESEUS *by Eisodos B with a pro-
cession carrying five draped corpses on biers.*

#### CHORUS LEADER
But now I behold the bodies of our perished sons! O how

91

795 τῶν οἰχομένων παίδων· μελέα
πῶς ἂν ὀλοίμην σὺν τοῖσδε τέκνοις
κοινὸν ἐς Ἅιδην καταβᾶσα;

στρ. β

ΑΔΡΑΣΤΟΣ

στεναγμόν, ὦ ματέρες,
τῶν κατὰ χθονὸς νεκρῶν
800 ἀύσατ᾽ ἀπύσατ᾽ ἀντίφων᾽ ἐμῶν
στεναγμάτων κλυοῦσαι.

ΧΟΡΟΣ

ὦ παῖδες, ὦ πικρὸν φίλων
προσηγόρημα ματέρων,
προσαυδῶ σε τὸν θανόντα.

ΑΔΡΑΣΤΟΣ

805 ἰὼ ἰώ.

⟨ΧΟΡΟΣ⟩

τῶν γ᾽ ἐμῶν κακῶν ἐγώ.

⟨ΑΔΡΑΣΤΟΣ⟩

αἰαῖ ⟨αἰαῖ⟩.

⟨ΧΟΡΟΣ

μεγάλα δ᾽ αἰάζειν πάρα.⟩

ΑΔΡΑΣΤΟΣ

ἐπάθομεν ὤ . . .

⟨ΧΟΡΟΣ⟩

. . . τὰ κύντατ᾽ ἄλγη κακῶν.

I wish I could die with these children, treading with them
the downward path to Hades!

ADRASTUS[26]

Utter, speak aloud, mothers,
a groan for your sons below the earth!
Listen to my groans
and answer!

CHORUS

O my son, a word
that gives pain to a loving mother,
I speak to you in death!

ADRASTUS

Alas, alas!

⟨CHORUS⟩

Yes, alas for my own woes!

⟨ADRASTUS⟩

Ah me, ⟨ah me⟩!

⟨CHORUS⟩

Terrible are the woes we must lament!⟩

ADRASTUS

We have suffered . . .

⟨CHORUS⟩

. . . the sharpest of griefs!

[26] From here to 837, Adrastus sings in answer to the Chorus.

---

805n ⟨Xo.⟩ Hermann    806nn ⟨Aδ.⟩ et ⟨Xo.⟩ Hermann
806 ⟨αἰαῖ⟩ Wilamowitz    lac. indic. Tr²
807n ⟨Xo.⟩ Hermann

ΑΔΡΑΣΤΟΣ

ὦ πόλις Ἀργεία, τὸν ἐμὸν πότμον οὐκ ἐσορᾶτε;

ΧΟΡΟΣ

ὁρῶσι κἀμὲ τὰν τάλαι-
810 ναν τέκνων ἄπαιδα.
ἀντ. β

ΑΔΡΑΣΤΟΣ

προσάγετ᾽ ⟨ἄγετε⟩ δυσπότμων
σώμαθ᾽ αἱματοσταγῆ,
σφαγέντας οὐκ ἄξι᾽ οὐδ᾽ ὑπ᾽ ἀξίων,
ἐν οἷς ἀγὼν ἐκράνθη.

ΧΟΡΟΣ

815 δόθ᾽ ὡς περιπτυχαῖσι δὴ
χέρας προσαρμόσασ᾽ ἐμοῖς
ἐν ἀγκῶσι τέκνα θῶμαι.

ΑΔΡΑΣΤΟΣ

ἔχεις ἔχεις . . .

ΧΟΡΟΣ

. . . πημάτων γ᾽ ἅλις βάρος.

ΑΔΡΑΣΤΟΣ

αἰαῖ ⟨αἰαῖ⟩.

⟨ΧΟΡΟΣ⟩

τοῖς τεκοῦσι δ᾽ οὐ λέγεις;

ΑΔΡΑΣΤΟΣ

820 ἀίετέ μου.

ADRASTUS

O city of Argos, do you not see the fate I suffer?

CHORUS

They see me too, the poor wretch
bereft of her children!

ADRASTUS

Bring near, ⟨bring near⟩ the blood-spattered
bodies of our unfortunate sons,
who died an undeserved death at undeserving hands!
In their death the contest was decided.

CHORUS

Let me put
my arms about my son
and embrace him!

ADRASTUS

You have, you have . . .

CHORUS

. . . a weight of grief that suffices!

ADRASTUS

Ah me, ⟨ah me⟩!

⟨CHORUS⟩

Is it not to his mother that you speak?

ADRASTUS

Hear me!

---

811 ⟨ἄγετε⟩ Diggle
813 σφαγέντας Fritzsche: σφαγέντ᾽ L
814 ἐν] ἐφ᾽ Wilamowitz      819 ⟨αἰαῖ⟩ Wilamowitz
819n ⟨Χο.⟩ Musgrave

ΧΟΡΟΣ

στένεις ἐπ' ἀμφοῖν ἄχη.

ΑΔΡΑΣΤΟΣ

εἴθε με Καδμείων ἔναρον στίχες ἐν κονίαισιν.

ΧΟΡΟΣ

ἐμὸν δὲ μήποτ' ἐζύγη
δέμας ἐς ἀνδρὸς εὐνάν.

ἐπῳδ

ΑΔΡΑΣΤΟΣ

ἴδετε κακῶν πέλαγος, ὦ
825   μᾰτέρες τάλαιναι τέκνων.

ΧΟΡΟΣ

κατὰ μὲν ὄνυξιν ἠλοκίσμεθ', ἀμφὶ δὲ
σποδὸν κάρᾳ κεχύμεθα.

ΑΔΡΑΣΤΟΣ

ἰὼ ἰώ μοί μοι·
κατά με πέδον γᾶς ἕλοι,
830   διὰ δὲ θύελλα σπάσαι,
πυρός τε φλογμὸς ὁ Διὸς ἐν κάρᾳ πέσοι.

ΧΟΡΟΣ

πικροὺς ἐσεῖδες γάμους,
πικρὰν δὲ Φοίβου φάτιν·
835   ἐς ἡμᾶς ἁ πολύστονος λιποῦσ'
Οἰδιπόδα δώματ' ἦλθ' Ἐρινύς.

<hr>

825 ἐλειναὶ Kayser      835 ἐς ἡμᾶς Bothe: ἔγημας L

96

**CHORUS**

You lament both your woes and mine!

**ADRASTUS**

Would that the Cadmean ranks had felled me in the dust!

**CHORUS**

And I, would that I had never
been brought to a man's bed!

**ADRASTUS**

Look on this sea of troubles,
O unhappy mothers of these sons!

**CHORUS**

Our cheeks are furrowed with our nails,
our heads besprinkled with dust!

**ADRASTUS**

Ah me, ah me!
May the earth swallow me up,
the whirlwind rend me in two,
the flash of Zeus's fire fall on my head!

**CHORUS**

Disastrous were the marriages you have seen,
disastrous the prophecy of Phoebus!
The grim Erinys,[27] has come to us, leaving
the house of Oedipus!

---

[27] Oedipus cursed his sons for filial impiety as he died, thereby letting loose upon them the Erinys, a spirit of destruction associated with Zeus.

---

835-6 λιποῦσ' Οἰδιπόδα δώματ' Wilamowitz (λ- Οἰδίπου δ-) et Collard: Οἰ- δ- λ- L

# EURIPIDES

## ΘΗΣΕΥΣ

μέλλων σ' ἐρωτᾶν, ἡνίκ' ἐξήντας στρατῷ
γόους ἀφήσων, τοὺς ἐκεῖ μὲν ἐκλιπὼν
840 εἴασα μύθους, νῦν δ', Ἄδραστ', ἀνιστορῶ·
πόθεν ποθ' οἴδε διαπρεπεῖς εὐψυχίᾳ
θνητῶν ἔφυσαν; εἰπὲ δ' ὡς σοφώτερος
843 νέοισιν ἀστῶν τῶνδ'· ἐπιστήμων γὰρ εἶ.
846 ἐν δ' οὐκ ἐρήσομαί σε, μὴ γέλωτ' ὄφλω,
ὅτῳ ξυνέστη τῶνδ' ἕκαστος ἐν μάχῃ
ἢ τραῦμα λόγχης πολεμίων ἐδέξατο.
κενοὶ γὰρ οὗτοι τῶν τ' ἀκουόντων λόγοι
850 καὶ τοῦ λέγοντος, ὅστις ἐν μάχῃ βεβὼς
λόγχης ἰούσης πρόσθεν ὀμμάτων πυκνῆς
σαφῶς ἀπήγγειλ' ὅστις ἐστὶν ἀγαθός.
οὐκ ἂν δυναίμην οὔτ' ἐρωτῆσαι τάδε
οὔτ' αὖ πιθέσθαι τοῖσι τολμῶσιν λέγειν·
855 μόλις γὰρ ἄν τις αὐτὰ τἀναγκαῖ' ὁρᾶν
δύναιτ' ἂν ἑστὼς πολεμίοις ἐναντίος.

## ΑΔΡΑΣΤΟΣ

ἄκουε δή νυν· καὶ γὰρ οὐκ ἄκοντί μοι
δίδως ἔπαινον ὧν ἔγωγε βούλομαι
859 φίλων ἀληθῆ καὶ δίκαι' εἰπεῖν πέρι.
844 εἶδον γὰρ αὐτῶν κρείσσον' ἢ λέξαι λόγῳ
845 τολμήμαθ', οἷς ἤλπιζον αἱρήσειν πόλιν.
860 ὁρᾷς τὸ λάβρον οὗ βέλος διέπτατο;
Καπανεὺς ὅδ' ἐστίν· ᾧ βίος μὲν ἦν πολύς,
ἥκιστα δ' ὄλβῳ γαῦρος ἦν· φρόνημα δὲ

98

### THESEUS

I intended to ask you when you came to meet the army and
shed your tears for the dead, but since I did not do so at
that time, now I ask you, Adrastus: how did it happen that
these men were so superior to other men in bravery? Tell
the young sons of these citizens, since you are wiser and
have the requisite skill. One thing I will not ask or I'd be
laughed at: whom each of these men stood facing in the
battle and by what foeman he was wounded. Such a recital
wastes the time of both hearers and speaker: can a man
stand in battle as the spears fly thick and fast before his
eyes and tell us clearly who was brave? I could not ask for
such a report nor believe anyone who ventured to give it.
When a man stands face to face with the enemy, he is
barely able to see what he needs to see.

### ADRASTUS

Listen, then. In fact the task you assign me of praising
these friends is not unwelcome since I want to say what is
true and just about them. I saw their bold deeds, greater
than words can describe, by which they expected to take
the city.

Do you see the man transfixed by the violent thunder-
bolt? That is Capaneus. Though he was rich, he did not at

---

838-9 ἐξήντας . . . ἀφήσων Bothe: ἐξήντλεις . . . ἀφήσω L

840 εἴασα Elmsley: εἰς τὰ σὰ L      Ἄδραστ', ἀνιστορῶ Ja-
cobs: Ἄδραστον εἰσορῶ L

842 εἰπὲ δ' Elmsley: εἰπέ γ' Tr¹: quid L habuerit incertum

844-5 vide post 859      854 αὖ Reiske: ἂν L

858 ὧν Pierson: τῶν L      844-5 post 859 trai. Camper

860 τὸ λάβρον Tyrwhitt: τὸν ἀβρὸν L: τὸ δῖον t

οὐδέν τι μεῖζον εἶχεν ἢ πένης ἀνήρ,
φεύγων τραπέζαις ὅστις ἐξογκοῖτ᾽ ἄγαν
865 τἀρκοῦντ᾽ ἀτίζων· οὐ γὰρ ἐν γαστρὸς βορᾷ
τὸ χρηστὸν εἶναι, μέτρια δ᾽ ἐξαρκεῖν ἔφη.
φίλοις τ᾽ ἀληθὴς ἦν φίλος, παροῦσί τε
καὶ μὴ παροῦσιν· ὧν ἀριθμὸς οὐ πολύς.
⟨πρὸς οὓς ἔδειξεν ἐν βίου συναλλαγαῖς⟩
ἀψευδὲς ἦθος, εὐπροσήγορον στόμα,
870 ἄκρατον οὐδὲν οὔτ᾽ ἐς οἰκέτας ἔχων
οὔτ᾽ ἐς πολίτας.
                    τὸν δὲ δεύτερον λέγω
Ἐτέοκλον, ἄλλην χρηστότητ᾽ ἠσκηκότα·
νεανίας ἦν τῷ βίῳ μὲν ἐνδεής,
πλείστας δὲ τιμὰς ἔσχ᾽ ἐν Ἀργείᾳ χθονί.
875 φίλων δὲ χρυσὸν πολλάκις δωρουμένων
οὐκ εἰσεδέξατ᾽ οἶκον ὥστε τοὺς τρόπους
δούλους παρασχεῖν χρημάτων ζευχθεὶς ὕπο.
τοὺς δ᾽ ἐξαμαρτάνοντας, οὐχὶ τὴν πόλιν,
ἤχθαιρ᾽· ἐπεί τοι κοὐδὲν αἰτία πόλις
880 κακῶς κλύουσα διὰ κυβερνήτην κακόν.
ὁ δ᾽ αὖ τρίτος τῶνδ᾽ Ἱππομέδων τοιόσδ᾽ ἔφυ·
παῖς ὢν ἐτόλμησ᾽ εὐθὺς οὐ πρὸς ἡδονὰς
Μουσῶν τραπέσθαι πρὸς τὸ μαλθακὸν βίου,
ἀγροὺς δὲ ναίων, σκληρὰ τῇ φύσει διδούς,
885 ἔβαινε πρὸς τἀνδρεῖον, ἔς τ᾽ ἄγρας ἰὼν
ἵπποις τε χαίρων τόξα τ᾽ ἐντείνων χεροῖν,
πόλει παρασχεῖν σῶμα χρήσιμον θέλων.
ὁ τῆς κυναγοῦ δ᾽ ἄλλος Ἀταλάντης γόνος

all give himself airs but had no more pride than a poor man.
He shunned men who boasted too much of their luxurious
fare and scorned mere sufficiency. The good life, he said,
does not consist in food for the belly: modest fare is
enough. He was true to his friends, both present and ab-
sent. These were few in number. <Toward them in his
dealings he displayed> a character that knew no falsehood
and a manner of speech that was approachable, behaving
with moderation toward both his family and his fellow citi-
zens.

The second man I mention is Eteoclus, who practiced
another sort of goodness. Though poor in means this young
man held many high offices in Argos. When his friends
repeatedly offered him money, he would not take it into
his house: that would enslave his way of life and halter it
with gold. His hatred was directed not at the city but at
those who did wrong. For, you know, the city is not at fault
if a bad steersman causes her to be ill spoken of.

The third of them, Hippomedon, was like this: right
from childhood he had the strength of mind to reject the
Muses' pleasures and the soft delights of life; dwelling in
the countryside and setting his nature harsh tasks he pro-
gressed toward manly valor by hunting, taking pleasure in
horses, and bending the bow with his hands. He wanted to
make his own body a useful gift to the city.

Another was the son of Atalanta the huntress, the splen-

---

867 φίλοις . . . παροῦσί Reiske: φίλος . . . τοῖς παροῦσί L
869 ante h. v. lac. indic. Kovacs
870 ἄκρατον Lenting: ἄκραντον L
885 ἔβαινε Hartung: ἔχαιρε L

παῖς Παρθενοπαῖος, εἶδος ἐξοχώτατος,
890  Ἀρκὰς μὲν ἦν, ἐλθὼν δ' ἐπ' Ἰνάχου ῥοὰς
παιδεύεται κατ' Ἄργος. ἐκτραφεὶς δ' ἐκεῖ
πρῶτον μέν, ὡς χρὴ τοὺς μετοικοῦντας ξένους,
λυπηρὸς οὐκ ἦν οὐδ' ἐπίφθονος πόλει
οὐδ' ἐξεριστὴς τῶν λόγων, ὅθεν βαρὺς
895  μάλιστ' ἂν εἴη δημότης τε καὶ ξένος.
λόχοις δ' ἐνεστὼς ὥσπερ Ἀργεῖος γεγὼς
ἤμυνε χώρᾳ, χὠπότ' εὖ πράσσοι πόλις
ἔχαιρε, λυπρῶς δ' ἔφερεν εἴ τι δυστυχοῖ.
πολλοὺς δ' ἐραστὰς κἀπὸ θηλειῶν †ὅσας†
900  ἔχων ἐφρούρει μηδὲν ἐξαμαρτάνειν.
    Τυδέως δ' ἔπαινον ἐν βραχεῖ θήσω μέγαν·
[οὐκ ἐν λόγοις ἦν λαμπρός, ἀλλ' ἐν ἀσπίδι
δεινὸς σοφιστὴς πολλά τ' ἐξευρεῖν σοφός.
γνώμῃ δ' ἀδελφοῦ Μελεάγρου λελειμμένος
905  ἴσον παρέσχεν ὄνομα διὰ τέχνης δορός,
εὑρὼν ἀκριβῆ μουσικὴν ἐν ἀσπίδι.]
φιλότιμον ἦθος πλούσιον, φρόνημα δὲ
ἐν τοῖσιν ἔργοις, οὐχὶ τοῖς λόγοις, †ἴσον†.
    ἐκ τῶνδε μὴ θαύμαζε τῶν εἰρημένων,
910  Θησεῦ, πρὸ πύργων τούσδε τολμῆσαι θανεῖν.
τὸ γὰρ τραφῆναι μὴ κακῶς αἰδῶ φέρει·
αἰσχύνεται δὲ τἀγάθ' ἀσκήσας ἀνὴρ
κακὸς γενέσθαι πᾶς τις. ἡ δ' εὐανδρία
διδακτόν, εἴπερ καὶ βρέφος διδάσκεται

didly handsome lad Parthenopaeus. He was an Arcadian, but he came to the streams of the Inachus and was raised in Argos. Since he was reared to manhood there, in the first place—as befits all foreign visitors—he caused no pain or resentment to the city and was never a wrangler in words, which is what most makes both citizen and foreigner hard to bear. He took his place in the military companies like an Argive born and fought for his country. When the city prospered, he was glad, but he grieved if it met with any misfortune. He had many admirers of both sexes, but he took care to avoid any wrongdoing.

As for Tydeus, I shall give him high praise in brief compass. [He was not brilliant in words but a great expert with the shield and wise at inventing many things. Though he was bested by his brother Meleager in intelligence, he won equal glory through the fine art of the spear, inventing subtle music on the shield.] His richly endowed mind was eager for honor, but the source of his pride was in deeds, not words.

From what I have said, Theseus, you should not be surprised that these men had the courage to die before the ramparts. A noble upbringing produces a sense of shame. Every man who is trained in good deeds is prevented by shame from becoming base. Courage is teachable: even a

---

896 ἐφεστὼς Blomfield cl. 755
899-900 del. L. Dindorf        899 τόσας England
902-6 om. t, del. Bruhn: 903 del. Porson, 904-8 Dindorf
903 σοφός Toup: σοφά L
908 ἴσον L: ἔχων t: fort. ἔχον

915   λέγειν ἀκούειν θ' ὧν μάθησιν οὐκ ἔχει.
     ἃ δ' ἂν μάθῃ τις, ταῦτα σῴζεσθαι φιλεῖ
     ἐς γῆρας. οὕτω παῖδας εὖ παιδεύετε.

ΧΟΡΟΣ

     ἰὼ τέκνον, δυστυχῆ
     σ' ἔτρεφον ἔφερον ὑφ' ἥπατος
920   πόνους ἐνεγκοῦσ' ἐν ὠδῖσι· καὶ
     νῦν τὸν ἐμὸν Ἅιδας
     ἔχει μόχθον ἀθλίας,
     ἐγὼ δὲ γηροβοσκὸν οὐκ ἔχω, τεκοῦσ'
     ἁ τάλαινα παῖδα.

ΘΗΣΕΥΣ

925   καὶ μὴν τὸν Οἰκλέους γε γενναῖον τόκον
     θεοὶ ζῶντ' ἀφαρπάσαντες ἐς μυχοὺς χθονὸς
     αὐτοῖς τεθρίπποις εὐλογοῦσιν ἐμφανῶς·
     τὸν Οἰδίπου δὲ παῖδα, Πολυνείκην λέγω,
     ἡμεῖς ἐπαινέσαντες οὐ ψευδοίμεθ' ἄν.
930   ξένος γὰρ ἦν μοι πρὶν λιπὼν Κάδμου πόλιν
     φυγῇ πρὸς Ἄργος διαβαλεῖν αὐθαιρέτῳ.
       ἀλλ' οἶσθ' ὃ δρᾶσαι βούλομαι τούτων πέρι;

ΑΔΡΑΣΤΟΣ

     οὐκ οἶδα πλὴν ἕν, σοῖσι πείθεσθαι λόγοις.

ΘΗΣΕΥΣ

     τὸν μὲν Διὸς πληγέντα Καπανέα πυρὶ . . .

917 ἐκπαιδεύετε Markland
921 τὸν ἐμὸν Ἅιδας Wilamowitz: Ἅιδας τὸν ἐμὸν L

babe learns to say and to hear things he does not yet understand. And what a man learns he tends to keep until he is old. Therefore raise your children well!

### CHORUS

Alas, my son, it was for misery
that I carried you next to my heart and nourished you,
bearing the pain of childbirth!
And now Hades has taken
the fruits of my labor, wretch that I am,
and I have no one to tend my old age, though I,
unhappy one, have borne a child!

### THESEUS

As regards the noble son of Oecles,[28] the gods by snatching him away alive, chariot and all, into the depths of the earth openly praise him. As for the son of Oedipus, I mean Polynices, it would be no lie if we were to praise him. He was my guest friend in the days before he left the city of Cadmus and came over to Argos in voluntary exile.

But do you know what I want to do about these men?

### ADRASTUS

I know only one thing, obedience to your words.

### THESEUS

Capaneus, struck down by the fire of Zeus . . .

[28] Amphiaraus: see note on line 158.

---

926 ἀφαρπάσαντες Paley: ἀν- L: ζῶνθ᾽ ἁρπάσαντες ἐς μ- χ-θεοὶ Baier
928 δὲ Hermann: τε L
931 αὐθαιρέτῳ Wecklein: -ος L
932 δρᾶν σε Markland

ΑΔΡΑΣΤΟΣ

935 ἦ χωρὶς ἱερὸν ὡς νεκρὸν θάψαι θέλεις;

ΘΗΣΕΥΣ

ναί· τοὺς δέ γ᾽ ἄλλους πάντας ἐν μιᾷ πυρᾷ.

ΑΔΡΑΣΤΟΣ

ποῦ δῆτα θήσεις μνῆμα τῷδε χωρίσας;

ΘΗΣΕΥΣ

αὐτοῦ παρ᾽ οἴκους τούσδε συμπήξας τάφον.

ΑΔΡΑΣΤΟΣ

οὗτος μὲν ἤδη δμωσὶν ἂν μέλοι πόνος.

ΘΗΣΕΥΣ

940 ἡμῖν δέ γ᾽ οἵδε· στειχέτω δ᾽ ἄχθη νεκρῶν.

ΑΔΡΑΣΤΟΣ

ἴτ᾽, ὦ τάλαιναι μητέρες, τέκνων πέλας.

ΘΗΣΕΥΣ

ἥκιστ᾽, Ἄδραστε, τοῦτο πρόσφορον λέγεις.

ΑΔΡΑΣΤΟΣ

πῶς; τὰς τεκούσας οὐ χρεὼν ψαῦσαι τέκνων;

ΘΗΣΕΥΣ

ὄλοιντ᾽ ἰδοῦσαι τούσδ᾽ ἂν ἠλλοιωμένους.

ΑΔΡΑΣΤΟΣ

945 πικρὰ γὰρ ὄψις αἷμα κἀτειλαὶ νεκρῶν.

938 οἴκους Reiske: οἰκτροὺς L
939 οὗτος Reiske: αὐτὸς L

ADRASTUS

Will you bury him apart from the others, as a corpse sacred
to the gods?

THESEUS

Yes: all the others I shall cremate on a single pyre.

ADRASTUS

Where will you put the tomb you are setting apart for him?

THESEUS

I shall build his grave here right beside this temple.

ADRASTUS

Servants will now concern themselves with this task.

THESEUS

And I with these. Let the bodies of the dead be carried
forth!

ADRASTUS

Draw near, unhappy mothers, to your sons!

THESEUS

That is not a good idea, Adrastus.

ADRASTUS

Why? Should mothers not touch their sons?

THESEUS

To see them so changed would be their death.

ADRASTUS

Yes, the blood and wounds of the dead are a painful sight.

---

945 πικρὰ γὰρ ὄψις Reiske: πικραὶ γὰρ ὄψεις L    αἷμα
κὠτειλαὶ νεκρῶν Toup: καὶ ἄμα τῷ τέλει νεκρῷ L

ΘΗΣΕΥΣ

τί δῆτα λύπην ταῖσδε προσθεῖναι θέλεις;

ΑΔΡΑΣΤΟΣ

νικᾷς. μένειν χρὴ τλημόνως· λέγει γὰρ εὖ
Θησεύς· ὅταν δὲ τούσδε προσθῶμεν πυρί,
ὀστᾶ προσάξεσθ'. ὦ ταλαίπωροι βροτῶν,
950 τί κτᾶσθε λόγχας καὶ κατ' ἀλλήλων φόνους
τίθεσθε; παύσασθ', ἀλλὰ λήξαντες πόνων
ἄστη φυλάσσεθ' ἥσυχοι μεθ' ἡσύχων.
σμικρὸν τὸ χρῆμα τοῦ βίου· τοῦτον δὲ χρὴ
ὡς ῥᾷστα καὶ μὴ σὺν πόνοις διεκπερᾶν.

ΧΟΡΟΣ

στρ.
955 οὐκέτ' εὔτεκνος, οὐκέτ' εὔ-
παις, οὐδ' εὐτυχίας μέτε-
στίν μοι κουροτόκοις ἐν Ἀργείαις·
οὐδ' Ἄρτεμις λοχία
προσφθέγξαιτ' ἂν τὰς ἀτέκνους.
960 δυσαίων δ' ὁ βίος,
πλαγκτὰ δ' ὡσεί τις νεφέλα
πνευμάτων ὑπὸ δυσχίμων ἀίσσω.

ἀντ.

ἑπτὰ ματέρες ἑπτὰ κού-
ρους ἐγεινάμεθ' αἱ ταλαί-
965 πωροι κλεινοτάτους ἐν Ἀργείοις·
καὶ νῦν ἄπαις ἄτεκνος

**THESEUS**

Why then do you want to add to these women's grief?

**ADRASTUS**

I yield to you. (*to the Chorus*) You must stay here and endure: Theseus is right. But when we have put the dead on the pyre, you shall take their bones in your embrace. O suffering mortals, why do you get yourselves spears and shed each other's blood? No more! Rest from toil and keep watch over your cities, sitting quietly with your quiet fellow citizens! The sum of our life is but short. We should pass through it as easily and with as little toil as we can.

*Exit* THESEUS, ADRASTUS, *and funeral procession, together with the Sons, by Eisodos A.*

**CHORUS**

No more mother of fair sons, of fair children,
am I, no more do I have a share
of happiness among the Argive women who have borne
    boys.
Artemis, goddess of childbirth,
will have no word for the childless.
Ill-starred is my life,
and I move like a wandering cloud
blown by harsh winds.

We seven unlucky mothers
to seven sons gave birth,
the most glorious among the Argives.
And now in utmost misery

109

γηράσκω δυστανοτάτα,
οὔτ᾽ ⟨οὖν⟩ ἐν φθιμένοις
οὐ ζωοῖς ἀριθμουμένα,
970 χωρὶς δή τινα τῶνδ᾽ ἔχουσα μοῖραν.
ἐπῳδ.

ὑπολελειμμένα μοι δάκρυα·
μέλεα παιδὸς ἐν οἴκοις
κεῖται μνήματα, πένθιμοι
κουραὶ κἀστέφανοι κόμαι
λοιβαί ⟨τε⟩ νεκύων φθιμένων
975 ἀοιδαί θ᾽ ἃς χρυσοκόμας
Ἀπόλλων οὐκ ἐνδέχεται·
γόοισι δ᾽ ὀρθρευομένα
δάκρυσι νοτερὸν ἀεὶ πέπλων
πρὸς στέρνῳ πτύχα τέγξω.

980 —καὶ μὴν θαλάμας τάσδ᾽ ἐσορῶ δὴ
Καπανέως ἤδη τύμβον θ᾽ ἱερὸν
μελάθρων τ᾽ ἐκτὸς
Θησέως ἀναθήματα νεκροῖς,
κλεινήν τ᾽ ἄλοχον τοῦ καπφθιμένου
985 τοῦδε κεραυνῷ πέλας Εὐάδνην,
ἣν Ἶφις ἄναξ παῖδα φυτεύει.

967 δυστανοτάτα Collard: δυστηνότατος L
968 ⟨οὖν⟩ Kirchhoff
969 οὐ ζωοῖς Hermann: οὔτ᾽ ἐν ζωοῖσιν L
974 κἀστέφανοι κόμαι Markland: καὶ στέφανοι κόμας L
974b ⟨τε⟩ Hermann, cetera t, om. L
975 θ᾽ ἃς Markland: τὰς L

we enter old age childless,
numbered neither among the dead
nor with the living:
my fate is set apart from both.

Tears are all I have left.
Sad memorials of my son
are kept in my house in store, the shorn
hair of mourning, my garlandless head,
the libations made for the dead and gone,
and the songs which golden-haired
Apollo does not welcome.
I shall wake at dawn in weeping
and ever drench with tears the folds
of my robe upon my breast.

*Enter* EVADNE *above the temple.*[29] *She is splendidly
dressed, perhaps as a bride.*

#### CHORUS LEADER
Look, I see the resting place and consecrated tomb of
Capaneus here and gifts from the temple Theseus has
dedicated to the dead. I also see near at hand Evadne, the
glorious wife of lightning-slain Capaneus and the daughter

---

[29] The roof of the *skene* is here apparently being used to represent the cliffs that stood directly behind the Temple of Demeter and Kore at Eleusis. Evadne must leap to her death from this spot at the end of the scene. How this was staged we do not know.

τί ποτ᾽ αἰθερίαν ἕστηκε πέτραν
ἢ τῶνδε δόμων ὑπερακρίζει,
τήνδ᾽ ἐμβαίνουσα κέλευθον;

ΕΥΑΔΝΗ

στρ.

990  τί φέγγος, τίν᾽ αἴγλαν
ἐδίφρευε τόθ᾽ ἅλιος
σελάνα τε κατ᾽ αἰθέρ᾽ ἃ
λαμπάσιν ὠκὺ θοαῖσι νυμφ-
φεῖ ἵππευε δι᾽ ὄρφνας,

995  ἁνίκ᾽ ⟨ἡδυθρόοις⟩ γάμων
τῶν ἐμῶν πόλις Ἄργους
ἀοιδαῖς εὐδαιμονίας
ἐπύργωσε καὶ γαμέτα
χαλκεοτευχέος Καπανέως;

1000  πρὸς ⟨ὅν γ᾽⟩ ἔβαν ⟨νῦν⟩ δρομὰς ἐξ
οἴκων ἐκβακχευσαμένα
πυρᾶς φῶς τάφον τ᾽ ἐμ-
βατεύσουσα τὸν αὐτόν,
ἐς Ἅιδαν καταλύσουσ᾽ ἄμοχθον

1005  βίοτον αἰῶνός τε πόνους·
ἥδιστος γάρ τοι θάνατος

991 ἐδίφρευε τόθ᾽ ἅλιος post Canter (-ετό γ᾽ ἅλιος) Matthiae: ἐδιφρεύετο τάλας L    992 αἰθέρ᾽ ἃ Grégoire: -ρα L
993 λαμπάσιν Kirchhoff: λαμπάδ᾽ ἵν᾽ L    ὠκὺ θοαῖσι Willink: ὠκυθόαι L
993–4 νυμφεῖ Murray: νύμφαι L    994 ἵππευε Willink: ἱππεύουσι L    ὄρφνας Hermann: ὀρφναίας L

112

of King Iphis. Why does she take this path and stand on
the high cliff that towers over this temple?

EVADNE[30]

What light, what gleam
did the sun on its chariot shine forth,
and likewise the moon, astride her steed,
swiftly accompanying my bridal celebration
through the dark night with her swift-moving torches?
On that day with songs ⟨sweet-resounding⟩
in honor of my marriage the city of Argos
raised tower-high my happiness
and that of my bridegroom,
Capaneus of the bronze panoply.
And ⟨now⟩ it is to him I have come, running
crazed from my house
to enter upon the same
pyre blaze and burial,
to bring my toilsome life and its labors
to a toilless end in Hades.
The most pleasurable death, you know,

[30] The two stanzas of Evadne's aria are notoriously corrupt,
and little confidence is to be felt in the Greek text I translate here.

---

995 ⟨ἡδυθρόοις⟩ Wilamowitz    996 fort. τὰς ἐμὰς
997 ἀοιδαῖς Musgrave: -δὰς L
999 χαλκεοτευχέος post Heath (del. τε) et Bothe (χαλκ-
οτευχέος) Page: χαλκεοτευχοῦς τε L
1000 πρὸς ⟨ὅν γ᾽⟩ ἔβαν Willink: προσέβαν L    ⟨νῦν⟩
Kovacs    1001 οἴκων Kovacs: ἐμῶν οἴκων L
1002 πυρᾶς Bothe: πυρὸς L    φῶς Hermann: φῶς
καθέξουσα L    1003 τ᾽ ἐμβατεύσουσα Kirchhoff: τε
βατεύσουσα L    1004 ἄμοχθον Hermann: ἔμμοχθον L

συνθνῄσκειν θνῄσκουσι φίλοις,
εἰ δαίμων τάδε κραίνοι.

ΧΟΡΟΣ

καὶ μὴν ὁρᾷς τήνδ᾽ ἧς ἐφέστηκας πέλας
1010 πυράν, Διὸς θησαυρόν, ἔνθ᾽ ἔνεστι σὸς
πόσις, δαμασθεὶς λαμπάσιν κεραυνίοις.

ΕΥΑΔΝΗ

ἀντ.

ὁρῶ δὴ τελευτὰν
ἵν᾽ ἔστακα (τύχα δέ μοι
ξυνάπτει ποδὸς ἀλλαγάς),
1015 εὐκλείας χάριν ἔνθεν ὁρ-
μάσω τᾶσδ᾽ ἀπὸ πέτρας·
πηδήσασα <δὲ> πυρὸς ἔσω
σῶμα τ᾽ αἴθοπι φλογμῷ
1020 πόσει συμμείξασα φίλῳ,
χρῶτα χρῷ πέλας θεμένα,
Φερσεφόνας ἥξω θαλάμους,
σὲ τὸν θανόντ᾽ οὔποτ᾽ ἐμᾷ
προδοῦσα ψυχᾷ κατὰ γᾶς.
1025 ἴτω φῶς γάμοι τ᾽· <εὐ-
τυχ>οῖθ᾽ αἵτινες εὐναὶ
δικαίων ὑμεναίων ἐν Ἄργει
φανῶσιν τέκνοις, ὅσιος δ᾽

1009 πέλας Scaliger: πύλας L
1013 ἵν᾽ Reiske: ἦν L
1014 ἀλλαγὰς Stinton: ἀλλὰ τῆς L

114

is to die with one's dearest as he dies,
if fate so ordains.

You see this pyre, above which you stand, the storehouse
of Zeus, where lies your husband, bested by the blaze of
the thunderbolt.

I see that my journey's end
is here where I stand (for fortune
is stepping along with me),
and it is here that to win glory
I shall launch myself from this cliff.
After leaping into the fire,
joining my body in the glowing flame
with my dear husband,
and laying my flesh near his,
I shall come to the marriage chamber of Persephone!
Never, where my life is concerned,
shall I abandon you lying dead beneath the earth!
Light the bridal torch, begin the marriage! ⟨May good luck
attend you,⟩ all lawful marriages
that may come to my children
in Argos! And may the wedded bridegroom,

---

1018 ⟨δὲ⟩ Wilamowitz
1020 φίλῳ Bothe: φίλον L
1021 χρῷ Hartung: χρωτὶ L
1022 Φερσεφόνας Elmsley: -νείας L
1025-6 ⟨εὐτυχ⟩οῖθ᾽ αἵτινες Stinton: εἴθε τινὲς L
1027 ὅσιος Hermann: ὁ σὸς L

εὐναῖος ⟨ναίοι⟩ γαμέτας
συντακεὶς αὔραις ἀδόλοις
1030　γενναίας ἀλόχοιο.

ΧΟΡΟΣ

καὶ μὴν ὅδ' αὐτὸς σὸς πατὴρ βαίνει πέλας
γεραιὸς Ἶφις ἐς νεωτέρους λόγους,
οὓς οὐ κατειδὼς πρόσθεν ἀλγήσει κλύων.

ΙΦΙΣ

ὦ δυστάλαιναι, δυστάλας ἐγὼ γέρων
1035　ἥκω διπλοῦν πένθημ' ὁμαιμόνων ἔχων,
τὸν μὲν θανόντα παῖδα Καδμείων δορὶ
Ἐτέοκλον ἐς γῆν πατρίδα ναυσθλώσων νεκρὸν
ζητῶν τ' ἐμὴν παῖδ', ἣ δόμων ἐξώπιος
βέβηκε πηδήσασα Καπανέως δάμαρ,
1040　θανεῖν ἐρῶσα σὺν πόσει. χρόνον μὲν οὖν
τὸν πρόσθ' ἐφρουρεῖτ' ἐν δόμοις· ἐπεὶ δ' ἐγὼ
φυλακὰς ἀνῆκα τοῖς παρεστῶσιν κακοῖς,
βέβηκεν. ἀλλὰ τῇδέ νιν δοξάζομεν
μάλιστ' ἂν εἶναι· φράζετ' εἰ κατείδετε.

ΕΥΑΔΝΗ

1045　τί τάσδ' ἐρωτᾷς; ἥδ' ἐγὼ πέτρας ἔπι
ὄρνις τις ὡσεὶ Καπανέως ὑπὲρ πυρᾶς
δύστηνον αἰώρημα κουφίζω, πάτερ.

1028 ⟨ναίοι⟩ Diggle
1029 συντακεὶς Diggle: -τηχθεὶς L
1030 ἀλόχοιο Wilamowitz: ψυχὰς ἀλόχῳ L

as goodness ordains, ⟨dwell⟩
fused in love to the pure impulse
of his noble wife!

*Enter* IPHIS *by Eisodos B.*

CHORUS LEADER

But look, here your father himself, aged Iphis, draws near
to receive new and unwelcome tidings, tidings he did not
know before and which will grieve him when he hears
them.

IPHIS

O unhappy women, unhappy old man that I am I have
come with a double burden of grief for my kin: I want to
transport my son Eteoclus, killed by the spears of the Cad-
means, back to his native land by ship and to find my
daughter, Capaneus' wife, who sprang up and left her
house, longing to die with her husband. Previously she was
guarded closely in the house. But because of our present
misfortunes I relaxed the watch, and she went off. But
we think she is most likely to be here. Tell me if you have
seen her.

EVADNE

Why do you ask *them*? Here I am upon the cliff like a bird,
perched high in my grief, father.

---

1034 δυστάλαιναι Markland: -α L     δυστάλας Kovacs:
δυσ- δ' L: v. del. Haslam
1035 πένθημ' ὁμαιμόνων Kirchhoff: πένθιμον δαιμόνων L
1037 γῆν Hermann: τὴν L
1039 λέληθε Wilamowitz

ΙΦΙΣ

τέκνον, τίς αὔρα; τίς στόλος; τίνος χάριν
δόμων ὑπεκβᾶσ' ἦλθες ἐς τήνδε χθόνα;

ΕΥΑΔΝΗ

1050 ὀργὴν λάβοις ἂν τῶν ἐμῶν βουλευμάτων
κλυών· ἀκοῦσαι δ' οὔ σε βούλομαι, πάτερ.

ΙΦΙΣ

τί δ'; οὐ δίκαιον πατέρα τὸν σὸν εἰδέναι;

ΕΥΑΔΝΗ

κριτὴς ἂν εἴης οὐ σοφὸς γνώμης ἐμῆς.

ΙΦΙΣ

σκευῇ δὲ τῇδε τοῦ χάριν κοσμεῖς δέμας;

ΕΥΑΔΝΗ

1055 θέλει τι κλεινὸν οὗτος ὁ στολμός, πάτερ.

ΙΦΙΣ

ὡς οὐκ ἐπ' ἀνδρὶ πένθιμος πρέπεις ὁρᾶν.

ΕΥΑΔΝΗ

ἐς γάρ τι πρᾶγμα νεοχμὸν ἐσκευάσμεθα.

ΙΦΙΣ

κἄπειτα τύμβῳ καὶ πυρᾷ φαίνῃ πέλας;

ΕΥΑΔΝΗ

ἐνταῦθα γὰρ δὴ καλλίνικος ἔρχομαι.

1049 ὑπεκβᾶσ' Kirchhoff: ὑπερβ- L
1050 ὀργὴν Reiske: ὁρμὴν L

IPHIS

My child, what impulse, what errand is this? Why have you
stolen from home and come to this land?

EVADNE

To learn my plans would make you angry, father. I do not
want you to hear them.

IPHIS

But is it not right for your father to know?

EVADNE

You would be a foolish judge of my intent.

IPHIS

But why have you adorned yourself with this finery?

EVADNE

These clothes have a glorious aim, father.

IPHIS

You do not look like a woman in mourning for her husband.

EVADNE

No: it is for a new purpose that I am decked out.

IPHIS

And yet you show yourself near his pyre and tomb?

EVADNE

Yes: I have come here in glorious victory.

---

1055 στολμός Markland: στόλος L
1056 πένθιμος Musgrave: -ίμῳ L

ΙΦΙΣ

1060  νικῶσα νίκην τίνα; μαθεῖν χρῄζω σέθεν.

ΕΥΑΔΝΗ

πάσας γυναῖκας ἃς δέδορκεν ἥλιος.

ΙΦΙΣ

ἔργοις Ἀθάνας ἢ φρενῶν εὐβουλίᾳ;

ΕΥΑΔΝΗ

ἀρετῇ· πόσει γὰρ συνθανοῦσα κείσομαι.

ΙΦΙΣ

τί φῄς; τί τοῦτ' αἴνιγμα σημαίνεις σαθρόν;

ΕΥΑΔΝΗ

1065  ᾄσσω θανόντος Καπανέως τήνδ' ἐς πυράν.

ΙΦΙΣ

ὦ θύγατερ, οὐ μὴ μῦθον ἐς πολλοὺς ἐρεῖς;

ΕΥΑΔΝΗ

τοῦτ' αὐτὸ χρῄζω, πάντας Ἀργείους μαθεῖν.

ΙΦΙΣ

ἀλλ' οὐδέ τοί σοι πείσομαι δρώσῃ τάδε.

ΕΥΑΔΝΗ

ὅμοιον· οὐ γὰρ μὴ κίχῃς μ' ἑλὼν χερί.
1070  καὶ δὴ πάρειται σῶμα, σοὶ μὲν οὐ φίλον,
ἡμῖν δὲ καὶ τῷ συμπυρουμένῳ πόσει.

1064 σημαίνει Markland
1066 ἐς Porson, Hermann: ἐπὶ L

**IPHIS**

What victory? I want to learn from your lips.

**EVADNE**

Over all women the sun looks on.

**IPHIS**

In the works of Athena or in prudence of thought?

**EVADNE**

In goodness: I shall lie next to my husband in death.

**IPHIS**

What do you mean? What is this diseased riddle you are telling?

**EVADNE**

I shall leap upon the pyre of dead Capaneus here.

**IPHIS**

My daughter, hush! Do not say this before the crowd.

**EVADNE**

But this is the very thing I want, that all the Argives should know it.

**IPHIS**

But I will not consent to your doing this.

**EVADNE**

That makes no difference. You will not be able to seize me in your grasp. See, my body is sped: this is unkind to you but kind to me and to the husband with whom I share the pyre.

*Exit EVADNE, leaping to a place behind the* skene.

ΧΟΡΟΣ

ἰώ,
γύναι, δεινὸν ἔργον ἐξειργάσω.

ΙΦΙΣ

ἀπωλόμην δύστηνος, Ἀργείων κόραι.

ΧΟΡΟΣ

ἒἔ,
σχέτλια τάδε παθών,
1075 τὸ πάντολμον ἔργον ὄψῃ τάλας;

ΙΦΙΣ

οὐκ ἄν τιν᾽ εὕροιτ᾽ ἄλλον ἀθλιώτερον.

ΧΟΡΟΣ

ἰὼ τάλας·
μετέλαχες τύχας Οἰδιπόδα, γέρον,
μέρος καὶ σὺ ⟨καὶ⟩ πόλις ἐμὰ τλάμων.

ΙΦΙΣ

1080 οἴμοι· τί δὴ βροτοῖσιν οὐκ ἔστιν τόδε,
νέους δὶς εἶναι καὶ γέροντας αὖ πάλιν;
ἀλλ᾽ ἐν δόμοις μὲν ἤν τι μὴ καλῶς ἔχῃ,
γνώμαισιν ὑστέραισιν ἐξορθούμεθα,
αἰῶνα δ᾽ οὐκ ἔξεστιν. εἰ δ᾽ ἦμεν νέοι
1085 δὶς καὶ γέροντες, εἴ τις ἐξημάρτανεν,
διπλοῦ βίου λαχόντες ἐξωρθούμεθ᾽ ἄν.
ἐγὼ γὰρ ἄλλους εἰσορῶν τεκνουμένους
παίδων ἐραστὴς ἦ πόθῳ τ᾽ ἀπωλλύμην.
εἰ δ᾽ εὖ τόδ᾽ ἤδη κἀξεπειράθην †τέκνων†

CHORUS

Alas,
woman, it is a dread deed you have accomplished!

IPHIS

My miserable life is at an end, Argive women!

CHORUS

Ah, ah!
Cruel are the griefs you have suffered!
Can you bear, poor man, to look on this deed of utmost
    daring?

IPHIS

You will never find another more hapless than me!

CHORUS

Poor man!
You have taken a share, old sir, in the fortunes of Oedipus,
both you ⟨and⟩ my luckless city!

IPHIS

Ah me! Why is it not possible for mortals to be twice young
and twice old? If something is amiss at home, with our
second thoughts we put it to rights, but we cannot do this
with our lives. If we were twice young and old, when any-
one made a mistake we could correct it when we had re-
ceived our life's second portion.

I, for example, saw others begetting children and
longed for them, and this longing was my undoing. If I had
known this and had experienced what a thing it is for a

---

1079 ⟨καὶ⟩ Bothe      1082 νόμοις Nauck
1089 εὖ τόδ᾽ ἤδη Haupt: ἐς τόδ᾽ ἦλθον L      πάρος Elmsley:
σαφῶς Hartung

1090   οἷον στέρεσθαι πατέρα γίγνεται τέκνων,
      οὐκ ἄν ποτ᾽ ἐς τόδ᾽ ἦλθον εἰς ὃ νῦν κακόν.
      [ὅστις φυτεύσας καὶ νεανίαν τεκὼν
      ἄριστον, εἶτα τοῦδε νῦν στερίσκομαι.]
      εἶέν· τί δὴ χρὴ τὸν ταλαίπωρόν με δρᾶν;
1095   στείχειν πρὸς οἴκους; κᾆτ᾽ ἐρημίαν ἴδω
      πολλὴν μελάθρων, ἀπορίαν τ᾽ ἐμῷ βίῳ;
      ἢ πρὸς μέλαθρα τοῦδε Καπανέως μόλω;
      ἥδιστα πρίν γε δῆθ᾽ ὅτ᾽ ἦν παῖς ἥδε μοι.
      ἀλλ᾽ οὐκέτ᾽ ἔστιν, ἥ γ᾽ ἐμὴν γενειάδα
1100   προσῆγετ᾽ αἰεὶ στόματι καὶ κάρα τόδε
      κατεῖχε χερσίν. οὐδὲν ἥδιον πατρὶ
      γέροντι θυγατρός· ἀρσένων δὲ μείζονες
      ψυχαί, γλυκεῖαι δ᾽ ἧσσον ἐς θωπεύματα.
      οὐχ ὡς τάχιστα δῆτά μ᾽ ἄξετ᾽ ἐς δόμους
1105   σκότῳ τε δώσετ᾽, ἔνθ᾽ ἀσιτίαις ἐμὸν
      δέμας γεραιὸν συντακεὶς ἀποφθερῶ;
      τί μ᾽ ὠφελήσει παιδὸς ὀστέων θιγεῖν;
      ὦ δυσπάλαιστον γῆρας, ὡς μισῶ σ᾽ ἔχων,
      μισῶ δ᾽ ὅσοι χρῄζουσιν ἐκτείνειν βίον,
1110   βρωτοῖσι καὶ ποτοῖσι καὶ μαγεύμασιν
      παρεκτρέποντες ὀχετὸν ὥστε μὴ θανεῖν·
      οὓς χρῆν, ἐπειδὰν μηδὲν ὠφελῶσι γῆν,
      θανόντας ἔρρειν κἀκποδὼν εἶναι νέοις.

1091 κακοῦ Toup
1092-3 del. Diggle
1096 πολλὴν Reiske: -ῶν L

father to lose his children, I would never have come to my
present pitch of misery. [I begot and fathered a brave
young man and now I am deprived of him.]

Well, then, what am I to do in my misery? Return
home? And then am I to look at the deep desolation of my
house and the emptiness of my life? Or should I go to the
house of Capaneus here? I loved to do so before when I
had my daughter. But she is gone, she who always used to
draw my cheek to her lips and hold my head in her hands.
Nothing is sweeter to an aged father than a daughter. Sons
are more spirited but not as endearing. Servants, take me
swiftly home and hide me in the dark! There I shall starve
my aged body and end my life! What good will it do me to
touch the bones of my son?

Old age, so hard to wrestle with, how I detest you! I
detest also those who wish to prolong their lives, using
meat and drink and magic potions to turn aside the stream
and avoid death. Since they do the earth no good, they
should vanish and die and get out of the way of the young!

*Exit* IPHIS *by Eisodos B. Enter* THESEUS *with retinue and
the* SONS *of the Seven, bearing urns of ashes, by Eisodos A.*

---

1098 δῆθ' ὅτ' Canter: δήποτ' L
1101 χερσίν Canter: χειρί L        οὐδὲν ἥδιον πατρὶ Burney:
πατρὶ δ' οὐδὲν ἥδιον L
1105 τε Markland: δὲ L
1110 ita t: νώτοισι καὶ στρώμναισι καὶ μαντεύμασιν L
1112 ὠφελῶσι γῆν t: ὠφέλουν πόλιν L

ΧΟΡΟΣ

ἰώ·
τάδε δὴ παίδων ἤδη φθιμένων
1115 ὀστᾶ φέρεται. λάβετ᾽, ἀμφίπολοι,
γραίας ἀμενοῦς (οὐ γὰρ ἔνεστιν
ῥώμη παίδων ὑπὸ πένθους)
πολλοῦ τε χρόνου ζώσης μέτρα δὴ
καταλειβομένης τ᾽ ἄλγεσι πολλοῖς.
1120 τί γὰρ ἂν μεῖζον τοῦδ᾽ ἔτι θνητοῖς
πάθος ἐξεύροις
ἢ τέκνα θανόντ᾽ ἐσιδέσθαι;

στρ. α

ΠΑΙΔΕΣ

φέρω φέρω,
τάλαινα μᾶτερ, ἐκ πυρᾶς πατρὸς μέλη,
1125 βάρος μὲν οὐκ ἀβριθὲς ἀλγέων ὕπο,
ἐν δ᾽ ὀλίγῳ τἀμὰ πάντα συνθείς.

ΧΟΡΟΣ

ἰὼ ἰώ,
πᾷ δάκρυα φέρεις φίλᾳ
ματρὶ τῶν ὀλωλότων
σποδοῦ τε πλῆθος ὀλίγον ἀντὶ σωμάτων
1130 εὐδοκίμων δή ποτ᾽ ἐν Μυκήναις;

ἀντ. α

ΠΑΙΔΕΣ

ἄπαις ἄπαις·
ἐγὼ δ᾽ ἔρημος ἀθλίου πατρὸς τάλας

#### CHORUS LEADER

Look! They are bringing the bones of our dead children!
Attendants, take hold of a weak old woman! Grief for my
son has left me strengthless. I have lived a long space of
years and been melted away with many woes. What grief
greater than seeing one's children slain could you find for
mortals?

#### SONS

I carry, I carry,
poor mother,[31] from the pyre my father's body,
a burden grief makes far from light:
all that is dear to me I have gathered in little compass.

#### CHORUS

Ah, ah,
how can you bring tears to the loving
mother of the slain
and a little dust in exchange for the bodies
of men once glorious in Mycenae?

#### SONS

Childless, childless
are you! But I, woefully bereft of my dear father,

31 Either used loosely for "grandmother," or addressed to
them as mothers of the slain.

---

1114 ἤδη Musgrave: καὶ δὴ L
1118 τε Reiske: δὴ L      μέτρα Musgrave: μέτα L
1124 πυρᾶς Markland: πυρὸς L
1125 ὕπο Markland: ὕπερ L
1131 παπαῖ παπαῖ Musgrave

ἔρημον οἶκον ὀρφανεύσομαι λαβών,
οὐ πατρὸς ἐν χερσὶ τοῦ τεκόντος.

ΧΟΡΟΣ

ἰὼ ἰώ·
ποῦ δὲ πόνος ἐμῶν τέκνων;
1135 ποῦ λοχευμάτων χάρις
τροφαί τε ματρὸς ἄυπνά τ᾽ ὀμμάτων τέλη
καὶ φίλιαι προσβολαὶ προσώπων;

στρ. β

ΠΑΙΔΕΣ

βεβᾶσιν, οὐκέτ᾽ εἰσίν· οἴμοι πάτερ·
βεβᾶσιν.

⟨ΧΟΡΟΣ⟩

αἰθὴρ ἔχει νιν ἤδη,
1140 πυρᾶς τετακότας σποδῷ,
ποτανοὶ δ᾽ ἤνυσαν τὸν Ἅιδαν.

⟨ΠΑΙΔΕΣ⟩

πάτερ, σῶν μὲν κλύεις τέκνων γόους;
ἆρ᾽ ἀσπιδοῦχος ἔτι ποτ᾽ ἀντιτείσομαι . . .

⟨ΧΟΡΟΣ⟩

. . . σὸν φόνον; εἰ γὰρ γένοιτο, τέκνον.

1134 ἐμὸς Wilamowitz
1135 ποῦ λοχευμάτων Musgrave: πολυχευμάτων L
1138 εἰσίν· οἴμοι Wilamowitz: εἰσί μοι L
1139n ⟨Χο.⟩ Murray

128

shall take his empty house and grow up as an orphan,
without the embrace of the father who begot me!

CHORUS

Ah me!
Where is the labor I spent on my sons?
Where is the thanks for the pains of childbirth?
Where is a mother's tendance, the sleepless devotion of her
eyes,
the sweet touch of her face?

SONS

Gone, here no more! Alas, my father!
They have gone.

⟨CHORUS⟩

They dwell now in the sky above,
dissolved in the pyre's hot ash!
They have taken wing and gone the road to Hades!

⟨SONS⟩

Father, do you hear your son's lamenting?
Shall the day ever come when I take up my shield and
avenge . . .

⟨CHORUS⟩

. . . your death? O may this be so, my son!

---

1140 πυρᾶς Markland: πυρὸς L
1142n ⟨Πα.⟩ Tyrwhitt
1142 σῶν μὲν Collard: σὺ μὲν σῶν L
1143 ἀντιτείσομαι Canter: -τάσσομαι L
1144n ⟨Χο.⟩ Grégoire

ἀντ. β

⟨ΠΑΙΔΕΣ⟩

1145 ἔτ' ἂν θεοῦ θέλοντος ἔλθοι δίκα
πατρῷος.

⟨ΧΟΡΟΣ⟩

οὔπω κακὸν τόδ' εὕδει.
ἅλις γόων (αἰαῖ τύχας)
ἅλις ⟨δ'⟩ ἀλγέων ἐμοὶ πάρεστιν.

⟨ΠΑΙΔΕΣ⟩

ἔτ' Ἀσωποῦ με δέξεται γάνος
1150 χαλκέοις ⟨ἐν⟩ ὅπλοις Δαναϊδᾶν στρατηλάταν . . .

⟨ΧΟΡΟΣ⟩

τοῦ φθιμένου πατρὸς ἐκδικαστάν.

στρ. γ

⟨ΠΑΙΔΕΣ⟩

ἔτ' εἰσορᾶν σε, πάτερ, ἐν ὄμμασιν δοκῶ . . .

⟨ΧΟΡΟΣ⟩

φίλαν φίλημα παρὰ γένυν τιθέντα σοί.

⟨ΠΑΙΔΕΣ⟩

λόγων δὲ παρακέλευσμα σῶν
1155 ἀέρι φερόμενον οἴχεται.

1145n ⟨Πα.⟩ Musgrave
1145 ἔτ' ἂν Musgrave: ὅταν L
1146n ⟨Χο.⟩ Murray
1147 ἅλις . . . αἰαῖ Willink: αἰαῖ . . . ἅλις L
1148 ⟨δ'⟩ Porson, Hermann
1149n ⟨Πα.⟩ Tyrwhitt

⟨SONS⟩

If heaven wills it, a father's vengeance
shall one day come.

⟨CHORUS⟩
                          This trouble is not yet laid to rest.
I have enough of tears (alas for my lot!),
enough of griefs!

⟨SONS⟩

One day the glistening Asopus[32]
will welcome me as general of Argives in bronze war
    gear . . .

⟨CHORUS⟩

. . . avenger of your dead father.

⟨SONS⟩

Father, I seem even now to see you before my eyes . . .

⟨CHORUS⟩

. . . planting a loving kiss on your cheek.

⟨SONS⟩

But the consolation of your words
has vanished, borne away on the air!

---

[32] One of the two principal rivers of Thebes.

---

1149 ἔτ᾽ Ἀσωποῦ Tyrwhitt (Ἀσωποῦ) et Elmsley: στάσω· ποῦ
L    1150 ⟨ἐν⟩ Markland
1151n ⟨Χο.⟩ Grégoire
1152n ⟨Πα.⟩ Hermann
1152 ἐν ὄμμασιν Diggle: ἐπ᾽ ὀμμάτων L
1153 ⟨Χο.⟩ Hermann    φίλαν Diggle: -ον L    σοί Page:
σόν L    1154n ⟨Πα.⟩ Hermann

ΧΟΡΟΣ

δυοῖν δ᾽ ἄχη, ματρί τ᾽ ἔλιπεν
σέ τ᾽ οὔποτ᾽ ἄλγη πατρῷα λείψει.

ἀντ. γ

⟨ΠΑΙΔΕΣ⟩

ἔχω τοσόνδε βάρος ὅσον μ᾽ ἀπώλεσεν.

⟨ΧΟΡΟΣ⟩

φέρ᾽, ἀμφὶ μαστὸν ὑποβάλω ⟨τέκνων⟩ σποδόν.

ΠΑΙΔΕΣ

1160 ἔκλαυσα τόδε κλυὼν ἔπος
στυγνότατον· ἔθιγέ μου φρενῶν.

ΧΟΡΟΣ

ὦ τέκνον, ἔβας· οὐκέτι φίλον
φίλας ἄγαλμ᾽ ὄψομαί σε ματρός.

ΘΗΣΕΥΣ

1165 Ἄδραστε καὶ γυναῖκες Ἀργεῖαι γένος,
ὁρᾶτε παῖδας τούσδ᾽ ἔχοντας ἐν χεροῖν
πατέρων ἀρίστων σώμαθ᾽ ὧν ἀνειλόμην·
τούτοις ἐγώ σφε καὶ πόλις δωρούμεθα.
ὑμᾶς δὲ τῶνδε χρὴ χάριν μεμνημένους
1170 σῴζειν, ὁρῶντας ὧν ἐκύρσατ᾽ ἐξ ἐμοῦ,
παισίν θ᾽ ὑπειπεῖν τοῖσδε τοὺς αὐτοὺς λόγους,
τιμᾶν πόλιν τήνδ᾽, ἐκ τέκνων ἀεὶ τέκνοις
μνήμην παραγγέλλοντας ὧν ἐκύρσατε.
Ζεὺς δὲ ξυνίστωρ οἵ τ᾽ ἐν οὐρανῷ θεοὶ
1175 οἵων ὑφ᾽ ἡμῶν στείχετ᾽ ἠξιωμένοι.

132

#### CHORUS

Both of us grieve: grief he has left his mother—
and pain for your father will never desert you!

#### ⟨SONS⟩

I have such a weight of grief as has destroyed me!

#### ⟨CHORUS⟩

Come, let me take ⟨my son's⟩ ashes to my breast!

#### SONS

I weep as I hear you say this word
most hateful: it tears my heart!

#### CHORUS

My son, you are gone! No more shall I see you,
beloved darling of a mother you loved!

#### THESEUS

Adrastus and women of Argive birth, you see these boys
holding in their arms the bodies of their valiant fathers,
bodies I have rescued. The city and I bestow these on
them. But you for your part must remember this and keep
gratitude for it in your hearts, seeing what you have re-
ceived at my hands, and you must say the same thing to
these children, telling them to honor this city and hand
down to their children's children the memory of what you
have received. Zeus and the gods in heaven are witnesses
that you go home deemed worthy of great benefits by us!

---

1156 ἔλιπεν Tyrwhitt: -ες L     1158n ⟨Πα.⟩ Musgrave
1159n ⟨Χο.⟩ Hermann     1159 ⟨τέκνων⟩ Fritzsche
1164 φίλας Musgrave: φίλος L     1168 σφε Elmsley: σε L
1171 παισίν θ᾽ ὑπειπεῖν Reiske: πᾶσίν θ᾽ ὑπεῖπον L
τοῖσδε Tyrwhitt: τούσδε L

ΑΔΡΑΣΤΟΣ

Θησεῦ, ξύνισμεν πάνθ᾽ ὅσ᾽ Ἀργείαν χθόνα
δέδρακας ἐσθλὰ δεομένην εὐεργετῶν,
χάριν τ᾽ ἀγήρων ἕξομεν· γενναῖα γὰρ
παθόντες ὑμᾶς ἀντιδρᾶν ὀφείλομεν.

ΘΗΣΕΥΣ

1180  τί δῆτ᾽ ἔθ᾽ ὑμῖν ἄλλ᾽ ὑπουργῆσαί με χρή;

ΑΔΡΑΣΤΟΣ

χαῖρ᾽· ἄξιος γὰρ καὶ σὺ καὶ πόλις σέθεν.

ΘΗΣΕΥΣ

ἔσται τάδ᾽· ἀλλὰ καὶ σὺ τῶν αὐτῶν τύχοις.

ΑΘΗΝΑ

ἄκουε, Θησεῦ, τῆσδ᾽ Ἀθηναίας λόγους,
ἃ χρή σε δρᾶσαι, δρῶντα δ᾽ ὠφελεῖν τὰ σά.
1185  μὴ δῷς τάδ᾽ ὀστᾶ τοῖσδ᾽ ἐς Ἀργείαν χθόνα
παισὶν κομίζειν ῥᾳδίως οὕτω μεθείς,
ἀλλ᾽ ἀντὶ τῶν σῶν καὶ πόλεως μοχθημάτων
πρῶτον λάβ᾽ ὅρκον. τόνδε δ᾽ ὀμνύναι χρεὼν
Ἄδραστον· οὗτος κύριος, τύραννος ὤν,
1190  πάσης ὑπὲρ γῆς Δαναϊδῶν ὁρκωμοτεῖν.
ὁ δ᾽ ὅρκος ἔσται μήποτ᾽ Ἀργείους χθόνα
ἐς τήνδ᾽ ἐποίσειν πολέμιον παντευχίαν
ἄλλων τ᾽ ἰόντων ἐμποδὼν θήσειν δόρυ.
ἢν δ᾽ ὅρκον ἐκλιπόντες ἔλθωσιν πόλιν,
1195  κακῶς ὀλέσθαι πρόστρεπ᾽ Ἀργείων χθόνα.

1180 δῆτ᾽ ἔθ᾽ Elmsley: δήποθ᾽ L

ADRASTUS

Theseus, we are conscious of all the good you have done
to the land of Argos when it needed a benefactor, and our
gratitude will never grow old. Since we have received such
noble treatment, we must treat you nobly in turn.

THESEUS

What further service can I perform for you?

ADRASTUS

Fare well! Faring well is what you and your city deserve!

THESEUS

I shall. And may you also do the same!

*Enter* ATHENA *from above the* skene.

ATHENA

Listen, Theseus, to my words, the words of Athena! Here
is what you must do and in doing benefit your own inter-
ests. Do not give these bones to these children to carry
away to the land of Argos, letting them go so lightly, but in
return for your labors and those of your city first exact an
oath. This man here, Adrastus, must swear: he has the
authority to take an oath on behalf of the whole land of
Danaus' sons since he is the king. This is the oath: that the
Argives will never move a hostile army against this land,
and that, if others do so, they will use their own might to
stop them. They must pray that the land of Argos may
perish miserably if they violate the oath and march against
the city.

---

1183 τῆσδ' Seidler: τούσδ' L
1184 τὰ σά Musgrave: τάδε L

135

EURIPIDES

ἐν ᾧ δὲ τέμνειν σφάγια χρή σ᾽, ἄκουέ μου.
ἔστιν τρίπους σοι χαλκόπους ἔσω δόμων,
ὃν Ἰλίου ποτ᾽ ἐξαναστήσας βάθρα
σπουδὴν ἐπ᾽ ἄλλην Ἡρακλῆς ὁρμώμενος
1200 στῆσαί σ᾽ ἐφεῖτο Πυθικῇ πρὸς ἐσχάρᾳ.
ἐν τῷδε λαιμοὺς τρεῖς τριῶν μήλων τεμὼν
ἔγγραψον ὅρκους τρίποδος ἐν κοίλῳ κύτει,
κἄπειτα σῴζειν θεῷ δὸς ᾧ Δελφῶν μέλει,
μνημεῖά θ᾽ ὅρκων μαρτύρημά θ᾽ Ἑλλάδι.
1205 ᾗ δ᾽ ἂν διοίξῃς σφάγια καὶ τρώσῃς φόνον
ὀξύστομον μάχαιραν ἐς γαίας μυχοὺς
κρύψον παρ᾽ αὐτὰς ἑπτὰ πυρκαιὰς νεκρῶν.
φόβον γὰρ αὐτοῖς, ἤν ποτ᾽ ἔλθωσιν πόλιν,
δειχθεῖσα θήσει καὶ κακὸν νόστον πάλιν.
1210 δράσας δὲ ταῦτα πέμπε γῆς ἔξω νεκρούς.
τεμένη δ᾽, ἵν᾽ αὐτῶν σώμαθ᾽ ἡγνίσθη πυρί,
μέθες παρ᾽ αὐτὴν τρίοδον Ἰσθμίαν θεῷ·
σοὶ μὲν τάδ᾽ εἶπον· παισὶ δ᾽ Ἀργείων λέγω·
πορθήσεθ᾽ ἡβήσαντες Ἰσμηνοῦ πόλιν,
1215 πατέρων θανόντων ἐκδικάζοντες φόνον,
σύ τ᾽ ἀντὶ πατρός, Αἰγιαλεῦ, στρατηλάτης
νέος καταστάς, παῖς τ᾽ ἀπ᾽ Αἰτωλῶν μολὼν
Τυδέως, ὃν ὠνόμαζε Διομήδη πατήρ.
ἀλλ᾽ οὐ φθάνειν χρὴ συσκιάζοντας γένυν
1220 καὶ χαλκοπληθῆ Δαναϊδῶν ὁρμᾶν στρατὸν

1196 σφάγια χρή Bothe: χ- σ- L

136

Now hear from me with what vessel you are to perform this sacrifice. In your house there is a bronze-footed tripod. When Heracles had destroyed the foundations of Troy, he bade you dedicate it near the Pythian hearth as he set off on another mission. Over this tripod you must cut the throats of three sheep and inscribe the oath on its curved hollow, and then give it for safekeeping to the god who rules Delphi, a memorial of the oath and a witness to it in the eyes of Hellas. The sharp-bladed knife with which you cut the throats and made the bloody wound you must bury in the depths of the earth right near the pyres of the seven dead. For if the Argives ever return to the city, this knife, when displayed, will make them afraid and cause them an evil journey home. When you have done these things, escort the bodies out of the country. The sanctuaries in which the bodies were purified by the fire, near the branching of the road that leads to the Isthmus, dedicate to the god.

Those are my instructions to you. To the children of the Argive champions I say this: when you come to manhood, you will sack the city of the Ismenus and exact vengeance for the blood of your fathers slain. You, Aegialeus,[33] shall be a young general in your father's stead, and Tydeus' son, whom his father called Diomedes, shall come from Aetolia and be general too. No sooner have your beards grown in than you must march the bronze-clad army of Danaus' sons

[33] Son of Adrastus.

---

1200 σ' Reiske: γ' L    Πυθικῇ . . . ἐσχάρᾳ Lenting: -ὴν . . . -άραν L
1211 ἡγνίσθη Heath: ἁγνισθῇ L
1212 Ἰσθμίαν θεῷ Tyrwhitt: Ἰσθμίας θεοῦ L

ἑπτάστομον πύργωμα Καδμείων ἔπι·
πικροὶ γὰρ αὐτοῖς ἥξετ᾽ ἐκτεθραμμένοι
σκύμνοι λεόντων, πόλεος ἐκπορθήτορες.
κοὐκ ἔστιν ἄλλως· Ἐπίγονοι δ᾽ ἂν᾽ Ἑλλάδα
1225 κληθέντες ᾠδὰς ὑστέροισι θήσετε·
τοῖον στράτευμα σὺν θεῷ πορεύσετε.

ΘΗΣΕΥΣ

δέσποιν᾽ Ἀθάνα, πείσομαι λόγοισι σοῖς·
σὺ γάρ μ᾽ ἀπορθοῖς ὥστε μὴ ᾽ξαμαρτάνειν.
καὶ τόνδ᾽ ἐν ὅρκοις ζεύξομαι· μόνον σύ με
1230 ἐς ὀρθὸν ἵστη· σοῦ γὰρ εὐμενοῦς πόλει
οὔσης τὸ λοιπὸν ἀσφαλῶς οἰκήσομεν.

ΧΟΡΟΣ

στείχωμεν, Ἄδρασθ᾽, ὅρκια δῶμεν
τῷδ᾽ ἀνδρὶ πόλει τ᾽· ἄξια δ᾽ ἡμῖν
προμεμοχθήκασι σέβεσθαι.

1221 ἑπτάστομον Heath: -στολον L
1224 Ἐπίγονοι Brodaeus: Ἔκγονοι L
1228 ἀπορθοῖς Markland: ἀν- L

138

to the seven-gated city of the Cadmeans. Unwelcome will you be to them as you arrive, lion cubs now full-grown, sackers of the city. It cannot be otherwise. Throughout Greece you will be called the Epigoni[34] and will make themes for song for generations to come: such, with the help of heaven, will be your expedition!

### THESEUS

Lady Athena, I shall obey your commands. You correct me so that I do not go astray. I shall bind this man with an oath. Only hold me upright! If you show goodwill toward the city, we will live in safety for all time to come.

*Exit ATHENA.*

### CHORUS LEADER

Let us go, Adrastus, and take the oath before this man and his city. For their labors on our behalf earn them our honor.

*Exit THESEUS with retinue, ADRASTUS, SONS, and CHORUS by Eisodos A.*

[34] I.e. the Successors in the next generation.

# ELECTRA

# INTRODUCTION

Euripides and Sophocles each wrote an *Electra*, covering the same portion of Argive myth Aeschylus had treated a generation earlier in his *Libation Bearers*, the second play of his *Oresteia*. One of the hardiest of the perennial problems of scholarship is which of the two *Electras* came first. Sophocles' play cannot be dated even approximately, though it is unlikely to be a very early play. Euripides' play was formerly dated with confidence to 413 on the basis of what was thought to be an allusion to the Sicilian expedition in lines 1347–8, but in recent years doubts have arisen whether the allusion is there, and many scholars would now date the play on the basis of its metrical practice to ca. 420. (On meter as evidence for the dates of Euripides' plays, see the general introduction, Volume One, pp. 16–17.) Yet while it would be nice to know whether Euripides first took up the challenge of emulating his great predecessor Aeschlyus and Sophocles was stirred by Euripides to a further version, or Sophocles was first and Euripides second, interpretation of our play is not much affected. Aeschylus' play is very much in the background for Euripides, but if he knew Sophocles' *Electra*, his own play shows few if any traces of it.

As noted in the general introduction, part of the biographical tradition regards Euripides as sharply anti-traditional in his artistic aims, and much of nineteenth- and twentieth-century scholarship has followed suit. The strongest case for Euripides as destroyer of tradition could be made on the basis of his *Electra*. It has seemed to many that in this play especially Euripides is bent on killing traditional tragedy and dancing on its grave. Here are the chief points. (1) Euripides goes out of his way to create an atmosphere of untragic realism. He invents the story that Aegisthus and Clytaemestra married Electra off to a poor farmer living in the mountains of the Argolid far from the city. The change of scene makes for homeliness rather than tragic grandeur. (2) He depicts his characters in a decidedly unheroic light. His Electra complains bitterly of her poverty and degradation and engages in what might be called self-martyrdom, wallowing in miseries that could have been partially alleviated. His Orestes is indecisive and cowardly, stealing into the Argolid with an eye always on the exit, not revealing himself to his sister even when he knows that it is safe to do so, needing to have his resolve strengthened by Electra. (3) Apollo's oracle, which had ordered Orestes to take revenge on his father's murderers, is shown to have disastrous results, and even Castor, despite qualms about criticizing Apollo, calls it "unwise." (4) At one point, in the notorious lines 518-44, Euripides goes out of his way to mock Aeschylus. When the old retainer of Agamemnon comes on, the man who will eventually recognize Orestes, he reports that he has seen footprints and a lock of hair at Agamemnon's tomb, thinks they may be those of Orestes, and invites Electra to compare her own hair and footprints with them and to think whether she could recognize her brother by some garment of his that she herself wove. These are the three signs, hair, foot-

143

print, and weaving, that help to effect the recognition in
Aeschylus' *Libation Bearers*. Electra pours commonsense
scorn on all three, and Orestes is finally recognized by a
scar he received in childhood. It looks as if Euripides is
engaged in making fun of his great predecessor and in the
process ruining whatever tragic seriousness his own play
still possessed.

It may not be Euripides but that prolific author Anony-
mous who is responsible for the last of these features. Lines
518-44 are not only destructive in the manner described
above but also intrusive in other ways that suggest they are
a later addition, and there is a strong case for excision, first
made by August Mau in 1877, seconded by Eduard
Fraenkel in 1950, and restated by M. L. West in 1980. (I
summarize the evidence and add new grounds in my arti-
cle of 1989.) As for the other items, there is more than one
way to look at Euripides' plot innovations and the way he
has portrayed his characters, both human and divine.

Euripides' big innovation is Electra's nominal marriage
to the Farmer and the consequent shift of the action of
the play from the palace of the Atridae to a humble cot-
tage in the hills of the Argolid. Why does he make this
change, which so essentially shapes his story? Do the deeds
of this story necessarily suffer a diminution in importance
or tragic grandeur by being enacted against this backdrop?
There is the best of precedents for a drama of return and
revenge taking place in such a venue: Homer's *Odyssey*, a
large part of which takes place in the hut of the swineherd
Eumaeus. When an absent hero returns home to regain his
rightful inheritance and punish usurpers, as both Odysseus
and Orestes are doing, one way of showing their legiti-
macy is to contrast the common folk like Eumaeus, who

are loyal to their absent lord, with the nobly born but arrogant usurpers. Aeschylus too makes use of this, for one of the homeliest characters in Greek tragedy is surely his Cilissa, who comes out lamenting that all her labor on Orestes—including washing his diapers—has been lost. Neither she nor the Chorus of slaves has acquiesced in the new regime, and they play an important role in the revenge.

In much the same way the common people in Euripides' play are shown to be on Orestes' side: the Farmer whose loyalty to Agamemnon and Orestes leads him to connive in a sham marriage with Electra; the Old Man, Agamemnon's old tutor, who ransacks his cupboards to bring food for Electra's guests and takes a large part in the plot against the usurpers; and even the anonymous attendants of Aegisthus, who welcome Orestes when they learn he is their rightful lord. The mythical shape of the plot is as visible here in the countryside as when the story is enacted before a palace, and new mythical connections become possible as well. The Chorus, for instance, sing of the arrival of the rustic god Pan in Argos, bringing a golden lamb to Atreus as the sign of his rightful kingship. Just a few lines earlier the audience had seen another rustic arrive, and he too was burdened with a lamb offered to a rightful king. Tragedy is most commonly enacted before a palace, as epic most commonly on a battlefield, but either can on occasion adopt a different location without ceasing to be itself.

Orestes has struck some critics of the play as deliberately sub-heroic, especially in his vacillation and indecisiveness, and the conclusion is drawn that he is a caricature of the more traditional Orestes of Aeschylus. One piece of evidence is particularly strong: the fact that, although he knows early on who Electra is and learns that the women of the Chorus are friendly and will keep any secrets entrusted to them, he nevertheless does not reveal his identity. It must be noted in general, however, that the essential thing about the Orestes story is that a young man is placed in an untenable position and confronted with an impossible choice. Hesitation and indecisiveness are inextricably bound up in the role, and an Orestes who exhibited a no-nonsense, take-charge attitude toward the matricide would have been quite untraditional. In Aeschylus, Orestes hesitates and has to have his resolution strengthened by the intervention of Pylades. Euripides means his audience to view the deed of matricide in a rather more tragic light than in Aeschylus, so that it is natural that one at least of the pair should exhibit hesitation. Orestes' hesitation even to reveal himself is harder to judge. No one comments on it one way or another in the play, and it may be that Euripides, who intended the Old Man to have a role not only in the murder plot but also in the recognition, has simply not bothered to motivate Orestes' silence. If we wish to supply motivation for him, we should note Orestes' stated purpose (100-1): "so that I may join with her, gain her as my accomplice in the murder, and learn reliably how matters stand inside the city." We might well imagine that, once he has been apprised of his sister's situation, he sees clearly that he can expect little help from her or her husband or, living as they do cut off from the city, any information from them about the situation in the palace. It may be that Orestes decides he must assess the situation more fully before committing himself, as a revelation would commit him, to action.

Euripides' Electra, though portrayed differently from either Aeschylus' or Sophocles', should not be judged as harshly as some critics have done. Her marriage to the Farmer really is a kind of social death, and the view that Aegisthus has committed an outrage against her in this is no private sense of grievance peculiar to her—evidence of snobbery or the like—but shared, among others, by the Farmer himself. And her refusal to borrow clothes from the Chorus and her insistence on carrying water for her nominal husband are less plausibly to be seen as psychologically interesting "self-martyrdom" than as refusal to come to terms with and make the best of the new order of things, a refusal also exhibited by Sophocles' Electra.

The divine ordering of events is visible throughout the action. Orestes is guided by the oracle to come to Argos in secret, as in other versions of the story. He finds his sister, a recognition is effected, and they plot to kill the usurpers. In Aeschylus, success depends upon a combination of resourcefulness and fortunate circumstance. Orestes gains entry into the palace by bringing news of his own death. By good fortune, Clytaemestra sends her servant Cilissa to tell Aegisthus, asking him to come with his bodyguard. Cilissa, grieving at the news of her charge's death, pours out her grief to the Chorus. They, knowing how important it is that Aegisthus arrive without his bodyguard, alter the message, telling him to come alone.

Euripides' play keeps the same elements of resourcefulness and luck. (Compare the Old Man's formulation in line 610.) But he has given much greater scope to luck. Electra lives out in the country, not in the palace, and it is explicitly said by the Old Man that it will be impossible for Orestes even to enter the city. Orestes has a price on his

head, and the guards are on the lookout for him. But by
good fortune Aegisthus is sacrificing to the Nymphs in the
countryside. It will be a simple matter, the Old Man says,
for Orestes and Pylades to get themselves invited to the
feast and there to watch for their chance. In the event,
everything goes splendidly. Orestes waits for the moment
when no one has a weapon nearby and kills Aegisthus with
a sacrificial cleaver. (Some scholars criticize him for this,
but captiously: there is no chance for a fair fight, and
stealth is the only route to success.) And though the two
young men are bravely prepared to fight against a band of
slaves, it does not prove necessary to do so. As for Clytae-
mestra, who cannot be killed at the same time, Electra's
resourcefulness assures that she will be on her way to the
cottage before she can learn the news of her husband's
death.

Euripides follows Aeschylus too in sharply distinguish-
ing between the murder of Aegisthus and that of Clytae-
mestra. The first brings unmixed joy to the two principals;
the second is matricide, and however much Clytaemestra
has deserved to die, death of a mother at the hands of her
own children cannot be the occasion of rejoicing but only
of horror. It is of the essence of the Orestes story that the
matricide should be tragic, embodying a conflict between
the duty to avenge one's father and the duty to honor one's
mother. In both Aeschylus and Euripides the horror of the
deed is brought into sharp focus, in Aeschylus by Orestes'
incipient madness as he sees the Erinyes, in Euripides by
the horror that comes over the agents after their deed. In
both plays there will be consequences for Orestes in the
pursuit of the Erinyes. In both, these consequences are

only temporary, and after a harrowing pursuit and a trial in Athens Orestes wins his freedom and has his fortunes restored.

Much is often made of the criticism of Apollo by Castor at the end of the play. Castor twice (1246, 1302) calls Apollo's command to Orestes unwise. But this is not as untraditional as it looks. The oracular command is unwise in that, as Castor points out, it is the right deed done by the wrong persons, and its consequences for Orestes and Electra are horrible. Apollo in tragedy is more than once portrayed as a god who pays insufficient attention to the realities of the mortal condition. (Compare Volume One, introduction to *Alcestis*.) That is his role in Aeschylus too, for in *Eumenides* Apollo takes the untragic view that there is nothing wrong with matricide since the mother is only the carrier of the father's seed. This view is implicitly repudiated by Athena, who thereby restores the tragic element to the story. Apollo's simplistic view of things is wrong. In similar fashion Euripides by the mouth of Castor criticizes Apollo and reasserts the tragic element of Orestes' action, even if tragedy for Orestes does not, in the great scheme of Zeus, have the last word.

## SELECT BIBLIOGRAPHY

### Editions

J. D. Denniston (Oxford, 1939).
M. Cropp (Warminster, 1988).
G. Basta Donzelli (Leipzig, 1995).

# EURIPIDES

## Literary Criticism

G. Basta Donzelli, *Studio sull'* Elettra *di Euripide* (Catania, 1978).

M. Cropp, *"Heracles, Electra* and the *Odyssey,"* in M. Cropp et al., edd., *Greek Tragedy and Its Legacy: Essays Presented to D. J. Conacher* (Calgary, 1986), pp. 187-99.

D. Kovacs, "Castor in Euripides' *Electra," CQ* 35 (1985), 306-14.

———— "Where is Aegisthus' Head?" *CP* 37 (1987), 139-41.

———— "Euripides, *Electra* 518-44: Further Doubts about Genuineness," *BICS* 36 (1989), 67-78.

M. Kubo, "The Norm of Myth: Euripides' *Electra," HSCP* 71 (1966), 15-31.

W. Steidle, *Studien zum antiken Drama* (Munich, 1968), pp. 63-95.

M. L. West, "Tragica IV," *BICS* 27 (1980), 9-22.

## Dramatis Personae

| | |
|---|---|
| ΑΥΤΟΥΡΓΟΣ | FARMER, Electra's nominal husband |
| ΗΛΕΚΤΡΑ | ELECTRA, daughter of Agamemnon and Clytaemestra |
| ΟΡΕΣΤΗΣ | ORESTES, exiled son of Agamemnon and Clytaemestra |
| ΧΟΡΟΣ | CHORUS of women of the rural Argolid |
| ΠΡΕΣΒΥΣ | OLD MAN |
| ΑΓΓΕΛΟΣ | Servant of Orestes as MESSENGER |
| ΚΛΥΤΑΙΜΗΣΤΡΑ | CLYTAEMESTRA, Queen of Argos |
| ΚΑΣΤΩΡ | CASTOR, deified brother of Clytaemestra |
| Nonspeaking roles: | Pylades, Orestes' friend; Polydeuces, Castor's brother |

## A Note on Staging

The *skene* represents the rustic home of the Farmer and Electra. Eisodos A leads to the Farmer's nearby fields and to the city of Argos, Eisodos B to Agamemnon's tomb, the Old Man's house, Aegisthus' country estate, and locations abroad. In front of the acting area there is an altar to Apollo with a statue of the god.

151

# ΗΛΕΚΤΡΑ

ΑΥΤΟΥΡΓΟΣ

Ὦ γῆς Πελασγῶν ἀρδμός, Ἰνάχου ῥοαί,
ὅθεν ποτ᾽ ἄρας ναυσὶ χιλίαις Ἄρη
ἐς γῆν ἔπλευσε Τρῳάδ᾽ Ἀγαμέμνων ἄναξ.
κτείνας δὲ τὸν κρατοῦντ᾽ ἐν Ἰδαίᾳ χθονὶ
5  Πρίαμον ἑλών τε Δαρδάνου κλεινὴν πόλιν
ἀφίκετ᾽ ἐς τόδ᾽ Ἄργος, ὑψηλῶν δ᾽ ἐπὶ
ναῶν ἔθηκε σκῦλα πλεῖστα βαρβάρων.
κἀκεῖ μὲν ηὐτύχησεν· ἐν δὲ δώμασιν
θνῄσκει γυναικὸς πρὸς Κλυταιμήστρας δόλῳ
10  καὶ τοῦ Θυέστου παιδὸς Αἰγίσθου χερί.
χὠ μὲν παλαιὰ σκῆπτρα Ταντάλου λιπὼν
ὄλωλεν, Αἴγισθος δὲ βασιλεύει χθονός,
ἄλοχον ἐκείνου Τυνδαρίδα κόρην ἔχων.
οὓς δ᾽ ἐν δόμοισιν ἔλιφ᾽ ὅτ᾽ ἐς Τροίαν ἔπλει,
15  ἄρσενά τ᾽ Ὀρέστην θῆλύ τ᾽ Ἠλέκτρας θάλος,
τὸν μὲν πατρὸς γεραιὸς ἐκκλέπτει τροφεὺς
μέλλοντ᾽ Ὀρέστην χερὸς ὑπ᾽ Αἰγίσθου θανεῖν
Στροφίῳ τ᾽ ἔδωκε Φωκέων ἐς γῆν τρέφειν·

---

1 Πελασγῶν Semitelos: παλαιὸν L    ἀρδμός Herwerden:
ἄργος L: ὄλβος Semitelos

# ELECTRA

*Enter from the* skene, *representing a rustic cottage, a* FARMER, *Electra's supposed husband.*

**FARMER**

Streams of Inachus, that water the land of the Pelasgians!
It was from you that King Agamemnon set forth for war
with a thousand ships and sailed to the land of Troy. When
he had killed Priam, Troy's ruler, and captured the glorious
city of Dardanus, he returned here to Argos, and on our
lofty temples he hung the rich spoils of the barbarian. In
Troy his fortunes were good, but at home he was treacher-
ously slain by his wife Clytaemestra and by the hand of
Thyestes' son, Aegisthus.

Now he has relinquished the ancient scepter of Tanta-
lus and is gone, and Aegisthus rules the land, having mar-
ried Agamemnon's wife, the daughter of Tyndareus. As
for the children he left behind when he sailed to Troy, his
son Orestes and his daughter Electra, the old servant who
raised Agamemnon snatched Orestes away as Aegisthus
was about to kill him, sending him to Strophius in Phocis

---

⁴ Ἰδαίᾳ Elmsley: Ἰλιάδι L
¹⁰ del. Klinkenberg

ἣ δ' ἐν δόμοις ἔμεινεν Ἠλέκτρα πατρός,
20 ταύτην ἐπειδὴ θαλερὸς εἶχ' ἥβης χρόνος,
μνηστῆρες ᾔτουν Ἑλλάδος πρῶτοι χθονός.
δείσας δὲ μή τῳ παῖδ' ἀριστέων τέκοι
Ἀγαμέμνονος ποινάτορ', εἶχεν ἐν δόμοις
Αἴγισθος οὐδ' ἥρμοζε νυμφίῳ τινί.
25   ἐπεὶ δὲ καὶ τοῦτ' ἦν φόβου πολλοῦ πλέων,
μή τῳ λαθραίως τέκνα γενναίῳ τέκοι,
κτανεῖν σφε βουλεύσαντος ὠμόφρων ὅμως
μήτηρ νιν ἐξέσωσεν Αἰγίσθου χερός.
ἐς μὲν γὰρ ἄνδρα σκῆψιν εἶχ' ὀλωλότα,
30 παίδων δ' ἔδεισε μὴ φθονηθείη φόνῳ.
ἐκ τῶνδε δὴ τοιόνδ' ἐμηχανήσατο
Αἴγισθος· ὃς μὲν γῆς ἀπηλλάχθη φυγὰς
Ἀγαμέμνονος παῖς, χρυσὸν εἶφ' ὃς ἂν κτάνῃ,
ἡμῖν δὲ δὴ δίδωσιν Ἠλέκτραν ἔχειν
35 δάμαρτα, πατέρων μὲν Μυκηναίων ἄπο
γεγῶσιν (οὐ δὴ τοῦτό γ' ἐξελέγχομαι·
λαμπροὶ γὰρ ἐς γένος γε, χρημάτων δὲ δὴ
πένητες, ἔνθεν ηὑγένει' ἀπόλλυται),
ὡς ἀσθενεῖ δοὺς ἀσθενῆ λάβοι φόβον.
40 εἰ γάρ νιν ἔσχεν ἀξίωμ' ἔχων ἀνήρ,
εὕδοντ' ἂν ἐξήγειρε τὸν Ἀγαμέμνονος
φόνον δίκη τ' ἂν ἦλθεν Αἰγίσθῳ τότε.
ἣν οὔποθ' ἁνὴρ ὅδε (σύνοιδέ μοι Κύπρις)
ᾔσχυν' ἐν εὐνῇ, παρθένος δ' ἔτ' ἐστὶ δή.

22 παῖδ' ἀριστέων Porson: παῖδας Ἀργείων L

to raise. As regards Electra, who still lived in her father's house, when the ripening season of youth came upon her, suitors, the most illustrious men of Greece, sought her hand. But Aegisthus was afraid she might bear to one of the nobility a son who would avenge Agamemnon's death, and so he kept her in the house and would not give her to a husband.

But even this plan involved the great danger that she might bear children to some nobleman in secret, and so Aegisthus determined to kill her. But her mother, cruel-minded though she was, rescued her from Aegisthus' hand. For as regards the husband she slew she had some excuse,[1] but she feared resentment if she killed her children. As a result, Aegisthus formed the following scheme: he announced a reward for whoever should kill the exiled Orestes, and he gave Electra in marriage to me. I come, to be sure, of good Mycenaean[2] parentage: no one can fault me here, for as regards ancestry I am distinguished, but I am poor, which brings an end to noble standing. This he did so that if he gave her to a weak man, the fear he felt might also be weak. For if a man of standing had married her, he would have awakened from its slumber the murder of Agamemnon, and punishment might have come thereafter to Aegisthus. To her in bed—Aphrodite is my witness—I have never done dishonor, and she is a virgin still: a sense

---

[1] Agamemnon sacrificed their daughter Iphigenia on his way to Troy in order to propitiate Artemis.

[2] Mycenae and Mycenaean are used throughout the play interchangeably with Argos and Argive.

---

23 ποινάτορ' Porson: -τορας L    42 ποτέ Reiske

45 αἰσχύνομαι γὰρ ὀλβίων ἀνδρῶν τέκνα
λαβὼν ὑβρίζειν, οὐ κατάξιος γεγώς.
στένω δὲ τὸν λόγοισι κηδεύοντ' ἐμοὶ
ἄθλιον Ὀρέστην, εἴ ποτ' εἰς Ἄργος μολὼν
γάμους ἀδελφῆς δυστυχεῖς ἐσόψεται.
50 ὅστις δέ μ' εἶναί φησι μῶρον, εἰ λαβὼν
νέαν ἐς οἴκους παρθένον μὴ θιγγάνω,
γνώμης πονηροῖς κανόσιν ἀναμετρούμενος
τὸ σῶφρον ἴστω καὐτὸς αὖ τοιοῦτος ὤν.

ΗΛΕΚΤΡΑ

ὦ νὺξ μέλαινα, χρυσέων ἄστρων τροφέ,
55 ἐν ᾗ τόδ' ἄγγος τῷδ' ἐφεδρεῦον κάρᾳ
φέρουσα πηγὰς ποταμίας μετέρχομαι—
οὐ δή τι χρείας ἐς τοσόνδ' ἀφιγμένη,
ἀλλ' ὡς ὕβριν δείξωμεν Αἰγίσθου θεοῖς—
γόους τ' ἀφίημ' αἰθέρ' ἐς μέγαν πατρί.
60 ἡ γὰρ πανώλης Τυνδαρίς, μήτηρ ἐμή,
ἐξέβαλέ μ' οἴκων, χάριτα τιθεμένη πόσει·
τεκοῦσα δ' ἄλλους παῖδας Αἰγίσθῳ πάρα
πάρεργ' Ὀρέστην κἀμὲ ποιεῖται δόμων.

ΑΥΤΟΥΡΓΟΣ

τί γὰρ τάδ', ὦ δύστην', ἐμὴν μοχθεῖς χάριν
65 πόνους ἔχουσα, πρόσθεν εὖ τεθραμμένη,
καὶ ταῦτ' ἐμοῦ λέγοντος οὐκ ἀφίστασαι;

56–8 sic distinxit Radermacher
59 ἀφίημ' Reiske: ἀφίην L
66 ψέγοντος Herwerden

of honor prevents me from taking the daughter of a wealthy man and committing outrage against her since I am not her equal. I groan also at the thought that poor Orestes, my supposed brother-in-law, should ever come to Argos and see the unlucky marriage his sister has made.

If anyone says I am a fool for taking a young virgin into my house and leaving her untouched, he should know that he measures modest behavior by his own mind's false standards and is himself a fool.

*Enter from the* skene ELECTRA, *carrying a water jug on her head.*

#### ELECTRA
O black night, nurse of the golden stars! In you, carrying this vessel poised on my head, I go to fetch water from a stream—I do this not from need but to show the gods Aegisthus' outrage against me—and utter my laments to the wide heaven for my father to hear! My mother, the accursed daughter of Tyndareus, has cast me out of my house to please her husband. Begetting other children by Aegisthus, she treats Orestes and me as the house's illegitimate offspring.

#### FARMER
Why, unlucky woman, do you do this work on my account, accepting toils though gently raised before? Why, when I have urged you to, do you not stop?

ΗΛΕΚΤΡΑ

ἐγώ σ᾽ ἴσον θεοῖσιν ἡγοῦμαι φίλον·
ἐν τοῖς ἐμοῖς γὰρ οὐκ ἐνύβρισας κακοῖς.
μεγάλη δὲ θνητοῖς μοῖρα συμφορᾶς κακῆς
70 ἰατρὸν εὑρεῖν, ὡς ἐγὼ σὲ λαμβάνω.
δεῖ δή με κἀκέλευστον εἰς ὅσον σθένω
μόχθου 'πικουφίζουσαν, ὡς ῥᾷον φέρῃς,
συνεκκομίζειν σοι πόνους. ἅλις δ᾽ ἔχεις
τἄξωθεν ἔργα· τἀν δόμοις δ᾽ ἡμᾶς χρεὼν
75 ἐξευτρεπίζειν. εἰσιόντι δ᾽ ἐργάτῃ
θύραθεν ἡδὺ τἄνδον εὑρίσκειν καλῶς.

ΑΥΤΟΥΡΓΟΣ

εἴ τοι δοκεῖ σοι, στεῖχε· καὶ γὰρ οὐ πρόσω
πηγαὶ μελάθρων τῶνδ᾽. ἐγὼ δ᾽ ἅμ᾽ ἡμέρᾳ
βοῦς εἰς ἀρούρας ἐσβαλὼν σπερῶ γύας.
80 ἀργὸς γὰρ οὐδεὶς θεοὺς ἔχων ἀνὰ στόμα
βίον δύναιτ᾽ ἂν ξυλλέγειν ἄνευ πόνου.

ΟΡΕΣΤΗΣ

Πυλάδη, σὲ γὰρ δὴ πρῶτον ἀνθρώπων ἐγὼ
πιστὸν νομίζω καὶ φίλον ξένον τ᾽ ἐμοί·
μόνος δ᾽ Ὀρέστην τόνδ᾽ ἐθαύμαζες φίλων,
85 πράσσονθ᾽ ἃ πράσσω δείν᾽ ὑπ᾽ Αἰγίσθου παθών,
ὅς μου κατέκτα πατέρα χἠ πανώλεθρος
μήτηρ. ἀφῖγμαι δ᾽ ἐκ θεοῦ μυστηρίων
Ἀργεῖον οὖδας οὐδενὸς ξυνειδότος,

---

83 πίστιν Camper cl. A. Pe. 443    καὶ φίλον] fort. σύννο-
μον

### ELECTRA

I regard you as no less a friend to me than the gods. You did not take advantage of my trouble. For mortals it is a great stroke of fortune to find one to heal their bad luck, as I have found you. So even without any urging from you I must with all my strength help you with your work, lightening your toil so that you may bear it more easily. The tasks you have out of doors are enough. I must look after the indoors. When a laborer comes in from outside, it is pleasant for him to find his house in good order.

### FARMER

If that is what you have decided, go. In fact the spring of water is not far from this house. At daybreak I shall take the bullocks to the fields and sow my crops. No idle man, just by talking always of the gods, can scrape together a living without work.

*Exit* ELECTRA *and* FARMER *by Eisodos A. Enter by Eisodos B* ORESTES *and Pylades accompanied by two slaves.*

### ORESTES

Pylades, you are the man I consider above all others to be faithful and a friend and host to me. You alone of my friends honored me, Orestes, though my fortunes are as ill as they are and I endure terrible treatment from Aegisthus, who with my murderous mother killed my father. Leaving the god's secret rites[3] I have come to Argive soil unbe-

---

[3] Orestes has come from Apollo's oracular shrine at Delphi.

φόνον φονεῦσι πατρὸς ἀλλάξων ἐμοῦ.
90 νυκτὸς δὲ τῆσδε πρὸς τάφον μολὼν πατρὸς
δάκρυά τ᾽ ἔδωκα καὶ κόμης ἀπηρξάμην
πυρᾷ τ᾽ ἐπέσφαξ᾽ αἷμα μηλείου φόνου,
λαθὼν τυράννους οἳ κρατοῦσι τῆσδε γῆς.
καὶ τειχέων μὲν ἐντὸς οὐ βαίνω πόδα,
95 δυοῖν δ᾽ ἅμιλλαν ξυντιθεὶς ἀφικόμην
πρὸς τέρμονας γῆς τῆσδ᾽, ἵν᾽ ἐκβάλω πόδα
ἄλλην ἐπ᾽ αἶαν, εἴ μέ τις γνοίη σκοπῶν,
ζητῶν τ᾽ ἀδελφήν (φασὶ γάρ νιν ἐν γάμοις
ζευχθεῖσαν οἰκεῖν οὐδὲ παρθένον μένειν),
100 ὡς συγγένωμαι καὶ φόνου συνεργάτιν
λάβω τά τ᾽ εἴσω τειχέων σαφῶς μάθω.
νῦν οὖν (ἕω γὰρ λευκὸν ὄμμ᾽ ἀναίρεται)
ἔξω τρίβου τοῦδ᾽ ἴχνος ἀλλαξώμεθα.
ἦ γάρ τις ἀροτὴρ ἤ τις οἰκέτις γυνὴ
105 φανήσεται νῷν, ἥντιν᾽ ἱστορήσομεν
εἰ τούσδε ναίει σύγγονος τόπους ἐμή.
ἀλλ᾽ εἰσορῶ γὰρ τήνδε πρόσπολόν τινα
πηγαῖον ἄχθος ἐν κεκαρμένῳ κάρᾳ
φέρουσαν, ἑζώμεσθα κἀκπυθώμεθα
110 δούλης γυναικός, ἤν τι δεξώμεσθ᾽ ἔπος
ἐφ᾽ οἷσι, Πυλάδη, τήνδ᾽ ἀφίγμεθα χθόνα.

ΗΛΕΚΤΡΑ

στρ. α

σύντειν᾽ ᾠδᾷ ποδὸς ὁρμάν· ὤ,

96 πόδα Dobree: ποδὶ L

160

knownst to any, to pay back my father's murderers with murder. This night, escaping the notice of those who rule this land, I have been to my father's tomb and given him tears and an offering of my hair, and upon his grave I shed the blood of a sheep. I do not set foot inside the city but have come to the border of this land, blending two competing aims: to make my escape to another country if one of the guards should recognize me,[4] and also to find my sister (for they say that she is married and no longer a virgin), so that I may join with her, gain her as my accomplice in the murder, and learn reliably how things stand inside the city.

So now, since the gleaming face of dawn is rising, let us step aside from this path. Some farmer or slave woman will come by here, and we will ask whether my sister lives in these parts.

*Orestes and Pylades and their slaves conceal themselves behind the altar of Apollo. Enter* ELECTRA *by Eisodos A.*

Look! I see a slave woman here carrying her burden of water on her close-cropped head. Let us crouch down, Pylades, and listen to her on the chance that we might catch some word to further the purpose that brought us to this land.

ELECTRA

Hasten the tread of your steps with song,

4 Or "if someone should know me by sight." In either case Orestes is aware that a reward has been offered for his death.

---

101 λάβω τά τ' Denniston: λαβὼν τά γ' L
112, 127 ᾠδᾷ Willink: ὥρα L

ἔμβα ἔμβα κατακλαίουσα.
ἰώ μοί μοι.
115 ἐγενόμαν Ἀγαμέμνονος
καί μ᾽ ἔτικτε Κλυταιμήστρα
στυγνὰ Τυνδάρεω κόρα,
κικλήσκουσι δέ μ᾽ ἀθλίαν
Ἠλέκτραν πολιῆται.
120 φεῦ φεῦ σχετλίων πόνων
καὶ στυγερᾶς ζόας.
ὦ πάτερ, σὺ δ᾽ ἐν Ἀίδα
κεῖσαι σᾶς ἀλόχου σφαγαῖς
Αἰγίσθου τ᾽, Ἀγάμεμνον.

μεσῳδ. α
125 ἴθι τὸν αὐτὸν ἔγειρε γόον,
ἄναγε πολύδακρυν ἀδονάν.

ἀντ. α
σύντειν᾽ ᾠδᾷ ποδὸς ὁρμάν· ὤ,
ἔμβα ἔμβας κατακλαίουσα.
ἰώ μοί μοι.
130 τίνα πόλιν, τίνα δ᾽ οἶκον, ὦ
τλᾶμον σύγγον᾽, ἀλατεύεις
οἰκτρὰν ἐν θαλάμοις λιπὼν
πατρῴοις ἐπὶ συμφοραῖς
ἀλγίσταισιν ἀδελφάν;
135 ἔλθοις δὲ πόνων ἐμοὶ
τᾷ μελέᾳ λυτήρ,

113, 128 fort. ἔμβα κατακλαίουσ᾽, ἔμβα

O march on, march on in tears!
Ah me!
By birth I am Agamemnon's child,
and my mother is Clytaemestra,
hateful daughter of Tyndareus,
and the citizens call me
Electra the unfortunate.
Alas for my cruel toil,
alas for my hateful life!
Father Agamemnon, you lie in the Underworld
slain by your wife
and by Aegisthus!

Come, raise the same lament once more,
stir up the delight that comes of much weeping!

Hasten the tread of your steps with song,
O march on, march on in tears!
Ah me!
In what city, what house,
unhappy brother, are you a wandering exile,
leaving your pitiable sister
in her father's halls
amidst grievous misfortune?
Come to free
me the unfortunate from trouble

---

115 Ἀγαμέμνονος Seidler: Ἀγ- κούρα L
123 σφαγαῖς Porson: σφαγεὶς L
131 σύγγον' ἀλατεύεις Hartung: σύγγονε λατρεύεις L
135 δὲ Hermann: τῶνδε L: τῶνδ' ἐλθὲ Willink

ὦ Ζεῦ Ζεῦ, πατρί θ᾽ αἱμάτων
αἰσχίστων ἐπίκουρος, Ἄρ-
γει κέλσας πόδ᾽ ἀλάταν.

μεσῳδ. β
140  θὲς τόδε τεῦχος ἐμᾶς ἀπὸ κρατὸς ἑ-
λοῦσ᾽, ἵνα πατρὶ γόους νυχίους
ὑπ᾽ ὄρθρον βοάσω·

στρ. β
    〈ἰώ μοί μοι·〉
ἰαχοῦσ᾽ Ἀίδα μέλος
σοί, πάτερ,
κάτω γᾶς ἐνέπω †γόους†
145  οἷς ἀεὶ τὸ κατ᾽ ἦμαρ
διέπομαι, κατὰ μὲν φίλαν
ὄνυχι τεμνομένα δέραν
χέρα τε κρᾶτ᾽ ἐπὶ κούριμον
τιθεμένα θανάτῳ σῷ.

μεσῳδ. γ
150  ἒ ἔ· δρύπτε κάρα·
οἷα δέ τις κύκνος ἀχέτας
ποταμίοις παρὰ χεύμασιν
πατέρα φίλτατον 〈ἀγ〉καλεῖ,

138 αἰσχίστων Seidler: ἐχθίστων L    142 ὑπ᾽ ὄρθρον βοά-
σω Willink: ἐπορθ*βοάσω L   〈ἰώ μοί μοι〉 Willink
143 ἰαχοῦσ᾽ Diggle: ἰαχὰν L   Ἀίδα μέλος Reiske: ἀοιδὰν
μέλος Ἀίδα L   σοί, πάτερ Hartung: π- σ- L
144 κάτω Seidler: κατὰ L   γό〈ων θρήν〉ους Willink
146 λείβομαι Wecklein, Herwerden

164

(O Zeus, Zeus!) and avenge your father
for his shameful murder,
setting your exiled foot on Argive soil!

*A female slave enters to take the water jar indoors.*

Take this vessel from my head and set it down
so that I may raise my night cry
before the dawn to my father!

<Ah, me, ah, me!>
Shouting a tune of death
to you, father,
beneath the earth I sing the laments
to which ceaselessly day by day
I devote myself, tearing my own throat
with my nails
and striking my shorn head with my hand
in grief at your murder!

Ah, ah, strike the head!
As the singing swan[5]
upon the riverbank
calls upon its dear father

[5] The usual conceit, that the swan sings at the approach of his
own death (Aeschylus, *Agamemnon* 1444–5, Euripides, *Heracles*
110–1), is here altered, perhaps in imitation of the familiar idea
(e.g. Sophocles, *Electra* 107, 147-9) that the song of the nightin-
gale is Procne lamenting her dead children.

---

148 ἐπὶ κούριμον Barnes: ἀποκούριμον L
153 <ἀγ>καλεῖ Hermann

ὀλόμενον δολίοις βρόχων
155 ἕρκεσιν, ὡς σὲ τὸν ἄθλιον,
πάτερ, ἐγὼ κατακλαίομαι,
λουτρὰ πανύσταθ᾽ ὑδρανάμενον χροῒ
κοίτᾳ ἐν οἰκτροτάτᾳ θανάτου.

ἀντ. β

ἰώ μοί μοι
160 πικρᾶς μὲν πελέκεως τομᾶς
σᾶς, πάτερ,
πικρᾶς δ᾽ ἐκ Τροΐας ὁδοῦ βουλᾶς·
οὐ μίτραις σε γυνὰ ⟨σὰ⟩
δέξατ᾽ οὐδ᾽ ἐπὶ στεφάνοις,
ξίφεσι δ᾽ ἀμφιτόμοις λυγρὰν
165 Αἰγίσθῳ λώβαν θεμένα
δόλιον ἔσχεν ἀκοίταν.

στρ.

ΧΟΡΟΣ

Ἀγαμέμνονος ὦ κόρα, ἤλυθον, Ἠλέκτρα,
ποτὶ σὰν ἀγρότειραν αὐλάν.
ἔμολέ τις ἔμολεν γαλακτοπότας ἀνὴρ
170 Μυκηναῖος οὐριβάτας,
ἀγγέλλει δ᾽ ὅτι νῦν τριταί-
αν καρύσσουσιν θυσίαν
Ἀργεῖοι, πᾶσαι δὲ παρ᾽ Ἥ-
ραν μέλλουσιν παρθενικαὶ στείχειν.

161 βουλᾶς] παυλᾶς Willink

166

slain in the guileful snare of meshes,
so I mourn for you,
my unhappy father.
You bathed yourself for the last time
in the pitiable place where you lay down in death.

Ah, me, ah, me,
how cruel the cut of the axe
that slew you, father,
how cruel the plot after your journey from Troy!
It was not with a crown that your wife
greeted you or with the garlands of victory:
with the two-edged sword she worked
for Aegisthus' sake grim outrage
and won as her mate that man of guile.

*Enter a group of Argive women as* CHORUS *by Eisodos B.*

#### CHORUS

Electra, daughter of Agamemnon,
I have come to your rustic abode.
There came, there came a drinker of milk,
a man of Mycenae, dweller in the mountains,
and he brought the news that for two days hence
the Argives are now proclaiming
a feast, and all the unmarried girls
will go to the temple of Hera.

---

ΗΛΕΚΤΡΑ

175  οὐκ ἐπ᾽ ἀγλαΐαις, φίλαι,
θυμὸν οὐδ᾽ ἐπὶ χρυσέοις
ὅρμοις ἐκπεπόταμαι
τάλαιν᾽, οὐδ᾽ ἐνστᾶσα χοροῖς
Ἀργείαις ἅμα νύμφαις
180  εἱλικτὸν κρούσω πόδ᾽ ἐμόν.
δάκρυσι νυχεύω, δακρύων δέ μοι μέλει
δειλαίᾳ τὸ κατ᾽ ἦμαρ.
σκέψαι μου πιναρὰν κόμαν
185  καὶ τρύχη τάδ᾽ ἐμῶν πέπλων,
εἰ πρέποντ᾽ Ἀγαμέμνονος
κούρᾳ τᾷ βασιλείᾳ
τᾷ Τροίᾳ θ᾽, ἃ ᾽μοῦ πατέρος
μέμναταί ποθ᾽ ἁλοῦσα.

ἀντ.

ΧΟΡΟΣ

190  μεγάλα θεός· ἀλλ᾽ ἴθι καὶ παρ᾽ ἐμοῦ χρῆσαι
πολύπηνα φάρεα δῦναι
χρύσεά τε χάρισιν προσθήματ᾽ ἀγλαΐας.
δοκεῖς τοῖσι σοῖς δακρύοις
μὴ τιμῶσα θεοὺς κρατή-
195  σειν ἐχθρῶν; οὔτοι στοναχαῖς
ἀλλ᾽ εὐχαῖσι θεοὺς σεβί-
ζουσ᾽ ἕξεις εὐαμερίαν, ὦ παῖ.

## ELECTRA

My heart is not aflutter, my friends,
at feasts or gold necklaces,
unhappy woman that I am,
nor shall I take my stand in a chorus
together with the wives of Argos
to whirl my feet about and strike the ground.
In tears my nights are spent, and tears
for me in my wretched state are the burden of my days.
Look at my filthy hair
and these tatters that are my clothes,
see if these befit a princess,
Agamemnon's daughter,
and Troy, which remembers
that my father once captured her!

## CHORUS

Great is the goddess. Come, then, and borrow from me
robes of thick weave to put on
and gold to add to the pleasures of the feast.
Do you think that by your tears alone,
giving no honor to the gods,
you can best your enemies? If you worship the gods
not with groans but with prayers
you will have prosperity, my child.

---

178 οὐδ' ἐνστᾶσα Diggle: οὐδὲ στᾶσα L    χοροῖς Seidler:
χοροὺς L
186 εἰ πρέποντ' Reiske: εἴ πέρ ποτ' L
1ο7 κούρᾳ τᾷ Reiske: κούρας τὰ L
191 φάρε' αὖ πολύπηνα vel πολύπηνα φάρεα ⟨τε⟩ Willink
192 χάρισιν Musgrave: χάρισαι L

ΗΛΕΚΤΡΑ

οὐδεὶς θεῶν ἐνοπᾶς κλύει
τᾶς δυσδαίμονος, οὐ παλαι-
200 ῶν πατρὸς σφαγιασμῶν.
οἴμοι τοῦ καταφθιμένου
τοῦ τε ζῶντος ἀλάτα,
ὅς που γᾶν ἄλλαν κατέχει,
205 μέλεος ἀλαίνων ποτὶ θῆσσαν ἑστίαν,
τοῦ κλεινοῦ πατρὸς ἐκφύς.
αὐτὰ δ' ἐν χερνῆσι δόμοις
ναίω ψυχὰν τακομένα
δωμάτων φυγὰς πατρίων
210 οὐρείας ἀν' ἐρίπνας.
μάτηρ δ' ἐν λέκτροις φονίοις
ἄλλῳ σύγγαμος οἰκεῖ.

ΧΟΡΟΣ

πολλῶν κακῶν Ἕλλησιν αἰτίαν ἔχει
σῆς μητρὸς Ἑλένη σύγγονος δόμοις τε σοῖς.

ΗΛΕΚΤΡΑ

215 οἴμοι, γυναῖκες, ἐξέβην θρηνημάτων.
ξένοι τινὲς παρ' οἶκον οἴδ' ἐφεστίους
εὐνὰς ἔχοντες ἐξανίστανται λόχου·
φυγῇ σὺ μὲν κατ' οἶμον, ἐς δόμους δ' ἐγὼ
φῶτας κακούργους ἐξαλύξωμεν ποδί.

209 φυγὰς π- Seidler: π- φυγὰς L
210 ἀν' Musgrave: ναίουσ' L
215 θρηνήμασιν Willink

ELECTRA

### ELECTRA

None of the gods pays heed
to this luckless woman's prayer
or to my father's murder long ago.
Alas for him who is slain
and for him who lives as an exile!
He dwells, I am sure, in another land,
a wretched wanderer to the hearths of laborers,
though he is the son of his glorious father.
And I myself in a toiler's cottage
dwell heart-worn,
exiled from my father's house,
on a mountain plot of ground,
while my mother lying in a blood-stained bed
lives as wife to another.

### CHORUS LEADER

Greece and your house can blame your mother's sister
Helen for many woes.

*Orestes and Pylades appear from hiding.*

### ELECTRA

Ah, women! I have left off lamenting! Strangers lying in
wait at the altar near my house are emerging from ambush!
Let's flee these criminals, you along the path and I into the
house!

*Orestes grasps Electra by the wrist.*

---

216 ἐπισκίους Jackson

ΟΡΕΣΤΗΣ

220 μέν᾽, ὦ τάλαινα· μὴ τρέσῃς ἐμὴν χέρα.

ΗΛΕΚΤΡΑ

ὦ Φοῖβ᾽ Ἄπολλον, προσπίτνω σε μὴ θανεῖν.

ΟΡΕΣΤΗΣ

ἄλλους κτάνοιμι μᾶλλον ἐχθίους σέθεν.

ΗΛΕΚΤΡΑ

ἄπελθε, μὴ ψαῦ᾽ ὧν σε μὴ ψαύειν χρεών.

ΟΡΕΣΤΗΣ

οὐκ ἔσθ᾽ ὅτου θίγοιμ᾽ ἂν ἐνδικώτερον.

ΗΛΕΚΤΡΑ

225 καὶ πῶς ξιφήρης πρὸς δόμοις λοχᾷς ἐμοῖς;

ΟΡΕΣΤΗΣ

μείνασ᾽ ἄκουσον, καὶ τάχ᾽ οὐκ ἄλλως ἐρεῖς.

ΗΛΕΚΤΡΑ

ἔστηκα· πάντως δ᾽ εἰμὶ σή· κρείσσων γὰρ εἶ.

ΟΡΕΣΤΗΣ

ἥκω φέρων σοι σοῦ κασιγνήτου λόγους.

ΗΛΕΚΤΡΑ

ὦ φίλτατ᾽, ἆρα ζῶντος ἢ τεθνηκότος;

ΟΡΕΣΤΗΣ

230 ζῇ· πρῶτα γάρ σοι τἀγάθ᾽ ἀγγέλλειν θέλω.

ΗΛΕΚΤΡΑ

εὐδαιμονοίης μισθὸν ἡδίστων λόγων.

**ORESTES**
Stay, unhappy woman! Do not fear my touch!

**ELECTRA**
O Phoebus Apollo, I pray I may not be killed!

**ORESTES**
May I kill others, much more my enemies than you are!

**ELECTRA**
Be gone! Do not touch what is not right for you to touch!

**ORESTES**
There is no one I may touch with greater right.

**ELECTRA**
Why then, sword in hand, do you wait near my house?

**ORESTES**
Stay and listen to me, and you will soon agree with me.

**ELECTRA**
I stay. I am yours in any case, for you are stronger.

**ORESTES**
I have come with word of your brother.

**ELECTRA**
O dearest of messengers, is he alive or dead?

**ORESTES**
Alive: it is the good news I wish to give you first.

**ELECTRA**
Good luck be yours in payment for your most welcome words!

ΟΡΕΣΤΗΣ
κοινῇ δίδωμι τοῦτο νῷν ἀμφοῖν ἔχειν.

ΗΛΕΚΤΡΑ
ποῦ γῆς ὁ τλήμων τλήμονας φυγὰς ἔχων;

ΟΡΕΣΤΗΣ
οὐχ ἕνα νομίζων φθείρεται πόλεως νόμον.

ΗΛΕΚΤΡΑ
235 οὔ που σπανίζων τοῦ καθ᾽ ἡμέραν βίου;

ΟΡΕΣΤΗΣ
ἔχει μέν, ἀσθενὴς δὲ δὴ φεύγων ἀνήρ.

ΗΛΕΚΤΡΑ
λόγον δὲ δὴ τίν᾽ ἦλθες ἐκ κείνου φέρων;

ΟΡΕΣΤΗΣ
εἰ ζῇς, ὅπως τε ζῶσα συμφορᾶς ἔχεις.

ΗΛΕΚΤΡΑ
οὔκουν ὁρᾷς μου πρῶτον ὡς ξηρὸν δέμας;

ΟΡΕΣΤΗΣ
240 λύπαις γε συντετηκός, ὥστε με στένειν.

ΗΛΕΚΤΡΑ
καὶ κρᾶτα πλόκαμόν τ᾽ ἐσκυθισμένον ξυρῷ.

ΟΡΕΣΤΗΣ
δάκνει σ᾽ ἀδελφὸς ὅ τε θανὼν ἴσως πατήρ.

237 fort. post h. v. lac. indicanda, e.g. ⟨Ορ. ἐς τήνδε γῆν μ᾽
ἔπεμψ᾽ ἵν᾽ ἐξεύρω σαφῶς . . . Ηλ. τὰ ποῖα; πάντ᾽ ἄν, εἴ τι
γιγνώσκω, μάθοις.⟩

174

**ORESTES**

May your wish hold good for the two of us in common!

**ELECTRA**

Where on earth is the poor man in his unhappy exile?

**ORESTES**

He goes about in misery, with no single city as his home.

**ELECTRA**

Surely he is not in want of daily necessities?

**ORESTES**

He has enough, but the rub is that an exile is powerless.

**ELECTRA**

But what message do you bring from him?

**ORESTES**

Are you alive? he asks. And if living, what are your fortunes?

**ELECTRA**

Can you not see yourself how withered my body is?

**ORESTES**

Yes, it is worn down by grief: I weep for you.

**ELECTRA**

And the hair of my head is cropped close with a sharp blade.

**ORESTES**

No doubt you grieve for your brother and your dead father.

---

238 ὅπως Elmsley: ὅπου L
240 γε Heath: τε L

ΗΛΕΚΤΡΑ

οἴμοι· τί γάρ μοι τῶνδέ γ᾽ ἐστὶ φίλτερον;

ΟΡΕΣΤΗΣ

φεῦ φεῦ· τί δ᾽ αὖ σοῦ σῷ κασιγνήτῳ δοκεῖς;

ΗΛΕΚΤΡΑ

245  ἀπὼν ἐκεῖνος, οὐ παρών, ἡμῖν φίλος.

ΟΡΕΣΤΗΣ

ἐκ τοῦ δὲ ναίεις ἐνθάδ᾽ ἄστεως ἑκάς;

ΗΛΕΚΤΡΑ

ἐγημάμεσθ᾽, ὦ ξεῖνε, θανάσιμον γάμον.

ΟΡΕΣΤΗΣ

ᾤμωξ᾽ ἀδελφὸν σόν. Μυκηναίων τίνι;

ΗΛΕΚΤΡΑ

οὐχ ᾧ πατήρ μ᾽ ἤλπιζεν ἐκδώσειν ποτέ.

ΟΡΕΣΤΗΣ

250  εἴφ᾽, ὡς ἀκούσας σῷ κασιγνήτῳ λέγω.

ΗΛΕΚΤΡΑ

ἐν τοῖσδ᾽ ἐκείνου τηλορὸς ναίω δόμοις.

ΟΡΕΣΤΗΣ

σκαφεύς τις ἢ βουφορβὸς ἄξιος δόμων.

ΗΛΕΚΤΡΑ

πένης ἀνὴρ γενναῖος ἔς τ᾽ ἔμ᾽ εὐσεβής.

244 δ᾽ αὖ σοῦ Seidler: δαὶ σὺ L
251 ἐκεῖνος . . . ναίει Broadhead

ELECTRA

Ah me! What is dearer to me than they are?

ORESTES

Ah yes! And what is dearer to your brother, do you think, than you are?

ELECTRA

To me he is an absent, not a present, friend.

ORESTES

Why do you live here, so far from the city?

ELECTRA

I have made a marriage, stranger, a marriage that is like death.

ORESTES

Ah! I groan for your brother. What man of Mycenae is it?

ELECTRA

Not the man to whom my father expected to marry me.

ORESTES

Tell me, so that I may hear and report it to your brother.

ELECTRA

I dwell far apart here in this man's house.

ORESTES

A ditchdigger or a cowherd would be a worthy tenant of this dwelling.

ELECTRA

The man is poor but noble and acts piously toward me.

ΟΡΕΣΤΗΣ

ἡ δ᾽ εὐσέβεια τίς πρόσεστι σῷ πόσει;

ΗΛΕΚΤΡΑ

255 οὐπώποτ᾽ εὐνῆς τῆς ἐμῆς ἔτλη θιγεῖν.

ΟΡΕΣΤΗΣ

ἄγνευμ᾽ ἔχων τι θεῖον ἤ σ᾽ ἀπαξιῶν;

ΗΛΕΚΤΡΑ

γονέας ὑβρίζειν τοὺς ἐμοὺς οὐκ ἠξίου.

ΟΡΕΣΤΗΣ

καὶ πῶς γάμον τοιοῦτον οὐχ ἥσθη λαβών;

ΗΛΕΚΤΡΑ

οὐ κύριον τὸν δόντα μ᾽ ἡγεῖται, ξένε.

ΟΡΕΣΤΗΣ

260 ξυνῆκ᾽· Ὀρέστῃ μή ποτ᾽ ἐκτείσῃ δίκην.

ΗΛΕΚΤΡΑ

τοῦτ᾽ αὐτὸ ταρβῶν· πρὸς δὲ καὶ σώφρων ἔφυ.

ΟΡΕΣΤΗΣ

φεῦ·
γενναῖον ἄνδρ᾽ ἔλεξας, εὖ τε δραστέον.

ΗΛΕΚΤΡΑ

εἰ δή ποθ᾽ ἥξει γ᾽ ἐς δόμους ὁ νῦν ἀπών.

ΟΡΕΣΤΗΣ

μήτηρ δέ σ᾽ ἡ τεκοῦσα ταῦτ᾽ ἠνέσχετο;

ΗΛΕΚΤΡΑ

265 γυναῖκες ἀνδρῶν, ὦ ξέν᾽, οὐ παίδων φίλαι.

178

**ORESTES**
This piety your husband has, what is it?

**ELECTRA**
Never yet has he brought himself to come to my bed.

**ORESTES**
Keeping some vow of purity, or thinking you unfit?

**ELECTRA**
He did not think it fit to commit an outrage against my parents.

**ORESTES**
But how is it he was not glad to make such a marriage?

**ELECTRA**
He thinks the man who gave me to him had no authority.

**ORESTES**
I see: he is afraid Orestes may punish him.

**ELECTRA**
Yes, he is afraid of that. But he is also naturally self-controlled.

**ORESTES**
Ah, what a noble man you describe! We must treat him well.

**ELECTRA**
Yes, if my absent brother returns home.

**ORESTES**
But did your own mother permit this to happen?

**ELECTRA**
Women, stranger, love their husbands, not their children.

ΟΡΕΣΤΗΣ
τίνος δέ σ' οὕνεχ' ὕβρισ' Αἴγισθος τάδε;

ΗΛΕΚΤΡΑ
τεκεῖν μ' ἐβούλετ' ἀσθενῆ, τοιῷδε δούς.

ΟΡΕΣΤΗΣ
ὡς δῆθε παῖδας μὴ τέκοις ποινάτορας;

ΗΛΕΚΤΡΑ
τοιαῦτ' ἐβούλευσ'· ὧν ἐμοὶ δοίη δίκην.

ΟΡΕΣΤΗΣ
270 οἶδεν δέ σ' οὖσαν παρθένον μητρὸς πόσις;

ΗΛΕΚΤΡΑ
οὐκ οἶδε· σιγῇ τοῦθ' ὑφαιρούμεσθά νιν.

ΟΡΕΣΤΗΣ
αἵδ' οὖν φίλαι σοι τούσδ' ἀκούουσιν λόγους;

ΗΛΕΚΤΡΑ
ὥστε στέγειν γε τἀμὰ καὶ σ' ἔπη καλῶς.

ΟΡΕΣΤΗΣ
τί δῆτ' Ὀρέστης πρὸς τάδ', Ἄργος ἢν μόλῃ;

ΗΛΕΚΤΡΑ
275 ἤρου τόδ'; αἰσχρόν γ' εἶπας· οὐ γὰρ νῦν ἀκμή;

ΟΡΕΣΤΗΣ
ἐλθὼν δὲ δὴ πῶς φονέας ἂν κτάνοι πατρός;

274 τάδ' Camper: τόδ' L    ἂν μόλοι Winnington-Ingram:
sed fort. post h. v. lac. indicanda

180

**ORESTES**

But why did Aegisthus abuse you so?

**ELECTRA**

He wanted me to bear powerless children and so gave me to a powerless husband.

**ORESTES**

So that you might not bear sons to avenge you?

**ELECTRA**

That was his plan. May I be able to pay him back for it!

**ORESTES**

Does your mother's husband know that you are a virgin?

**ELECTRA**

No: we have kept this knowledge from him.

**ORESTES**

Then these women[6] who are listening here are friends?

**ELECTRA**

Yes, and they will keep your words and mine a firm secret.

**ORESTES**

What will Orestes do about this if he comes to Argos?

**ELECTRA**

Can you ask this? Shame! Is it not high time?

**ORESTES**

But if he does come, how could he kill his father's murderers?

---

[6] The Chorus.

ΗΛΕΚΤΡΑ

τολμῶν ὑπ' ἐχθρῶν οἷ' ἐτολμήθη ποτέ.

ΟΡΕΣΤΗΣ

ἦ καὶ μετ' αὐτοῦ μητέρ' ἂν τλαίης κτανεῖν;

ΗΛΕΚΤΡΑ

ταὐτῷ γε πελέκει τῷ πατὴρ ἀπώλετο.

ΟΡΕΣΤΗΣ

280 λέγω τάδ' αὐτῷ, καὶ βέβαια τἀπὸ σοῦ;

ΗΛΕΚΤΡΑ

θάνοιμι μητρὸς αἷμ' ἐπισφάξασ' ἐμῆς.

ΟΡΕΣΤΗΣ

φεῦ·
εἴθ' ἦν Ὀρέστης πλησίον κλύων τάδε.

ΗΛΕΚΤΡΑ

ἀλλ', ὦ ξέν', οὐ γνοίην ἂν εἰσιδοῦσά νιν.

ΟΡΕΣΤΗΣ

νέα γάρ, οὐδὲν θαῦμ', ἀπεζεύχθης νέου.

ΗΛΕΚΤΡΑ

285 εἷς ἂν μόνος νιν τῶν ἐμῶν γνοίη φίλων.

ΟΡΕΣΤΗΣ

ἆρ' ὃν λέγουσιν αὐτὸν ἐκκλέψαι φόνου;

ΗΛΕΚΤΡΑ

πατρός γε παιδαγωγὸς ἀρχαῖος γέρων.

---

[277] ποτέ Nauck: πατήρ L    [282] κλύειν Camper

**ELECTRA**
By showing the same boldness his enemies once showed.

**ORESTES**
Would you also have the hardihood to kill your mother with his help?

**ELECTRA**
Yes, with the same ax with which my father met his death!

**ORESTES**
Shall I tell him this, and that he can rely on you?

**ELECTRA**
When I have shed my mother's blood, then let me die!

**ORESTES**
Ah me! If only Orestes were nearby to hear this!

**ELECTRA**
Well, I would not recognize him by sight, stranger.

**ORESTES**
No wonder: you and he were young when you were separated.

**ELECTRA**
Only one of my friends would know him.

**ORESTES**
Is this the man they say snatched him from death?

**ELECTRA**
Yes: he was my father's tutor and is now an old man.

ΟΡΕΣΤΗΣ

ὁ κατθανὼν δὲ σὸς πατὴρ τύμβου κυρεῖ;

ΗΛΕΚΤΡΑ

ἔκυρσεν ὡς ἔκυρσεν, ἐκβληθεὶς δόμων.

ΟΡΕΣΤΗΣ

290   οἴμοι, τόδ᾽ οἷον εἶπας· αἴσθησις γὰρ οὖν
291   καὶ τῶν θυραίων πημάτων δάκνει βροτούς.
294   ἔνεστι δ᾽ οἶκτος ἀμαθίᾳ μὲν οὐδαμοῦ,
295   σοφοῖσι δ᾽ ἀνδρῶν· καὶ γὰρ οὐδ᾽ ἀζήμιον
296   γνώμην ἐνεῖναι τοῖς σοφοῖς λίαν σοφήν.
292     λέξον δ᾽, ἵν᾽ εἰδὼς σῷ κασιγνήτῳ φέρω
293   λόγους ἀτερπεῖς ἀλλ᾽ ἀναγκαίους κλυεῖν.

ΧΟΡΟΣ

297   κἀγὼ τὸν αὐτὸν τῷδ᾽ ἔρον ψυχῆς ἔχω.
    πρόσω γὰρ ἄστεως οὖσα τὰν πόλει κακὰ
    οὐκ οἶδα, νῦν δὲ βούλομαι κἀγὼ μαθεῖν.

ΗΛΕΚΤΡΑ

300   λέγοιμ᾽ ἄν, εἰ χρή (χρὴ δὲ πρὸς φίλον λέγειν),
    τύχας βαρείας τὰς ἐμὰς κἀμοῦ πατρός.
    ἐπεὶ δὲ κινεῖς μῦθον, ἱκετεύω, ξένε,
    ἄγγελλ᾽ Ὀρέστῃ τἀμὰ κἀκείνου κακά,
    πρῶτον μὲν οἵοις ἐν πέπλοις αὐλίζομαι,
305   πίνῳ θ᾽ ὅσῳ βέβριθ᾽, ὑπὸ στέγαισί τε
    οἵαισι ναίω βασιλικῶν ἐκ δωμάτων,
    αὐτὴ μὲν ἐκμοχθοῦσα κερκίσιν πέπλους,

291 καὶ Dobree κἀκ L

**ORESTES**

Has your dead father received a tomb?

**ELECTRA**

Yes, such as it is: he was cast forth from the house.[7]

**ORESTES**

Ah, what a terrible thing you tell me! For mortals feel a sting when they learn of misfortune, even when it is not their own. Pity is found not in ill-bred ignorance but only in the wise. And in fact when the wise possess minds that are too wise, there is a price to be paid.

But tell me, so that I may learn and carry to your brother words that give no pleasure but which one must hear.

**CHORUS LEADER**

My heart feels the same desire as his. Since I live far off from the city and know nothing of the troubles there, I too would like to know.

**ELECTRA**

I shall tell, if I must (and to a friend I must), the heavy woes that are mine and my father's. But since you stir me to talk of them, I beg you, stranger, tell Orestes of my troubles and his. Tell him first in what clothing I am dressed, with what dirt I am encrusted, in what kind of a house I dwell after life in a royal palace, myself toiling at the loom to

[7] I.e. he was not buried near the palace but off in an isolated spot.

---

294–6 post 291 trai. Bothe: del. Steinberg

[ἢ γυμνὸν ἔξω σῶμα καὶ στερήσομαι,]
αὐτὴ δὲ πηγὰς ποταμίους φορουμένη,
310 ἀνέορτος ἱερῶν καὶ χορῶν τητωμένη.
ἀναίνομαι δὲ γυμνὰς οὖσα παρθένους,
ἀναίνομαι δὲ Κάστορ᾽, ᾧ πρὶν ἐς θεοὺς
ἐλθεῖν ἔμ᾽ ἐμνήστευον, οὖσαν ἐγγενῆ.

μήτηρ δ᾽ ἐμὴ Φρυγίοισιν ἐν σκυλεύμασιν
315 θρόνῳ κάθηται, πρὸς δ᾽ ἕδραισιν Ἀσίδες
δμωαὶ στατίζουσ᾽, ἃς ἔπερσ᾽ ἐμὸς πατήρ,
Ἰδαῖα φάρη χρυσέαις ἐζευγμέναι
πόρπαισιν. αἷμα δ᾽ ἔτι πατρὸς κατὰ στέγας
μέλαν σέσηπεν, ὃς δ᾽ ἐκεῖνον ἔκτανεν
320 ἐς ταὐτὰ βαίνων ἅρματ᾽ ἐκφοιτᾷ πατρί,
καὶ σκῆπτρ᾽ ἐν οἷς Ἕλλησιν ἐστρατηλάτει
μιαιφόνοισι χερσὶ γαυροῦται λαβών.

Ἀγαμέμνονος δὲ τύμβος ἠτιμασμένος
οὔπω χοάς ποτ᾽ οὐδὲ κλῶνα μυρσίνης
325 ἔλαβε, πυρᾶ δὲ χέρσος ἀγλαϊσμάτων.
μέθῃ δὲ βρεχθεὶς τῆς ἐμῆς μητρὸς πόσις
ὁ κλεινός, ὡς λέγουσιν, ἐνθρῴσκει τάφῳ
πέτροις τε λεύει μνῆμα λάινον πατρός,
καὶ τοῦτο τολμᾷ τοὔπος εἰς ἡμᾶς λέγειν·
330 Ποῦ παῖς Ὀρέστης; ἆρά σοι τύμβῳ καλῶς
παρὼν ἀμύνει; ταῦτ᾽ ἀπὼν ὑβρίζεται.

308 del. Camper
311 δὲ γυμνὰς L: δὲ γυναῖκας Tr², unde [δὲ] γυναῖκας Barnes
παρθένους Kirchhoff: -ος L

186

make my garments, [or I shall be naked and go without,] myself carrying water from the river, bereft of festivals and deprived of dances. For since I have no clothes I shun the maidens, shun likewise Castor and Polydeuces,[8] who before they went up to heaven were suitors for my hand since I was their kinswoman.

My mother sits on a throne in the midst of the spoils of Troy, and near her place Asian slaves, whom my father took as booty, stand with their Trojan garments pinned with gold brooches. The black blood of my father still lies rotting in the house, and the man who killed him mounts and rides out on the same chariot my father drove and assumes a haughty air as he takes in his murderous hands the scepter with which my father used to command the Greek host.

Agamemnon's tomb lies neglected and to this day has received no libation or spray of myrtle, and the altar at his tomb is empty of offerings. They tell me that my mother's new husband, when he is steeped in drink, leaps upon the grave and throws stones at my father's monument and has the gall to say against us, "Where is your son Orestes? A fine job he does of standing by your tomb and defending it!" Such is the outrage Orestes endures in his absence.

[8] I.e. their worship and festivals.

---

312 Κάστορ' (i.e. Κάστορε) ὦ Scaliger: Κάστορ' ὦ L: Κάστορ' ὅς (et 313 ἐμνήστευεν) Nauck: vide *CQ* 35 (1985), 306–10
314 fort. μήτηρ δὲ Φρυγίοις ⟨γαῦρος⟩
315 ἕδραισιν Ἀσίδες Hermann: ἕδρας Ἀσιήτιδες L
324 οὔπω χοάς ποτ' Porson: οὐπώποτ' οὐ χοὰς L
327 καινός Kirchhoff: κλεινός L

ἀλλ᾽, ὦ ξέν᾽, ἱκετεύω σ᾽, ἀπάγγειλον τάδε.
πολλοὶ δ᾽ ἐπιστέλλουσιν, ἑρμηνεὺς δ᾽ ἐγώ,
αἱ χεῖρες ἡ γλῶσσ᾽ ἡ ταλαίπωρός τε φρὴν
335  κάρα τ᾽ ἐμὸν ξυρῆκες ὅ τ᾽ ἐκεῖνον τεκών.
αἰσχρὸν γάρ, εἰ πατὴρ μὲν ἐξεῖλεν Φρύγας,
ὁ δ᾽ ἄνδρ᾽ ἕν᾽ εἷς ὢν οὐ δυνήσεται κτανεῖν,
νέος πεφυκὼς κἀξ ἀμείνονος πατρός.

ΧΟΡΟΣ

καὶ μὴν δέδορκα τόνδε, σὸν λέγω πόσιν,
340  λήξαντα μόχθου πρὸς δόμους ὁρμώμενον.

ΑΥΤΟΥΡΓΟΣ

ἔα· τίνας τούσδ᾽ ἐν πύλαις ὁρῶ ξένους;
τίνος δ᾽ ἕκατι τάσδ᾽ ἐπ᾽ ἀγραύλους πύλας
προσῆλθον; ἦ 'μοῦ δεόμενοι; γυναικί τοι
αἰσχρὸν μετ᾽ ἀνδρῶν ἑστάναι νεανιῶν.

ΗΛΕΚΤΡΑ

345  ὦ φίλτατ᾽, εἰς ὕποπτα μὴ μόλῃς ἐμοί·
τὸν ὄντα δ᾽ εἴσῃ μῦθον· οἵδε γὰρ ξένοι
ἥκουσ᾽ Ὀρέστου πρὸς ἐμὲ κήρυκες λόγων.
ἀλλ᾽, ὦ ξένοι, σύγγνωτε τοῖς εἰρημένοις.

ΑΥΤΟΥΡΓΟΣ

τί φασίν; ἀνὴρ ἔστι καὶ λεύσσει φάος;

ΗΛΕΚΤΡΑ

350  ἔστιν λόγῳ γοῦν, φασὶ δ᾽ οὐκ ἄπιστ᾽ ἐμοί.

340 ὁρμώμενον Paley· ὡρμημένον L

188

So I beg you, stranger, take this message back. Its send-
ers are many, and I am their interpreter: my hands, my
tongue, my suffering heart, my close-cropped head, and
the father who begot him. It is a disgrace if his father
destroyed the Trojans but he himself cannot kill his man,
one against one, though he is young and born of a nobler
father.

*Enter* FARMER *by Eisodos A.*

#### CHORUS LEADER
But look, I see him coming home, your husband, I mean,
having finished his work.

#### FARMER
What is this? Who are these strangers I see at my door?
Why have they come to my house so far from the city? Do
they want something from me? It is quite shameful for a
woman to stand about with young men.

#### ELECTRA
Dearest husband, do not be suspicious of me, for you shall
hear the truth: these strangers have come to me bearing
a message from Orestes. Strangers, please excuse these
words.

#### FARMER
What do they say? Does the man live and look upon the
light?

#### ELECTRA
In their report, at least, he lives, and what they say seems
credible.

# EURIPIDES

ΑΥΤΟΥΡΓΟΣ

ἦ καί τι πατρὸς σῶν τε μέμνηται κακῶν;

ΗΛΕΚΤΡΑ

ἐν ἐλπίσιν ταῦτ'· ἀσθενὴς φεύγων ἀνήρ.

ΑΥΤΟΥΡΓΟΣ

ἦλθον δ' Ὀρέστου τίνα πορεύοντες λόγον;

ΗΛΕΚΤΡΑ

σκοποὺς ἔπεμψε τούσδε τῶν ἐμῶν κακῶν.

ΑΥΤΟΥΡΓΟΣ

355    οὔκουν τὰ μὲν λεύσσουσι, τὰ δὲ σύ που λέγεις;

ΗΛΕΚΤΡΑ

ἴσασιν, οὐδὲν τῶνδ' ἔχουσιν ἐνδεές.

ΑΥΤΟΥΡΓΟΣ

οὔκουν πάλαι χρῆν τοῖσδ' ἀνεπτύχθαι πύλας;
    χωρεῖτ' ἐς οἴκους· ἀντὶ γὰρ χρηστῶν λόγων
ξενίων κυρήσεθ', οἷ' ἐμὸς κεύθει δόμος.
360    [αἴρεσθ', ὀπαδοί, τῶνδ' ἔσω τεύχη δόμων.]
    καὶ μηδὲν ἀντείπητε, παρὰ φίλου φίλοι
μολόντες ἀνδρός· καὶ γὰρ εἰ πένης ἔφυν,
οὔτοι τό γ' ἦθος δυσγενὲς παρέξομαι.

ΟΡΕΣΤΗΣ

πρὸς θεῶν, ὅδ' ἀνὴρ ὃς συνεκκλέπτει γάμους
365    τοὺς σούς, Ὀρέστην οὐ καταισχύνειν θέλων;

353 τίνα πορεύοντες Reiske: τίν' ἀγορεύοντες L
360 del. Barrett

190

**FARMER**

And does he think of his father's troubles and of yours?

**ELECTRA**

That lies in the realm of hope: an exile is powerless.

**FARMER**

What message have they brought from Orestes?

**ELECTRA**

He sent them to spy out my misery.

**FARMER**

Do they not see some of it, while you doubtless are telling them the rest?

**ELECTRA**

They know, they have the story in full.

**FARMER**

Then should not our door have long ago been opened to them?

(*to Orestes and Pylades*) Go into the house. In return for your noble words you will get such hospitality as my house affords. [Take the gear, attendants, into this house.] And do not refuse since you are friends come from a friend. Though I am poor, I shall not show my nature to be ignoble.

**ORESTES**

By the gods, is this the man who joins in your pretense of marriage, not wishing to dishonor Orestes?

ΗΛΕΚΤΡΑ

οὗτος κέκληται πόσις ἐμὸς τῆς ἀθλίας.

ΟΡΕΣΤΗΣ

φεῦ·
οὐκ ἔστ᾽ ἀκριβὲς οὐδὲν εἰς εὐανδρίαν·
[ἔχουσι γὰρ ταραγμὸν αἱ φύσεις βροτῶν.
ἤδη γὰρ εἶδον ἄνδρα γενναίου πατρὸς
370  τὸ μηδὲν ὄντα, χρηστά τ᾽ ἐκ κακῶν τέκνα,
λιμόν τ᾽ ἐν ἀνδρὸς πλουσίου φρονήματι,
γνώμην δὲ μεγάλην ἐν πένητι σώματι.
πῶς οὖν τις αὐτὰ διαλαβὼν ὀρθῶς κρινεῖ;
πλούτῳ; πονηρῷ τἆρα χρήσεται κριτῇ.
375  ἢ τοῖς ἔχουσι μηδέν; ἀλλ᾽ ἔχει νόσον
πενία, διδάσκει δ᾽ ἄνδρα τῇ χρείᾳ κακόν.
ἀλλ᾽ εἰς ὅπλ᾽ ἐλθών; τίς δὲ πρὸς λόγχην βλέπων
μάρτυς γένοιτ᾽ ἂν ὅστις ἐστὶν ἀγαθός;
κράτιστον εἰκῇ ταῦτ᾽ ἐᾶν ἀφειμένα.]
380  οὗτος γὰρ ἀνὴρ οὔτ᾽ ἐν Ἀργείοις μέγας
οὔτ᾽ αὖ δοκήσει δωμάτων ὠγκωμένος,
ἐν τοῖς δὲ πολλοῖς ὤν, ἄριστος ηὑρέθη.
οὐ μὴ ἀφρονήσεθ᾽, οἳ κενῶν δοξασμάτων
πλήρεις πλανᾶσθε, τῇ δ᾽ ὁμιλίᾳ βροτῶν
385  κρινεῖτε καὶ τοῖς ἤθεσιν τοὺς εὐγενεῖς;
[οἱ γὰρ τοιοῦτοι τὰς πόλεις οἰκοῦσιν εὖ
καὶ δώμαθ᾽· αἱ δὲ σάρκες αἱ κεναὶ φρενῶν
ἀγάλματ᾽ ἀγορᾶς εἰσιν. οὐδὲ γὰρ δόρυ
μᾶλλον βραχίων σθεναρὸς ἀσθενοῦς μένει·

## ELECTRA

This is the man they call the husband of unhappy Electra.

### ORESTES

Oh my! There is no reliable way to predict nobility. [The natural endowments of mortals suffer confusion. I have seen a man born of a noble father but himself a nullity, and noble children sprung from those of low estate; I have seen resourcelessness in a rich man's pride and greatness in the body of a poor one. How then shall a man distinguish and judge these things aright? By wealth? It is a sorry judge he will be making use of. By poverty? But poverty is unhealthy and teaches a man to be base from need. By considering his conduct in war? Yet who, as he stands facing a spear point, can bear testimony to the bravery of others? It is best to let this subject go as it will.] For this man, not one of the great among the Argives, nor yet impressive because of his family's reputation, a man of the people, has been shown to be noble. All you who wander about full of vain notions, come to your senses and judge the nobility of mortals by their way of life and their character! [Men of this kind are good at administering cities and households, while physiques lacking in brains are good only at adorning the marketplace. For a strong arm is not even better at withstanding the spear in battle than a weak one, but this is purely a

---

368–72 del. Reeve        373–9 del. Wilamowitz
377 ἐλθών Heath: ἔλθω L
383–5 suspectos habuit Murray
383 ἀφρονήσεθ' Badham: φρονήσεθ' L
384 βροτῶν Keene: -ούς L
386–90 del. Wilamowitz

193

390 ἐν τῇ φύσει δὲ τοῦτο κἀν εὐψυχίᾳ.]
   ἀλλ᾽ ἄξιος γὰρ ὅ τε παρὼν ὅ τ᾽ οὐ παρὼν
   Ἀγαμέμνονος παῖς, οὗπερ οὕνεχ᾽ ἥκομεν,
   δεξώμεθ᾽ οἴκων καταλύσεις. χωρεῖν χρεών,
   δμῶες, δόμων τῶνδ᾽ ἐντός. ὡς ἐμοὶ πένης
395 εἴη πρόθυμος πλουσίου μᾶλλον ξένος.
   αἰνῶ μὲν οὖν τοῦδ᾽ ἀνδρὸς ἐσδοχὰς δόμων,
   ἐβουλόμην δ᾽ ἂν εἰ κασίγνητός με σὸς
   ἐς εὐτυχοῦντας ἦγεν εὐτυχῶν δόμους.
   ἴσως δ᾽ ἂν ἔλθοι· Λοξίου γὰρ ἔμπεδοι
400 χρησμοί, βροτῶν δὲ μαντικὴν χαίρειν ἐῶ.

ΧΟΡΟΣ
   νῦν ἢ πάροιθε μᾶλλον, Ἠλέκτρα, χαρᾷ
   θερμαινόμεσθα καρδίαν· ἴσως γὰρ ἂν
   μόλις προβαίνουσ᾽ ἡ τύχη σταίη καλῶς.

ΗΛΕΚΤΡΑ
   ὦ τλῆμον, εἰδὼς δωμάτων χρείαν σέθεν
405 τί τούσδ᾽ ἐδέξω μείζονας σαυτοῦ ξένους;

ΑΥΤΟΥΡΓΟΣ
   τί δ᾽; εἴπερ εἰσὶν ὡς δοκοῦσιν εὐγενεῖς,
   οὐκ ἔν τε μικροῖς ἔν τε μὴ στέρξουσ᾽ ὁμῶς;

391 fort. ἄξενος (sine hospite) vel ἄστεγος
396–400 del. Reeve
400 μᾶλλον ἢ πάροιθεν Diggle

matter of character and courage.]

Well, since your present guest and the absent son of Agamemnon, for whose sake we have come,[9] are his worthy guests, let us accept the lodging this house affords. Go into the house, servants! Rather than a rich host, may I have a poor one who is well disposed! I gratefully accept the hospitality of this man. But I wish your brother, returned to prosperity, were leading me into his prosperous house. Perhaps he will come. The oracles of Loxias are unfailing, though I dismiss the divination of mortal men.

*Exit* ORESTES, *Pylades, and slaves into the house.*

### CHORUS LEADER
Now more than before, Electra, my heart is warmed with joy. Perhaps our fate, after marching forward with difficulty, will now stand on fair ground.

### ELECTRA
Heedless man, why have you received guests of higher standing than yourself, although you are aware your house is poor?

### FARMER
Why not? If they are as noble as they appear to be, will they not be content equally in modest and in grand circumstances?

---

[9] Orestes wants to be understood as speaking of two people, the man who is here (himself as Orestes' envoy) and the absent son of Agamemnon, but the secret sense of his words is "the son of Agamemnon who is both absent (since here in concealment) and present (in reality)."

ΗΛΕΚΤΡΑ

ἐπεί νυν ἐξήμαρτες ἐν σμικροῖσιν ὤν,
ἔλθ' ὡς παλαιὸν τροφέα μοι φίλου πατρός,
410 ὃς ἀμφὶ ποταμὸν Τάναον Ἀργείας ὅρους
τέμνοντα γαίας Σπαρτιάτιδός τε γῆς
ποίμναις ὁμαρτεῖ πόλεος ἐκβεβλημένος·
κέλευε δ' αὐτὸν ἐς δόμους ἀφιγμένος
ἐλθεῖν ξένιά τ' ἐς δαῖτα πορσῦναί τινα.
415 ἡσθήσεταί τοι καὶ προσεύξεται θεοῖς,
ζῶντ' εἰσακούσας παῖδ' ὃν ἐκσῴζει ποτέ.
οὐ γὰρ πατρῴων ἐκ δόμων μητρὸς πάρα
λάβοιμεν ἄν τι· πικρὰ δ' ἀγγείλαιμεν ἄν,
εἰ ζῶντ' Ὀρέστην ἡ τάλαιν' αἴσθοιτ' ἔτι.

ΑΥΤΟΥΡΓΟΣ

420 ἀλλ', εἰ δοκεῖ σοι, τούσδ' ἀπαγγελῶ λόγους
γέροντι· χώρει δ' ἐς δόμους ὅσον τάχος
καὶ τἄνδον ἐξάρτυε. πολλά τοι γυνὴ
χρῄζουσ' ἂν εὕροι δαιτὶ προσφορήματα.
ἔστιν δὲ δὴ τοσαῦτά γ' ἐν δόμοις ἔτι
425 ὥσθ' ἕν γ' ἐπ' ἦμαρ τούσδε πληρῶσαι βορᾶς.
ἐν τοῖς τοιούτοις δ' ἡνίκ' ἂν γνώμη πέσῃ,
σκοπῶ τὰ χρήμαθ' ὡς ἔχει μέγα σθένος
ξένοις τε δοῦναι σῶμά τ' ἐς νόσους πεσὸν
δαπάναισι σῶσαι· τῆς δ' ἐφ' ἡμέραν βορᾶς
430 ἐς σμικρὸν ἥκει· πᾶς γὰρ ἐμπλησθεὶς ἀνὴρ
ὁ πλούσιός τε χὠ πένης ἴσον φέρει.

---

409 τροφέα μοι Diggle: τροφὸν ἐμὸν L

196

### ELECTRA

Since you have made a blunder in your modest circumstances, go to my father's beloved old tutor. He has been cast out of the city and pastures sheep near the Tanaus River, which divides the Argolid from Spartan territory. When you get to his house, tell him to come and bring some guest provisions for a feast. He will surely be overjoyed and offer prayers to the gods when he hears that the child he once rescued is alive. We would never get anything out of my ancestral home from my mother. It would be unwelcome news to that cruel woman if she learned that Orestes is still alive.

### FARMER

Well, if that is what you think best, I will bring this message to the old man. But go into the house as quickly as you can, and prepare what you find there. Surely a woman who wants to can find something to add to the feast. There is still enough in the house to fill these men with food for a single day.

*Exit ELECTRA into the house.*

When my thought lights on matters like these, I observe that while money has great power and allows you to give gifts to your guests and to keep your body alive when it has fallen into disease, it makes little difference to daily sustenance. When his belly is full, everyone, rich man and poor alike, holds an equal amount.

---

413 αὐτὸν Scaliger: αὐτὸν τόνδ' L: possis etiam αὐτὸν τόνδ' ἐκεῖσ'    ἀφιγμένος Musgrave: -ον L
414 ξένιά Weil: ξένων L

# EURIPIDES

ΧΟΡΟΣ

στρ. α

 κλειναὶ νᾶες, αἵ ποτ' ἔβατε Τροίαν
 τοῖς ἀμετρήτοις ἐρετμοῖς
 πέμπουσαι χορεύματα Νηρῄδων,
435 ἵν' ὁ φίλαυλος ἔπαλλε δελ-
 φὶς πρώραις κυανεμβόλοις
 ⟨συν⟩ειλισσόμενος, πορεύ-
 ουσαι τὸν τᾶς Θέτιδος
 κοῦφον ἅλμα ποδῶν Ἀχιλῆ
440 σὺν Ἀγαμέμνονι Τρῳάς
 ἐπὶ Σιμουντίδας ἀκτάς.

ἀντ. α

 Νηρῇδες δ' Εὐβοῖδας ἄκρας λιποῦσαι
 μόχθους ἀσπιστὰς ἀκμόνων
 Ἡφαίστου χρυσέων ἔφερον τευχέων,
445 ἀνὰ δὲ Πήλιον ἀνά τ' ἐρυ-
 μνὰς Ὄσσας ἱερᾶς νάπας
 Νυμφαίας σκοπιάς, κόραι
 μάτευσαν ἔνθα πατὴρ
 ἱππότας τρέφεν Ἑλλάδι φῶς
450 Θέτιδος εἰναλίας γόνον

<hr>

434 χορεύματα Diggle: χοροὺς μετὰ L
437 ⟨συν⟩ειλισσόμενος post Musgrave (⟨ἐν-⟩) Willink
437–8 πορεύουσαι Wecklein: πορεύων L
442 ἄκρας Orelli: ἀκτὰς L
443–4 sic Headlam: Ἡφαίστου χρυσέων ἀκμόνων μόχθους
ἀσπιστὰς L

198

*Exit* FARMER *by Eisodos B.*

CHORUS

Glorious ships that once went to Troy,
ships that with those numberless oars
escorted the dances of the Nereids,
dances wherein the dolphin that loves the sound of the
    pipe[10]
gamboled in company
with the dark-blue prows:
you ferried Thetis' son,
Achilles of the swiftly leaping feet,
with Agamemnon to the banks
of the Simois, Troy's river.

The Nereids, leaving the headlands of Euboea,
carried the warrior produce
of Hephaestus' anvil, a panoply of gold,
and on Mount Pelion and in holy
Ossa's sheer dells,
the lookouts of the nymphs, these maidens
sought him out where his father,
the horseman, was nurturing, as a beacon of light to the
    Greeks,
the sea goddess Thetis' son

[10] A tune played on the pipe (*aulos*) was used to set the rowers'
beat.

---

445 δὲ Bothe: τε L      ἐρυμνὰς Musgrave: πρυμνὰς L
447 κόραι Milton: κόρας L      448 μάτευσαν Reiter: μάτευσ᾽ L
450 εἰναλίας Kvíčala: ἐνάλιον L

ταχύπορον πόδ᾽ Ἀτρείδαις.

στρ. β

Ἰλιόθεν δ᾽ ἔκλυόν τινος ἐν λιμέσιν
Ναυπλίοις βεβῶτος
τᾶς σᾶς, ὦ Θέτιδος παῖ,
455 κλεινᾶς ἀσπίδος ἐν κύκλῳ
τοιάδε σήματα, δείματα ⟨γᾷ⟩ Φρυγίᾳ, τετύχθαι·
περιδρόμῳ μὲν ἴτυος ἕδρᾳ
Περσέα λαιμοτόμαν ὑπὲρ ἅλμας
460 ποτανοῖσι πεδίλοις κορυφὰν Γοργόνος ἴσχειν,
Διὸς ἀγγέλῳ σὺν Ἑρμᾷ,
τῷ Μαίας ἀγροτῆρι κούρῳ.

ἀντ. β

ἐν δὲ μέσῳ κατέλαμπε σάκει φαέθων
465 κύκλος ἁλίοιο
ἵπποις ἂμ πτεροέσσαις
ἄστρων τ᾽ αἰθέριοι χοροί,
Πλειάδες, Ὑάδες, ὄμμασιν Ἑκτορέοις τροπαῖοι·
470 ἐπὶ δὲ χρυσοτύπῳ κράνει
Σφίγγες ὄνυξιν ἀοίδιμον ἄγραν
φέρουσαι· περιπλεύρῳ δὲ κύτει πύρπνοος ἔσπευ-
δε δρόμῳ λέαινα χαλαῖς
475 Πειρηναῖον ὁρῶσα πῶλον.

456–7 ⟨γᾷ⟩ Φρυγίᾳ Diggle: Φρύγια L
459 λαιμοτόμαν Seidler: -τόμον L      ἅλμας Weil: ἁλὸς L
460 πεδίλοις κορυφὰν Herwerden: πεδίλοισι φυὰν L
468 ὄμμασιν Ἑκτορέοις Diggle: Ἕκτορος ὄμμασι L
475 ὁρῶσα Bothe: θ᾽ ὁρῶσα L

swift-footed, for the sons of Atreus.

I have heard from a man who came from Troy
and disembarked in the harbor of Nauplia
that on the circle
of your famous shield, Achilles,
figures like these were fashioned to affright the land of
    Troy:
on the round rim of the shield
Perseus skimming above the sea,
shod in winged sandals, holds the Gorgon's severed head,
traveling in company with Hermes, Zeus's messenger,
the rustic[11] son of Maia.

In the center of the shield glowed the burning
circle of the sun
with his winged steeds,
and the choruses of stars on high,
Pleiades and Hyades, to turn Hector's eyes to flight.
On his helmet of beaten gold,
Sphinxes bear in their talons the prey their song has won.
On the breastplate that encircled his flanks the fire-breath-
    ing
lioness[12] hurries away on her paws in swift flight
as she spies Peirene's colt.[13]

[11] Hermes is especially worshipped in pastoral Arcadia.
[12] The Chimaera, a mythical monster, lion in front, serpent
behind, and she-goat in the middle.
[13] Pegasus, ridden by Bellerophon, who slew the Chimaera.

ἐπῳδ.

ἄορι δ᾽ ἐν φονίῳ τετραβάμονες ἵπποι ἔπαλλον,
κελαινὰ δ᾽ ἀμφὶ νῶθ᾽ ἵετο κόνις.
τοιῶνδ᾽ ἄνακτα δοριπόνων
480 ἔκανεν ἀνδρῶν, Τυνδαρί,
σὰ λέχεα, κακόφρον κόρα.
τοιγάρ σοί ποτ᾽ οὐρανίδαι
πέμψουσιν θανάτου δίκαν.
485 ἔτ᾽ ἔτι φόνιον ὑπὸ δέραν
ὄψομαι αἷμα χυθὲν σιδάρῳ.

ΠΡΕΣΒΥΣ

ποῦ ποῦ νεᾶνις πότνι᾽ ἐμὴ δέσποινά τε,
Ἀγαμέμνονος παῖς, ὅν ποτ᾽ ἐξέθρεψ᾽ ἐγώ;
ὡς πρόσβασιν τῶνδ᾽ ὀρθίαν οἴκων ἔχει
490 ῥυσῷ γέροντι τῷδε προσβῆναι ποδί.
ὅμως δὲ πρός γε τοὺς φίλους ἐξελκτέον
διπλῆν ἄκανθαν καὶ παλίρροπον γόνυ.
    ὦ θύγατερ (ἄρτι γάρ σε πρὸς δόμοις ὁρῶ),
ἥκω φέρων σοι τῶν ἐμῶν βοσκημάτων
495 ποίμνης νεογνὸν θρέμμ᾽ ὑποσπάσας τόδε
στεφάνους τε τευχέων τ᾽ ἐξελὼν τυρεύματα,
πολιόν τε θησαύρισμα Διονύσου τόδε
ὀσμῇ κατῆρες, σμικρὸν ἀλλ᾽ ἐπεσβαλεῖν
ἡδὺ σκύφον τοῦδ᾽ ἀσθενεστέρῳ ποτῷ.

---

476 ἄορι δ᾽ ἐν Hartung: ἐν δὲ δορὶ L
483 σοί Murray: σέ L    484 θανάτου δίκαν Murray (δίκαν)
et Diggle: θανάτοισι· κἂν L

On his deadly sword four-footed horses pranced,
and behind them the black dust was rising.
The lord of warriors like these,
Clytaemestra, woman of evil thoughts,
your adultery has slain.
For this the gods will send upon you
the judgment of death.
One day, one day beneath your neck
I shall see blood spilled upon the ground by the sword.

*Enter* OLD MAN *by Eisodos B carrying a lamb on his shoulders and other provisions in his hands.*

#### OLD MAN

Where, O where is the young princess, my lady, daughter of Agamemnon, the man I once reared up? What an approach she has to her house, so steep for this withered old man to climb on foot! Still, to reach my friends I must drag along my stooping back and tottering legs.

*Enter* ELECTRA *from the house.*

My daughter—now I see you near the house—I bring you a young lamb I have pulled away from my flocks and garlands and cheeses taken from the press, and some old and fragrant wine I have treasured, not a great deal of it—but it is a pleasant thing to put a cup of this in a wine

---

485 δέρας Wecklein    497 πολιόν Scaliger: παλαιόν L
498 ὀσμῇ κατῆρες suspectum
499 τοῦδ' Reiske: τῷδ' L

500 ἴτω φέρων τις τοῖς ξένοις τάδ᾽ ἐς δόμους.
ἐγὼ δὲ τρύχει τῷδ᾽ ἐμῶν πέπλων κόρας
δακρύοισι τέγξας ἐξομόρξασθαι θέλω.

ΗΛΕΚΤΡΑ

τί δ᾽, ὦ γεραιέ, διάβροχον τόδ᾽ ὄμμ᾽ ἔχεις;
μῶν τἀμὰ διὰ χρόνου σ᾽ ἀνέμνησαν κακὰ
<τηλουρὸς οἶκος καὶ πέπλων ἐμῶν ῥάκη>;
505 ἢ τὰς Ὀρέστου τλήμονας φυγὰς στένεις
καὶ πατέρα τὸν ἐμόν, ὅν ποτ᾽ ἐν χεροῖν ἔχων
ἀνόνητ᾽ ἔθρεψάς σοί τε καὶ τοῖς σοῖς φίλοις;

ΠΡΕΣΒΥΣ

ἀνόνηθ᾽· ὅμως δ᾽ οὖν τοῦτό γ᾽ οὐκ ἠνεσχόμην,
<ὁρῶν πατέρα σὸν ἐστερημένον χοῶν>.
ἦλθον γὰρ αὐτοῦ πρὸς τάφον πάρεργ᾽ ὁδοῦ
510 καὶ προσπεσὼν ἔκλαυσ᾽ ἐρημίας τυχών,
σπονδάς τε, λύσας ἀσκὸν ὃν φέρω ξένοις,
ἔσπεισα, τύμβῳ δ᾽ ἀμφέθηκα μυρσίνας.
πυρᾶς δ᾽ ἐπ᾽ αὐτῆς οἶν μελάγχιμον πόκῳ
σφάγιον ἐσεῖδον αἷμά τ᾽ οὐ πάλαι χυθὲν
515 ξανθῆς τε χαίτης βοστρύχους κεκαρμένους.
κἀθαύμασ᾽, ὦ παῖ, τίς ποτ᾽ ἀνθρώπων ἔτλη
πρὸς τύμβον ἐλθεῖν· οὐ γὰρ Ἀργείων γέ τις.
[ἀλλ᾽ ἦλθ᾽ ἴσως που σὸς κασίγνητος λάθρᾳ,

504 post h. v. lac. indic. Kovacs
508 post h. v. lac. indic. Schenkl
518–44 del. Mau

of weaker vintage. Let someone take these things into the house for the guests! Since I have drenched my eyes with weeping, I want to wipe them on these tattered garments of mine.

*A servant takes the provisions into the house. The Old Man wipes his eyes.*

ELECTRA

Why, old sir, is your face wet with tears? Has ‹the sight of this lonely dwelling and my ragged clothing› after so long a time reminded you of my troubles? Or do you weep for the wretched exile of Orestes and for my father? You took him in your arms and reared him, yet your labor has proved useless to you and those you hold dear.

OLD MAN

Yes, useless. Yet the thing I could not endure was this, ‹to see your father deprived of funeral libations›. For as a detour on my journey I went to his tomb, and finding myself alone I fell down and wept for him: I opened the wineskin I was bringing for your guests and poured him a libation and put myrtle branches about his tomb. But on the altar itself I saw a black lamb, its blood recently shed, and shorn locks of blond hair. I wondered, daughter, what mortal had had the courage to visit the tomb. Certainly it was no citizen of Argos.[14] [But perhaps your brother has

---

[14] The 27 lines that follow have been suspected of being an interpolation since the nineteenth century, and Fraenkel in his *Agamemnon* commentary (vol. 3, pp. 821ff.) argued strongly for deletion. Since then several discussions, for and against deletion, have appeared. For a history of the question and further arguments for excision, see Kovacs 1989.

μολὼν δ᾽ ἐθαύμασ᾽ ἄθλιον τύμβον πατρός.
520 σκέψαι δὲ χαίτην προστιθεῖσα σῇ κόμῃ,
εἰ χρῶμα ταὐτὸν κουρίμης ἔσται τριχός·
φιλεῖ γάρ, αἷμα ταὐτὸν οἷς ἂν ᾖ πατρός,
τὰ πόλλ᾽ ὅμοια σώματος πεφυκέναι.

ΗΛΕΚΤΡΑ
οὐκ ἄξι᾽ ἀνδρός, ὦ γέρον, σοφοῦ λέγεις,
525 εἰ κρυπτὸν ἐς γῆν τήνδ᾽ ἂν Αἰγίσθου φόβῳ
δοκεῖς ἀδελφὸν τὸν ἐμὸν εὐθαρσῆ μολεῖν.
ἔπειτα χαίτης πῶς συνοίσεται πλόκος,
ὁ μὲν παλαίστραις ἀνδρὸς εὐγενοῦς τραφείς,
ὁ δὲ κτενισμοῖς θῆλυς; ἀλλ᾽ ἀμήχανον.
530 πολλοῖς δ᾽ ἂν εὕροις βοστρύχους ὁμοπτέρους
καὶ μὴ γεγῶσιν αἵματος ταὐτοῦ, γέρον.

ΠΡΕΣΒΥΣ
σὺ δ᾽ εἰς ἴχνος βᾶσ᾽ ἀρβύλης σκέψαι βάσιν
εἰ σύμμετρος σῷ ποδὶ γενήσεται, τέκνον.

ΗΛΕΚΤΡΑ
πῶς δ᾽ ἂν γένοιτ᾽ ἂν ἐν κραταιλέῳ πέδῳ
535 γαίας ποδῶν ἔκμακτρον; εἰ δ᾽ ἔστιν τόδε,
δυοῖν ἀδελφοῖν ποὺς ἂν οὐ γένοιτ᾽ ἴσος
ἀνδρός τε καὶ γυναικός, ἀλλ᾽ ἄρσην κρατεῖ.

ΠΡΕΣΒΥΣ
οὐκ ἔστιν, εἰ καὶ γῆν κασίγνητος μόλοι,
κερκίδος ὅτῳ γνοίης ἂν ἐξύφασμα σῆς,
540 ἐν ᾧ ποτ᾽ αὐτὸν ἐξέκλεψα μὴ θανεῖν;

come in secret and on his arrival honored the wretched tomb of his father. Put the lock up against your hair and see whether the color of the shorn tress is the same. For it commonly happens that those who have the same paternal blood in them show physical similarity in most things.

### ELECTRA

What you say, old sir, is unworthy of a wise man if you imagine that my brave brother would come to this land in secret because he feared Aegisthus. Furthermore, how should his hair be like mine since his was grown in the wrestling schools of young noblemen while mine is feminine and combed? It is impossible. You will find that many people possess locks that are similar, old man, who are not of the same blood.

### OLD MAN

Step into his footprint and see whether the mark of his boot agrees with your foot, my child.

### ELECTRA

But how could a footprint be made on ground well-stoned?[15] And if there is one, the feet of siblings will not be of equal size when one is male and the other female: the male will be larger.

### OLD MAN

But if in fact your brother should come to this land, is there not some bit of your weaving by which you could recognize him, weaving in which I spirited him away from death?

[15] The phrase probably comes from the lost opening lines of Aeschylus' *Libation Bearers*.

---

538 μόλοι Musgrave: μολὼν L

ΗΛΕΚΤΡΑ

οὐκ οἶσθ᾽, Ὀρέστης ἡνίκ᾽ ἐκπίπτει χθονός,
νέαν μ᾽ ἔτ᾽ οὖσαν; εἰ δὲ κἄκρεκον πέπλους,
πῶς ἂν τότ᾽ ὢν παῖς ταὐτὰ νῦν ἔχοι φάρη,
εἰ μὴ ξυναύξοινθ᾽ οἱ πέπλοι τῷ σώματι;]

⟨ΗΛΕΚΤΡΑ⟩

545  ἀλλ᾽ ἤ τις αὐτοῦ τάφον ἐποικτίρας ξένος
σκοποὺς λαθὼν ἐκείρατ᾽ ἢ τῆσδε χθονὸς
⟨ἐς ὄρι᾽ ἀδελφοῦ βοστρύχους ἐσήγαγεν⟩.

ΠΡΕΣΒΥΣ

οἱ δὲ ξένοι ποῦ; βούλομαι γὰρ εἰσιδὼν
αὐτοὺς ἐρέσθαι σοῦ κασιγνήτου πέρι.

ΗΛΕΚΤΡΑ

οἵδ᾽ ἐκ δόμων βαίνουσι λαιψηρῷ ποδί.

ΠΡΕΣΒΥΣ

550  ἀλλ᾽ εὐγενεῖς μέν, ἐν δὲ κιβδήλῳ τόδε·
πολλοὶ γὰρ ὄντες εὐγενεῖς εἰσιν κακοί.
ὅμως δὲ χαίρειν τοὺς ξένους προσεννέπω.

ΟΡΕΣΤΗΣ

χαῖρ᾽, ὦ γεραιέ. τοῦ ποτ᾽, Ἠλέκτρα, τόδε
παλαιὸν ἀνδρὸς λείψανον φίλων κυρεῖ;

ΗΛΕΚΤΡΑ

555  οὗτος τὸν ἀμὸν πατέρ᾽ ἔθρεψεν, ὦ ξένε.

545 fort. ξένων    546 σκοποὺς λαθὼν ἐκείρατ᾽ ἢ τῆσδε
χθονός post Victorium (λαθὼν) Elmsley: ἐκείρατ᾽ ἢ τῆσδε
σκοποὺς λαβὼν χθονός L    post h. v. lac. indic. Mau

### ELECTRA

Do you not know that when Orestes went into exile I was
still a child? And even if I had been weaving clothes, how
could a man who was a child at that time be wearing the
same garments unless his clothing were to grow with his
body?]

### ⟨ELECTRA⟩

Well, some foreigner either took pity on his tomb and
cut his hair, escaping the guards' notice, or ⟨brought my
brother's hair offering into the territory⟩ of this land.

### OLD MAN

But where are our foreign guests? I want to see them and
ask them about your brother.

*ORESTES, Pylades, and attendants come out of the house.*

### ELECTRA

Here they come with nimble step out of the house.

### OLD MAN

Well, they are gentlemen, to be sure, but that's a deceptive
matter. Many who are well born are worthless characters.
Still, my greeting to the strangers!

### ORESTES

Greeting to you, old sir. Which one of your friends, Electra,
owns this ancient relic of a man?

### ELECTRA

This is the man who reared my father, stranger.

ΟΡΕΣΤΗΣ

τί φῄς; ὅδ᾽ ὃς σὸν ἐξέκλεψε σύγγονον;

ΗΛΕΚΤΡΑ

ὅδ᾽ ἔσθ᾽ ὁ σώσας κεῖνον, εἴπερ ἔστ᾽ ἔτι.

ΟΡΕΣΤΗΣ

ἔα·
τί μ᾽ ἐσδέδορκεν ὥσπερ ἀργύρου σκοπῶν
λαμπρὸν χαρακτῆρ᾽; ἢ προσεικάζει μέ τῳ;

ΗΛΕΚΤΡΑ

560    ἴσως Ὀρέστου σ᾽ ἥλιχ᾽ ἥδεται βλέπων.

ΟΡΕΣΤΗΣ

φίλου γε φωτός. τί δὲ κυκλεῖ πέριξ πόδα;

ΗΛΕΚΤΡΑ

καὐτὴ τόδ᾽ εἰσορῶσα θαυμάζω, ξένε.

ΠΡΕΣΒΥΣ

ὦ πότνι᾽, εὔχου, θύγατερ Ἠλέκτρα, θεοῖς.

ΗΛΕΚΤΡΑ

τί τῶν ἀπόντων ἢ τί τῶν ὄντων πέρι;

ΠΡΕΣΒΥΣ

565    λαβεῖν φίλον θησαυρόν, ὃν φαίνει θεός.

ΗΛΕΚΤΡΑ

ἰδού· καλῶ θεούς. ἢ τί δὴ λέγεις, γέρον;

ΠΡΕΣΒΥΣ

βλέψον νυν ἐς τόνδ᾽, ὦ τέκνον, τὸν φίλτατον.

556 ἐξέκλεψε Pierson: ἐξέθρεψε L

**ORESTES**
What? The man who spirited your brother away?

**ELECTRA**
This is the man who saved his life, if life he still has.

**ORESTES**
What's this? Why is he staring at me as if he were looking
at the hallmark on silver? Does he think I look like some-
one else?

**ELECTRA**
Perhaps he is happy to see a man Orestes' age.

*The Old Man walks around Orestes.*

**ORESTES**
The man we love. But why is he circling around me?

**ELECTRA**
I see this too and wonder at it, stranger.

**OLD MAN**
Daughter Electra, my lady, offer prayers to the gods!

**ELECTRA**
For what? Something I lack or something I have?

**OLD MAN**
Pray you may grasp the precious treasure the god is show-
ing you!

**ELECTRA**
All right: I call on the gods. Or did you mean something
different, old man?

**OLD MAN**
Then look, my daughter, at this man you love best.

211

ΗΛΕΚΤΡΑ

πάλαι δέδορκα· μὴ σύ γ᾽ οὐκέτ᾽ εὖ φρονεῖς;

ΠΡΕΣΒΥΣ

οὐκ εὖ φρονῶ ᾽γὼ σὸν κασίγνητον βλέπων;

ΗΛΕΚΤΡΑ

570 πῶς εἶπας, ὦ γεραί᾽, ἀνέλπιστον λόγον;

ΠΡΕΣΒΥΣ

ὁρᾶν Ὀρέστην τόνδε τὸν Ἀγαμέμνονος.

ΗΛΕΚΤΡΑ

ποῖον χαρακτῆρ᾽ εἰσιδών, ᾧ πείσομαι;

ΠΡΕΣΒΥΣ

οὐλὴν παρ᾽ ὀφρύν, ἥν ποτ᾽ ἐν πατρὸς δόμοις
νεβρὸν διώκων σοῦ μέθ᾽ ἡμάχθη πεσών.

ΗΛΕΚΤΡΑ

575 πῶς φῄς; ὁρῶ μὲν πτώματος τεκμήριον.

ΠΡΕΣΒΥΣ

ἔπειτα μέλλεις προσπίτνειν τοῖς φιλτάτοις;

ΗΛΕΚΤΡΑ

ἀλλ᾽ οὐκέτ᾽, ὦ γεραιέ· συμβόλοισι γὰρ
τοῖς σοῖς πέπεισμαι θυμόν. ὦ χρόνῳ φανείς,
ἔχω σ᾽ ἀέλπτως . . .

569 ᾽γὼ] γὰρ Denniston
568 interrogationis notam add. Diggle
570 πῶς] τίν᾽ Wecklein

### ELECTRA

I have been looking for some time: have you gone mad?

### OLD MAN

Am I mad if I see your brother?

### ELECTRA

What do you mean, old man, by this extraordinary claim?

### OLD MAN

That I see Orestes, Agamemnon's son.

### ELECTRA

What mark have you seen that deserves my trust?

### OLD MAN

The scar next to his eyebrow: once in your father's house
he fell and cut it as you and he chased a fawn.

### ELECTRA

What is this you say? I see the evidence of his fall.

### OLD MAN

Then can you hesitate to fling yourself into your dear
brother's embrace?

### ELECTRA

I hesitate no longer, old man. My heart is persuaded by the
tally you point out.

*Electra and Orestes embrace.*

O brother long in coming, I embrace you though I no
longer hoped to . . .

ΟΡΕΣΤΗΣ
κἀξ ἐμοῦ γ' ἔχῃ χρόνῳ.

ΗΛΕΚΤΡΑ
580    . . . οὐδέποτε δόξασ'.

ΟΡΕΣΤΗΣ
οὐδ' ἐγὼ γὰρ ἤλπισα.

ΗΛΕΚΤΡΑ
ἐκεῖνος εἶ σύ;

ΟΡΕΣΤΗΣ
σύμμαχός γέ σοι μόνος,
ἢν δ' ἀνσπάσωμαί γ' ὃν μετέρχομαι βόλον,
⟨σωτὴρ ἂν εἴην ἐξ ἀμηχάνων κακῶν⟩.
πέποιθα δ'· ἢ χρὴ μηκέθ' ἡγεῖσθαι θεούς,
εἰ τἄδικ' ἔσται τῆς δίκης ὑπέρτερα.

ΧΟΡΟΣ
585    ἔμολες ἔμολες, ὤ, χρόνιος ἁμέρα,
κατέλαμψας, ἔδειξας ἐμφανῆ
πόλει πυρσόν, ὃς παλαιᾷ φυγᾷ
πατρίων ἀπὸ δωμάτων τάλας
ἀλαίνων ἔβα.
590    θεὸς αὖ θεὸς ἁμετέραν τις ἄγει
νίκαν, ὦ φίλα.
ἄνεχε χέρας, ἄνεχε λόγον, ἵει
λιτὰς ἐς θεούς, τύχᾳ σοι τύχᾳ
595    κασίγνητον ἐμβατεῦσαι πόλιν.

582 post h. v. lac. indic. Vitelli

214

**ORESTES**

And at long last I too embrace you!

**ELECTRA**

. . . and never thought this would happen!

**ORESTES**

No, for not even I had hope.

**ELECTRA**

Are you the very man?

**ORESTES**

Yes, your only ally, and if I succeed in hauling in the catch
of fish I have come for, ⟨I will prove your savior from
grievous troubles⟩. I am confident: otherwise we must no
longer believe in the gods if injustice is triumphant over
justice.

**CHORUS**

You have arrived, have arrived, O long-awaited day!
You have dawned and shown clearly
to the city the torch that in long exile
went wandering unhappy
far from his father's house.
Some god, some god is bringing us
victory, dear friend!
Lift up hands and voice, utter
prayers to the gods that with good luck, good luck
your brother may tread upon the city's soil!

*Orestes releases Electra from his embrace.*

---

ΟΡΕΣΤΗΣ

εἶἑν· φίλας μὲν ἡδονὰς ἀσπασμάτων
ἔχω, χρόνῳ δὲ καῦθις αὐτὰ δώσομεν.
σὺ δ', ὦ γεραιέ, καίριος γὰρ ἦλυθες,
λέξον, τί δρῶν ἂν φονέα τεισαίμην πατρὸς
600  μητέρα τε ⟨τὴν⟩ κοινωνὸν ἀνοσίων γάμων;
ἔστιν τί μοι κατ' Ἄργος εὐμενὲς φίλων;
ἢ πάντ' ἀνεσκευάσμεθ', ὥσπερ αἱ τύχαι;
τῷ ξυγγένωμαι; νύχιος ἢ καθ' ἡμέραν;
ποίαν ὁδὸν τραπώμεθ' εἰς ἐχθροὺς ἐμούς;

ΠΡΕΣΒΥΣ

605  ὦ τέκνον, οὐδεὶς δυστυχοῦντί σοι φίλος.
εὕρημα γάρ τοι χρῆμα γίγνεται τόδε,
κοινῇ μετασχεῖν τἀγαθοῦ καὶ τοῦ κακοῦ.
σὺ δ' (ἐκ βάθρων γὰρ πᾶς ἀνήρησαι φίλοις
οὐδ' ἐλλέλοιπας ἐλπίδ') ἴσθι μου κλυών·
610  ἐν χειρὶ τῇ σῇ πάντ' ἔχεις καὶ τῇ τύχῃ,
πατρῷον οἶκον καὶ πόλιν λαβεῖν σέθεν.

ΟΡΕΣΤΗΣ

τί δῆτα δρῶντες τοῦδ' ἂν ἐξικοίμεθα;

ΠΡΕΣΒΥΣ

κτανὼν Θυέστου παῖδα σήν τε μητέρα.

ΟΡΕΣΤΗΣ

ἥκω 'πὶ τόνδε στέφανον· ἀλλὰ πῶς λάβω;

ΠΡΕΣΒΥΣ

615  τειχέων μὲν ἐλθὼν ἐντὸς οὐδ' ἂν εἰ θέλοις.

ORESTES

Well, though I enjoy the pleasure of your embrace, still we
shall put off such embraces until the future. You, old sir,
since your arrival was most timely, tell me: how can I pun-
ish the man who slew my father and also my mother who
shares an unholy union with him? Do I have at Argos any
friends who wish me well? Or am I as bankrupt as are my
circumstances? With whom shall I join forces? Shall I meet
them by night or by day? What route am I to take against
my enemies?

OLD MAN

My son, no one is loyal to you in your troubles. It is a rare
piece of fortune, you know, if a friend stands by you in bad
luck as well as good. But—since your friends find you ut-
terly undone and you have left them no hope—hear me
and know how matters stand: the recovery of your father's
house and your city lies in your hands and fortune's.

ORESTES

What must I do to arrive at that goal?

OLD MAN

Kill Aegisthus and your mother.

ORESTES

That is the crown I have come for. But how am I to win it?

OLD MAN

Not by entering the city, even if you wanted to.

---

600 ⟨τὴν⟩ Canter    603 τῷ] πῶς Porson
606 τοι Seidler: τὸ L
609 ἐλλελοίπασ' A. Schmidt

ΟΡΕΣΤΗΣ

φρουραῖς κέκασται δεξιαῖς τε δορυφόρων;

ΠΡΕΣΒΥΣ

ἔγνως· φοβεῖται γάρ σε κοὐχ εὕδει σαφῶς.

ΟΡΕΣΤΗΣ

εἶέν· σὺ δὴ τοὐνθένδε βούλευσον, γέρον.

ΠΡΕΣΒΥΣ

τἄμ' οὖν ἄκουσον· ἄρτι γάρ μ' ἐσῆλθέ τι.

ΟΡΕΣΤΗΣ

620  ἐσθλόν τι μηνύσειας, αἰσθοίμην δ' ἐγώ.

ΠΡΕΣΒΥΣ

Αἴγισθον εἶδον, ἡνίχ' εἶρπον ἐνθάδε.

ΟΡΕΣΤΗΣ

προσηκάμην τὸ ῥηθέν. ἐν ποίοις τόποις;

ΠΡΕΣΒΥΣ

ἀγρῶν πέλας τῶνδ' ἱπποφορβίων ἔπι.

ΟΡΕΣΤΗΣ

τί δρῶνθ'; ὁρῶ γὰρ ἐλπίδ' ἐξ ἀμηχάνων.

ΠΡΕΣΒΥΣ

625  Νύμφαις ἐπόρσυν' ἔροτιν, ὡς ἔδοξέ μοι.

ΟΡΕΣΤΗΣ

τροφεῖα παίδων ἢ πρὸ μέλλοντος τόκου;

ΠΡΕΣΒΥΣ

οὐκ οἶδα πλὴν ἕν· βουσφαγεῖν ὡπλίζετο.

619 τἄμ' οὖν Weil: κἀμοῦ γ' L: καὶ μὴν Kirchhoff

218

ORESTES
He is protected by watchmen and a bodyguard?

OLD MAN
Exactly: he is afraid of you and does not sleep soundly.

ORESTES
Well then, old sir, please advise me on the next step.

OLD MAN
Listen to what I have to say: I have just had an idea.

ORESTES
May the plan you reveal—and I listen to—be a good one!

OLD MAN
I saw Aegisthus when I was on my way here.

ORESTES
I welcome what you are saying. Where was he?

OLD MAN
In his horse pastures not far from this farm.

ORESTES
What was he doing? I begin to see hope after despair.

OLD MAN
He was preparing a sacrifice for the Nymphs, as it seemed to me.

ORESTES
In payment for nurturing his children or for a child as yet unborn?

OLD MAN
I only know one thing: he had the gear for sacrificing a bullock.

ΟΡΕΣΤΗΣ

πόσων μετ᾽ ἀνδρῶν; ἢ μόνος δμώων μέτα;

ΠΡΕΣΒΥΣ

οὐδεὶς παρῆν Ἀργεῖος, οἰκεία δὲ χείρ.

ΟΡΕΣΤΗΣ

630  οὔ πού τις ὅστις γνωριεῖ μ᾽ ἰδών, γέρον;

ΠΡΕΣΒΥΣ

δμῶες μέν εἰσιν οὓς ἐγὼ οὐκ εἶδόν ποτε.

ΟΡΕΣΤΗΣ

ἡμῖν ⟨δ᾽⟩ ἂν εἶεν, εἰ κρατοῖμεν, εὐμενεῖς;

ΠΡΕΣΒΥΣ

δούλων γὰρ ἴδιον τοῦτο, σοὶ δὲ σύμφορον.

ΟΡΕΣΤΗΣ

πῶς οὖν ἂν αὐτῷ πλησιασθείην ποτέ;

ΠΡΕΣΒΥΣ

635  στείχων ὅθεν σε βουθυτῶν ἐσόψεται.

ΟΡΕΣΤΗΣ

ὁδὸν παρ᾽ αὐτήν, ὡς ἔοικ᾽, ἀγροὺς ἔχει;

ΠΡΕΣΒΥΣ

ὅθεν ⟨γ᾽⟩ ἰδών σε δαιτὶ κοινωνὸν καλεῖ.

ΟΡΕΣΤΗΣ

πικρόν γε συνθοινάτορ᾽, ἢν θεὸς θέλῃ.

631 fort. δμώων μὲν εἷς τις (Kovacs, cl. 852–3), οἱ δέ σ᾽ οὐκ
(Willink): etiam δμώων μέν εἰσὶν οἵ γε σ᾽ (aliqui saltem ex servis)
Willink      632 ⟨δ᾽⟩ Victorius      637 ⟨γ᾽⟩ Barnes

**ORESTES**

How many men were with him? Or was he accompanied only by slaves?

**OLD MAN**

No Argive citizen was present, only his household band.

**ORESTES**

No one, I suppose, who will recognize me on sight?

**OLD MAN**

The slaves are ones I have never seen.

**ORESTES**

But would they take our side if we should be victorious?

**OLD MAN**

Yes, for that is the nature of slaves and advantageous for you.

**ORESTES**

How then am I to get near him?

**OLD MAN**

Walk to a place from which he will see you as he sacrifices.

**ORESTES**

His fields, it seems, are right next to the road?

**OLD MAN**

Yes, and from there he will invite you to share in his feast.

**ORESTES**

And an unwelcome fellow feaster I shall prove, if heaven is willing!

ΠΡΕΣΒΥΣ

τοὐνθένδε πρὸς τὸ πῖπτον αὐτὸς ἐννόει.

ΟΡΕΣΤΗΣ

640    καλῶς ἔλεξας. ἡ τεκοῦσα δ᾽ ἐστὶ ποῦ;

ΠΡΕΣΒΥΣ

Ἄργει· παρέσται δ᾽ ἐν σκότῳ θοίνην ἔπι.

ΟΡΕΣΤΗΣ

τί δ᾽ οὐχ ἅμ᾽ ἐξώρμᾱτ᾽ ἐμὴ μήτηρ πόσει;

ΠΡΕΣΒΥΣ

ψόγον τρέμουσα δημοτῶν ἐλείπετο.

ΟΡΕΣΤΗΣ

ξυνῆχ᾽· ὕποπτος οὖσα γιγνώσκει πόλει.

ΠΡΕΣΒΥΣ

645    τοιαῦτα· μισεῖται γὰρ ἀνόσιος γυνή.

ΟΡΕΣΤΗΣ

πῶς οὖν ἐκεῖνον τήνδε τ᾽ ἐν ταὐτῷ κτάνω;

ΗΛΕΚΤΡΑ

ἐγὼ φόνον γε μητρὸς ἐξαρτύσομαι.

ΟΡΕΣΤΗΣ

καὶ μὴν ἐκεῖνά γ᾽ ἡ τύχη θήσει καλῶς.

ΗΛΕΚΤΡΑ

ὑπηρετείτω μὲν δυοῖν ὄντοιν ὅδε.

641 σκότῳ Weil: πόσει L        646 κτάνω Cobet: κτενῶ L
648 fort. θείη cl. Alc. 713
649 μὲν] δ᾽ εἷς Weil        ὅδε Tyrwhitt: τόδε L

222

**OLD MAN**

After that you yourself must improvise to suit the dice's fall.

**ORESTES**

Your advice is good. And where is my mother?

**OLD MAN**

In Argos. But she will join her husband for the feast when it is dark.

**ORESTES**

Why did my mother not set out with her husband?

**OLD MAN**

She stayed behind for fear of criticism from the people.

**ORESTES**

I understand: she knows the city looks askance at her.

**OLD MAN**

Right: they hate her as a godless woman.

**ORESTES**

How then can I kill the two of them at the same time?[16]

**ELECTRA**

I shall manage my mother's death.

**ORESTES**

Yes, and good luck will further your design.

**ELECTRA**

To begin with, let this man assist the two of us.

[16] I.e. so that one will not learn of the other's death and be on guard.

ΠΡΕΣΒΥΣ

650 ἔσται τάδ᾿· εὑρίσκεις δὲ μητρὶ πῶς φόνον;

ΗΛΕΚΤΡΑ

[λέγ᾿, ὦ γεραιέ, τάδε Κλυταιμήστρᾳ μολών·]
λεχώ μ᾿ ἀπάγγελλ᾿ οὖσαν ἄρσενος τόκῳ.

ΠΡΕΣΒΥΣ

πότερα πάλαι τεκοῦσαν ἢ νεωστὶ δή;

ΗΛΕΚΤΡΑ

δέχ᾿ ἡλίους, ἐν οἷσιν ἁγνεύει λεχώ.

ΠΡΕΣΒΥΣ

655 καὶ δὴ τί τοῦτο μητρὶ προσβάλλει φόνον;

ΗΛΕΚΤΡΑ

ἥξει κλυοῦσα λόχιά μου νοσήματα.

ΠΡΕΣΒΥΣ

πόθεν; †τί δ᾿ αὐτῇ† σοῦ μέλειν δοκεῖς, τέκνον;

ΗΛΕΚΤΡΑ

ναί· καὶ δακρύσει γ᾿ ἀξίωμ᾿ ἐμῶν τόκων.

ΠΡΕΣΒΥΣ

ἴσως· πάλιν μοι μῦθον ἐς καμπὴν ἄγε.

ΗΛΕΚΤΡΑ

660 ἐλθοῦσα μέντοι δῆλον ὡς ἀπόλλυται.

651 del. Matthiae
654 δέχ᾿ Elmsley: λέγ᾿ L
657 σὺ δ᾿ αὐτῇ Weil: τοιαύτη Diggle
659 μοι Diggle: τοι L: δὲ Camper    ἄγε Jortin: ἄγω L

224

OLD MAN

It shall be so. But how will you find a way to murder your mother?

ELECTRA

[Go to Clytaemestra, old man, and say the following to her.] Tell her that I have just given birth to a boy.

OLD MAN

Some time ago, or very recently?

ELECTRA

Ten days ago, the time a women who has given birth keeps pure.[17]

OLD MAN

But how will this lead to your mother's death?

ELECTRA

When she hears of my being in childbed, she will come.

OLD MAN

Why do you think so? Do you imagine that she cares about you, my child?

ELECTRA

Yes, and she will weep for the low standing of my baby.

OLD MAN

Perhaps: bring your tale to its last lap.

ELECTRA

If she comes, she will clearly be killed.

---

[17] In the Greek view birth, like death, produces a taint (*miasma*), and a woman abstains from intercourse with her husband to avoid passing it on. After ten days she is ritually purified by a sacrifice.

ΠΡΕΣΒΥΣ

καὶ μὴν ἐς αὐτάς γ' εἰσίτω δόμων πύλας.

ΗΛΕΚΤΡΑ

οὔκουν τραπέσθαι σμικρὸν εἰς Ἅιδου τότε;

ΠΡΕΣΒΥΣ

εἰ γὰρ θάνοιμι τοῦτ' ἰδὼν ἐγώ ποτε.

ΗΛΕΚΤΡΑ

πρώτιστα μέν νυν τῷδ' ὑφήγησαι, γέρον.

ΠΡΕΣΒΥΣ

665   Αἴγισθος ἔνθα νῦν θυηπολεῖ θεοῖς;

ΗΛΕΚΤΡΑ

ἔπειτ' ἀπαντῶν μητρὶ τἀπ' ἐμοῦ φράσον.

ΠΡΕΣΒΥΣ

ὥστ' αὐτά γ' ἐκ σοῦ στόματος εἰρῆσθαι δοκεῖν.

ΗΛΕΚΤΡΑ

σὸν ἔργον ἤδη· πρόσθεν εἴληχας φόνου.

ΟΡΕΣΤΗΣ

στείχοιμ' ἄν, εἴ τις ἡγεμὼν γίγνοιθ' ὁδοῦ.

ΠΡΕΣΒΥΣ

670   καὶ μὴν ἐγὼ πέμποιμ' ἂν οὐκ ἀκουσίως.

ΟΡΕΣΤΗΣ

ὦ Ζεῦ Πατρῷε καὶ Τροπαῖ' ἐχθρῶν ἐμῶν,
οἴκτιρον ἡμᾶς· οἰκτρὰ γὰρ πεπόνθαμεν.

---

661 ἐς Fix: ἐπ' L     εἰσίτω Musgrave: εἰσίω L     662 τότε
Kvíčala: τόδε L     672 οἴκτιρον Dobree: οἰκτίρεθ' L

**OLD MAN**

Well then, suppose she comes into the very gates of your house.

**ELECTRA**

Is not the journey thence to Hades brief?

**OLD MAN**

Once I have seen this, then may death come!

**ELECTRA**

So first, old man, lead Orestes on his way.

**OLD MAN**

To where Aegisthus is now sacrificing to the gods?

**ELECTRA**

Then go to see my mother and give her my message.

**OLD MAN**

I shall, so that it seems to come from your mouth.

**ELECTRA**

(*to Orestes*) Now it is your turn to work: you have drawn the first murder trial.[18]

**ORESTES**

I will go if someone will show me the way.

**OLD MAN**

I shall conduct you gladly.

**ORESTES**

Zeus, my fathers' god and router of my enemies, have pity on us, for our sufferings deserve pity!

[18] The language suggests Athenian legal procedure where prosecutors were assigned their time to appear in court by lot: cf. J. H. Kells, *CQ* 16 (1966), 51-2.

ΗΛΕΚΤΡΑ

οἴκτιρε δῆτα σοῦ γε φύντας ἐκγόνους.

ΟΡΕΣΤΗΣ

Ἥρα τε, βωμῶν ἢ Μυκηναίων κρατεῖς,
675  νίκην δὸς ἡμῖν, εἰ δίκαι᾽ αἰτούμεθα.

ΗΛΕΚΤΡΑ

δὸς δῆτα πατρὸς τοῖσδε τιμωρὸν δίκην.

ΟΡΕΣΤΗΣ

σύ τ᾽, ὦ κάτω γῆς ἀνοσίως οἰκῶν πάτερ
καὶ Γαῖ᾽ ἄνασσα, χεῖρας ᾗ δίδωμ᾽ ἐμάς,
ἄμυν᾽ ἄμυνε τοῖσδε φιλτάτοις τέκνοις·
680  νῦν πάντα νεκρὸν ἐλθὲ σύμμαχον λαβὼν
οἵπερ γε σὺν σοὶ Φρύγας ἀνήλωσαν δορὶ
683  χὤσοι στυγοῦσιν ἀνοσίους μιάστορας.
682  ἤκουσας, ὦ δείν᾽ ἐξ ἐμῆς μητρὸς παθών;

ΗΛΕΚΤΡΑ

πάντ᾽, οἶδ᾽, ἀκούει τάδε πατήρ· στείχειν δ᾽ ἀκμή.
685  καί σοι προφωνῶ πρὸς τάδ᾽ Αἴγισθον κτανεῖν,
ὡς εἰ παλαισθεὶς πτῶμα θανάσιμον πεσῇ,
τέθνηκα κἀγὼ μηδέ με ζῶσαν λέγε.
[παίσω κάρα γὰρ τοὐμὸν ἀμφήκει ξίφει·
δόμων ἔσω βᾶσ᾽ εὐτρεπὲς ποήσομαι.
690  ὡς ἢν μὲν ἔλθῃ πύστις εὐτυχὴς σέθεν,
ὀλολύξεται πᾶν δῶμα· θνήσκοντος δέ σου
τἀναντί᾽ ἔσται τῶνδε· ταῦτά σοι λέγω.]

---

673 σοῦ Barnes: σούς L     678 Γαῖ᾽ Musgrave: γῆ τ᾽ L

### ELECTRA
Yes, pity these descendants of yours![19]

### ORESTES
And Hera, ruler of Mycenae's altars, grant us victory if our prayer is just!

### ELECTRA
Yes, grant to these children here vengeance for their father!

### ORESTES
And you, father, impiously made to dwell under the ground, and Lady Earth, whom I strike with my hands, protect, O protect these beloved children of yours! Come with all the dead as your allies, those who helped you destroy the Trojans with the spear and those who detest unholy defilers! Father, who suffered dreadful things at my mother's hands, do you hear me?

### ELECTRA
He hears it all, I am sure. But now it is time to go. Be sure to kill Aegisthus! I tell you this beforehand in light of this: if in your wrestling match you take a deadly fall, I too am dead and you may speak of me as one who lives no more. [For I shall strike my heart with a two-edged sword. I shall go into the house and make it ready. If tidings of your good fortune are brought, the whole house will shout in triumph: if you die, it will be the reverse. I say this to you.]

---

[19] Zeus was the father of Tantalus, the great-great-grandfather of Orestes and Electra.

---

683 ante 682 trai. Reiske    685 κτανεῖν Seidler: θανεῖν L
688–92 del. Kovacs, 689–93 Wilamowitz

ΟΡΕΣΤΗΣ

πάντ᾽ οἶδα.

ΗΛΕΚΤΡΑ

πρὸς τάδ᾽ ἄνδρα γίγνεσθαί σε χρή.
ὑμεῖς δέ μοι, γυναῖκες, εὖ πυρσεύετε
695 κραυγὴν ἀγῶνος τοῦδε· φρουρήσω δ᾽ ἐγὼ
πρόχειρον ἔγχος χειρὶ βαστάζουσ᾽ ἐμῇ.
οὐ γάρ ποτ᾽ ἐχθροῖς τοῖς ἐμοῖς νικωμένη
δίκην ὑφέξω, σῶμ᾽ ἐμὸν καθυβρίσαι.

ΧΟΡΟΣ

στρ. α

ἀταλὰν ὑπὸ †ματέρος Ἀργείων†
700 ὀρέων ποτὲ κληδὼν
ἐν πολιαῖσι μένει φήμαις
εὐαρμόστοις ἐν καλάμοις
Πᾶνα μοῦσαν ἡδύθροον
πνέοντ᾽, ἀγρῶν ταμίαν,
705 χρυσέαν ἄρνα καλλίποκον
πορεῦσαι. πετρίνοις δ᾽ ἐπι-
στὰς κᾶρυξ ἴαχεν βάθροις·
Ἀγορὰν ἀγοράν, Μυκη-
ναῖοι, στείχετε μακαρίων
710 ὀψόμενοι τυράννων
φάσματα δεινά· χοροὶ δ᾽
⟨αὐτίκ᾽⟩ Ἀτρειδᾶν ἐγέραιρον οἴκους.

699 ἀταλὰν Page: ἀταλᾶς L      lac. indic. Willink, e.g.
⟨μηκάδος⟩ (Kovacs) Ἀργείων, tum 713 χρυσηλάτῳ ⟨ἀγλαΐᾳ⟩

230

**ORESTES**

I understand you perfectly.

**ELECTRA**

Therefore you must be brave.

But you, women, must cry out with beacon clarity the
result of this contest. I shall be on guard, a sword at the
ready in my hand. If I am defeated, I shall not allow my
enemies the satisfaction of outraging my body.

*Exit ELECTRA into the* skene, ORESTES, *Pylades, and* OLD
MAN *with retinue by Eisodos B.*

**CHORUS**

Once on a time a tender lamb taken from its mother
in the Argive mountains
(so runs the tale in our age-old legends)
did Pan, warder of the fields,
breathing sweet-voiced music
on well-joined reeds,
bring forth, a lamb with lovely fleece of gold.
And standing on a platform
of stone a herald shouted,
"To assembly, to assembly,
men of Mycenae,
to see the august portent
of your blessed rulers!" And choruses
⟨straightway⟩ hailed the house of the Atridae.

---

705 καλλίποκον Heath: καλλιπλόκαμον L
707 ἴαχεν Elmsley: ἰάχει L
711 δεινά Denniston: δείματα L
712 ⟨αὐτίκ᾽⟩ Denniston

231

ἀντ. α

θυμέλαι δ᾽ †ἐπίτναντο χρυσήλατοι†,
σελαγεῖτο δ᾽ ἀν᾽ ἄστυ
715   πῦρ ἐπιβώμιον Ἀργείων·
λωτὸς δὲ φθόγγον κελάδει
κάλλιστον, Μουσᾶν θεράπων.
μολπαὶ δ᾽ ηὔξονθ᾽ ἕτεραι
χρυσέας ἀρνὸς ἀμφὶ λόγοις
720   Θυέστου· κρυφίαις γὰρ εὐ-
ναῖς πείσας ἄλοχον φίλαν
Ἀτρέως, τέρας ἐκκομί-
ζει πρὸς δώματα, νεόμενος δ᾽
εἰς ἀγόρους αὐτεῖ
725   τὰν κερόεσσαν ἔχειν
στρ. β   χρυσεόμαλλον κατὰ δῶμα ποίμναν.

τότε δὴ τότε ⟨τὰς⟩ φαεν-
νὰς ἄστρων μετέβασ᾽ ὁδοὺς
Ζεὺς καὶ φέγγος ἀελίου
730   λευκόν τε πρόσωπον ἀ-
οῦς, τὰ δ᾽ ἕσπερα νῶτ᾽ ἐλαύ-
νει θερμᾷ φλογὶ θεοπύρῳ.
νεφέλαι δ᾽ ἔνυδροι πρὸς ἄρ-
κτον, ξηραί τ᾽ Ἀμμωνίδες ἔ-

---

713 vide 699      719 ἕτεραι Murray: ἐραταὶ L      ἀμφὶ
λόγοις Kovacs: ἐπίλογοι L      727 ⟨τὰς⟩ Willink
728 μετέβασ᾽ Musgrave: μεταβὰς L

The temples of wrought gold were opened,
and in Argos fire gleamed
on many an altar.
The pipe, servant of the Muses,
gave forth its fair melody.
But other were the songs that swelled in praise
of the golden lamb because of the words
of Thyestes: for with illicit love
he won over the dear wife
of Atreus and removed
this portent to his own house, and then coming
into the assembly he cried out
that he had in his house
the horned lamb with fleece of gold.

Then, then it was
that Zeus changed the bright courses of the stars,
the light of the sun
and the pale visage of the dawn
and made it march to the West's expanse
with its divine and burning heat.[20]
The clouds heavy with rain went toward the Bear,
and the dwelling place of Ammon wasted away

[20] Euripides alludes here, as at *Orestes* 1001-6, to the legend
that the sun used to rise in the west and set in the east until Zeus,
to show his disapproval of Thyestes' theft, caused it to change to
its present course. See M. L. West's edition of *Orestes* ad loc.

735 δραι φθίνουσ' ἀπειρόδροσοι,
κἀλλίστων ὄμβρων Διόθεν στερεῖσαι.

ἀντ. β

λέγεται ⟨τάδε⟩, τὰν δὲ πί-
στιν σμικρὰν παρ' ἔμοιγ' ἔχει,
στρέψαι θερμὰν ἀέλιον

740 χρυσωπὸν ἕδραν ἀλλά-
ξαντα δυστυχίᾳ βροτεί-
ῳ θνατᾶς ἕνεκεν δίκας.
φοβεροὶ δὲ βροτοῖσι μῦ-
θοι κέρδος πρὸς θεῶν θεραπεί-

745 ας. ὧν οὐ μνασθεῖσα πόσιν
κτείνεις, κλεινῶν συγγενέτειρ' ἀδελφῶν.

—ἔα ἔα·
φίλαι, βοῆς ἠκούσατ', ἢ δοκῶ κενὴ
ὑπῆλθέ μ', ὥστε νερτέρας βροντῆς Διός;
ἰδού, τάδ' οὐκ ἄσημα πνεύματ' αἴρεται·

750 δέσποιν', ἄμειψον δώματ', Ἠλέκτρα, τάδε.

HΛΕΚΤΡΑ

φίλαι, τί χρῆμα; πῶς ἀγῶνος ἥκομεν;

737 ⟨τάδε⟩ Weil
739 ἀέλιον Canter: -ίου L
740–1 ἀμείψαντα Dindorf
744–5 θεραπείας Matthiae: -είαις L
748 νερτέρας βροντῆς Bothe: -α -ῇ L

dry and bereft of water,[21]
robbed of the lovely rain that falls from Zeus.

That is the story men tell, but the credit
it receives from me is but slight,
that the gold-visaged sun should turn,
altering its torrid station
to cause mortals grief
for the punishment of their wrongdoing.
But fearful tales benefit mortals,
making them worship the gods,
the gods you forgot, kinswoman of glorious brothers,
when you murdered your husband.

*A distant cry is heard offstage.*

CHORUS LEADER
Ah! What is this? Friends, did you hear a shout (or was it
a mere fancy passing over me), like the roar of Zeus's thun-
der beneath the earth?

*Another cry is heard.*

There, that was a breath of air with a message on it! My
lady Electra, come out of the house!

*Enter* ELECTRA *from the house.*

ELECTRA
Friends, what has happened? How do we stand in the
battle?

[21] Ammon lies southward, in Libya; the Bear is in the north.

ΧΟΡΟΣ

οὐκ οἶδα πλὴν ἕν· φόνιον οἰμωγὴν κλύω.

ΗΛΕΚΤΡΑ

ἤκουσα κἀγώ, τηλόθεν μὲν ἀλλ᾽ ὅμως.

ΧΟΡΟΣ

μακρὰν γὰρ ἕρπει γῆρυς, ἐμφανής γε μήν.

ΗΛΕΚΤΡΑ

755  Ἀργεῖος ὁ στεναγμὸς ἢ φίλων ἐμῶν;

ΧΟΡΟΣ

οὐκ οἶδα· πᾶν γὰρ μείγνυται μέλος βοῆς.

ΗΛΕΚΤΡΑ

σφαγὴν ἀυτεῖς τήνδε μοι· τί μέλλομεν;

ΧΟΡΟΣ

ἔπισχε, τρανῶς ὡς μάθῃς τύχας σέθεν.

ΗΛΕΚΤΡΑ

οὐκ ἔστι· νικώμεσθα· ποῦ γὰρ ἄγγελοι;

ΧΟΡΟΣ

760  ἥξουσιν· οὗτοι βασιλέα φαῦλον κτανεῖν.

ΑΓΓΕΛΟΣ

ὦ καλλίνικοι παρθένοι Μυκηνίδες,
νικῶντ᾽ Ὀρέστην πᾶσιν ἀγγέλλω φίλοις,
Ἀγαμέμνονος δὲ φονέα κείμενον πέδῳ
Αἴγισθον· ἀλλὰ θεοῖσιν εὔχεσθαι χρεών.

755 στεναγμός· ἢ Willink
757 τῇδέ F. W. Schmidt

**CHORUS LEADER**

I know one thing only: I heard a cry of death.

**ELECTRA**

I heard it too, far off but audible.

**CHORUS LEADER**

The sound has far to travel, but it is clear.

**ELECTRA**

Was it the cry of an Argive or of those I love?

**CHORUS LEADER**

I don't know. The whole tune of the shouting was confused.

**ELECTRA**

Your words mean slaughter for me: why do I delay?

**CHORUS LEADER**

But stay, so that you may learn your fate for sure.

**ELECTRA**

I cannot. We are beaten. For where are our messengers?

**CHORUS LEADER**

They will come. It is no slight thing, you know, to kill a king.

*Enter servant of Orestes as* MESSENGER *by Eisodos B.*

**MESSENGER**

Maids of Mycenae, glorious in victory, I bring news to all who love him that Orestes is victorious and that Aegisthus, Agamemnon's murderer, has been struck down! So we must offer thanks to the gods.

ΗΛΕΚΤΡΑ

765 τίς δ' εἶ σύ; πῶς μοι πιστὰ σημαίνεις τάδε;

ΑΓΓΕΛΟΣ

οὐκ οἶσθ' ἀδελφοῦ μ' εἰσορῶσα πρόσπολον;

ΗΛΕΚΤΡΑ

ὦ φίλτατ', ἔκ τοι δείματος δυσγνωσίαν
εἶχον προσώπου· νῦν δὲ γιγνώσκω σε δή.
τί φής; τέθνηκε πατρὸς ἐμοῦ στυγνὸς φονεύς;

ΑΓΓΕΛΟΣ

770 τέθνηκε· δίς σοι ταῦθ', ἃ γοῦν βούλῃ, λέγω.

ΗΛΕΚΤΡΑ

ὦ θεοί, Δίκη τε πάνθ' ὁρῶσ', ἦλθές ποτε.
ποίῳ τρόπῳ δὲ καὶ τίνι ῥυθμῷ φόνου
κτείνει Θυέστου παῖδα; βούλομαι μαθεῖν.

ΑΓΓΕΛΟΣ

ἐπεὶ μελάθρων τῶνδ' ἀπήραμεν πόδα,
775 ἐσβάντες ἦμεν δίκροτον εἰς ἁμαξιτὸν
ἔνθ' ἦν ὁ καινὸς τῶν Μυκηναίων ἄναξ.
κυρεῖ δὲ κήποις ἐν καταρρύτοις βεβώς,
δρέπων τερείνης μυρσίνης κάρα πλόκους·
ἰδὼν δ' αὐτεῖ· Χαίρετ', ὦ ξένοι· τίνες
780 πόθεν πορεύεσθ' ἔστε τ' ἐκ ποίας χθονός;
ὁ δ' εἶπ' Ὀρέστης· Θεσσαλοί· πρὸς δ' Ἀλφεὸν
θύσοντες ἐρχόμεσθ' Ὀλυμπίῳ Διί.
κλυὼν δὲ ταῦτ' Αἴγισθος ἐννέπει τάδε·

776 καινὸς Kvíčala: κλεινὸς L

238

ELECTRA

Who are you? How can I trust what you tell me?

MESSENGER

Do you not know me, your brother's servant, by sight?

ELECTRA

Dear man, fear made me slow to recognize your face, but now I see who you are. What is this you say? My father's hateful murderer is dead?

MESSENGER

Yes, dead: I tell you the same welcome news twice.

ELECTRA

O gods and all-seeing Justice, at last you have come! But I want to know how and with what murderous stroke he killed Thyestes' son.

MESSENGER

After we left this house, we entered a broad wagon road and came to where the new king of Mycenae was. He happened to be standing in a well-watered garden, plucking tender myrtle to weave as a garland for his head. He saw us and shouted, "Hail, strangers! Who are you, where have you come from, and what is your native land?" Orestes said, "We are Thessalians, bound for the Alpheus River to make sacrifice to Olympian Zeus."[22] When Aegisthus heard this, he said, "Today you must share with me in

---

[22] Orestes represents himself as an athlete headed for the Olympic games.

---

<sup>780</sup> πορεύεσθ᾽ ἔστε Musgrave: πορεύεσθέ τ᾽ L

Νῦν μὲν παρ' ἡμῖν χρὴ συνεστίους ἐμοὶ
785 θοίνης γενέσθαι· τυγχάνω δὲ βουθυτῶν
Νύμφαις· ἑῷοι δ' ἐξαναστάντες λέχους
ἐς ταὐτὸν ἥξετ'. ἀλλ' ἴωμεν ἐς δόμους—
καὶ ταῦθ' ἅμ' ἠγόρευε καὶ χερὸς λαβὼν
παρῆγεν ἡμᾶς—οὐδ' ἀπαρνεῖσθαι χρεών.
790 ἐπεὶ δ' ἐν οἴκοις ἦμεν, ἐννέπει τάδε·
λούτρ' ὡς τάχιστα τοῖς ξένοις τις αἱρέτω,
ὡς ἀμφὶ βωμὸν στῶσι χερνίβων πέλας.
ἀλλ' εἶπ' Ὀρέστης· Ἀρτίως ἡγνίσμεθα
λουτροῖσι καθαροῖς ποταμίων ῥείθρων ἄπο.
795 εἰ δὲ ξένους ἀστοῖσι συνθύειν χρεών,
Αἴγισθ', ἕτοιμοι κοὐκ ἀπαρνούμεσθ', ἄναξ.
τοῦτον μὲν οὖν μεθεῖσαν ἐκ μέσου λόγον·
λόγχας δὲ θέντες δεσπότου φρουρήματα
δμῶες πρὸς ἔργον πάντες ἵεσαν χέρας·
800 οἱ μὲν σφαγεῖον ἔφερον, οἱ δ' ἦρον κανᾶ,
ἄλλοι δὲ πῦρ ἀνῆπτον ἀμφί τ' ἐσχάραις
λέβητας ὤρθουν· πᾶσα δ' ἐκτύπει στέγη.
λαβὼν δὲ προχύτας μητρὸς εὐνέτης σέθεν
ἔβαλλε βωμούς, τοιάδ' ἐννέπων ἔπη·
805 Νύμφαι πετραῖαι, πολλάκις με βουθυτεῖν
καὶ τὴν κατ' οἴκους Τυνδαρίδα δάμαρτ' ἐμὴν
πράσσοντας ὡς νῦν, τοὺς δ' ἐμοὺς ἐχθροὺς κακῶς—
λέγων Ὀρέστην καὶ σέ. δεσπότης δ' ἐμὸς

784 παρ' ἡμῖν] μένοντας L. v. Sybel     ἐμοὶ] ὁμοῦ Musgrave     785 θοίνης Reiske: θοίνην L

240

the feast at our house. I happen to be sacrificing a bullock to the Nymphs. Tomorrow if you get up at dawn, you will arrive just as quickly at your journey's end. But let us go into the house"—and as he spoke he took us by the hand and began to lead us from the road—"and you must not say no."

When we were inside the house, he said, "Someone quickly bring purifying water for the guests so that they may stand around the altar next to the lustral basins." But Orestes said, "We have but recently been cleansed by a pure bath in the running streams of a river.[23] So if it is right for strangers to help citizens at a sacrifice, Aegisthus, we are ready and do not refuse, my lord."

Thus they spoke standing in their midst, and the slaves laid aside the spears that guarded their master and put forth their hands to their work: some brought a bowl to catch the blood, others brought baskets, still others proceeded to light the fire and set cauldrons upright about the altar. The whole house resounded with activity.

Then your mother's husband took barley grains and cast them at the altar, saying as he did so, "You nymphs of the rock, may I and my wife, Tyndareus' daughter, who is at home, live to offer many such sacrifices while we enjoy our present good fortune, but may my enemies"—he meant you and Orestes—"fare badly." But my master prayed in-

---

[23] Orestes cleverly avoids accepting hospitality from Aegisthus and thereby becoming his guest, which would have made his murder the killing of a host.

---

[786] fort. τάχους    [797] ἐς μέσον Keene
[801] ἐσχάραις Wecklein: -ας L

τἀναντί’ ηὔχετ’, οὐ γεγωνίσκων λόγους,
810　λαβεῖν πατρῷα δώματ’. ἐκ κανοῦ δ’ ἑλὼν
Αἴγισθος ὀρθὴν σφαγίδα, μοσχείαν τρίχα
τεμὼν ἐφ’ ἁγνὸν πῦρ ἔθηκε δεξιᾷ,
κᾆσφαξ’ ἐπ’ ὤμων μόσχον ὡς ἦραν χεροῖν
δμῶες, λέγει δὲ σῷ κασιγνήτῳ τάδε·
815　Ἐν τῶν καλῶν κομποῦσι τοῖσι Θεσσαλοῖς
εἶναι τόδ’, ὅστις ταῦρον ἀρταμεῖ καλῶς
ἵππους τ’ ὀχμάζει· λαβὲ σίδηρον, ὦ ξένε,
δεῖξόν τε φήμην ἔτυμον ἀμφὶ Θεσσαλῶν.
　　ὁ δ’ εὐκρότητον Δωρίδ’ ἁρπάσας χεροῖν,
820　ῥίψας ἀπ’ ὤμων εὐπρεπῆ πορπάματα,
Πυλάδην μὲν εἵλετ’ ἐν πόνοις ὑπηρέτην,
δμῶας δ’ ἀπωθεῖ· καὶ λαβὼν μόσχου πόδα
λευκὰς ἐγύμνου σάρκας ἐκτείνων χερί·
θᾶσσον δὲ βύρσαν ἐξέδειρεν ἢ δρομεὺς
825　δισσοὺς διαύλους ἱππίους διήνυσ’ ἄν,
κἀνεῖτο λαγόνας. ἱερὰ δ’ ἐς χεῖρας λαβὼν
Αἴγισθος ἤθρει. καὶ λοβὸς μὲν οὐ προσῆν
σπλάγχνοις, πύλαι δὲ καὶ δοχαὶ χολῆς πέλας
κακὰς ἔφαινον τῷ σκοποῦντι προσβολάς.
830　χὠ μὲν σκυθράζει, δεσπότης δ’ ἀνιστορεῖ·
Τί χρῆμ’ ἀθυμεῖς; Ὦ ξέν’, ὀρρωδῶ τινα
δόλον θυραῖον. ἔστι δ’ ἔχθιστος βροτῶν
Ἀγαμέμνονος παῖς πολέμιός τ’ ἐμοῖς δόμοις·
ὁ δ’ εἶπε· Φυγάδος δῆτα δειμαίνεις δόλον,

823 χερί Musgrave: χέρα L

audibly for the opposite, that he should get back his father's house. Aegisthus took from a basket a straight-bladed sacrificial knife, cut off a hair of the calf and put it on the pure fire with his right hand, and then when the servants had lifted the calf onto their shoulders, he cut its throat. Then he said to your brother: "They say that the Thessalians regard it as a fine accomplishment to butcher a bullock or break a horse. Take the knife, stranger, and show the truth of the Thessalians' reputation."

Orestes took the well-wrought Doric blade in his hand and stripped his handsome cloak from his shoulders, and choosing Pylades as his assistant in the work he pushed the slaves back. Then he took the calf's foot and laid bare the white flesh beneath the skin by tugging at it with his hand. And in less time than a runner could have finished both legs of a hippodrome[24] he flayed off the hide and loosened the flanks. Aegisthus took the sacred portions into his hands and proceeded to inspect them. In the entrails the lobe of the liver was missing, and the portal vein and gall bladder showed that an attack of trouble for the observer was near at hand.

Aegisthus scowled, and my master asked him, "Why are you downcast?" "Stranger," he said, "I fear deceit from abroad. The son of Agamemnon is my bitterest personal enemy and is a foe to my house." But Orestes said, "Do you really fear the trickery of an exile when you are in

[24] Two legs of a hippodrome (twice the length of an ordinary race course) equal about 400 yards.

---

825 διήνυσ' ἄν Kovacs cl. *Med.* 1181–2: διήνυσεν L

835 πόλεως ἀνάσσων; οὐχ, ὅπως παστήρια
θοινασόμεσθα, Φθιάδ᾽ ἀντὶ Δωρικῆς
οἴσει τις ἡμῖν κοπίδ᾽ ἀναρρῆξαι χέλυν;
λαβὼν δὲ κόπτει. σπλάγχνα δ᾽ Αἴγισθος λαβὼν
ἤθρει διαιρῶν. τοῦ δὲ νεύοντος κάτω

840 ὄνυχας ἐπ᾽ ἄκρους στὰς κασίγνητος σέθεν
ἐς σφονδύλους ἔπαισε, νωτιαῖα δὲ
ἔρρηξεν ἄρθρα· πᾶν δὲ σῶμ᾽ ἄνω κάτω
ἤσπαιρεν ἠλέλιζε δυσθνήσκων φόνῳ.

     δμῶες δ᾽ ἰδόντες εὐθὺς ᾖξαν ἐς δόρυ,
845 πολλοὶ μάχεσθαι πρὸς δύ᾽· ἀνδρείας δ᾽ ὕπο
ἔστησαν ἀντίπρωρα σείοντες βέλη
Πυλάδης Ὀρέστης τ᾽. εἶπε δ᾽· Οὐχὶ δυσμενὴς
ἥκω πόλει τῇδ᾽ οὐδ᾽ ἐμοῖς ὀπάοσιν,
φονέα δὲ πατρὸς ἀντετιμωρησάμην

850 τλήμων Ὀρέστης· ἀλλὰ μή με καίνετε,
πατρὸς παλαιοὶ δμῶες. οἱ δ᾽, ἐπεὶ λόγων
ἤκουσαν, ἔσχον κάμακας· ἐγνώσθη δ᾽ ὑπὸ
γέροντος ἐν δόμοισιν ἀρχαίου τινός.

     στέφουσι δ᾽ εὐθὺς σοῦ κασιγνήτου κάρα
855 χαίροντες ἀλαλάζοντες. ἔρχεται δὲ σοὶ
κάρα 'πιδείξων οὐχὶ Γοργόνος φέρων
ἀλλ᾽ ὃν στυγεῖς Αἴγισθον· αἷμα δ᾽ αἵματος
πικρὸς δανεισμὸς ἦλθε τῷ θανόντι νῦν.

ΧΟΡΟΣ

στρ.
860 θὲς ἐς χορόν, ὦ φίλα, ἴχνος, ὡς νεβρὸς οὐράνιον

command of the city? Someone bring me a Phthian cleaver
in place of this Doric knife to break open the breast bone
so that we may feast on the innards!" When he had received
it, he smashed the breast bone. Aegisthus took the innards
and began to divide and inspect them. And as he was bend-
ing down, your brother standing on tip-toe struck him in
the spine and smashed his vertebrae: his whole body from
head to toe convulsed and shook in a bloody death agony.

When the slaves saw this, they rushed to their weapons,
a large number for two men to fight against. But Pylades
and Orestes courageously stood their ground, brandish-
ing their weapons in front of them. Then Orestes said, "I
have not come as the enemy of this city or of my servants.
Rather, I, Orestes the unfortunate, have taken vengeance
on my father's murderer. Do not kill me, former servants
of my father!" The slaves, when they had heard his words,
checked their spears, and Orestes was recognized by an old
servant in the house.

Immediately with rejoicing and shouts of joy they gar-
landed your brother's head. He is coming with something
to show you, not a Gorgon's head but Aegisthus whom you
hate. For the one who has died bloodshed has come as the
bitter return for bloodshed.

*Exit* MESSENGER *by Eisodos B.*

CHORUS

Lift your feet in dancing, dear friend, leap heaven-high

---

837 ἀναρρῆξαι Wecklein: ἀπορρήξω L
843 ἠλέλιζε Schenkl: ἠλάλαζεν L
850 καίνετε Elmsley: κτείν- L

πήδημα κουφίζουσα σὺν ἀγλαΐᾳ.
νικᾷ στεφαναφορίαν
†κρείσσω τοῖς† παρ' Ἀλφειοῦ ῥεέθροισι τελέσ-
σας κασίγνητος σέθεν· ἀλλ' ὑπάειδε
865   καλλίνικον ᾠδὰν ἐμῷ χορῷ.

ΗΛΕΚΤΡΑ

ὦ φέγγος, ὦ τέθριππον ἡλίου σέλας,
ὦ γαῖα καὶ νὺξ ἣν ἐδερκόμην πάρος,
νῦν ὄμμα τοὐμὸν ἀμπτυχαί τ' ἐλεύθεροι,
ἐπεὶ πατρὸς πέπτωκεν Αἴγισθος φονεύς.
870   φέρ', οἷα δὴ 'χω καὶ δόμοι κεύθουσί μου
κόμης ἀγάλματ' ἐξενέγκωμεν, φίλαι,
στέψω τ' ἀδελφοῦ κρᾶτα τοῦ νικηφόρου.

ΧΟΡΟΣ

ἀντ.

σὺ μέν νυν ἀγάλματ' ἄειρε κρατί· τὸ δ' ἀμέτερον
875   χωρήσεται Μούσαισι χόρευμα φίλον.
νῦν οἱ πάρος ἀμετέρας
γαίας τυραννεύσουσι φίλοι βασιλῆ-
ες δικαίως, τοὺς ἀδίκους καθελόντες.
ἀλλ' ἴτω ξύναυλος βοὰ χαρᾷ.

ΗΛΕΚΤΡΑ

880   ὦ καλλίνικε, πατρὸς ἐκ νικηφόρου

863 οὐ τὰν vel οὐχ ὡς Wecklein olim: οἴαν Dindorf
864 ὑπάειδε Blaydes: ἐπ- L
871 ἐξενέγκωμεν Lenting: -ωμαι L
876 ἀμετέρας Wecklein: -οι L

246

like a fawn in your rejoicing!
Your brother has completed, has won a crown of victory
greater than that by the streams of the Alpheus![25]
Accompany with your song of triumph
the steps of my dance!

ELECTRA

O light, O chariot-drawn blaze of the sun, O earth and the
night my gaze once looked upon, now I can open my eyes
in freedom since Aegisthus, my father's killer, has fallen!
Come, friends, let us bring out such adornments for his
hair as I possess and my house contains, and let me garland
the head of my victorious brother!

*Exit* ELECTRA *into the house.*

CHORUS

You, then, bring the adornments for his head.
But our dancing shall go on, dancing the Muses love.
Now shall our beloved kings of old
rule over our land
in justice since they have destroyed the wicked!
So let the cry of our voices go in concert with our joy!

*Enter* ELECTRA *with garlands from the house,* ORESTES
*and Pylades by Eisodos B, accompanied by attendants
bearing the body of Aegisthus, which they set down before
the house.*

ELECTRA

O Orestes, glorious in victory, son of the man who won the

---

[25] I.e. at the Olympic Games.

γεγώς, Ὀρέστα, τῆς ὑπ' Ἰλίῳ μάχης,
δέξαι κόμης σῆς βοστρύχων ἀνδήματα.
ἥκεις γὰρ οὐκ ἀχρεῖον ἔκπλεθρον δραμὼν
ἀγῶν' ἐς οἴκους ἀλλὰ πολέμιον κτανὼν
885  Αἴγισθον, ὃς σὸν πατέρα κἀμὸν ὤλεσεν.
       σύ τ', ὦ παρασπίστ', ἀνδρὸς εὐσεβεστάτου
παίδευμα Πυλάδη, στέφανον ἐξ ἐμῆς χερὸς
δέχου· φέρῃ γὰρ καὶ σὺ τῷδ' ἴσον μέρος
ἀγῶνος· αἰεὶ δ' εὐτυχεῖς φαίνοισθέ μοι.

ΟΡΕΣΤΗΣ

890  θεοὺς μὲν ἡγοῦ πρῶτον, Ἠλέκτρα, τύχης
ἀρχηγέτας τῆσδ', εἶτα κἄμ' ἐπαίνεσον
τὸν τῶν θεῶν τε τῆς τύχης θ' ὑπηρέτην.
ἥκω γὰρ οὐ λόγοισιν ἀλλ' ἔργοις κτανὼν
Αἴγισθον· †ὡς δὲ τῷ σάφ' εἰδέναι τάδε
895  προσθῶμεν†, αὐτὸν τὸν θανόντα σοι φέρω,
ὃν εἴτε χρῄζεις θηρσὶν ἁρπαγὴν πρόθες,
ἢ σκῦλον οἰωνοῖσιν, αἰθέρος τέκνοις,
πήξασ' ἔρεισον σκόλοπι· σὸς γάρ ἐστι νῦν
δοῦλος, πάροιθε δεσπότης κεκλημένος.

ΗΛΕΚΤΡΑ

900  αἰσχύνομαι μέν, βούλομαι δ' εἰπεῖν ὅμως.

ΟΡΕΣΤΗΣ

τί χρῆμα; λέξον· ὡς φόβου γ' ἔξωθεν εἶ.

‹ΗΛΕΚΤΡΑ›

νεκρόν περ ὄντα τόνδ' ὀνειδίσαι θέλω.

prize of victory in the war at Troy, accept this garland for
the tresses of your hair! You have come home: you have
run no futile furlong but have destroyed your enemy Aeg-
isthus, who killed your father and mine! (*She garlands
Orestes' head.*) And you, Pylades, his companion in arms,
nursling of a man most god-fearing, accept a garland from
my hand! For you win from this contest a prize equal to
his. Ever may I see you both in prosperity! (*She garlands
Pylades' head.*)

### ORESTES
Regard the gods first, Electra, as the authors of this turn
of fate, and thereafter praise me also, the servant of the
gods and of fate. I arrive having killed Aegisthus, not in
word but in deed: and in order to add to your clear knowl-
edge of this, I bring you the dead man himself. You may,
if you like, expose him as food for the wild beasts or spit
him on a crag as spoil for birds, the children of the air. For
he is now your slave, though formerly called your master.

### ELECTRA
I want to speak, but shame prevents me.

### ORESTES
What is it? Speak, since you are out of danger.

### ‹ELECTRA
I want to hurl abuse at this man, although he is dead.

---

894–5 τῳ . . . προθῶμεν Barnes: ὡς . . . προσθῶμεν delere
malebat Diggle
899 del. Naber
901 post h.v. lac. indic. Kovacs

ΟΡΕΣΤΗΣ

καὶ μὴν πάρεστι, τῇ τύχῃ τε χρηστέον.

ΗΛΕΚΤΡΑ

καὶ βούλομαι μὲν ταῦτα δρᾶν, δέδοικα δὲ . . .

ΟΡΕΣΤΗΣ

τί χρῆμα δρᾶσαι, σύγγον᾽, ἢ παθεῖν φοβῇ;>

ΗΛΕΚΤΡΑ

νεκροὺς ὑβρίζειν, μή μέ τις φθόνος βάλῃ.

ΟΡΕΣΤΗΣ

οὐκ ἔστιν οὐδεὶς ὅστις ἂν μέμψαιτό σε.

ΗΛΕΚΤΡΑ

δυσάρεστος ἡμῶν καὶ φιλόψογος πόλις.

ΟΡΕΣΤΗΣ

905  λέγ᾽, εἴ τι χρῄζεις, σύγγον᾽· ἀσπόνδοισι γὰρ
νόμοισιν ἔχθραν τῷδε συμβεβλήκαμεν.

ΗΛΕΚΤΡΑ

εἶέν· τίν᾽ ἀρχὴν πρῶτά σ᾽ ἐξείπω κακῶν,
ποίας τελευτάς; τίνα μέσον τάξω λόγον;
καὶ μὴν δι᾽ ὄρθρων γ᾽ οὔποτ᾽ ἐξελίμπανον
910  θρυλοῦσ᾽ ἅ γ᾽ εἰπεῖν ἤθελον κατ᾽ ὄμμα σόν,
εἰ δὴ γενοίμην δειμάτων ἐλευθέρα
τῶν πρόσθε. νῦν οὖν ἐσμεν· ἀποδώσω δέ σοι
ἐκεῖν᾽ ἅ σε ζῶντ᾽ ἤθελον λέξαι κακά.

---

902 φθόνος Tyrwhitt: -ῳ L

ORESTES

You may: make use of your good fortune.

ELECTRA

I want to, but I am afraid . . .

ORESTES

Of doing or suffering what, sister?›

ELECTRA

. . . to insult the dead lest I be struck by some ill will.

ORESTES

There is no one who will find fault with you.

ELECTRA

Our city is peevish and inclined to criticize.

ORESTES

Speak if you want, sister. For our enmity against this man admits no truce.

ELECTRA

Well then.[26] What beginning shall I make of insult, what end? What theme shall I put in the center? Yet in the early morning hours I never ceased from rehearsing what I wanted to say to your face if ever I should be freed from the fears that are now past. Now I am free, and I shall pay out to you the insults that I wanted to pay you while you lived.

[26] Several portions of this speech, addressed to the dead Aegisthus, have been suspected of being interpolated, and I have bracketed the likeliest suspects and recorded others in the notes to the Greek. In addition there seems to be a lacuna after line 914 (the join with 915 seems to me impossible), and I have supplied lines that would be appropriate in the speech, restore the grammar, and account for the omission.

251

ἀπώλεσάς με κὠρφανὴν φίλου πατρὸς
&lt;πικρῶς ἔθηκας· ὅν γ' ἄφαρκτον ἐκ λόχου
ἔκτεινας, ἔργου δ' ἦν σύνεργός σοι γυνή.
κοὐκ ἤρκεσεν ταῦτ', ἀλλ' ἐπεί μ' ὥρα γάμου
εἶχ', ἐξέδωκας εὐγενῶν μὲν οὐδενί,
χέρνητι δ' ἀνδρὶ τῷδε, θανάσιμον γάμον,
φυγάδα δ' Ὀρέστην ἐξεκήρυξας κτανεῖν,
τὸν δὲ κτανόντα δυσσεβῶς χρυσὸν πολὺν
λαβεῖν· πατρῴων κἀμὲ τητᾶσθαι δόμων&gt;
915   καὶ τόνδ' ἔθηκας, οὐδὲν ἠδικημένος.

κἄγημας αἰσχρῶς μητέρ' ἄνδρα τ' ἔκτανες
στρατηλατοῦνθ' Ἕλλησιν, οὐκ ἐλθὼν Φρύγας.
ἐς τοῦτο δ' ἦλθες ἀμαθίας ὥστ' ἤλπισας
ὡς ἐς σὲ μὲν δὴ μητέρ' οὐχ ἕξοις κακὴν
920   γήμας, ἐμοῦ δὲ πατρὸς ἠδίκει λέχη.
[ἴστω δ', ὅταν τις διολέσας δάμαρτά του
κρυπταῖσιν εὐναῖς εἶτ' ἀναγκασθῇ λαβεῖν,
δύστηνός ἐστιν, εἰ δοκεῖ τὸ σωφρονεῖν
ἐκεῖ μὲν αὐτὴν οὐκ ἔχειν, παρ' οἷ δ' ἔχειν.]
925   ἄλγιστα δ' ᾤκεις, οὐ δοκῶν οἰκεῖν κακῶς·
ᾔδησθα γὰρ δῆτ' ἀνόσιον γήμας γάμον,
μήτηρ δὲ σ' ἄνδρα δυσσεβῆ κεκτημένη.
ἄμφω πονηρὼ δ' ὄντ' ἀνηρεῖσθον τύχην
κείνη τε τὴν σὴν καὶ σὺ τοὐκείνης κακόν.
930   πᾶσιν δ' ἐν Ἀργείοισιν ἤκουες τάδε·
ὁ τῆς γυναικός, οὐχὶ τἀνδρὸς ἡ γυνή.

914 post h. v. lac. indic. Kovacs, diffidenter suppl.

You destroyed my life and ⟨cruelly⟩ bereft me of my father, ⟨for you caught him off his guard from an ambush with a woman as your helper. But that was not enough for you: when I came of age you married me to none of the nobility but to this laboring man, a marriage like a death, and the proclamation was made to kill the exiled Orestes and that his impious killer should be richly rewarded. Both me⟩ and him you have caused ⟨to be deprived of our paternal home⟩ though we had done you no wrong.

You shamefully married my mother and killed the man who was general over the Greeks though you had not gone to Troy. And you were so far gone in folly that you imagined that if you married my mother you would find in her no bad wife, though she was unfaithful to the bed of my father. [If a man corrupts another's wife by illicit love and then is compelled to take her as wife, he should know that he is a poor fool if he imagines that in her former marriage she had no chastity but has it in his house.]

The life you lived was miserable, although people did not think you lived badly. You knew that you had made an impious marriage, and my mother knew that in you she possessed a godless husband. Wicked both, the pair of you took on each other's lot, she yours and you her villainy. And among all the Argives this was said of you, "The man belongs to his wife, not she to him." Yet it is a disgrace for the

---

916–20 suspectos hab. Kovacs     920 ἠδίκει Canter: -εις L
921–4 del. Hartung     928 ἀνηρεῖσθον Walberg: ἀφαιρ- L
929 fort. τοῦ σοῦ . . . τοῦ κείνης κακοῦ
930–7 suspectos hab. Kovacs (932–7 Wecklein)

καίτοι τόδ᾽ αἰσχρόν, προστατεῖν γε δωμάτων
γυναῖκα, μὴ τὸν ἄνδρα· κἀκείνους στυγῶ
τοὺς παῖδας, ὅστις τοῦ μὲν ἄρσενος πατρὸς
935 οὐκ ὠνόμασται, τῆς δὲ μητρὸς ἐν πόλει.
ἐπίσημα γὰρ γήμαντι καὶ μείζω λέχη
τἀνδρὸς μὲν οὐδείς, τῶν δὲ θηλειῶν λόγος.

ὃ δ᾽ ἠπάτα σε πλεῖστον οὐκ ἐγνωκότα,
ηὔχεις τις εἶναι τοῖσι χρήμασι σθένων·
940 τὰ δ᾽ οὐδὲν εἰ μὴ βραχὺν ὁμιλῆσαι χρόνον.
ἡ γὰρ φύσις βέβαιος, οὐ τὰ χρήματα.
ἡ μὲν γὰρ αἰεὶ παραμένουσ᾽ αἴρει κακά·
ὃ δ᾽ ὄλβος ἀδίκως καὶ μετὰ σκαιῶν ξυνὼν
ἐξέπτατ᾽ οἴκων, σμικρὸν ἀνθήσας χρόνον.

945 ἃ δ᾽ ἐς γυναῖκας (παρθένῳ γὰρ οὐ καλὸν
λέγειν) σιωπῶ, γνωρίμως δ᾽ αἰνίξομαι·
ὕβριζες, ὡς δὴ βασιλικοὺς ἔχων δόμους
κάλλει τ᾽ ἀραρώς. ἀλλ᾽ ἔμοιγ᾽ εἴη πόσις
μὴ παρθενωπὸς ἀλλὰ τἀνδρείου τρόπου.
950 τὰ γὰρ τέκν᾽ αὐτῶν Ἄρεος ἐκκρεμάννυται,
τὰ δ᾽ εὐπρεπῆ δὴ κόσμος ἐν χοροῖς μόνον.

ἔρρ᾽, οὐδὲν εἰδὼς σῶν· ἐφευρεθεὶς χρόνῳ
δίκην δέδωκας. ὧδέ τις κακοῦργος ὢν
μή μοι τὸ πρῶτον βῆμ᾽ ἐὰν δράμῃ καλῶς
955 νικᾶν δοκείτω τὴν Δίκην, πρὶν ἂν πέρας
γραμμῆς ἵκηται καὶ τέλος κάμψῃ βίου.

934 πατρὸς] παρὸν Camper
941–4 del. Bruhn

254

woman, rather than the man, to be the head of a house. I loathe any child who derives his name in the city not from his father but from his mother. For when a man marries a wife of greater eminence than himself, no account is taken of the man but only of his wife.

But where you were most deceived and mistaken was that you thought you were really someone on the strength of your money. But money does nothing except to stay with us a short while. It is character that is reliable, not money. Character stands beside us always and shoulders our troubles, while wealth lives unjustly with fools and then flies off from their houses, having blossomed for only a short time.

Your conduct toward women (since it ill befits a virgin to describe it) I pass over in silence, but I shall give an intelligible hint. You acted with outrage thinking that you had a king's house and were well provided with good looks. But I would rather have a husband who is not girlish in his looks but of the manly sort. For children of the manly hold fast to valor, while the pretty ones are only good to adorn a chorus.

Be gone, then, man of unsound thoughts: unmasked by Time, you have paid the penalty! Therefore let not the criminal imagine, just because he has run his first steps well, that he is victorious over Justice until he reaches the finish line and runs life's final lap!

---

952 σῶν Radermacher: ὧν L
955 πέρας Weil: πέλας L: τέλος tt

ΧΟΡΟΣ

ἔπραξε δεινά, δεινὰ δ᾿ ἀντέδωκε σοὶ
καὶ τῷδ᾿· ἔχει γὰρ ἡ Δίκη μέγα σθένος.

ΟΡΕΣΤΗΣ

εἶέν· κομίζειν τοῦδε σῶμ᾿ ἔσω χρεὼν
960  σκότῳ τε δοῦναι, δμῶες, ὡς, ὅταν μόλῃ
μήτηρ, σφαγῆς πάροιθε μὴ ᾿σίδῃ νεκρόν.

ΗΛΕΚΤΡΑ

ἐπίσχες· ἐμβάλωμεν εἰς ἄλλον λόγον.

ΟΡΕΣΤΗΣ

τί δ᾿; ἐκ Μυκηνῶν μῶν βοηδρόμους ὁρᾷς;

ΗΛΕΚΤΡΑ

οὔκ, ἀλλὰ τὴν τεκοῦσαν ἥ μ᾿ ἐγείνατο.

ΟΡΕΣΤΗΣ

966  καὶ μὴν ὄχοις γε καὶ στολῇ λαμπρύνεται.

ΗΛΕΚΤΡΑ

965  καλῶς ἄρ᾿ ἄρκυν ἐς μέσην πορεύεται.

ΟΡΕΣΤΗΣ

τί δῆτα δρῶμεν; μητέρ᾿ ἦ φονεύσομεν;

ΗΛΕΚΤΡΑ

μῶν σ᾿ οἶκτος εἷλε, μητρὸς ὡς εἶδες δέμας;

962 ἐσβάλλωμεν Diggle
963 ὁρᾷς Bothe: ὁρῶ L
965, 966 invicem transposuit Kirchhoff
966 γε Schaefer: τε L

**CHORUS LEADER**

Terrible were his deeds, and terrible the recompense he has paid you and Orestes. Justice is mighty indeed.

**ORESTES**

Well then, servants, now you must take this man's body into the house and consign it to the dark so that when my mother comes she may not see the corpse before she is killed.

*The attendants take Aegisthus' body into the house.*

**ELECTRA**

(*looking toward Eisodos A*) Stay! Let us talk of another subject!

**ORESTES**

What is it? Do you perhaps see soldiers from Mycenae[27] come to Aegisthus' aid?

**ELECTRA**

No: it is the mother who gave me birth.

**ORESTES**

And see how splendidly she goes in her chariot and finery!

**ELECTRA**

How grandly, then, she walks into the middle of our trap!

**ORESTES**

What then shall we do? Shall we kill our mother?

**ELECTRA**

Surely you are not seized by pity since you caught sight of your mother in person?

[27] See note on line 35 above.

ΟΡΕΣΤΗΣ

φεῦ·

πῶς γὰρ κτάνω νιν, ἥ μ' ἔθρεψε κἄτεκεν;

ΗΛΕΚΤΡΑ

970 ὥσπερ πατέρα σὸν ἥδε κἀμὸν ὤλεσεν.

ΟΡΕΣΤΗΣ

ὦ Φοῖβε, πολλήν γ' ἀμαθίαν ἐθέσπισας . . .

ΗΛΕΚΤΡΑ

ὅπου δ' Ἀπόλλων σκαιὸς ᾖ, τίνες σοφοί;

ΟΡΕΣΤΗΣ

. . . ὅστις μ' ἔχρησας μητέρ', ἣν οὐ χρή, κτανεῖν.

ΗΛΕΚΤΡΑ

βλάπτῃ δὲ δὴ τί πατρὶ τιμωρῶν σέθεν;

ΟΡΕΣΤΗΣ

975 μητροκτόνος νῦν φεύξομαι, τόθ' ἁγνὸς ὤν.

ΗΛΕΚΤΡΑ

καὶ μή γ' ἀμύνων πατρὶ δυσσεβὴς ἔσῃ.

ΟΡΕΣΤΗΣ

ἐγῷδα· μητρὸς δ' οὐ φόνου δώσω δίκας;

ΗΛΕΚΤΡΑ

τί δ' ἦν πατρῴαν διαμεθῇς τιμωρίαν;

973 χρή Kovacs: χρῆν L
977 ἐγῷδα Musgrave: ἐγὼ δὲ L     δ' οὐ Herwerden: τοῦ L
978 τί δ' ἦν Nauck: τῷ; δαὶ L

**ORESTES**

Ah me! How can I kill her, the woman who bore and nurtured me?

**ELECTRA**

In just the way she killed your father and mine.

**ORESTES**

Phoebus Apollo, there was much folly in your oracle . . .

**ELECTRA**

But where Apollo is foolish, who is wise?

**ORESTES**

. . . seeing that you bade me kill one I should not kill, my mother.

**ELECTRA**

But what harm will you suffer if you avenge your father?

**ORESTES**

I shall be exiled as a matricide, though formerly I was free of stain.

**ELECTRA**

And if you do not avenge your father, you will be guilty of impiety.

**ORESTES**

I know. But shall I not be punished for my mother's murder?

**ELECTRA**

But what will happen if you neglect to avenge your father?

ΟΡΕΣΤΗΣ

ἆρ' αὔτ' ἀλάστωρ εἶπ' ἀπεικασθεὶς θεῷ;

ΗΛΕΚΤΡΑ

980 ἱερὸν καθίζων τρίποδ'; ἐγὼ μὲν οὐ δοκῶ.

ΟΡΕΣΤΗΣ

οὔ τἂν πιθοίμην εὖ μεμαντεῦσθαι τάδε.

ΗΛΕΚΤΡΑ

οὐ μὴ κακισθεὶς εἰς ἀνανδρίαν πεσῇ,
ἀλλ' εἶ τὸν αὐτὸν τῇδ' ὑποστήσων δόλον
ᾧ καὶ πόσιν καθεῖλες Αἴγισθον κτανών;

ΟΡΕΣΤΗΣ

985 ἔσειμι· δεινοῦ δ' ἄρχομαι προβλήματος
καὶ δεινὰ δράσω. θεοῖσι δ' εἰ δοκεῖ τάδε,
ἔστω· πικρὸν δ', οὐχ ἡδύ, τἀγώνισμά μοι.

ΧΟΡΟΣ

ἰὼ ⟨ἰώ⟩,
βασίλεια γύναι χθονὸς Ἀργείας,
παῖ Τυνδάρεω,
990 καὶ τοῖν ἀγαθοῖν ξύγγονε κούροιν
Διός, οἳ φλογερὰν αἰθέρ' ἐν ἄστροις
ναίουσι, βροτῶν ἐν ἁλὸς ῥοθίοις
τιμὰς σωτῆρας ἔχοντες·

981 οὔ τἂν Hermann: οὐδ' ἂν L
982 πεσῇ Elmsley: πέσῃς L
983–4 Electrae contin. Weil: 983 Oresti, 984 Electrae trib. L
983 εἶ . . . ὑποστήσων Weil: εἰς . . . -σω L     984 καθεῖλες
Tr²: -εν L, quo servato Αἰγίσθου μέτα Wilamowitz

ORESTES

Were these commands spoken by a spirit of destruction
disguised as the god?

ELECTRA

Seated on the holy tripod? I scarcely think so.

ORESTES

I cannot believe that such an oracle is good.

ELECTRA

Don't play the coward and be unmanly but go practice the
same guile on her as you used to kill Aegisthus, her hus-
band!

ORESTES

I will go inside. Dreadful is the sacrifice I am beginning,
and dreadful is the deed I shall do. But if it is the gods' will,
so be it. Yet this contest to me is not sweet but bitter.

*Exit* ORESTES *and Pylades into the house. Enter by Eisodos
A* CLYTAEMESTRA *in a chariot, followed by a wagon bear-
ing slaves.*

CHORUS LEADER

Hail, queen of Argos, daughter of Tyndareus, sister to the
noble sons of Zeus, who dwell in the fiery upper air amid
the stars and are worshiped as saviors of mortals amid

---

985 προβήματος Denniston

986 δράσω. θεοῖσι δ᾽ εἰ Weil: δράσω. εἰ θεοῖς L: δράσω γ᾽. εἰ
θ. Tr¹

987 δ᾽ οὐχ ἡδὺ Musgrave: δὲ καὶ ἡδὺ L

988 ⟨ἰώ⟩ Wilamowitz

χαῖρε, σεβίζω σ᾿ ἴσα καὶ μάκαρας
995   πλούτου μεγάλης τ᾿ εὐδαιμονίας.
τὰς σὰς δὲ τύχας θεραπεύεσθαι
καιρός, ‹πότνι᾿› ὦ βασίλεια.

ΚΛΥΤΑΙΜΗΣΤΡΑ

ἔκβητ᾿ ἀπήνης, Τρῳάδες, χειρὸς δ᾿ ἐμῆς
λάβεσθ᾿, ἵν᾿ ἔξω τοῦδ᾿ ὄχου στήσω πόδα.
1000  σκύλοισι μὲν γὰρ θεῶν κεκόσμηνται δόμοι
Φρυγίοις, ἐγὼ δὲ τάσδε, Τρῳάδος χθονὸς
ἐξαίρετ᾿, ἀντὶ παιδὸς ἣν ἀπώλεσα
σμικρὸν γέρας, καλὸν δὲ κέκτημαι δόμοις.

ΗΛΕΚΤΡΑ

οὔκουν ἐγώ (δούλη γὰρ ἐκβεβλημένη
1005  δόμων πατρῴων δυστυχεῖς οἰκῶ δόμους),
μῆτερ, λάβωμαι μακαρίας τῆς σῆς χερός;

ΚΛΥΤΑΙΜΗΣΤΡΑ

δοῦλαι πάρεισιν αἵδε· μὴ σύ μοι πόνει.

ΗΛΕΚΤΡΑ

τί δ᾿; αἰχμάλωτόν τοί μ᾿ ἀπῴκισας δόμων,
ἠρημένων δὲ δωμάτων ἠρήμεθα,
1010  ὡς αἵδε, πατρὸς ὀρφανοὶ λελειμμένοι.

ΚΛΥΤΑΙΜΗΣΤΡΑ

τοιαῦτα μέντοι σὸς πατὴρ βουλεύματα

997 ‹πότνι᾿› Diggle
1010 ὀρφανοὶ λελειμμένοι praemonente Seidler Fix: -αὶ -αι L
1011 βουλεύματα Victorius: -εύεται L

the waves of the sea! Greeting: I worship you as I do the blessed gods for your great wealth and good fortune! And now, my ⟨lady⟩ queen, is the time for your fortunes to be honored!

### CLYTAEMESTRA

Get down from the wagon, Trojan maids, and take my hand in order that I may step from this car! The temples of the gods are adorned with Trojan spoils, and I have acquired for my house these slaves, pick of the land of Troy, a small badge of honor but a fine one, to replace the daughter I lost.[28]

*The attendants get down and help Clytaemestra to descend.*

### ELECTRA

Since I am a slave, cast out of my father's house, and live in a house of misery, shall not I, mother, take your heaven-blessed hand?

### CLYTAEMESTRA

There are slaves here for that. Do not give yourself toil on my account.

### ELECTRA

Why not? After all, you have made me live far from my home like a captive: with my house destroyed I am destroyed as well, and like these slaves, left orphaned of my father.

### CLYTAEMESTRA

Well, that is the kind of plot your father made against those

---

[28] See note on line 29 above.

ἐς οὓς ἐχρῆν ἥκιστ᾽ ἐβούλευσεν φίλων.
λέξω δέ. καίτοι δόξ᾽ ὅταν λάβῃ κακὴ
γυναῖκα, γλώσσῃ πικρότης ἔνεστί τις,
1015  ὡς μὲν παρ᾽ ἡμῖν, οὐ καλῶς· τὸ πρᾶγμα δὲ
μαθόντας, ἢν μὲν ἀξίως μισεῖν ἔχῃ,
στυγεῖν δίκαιον· εἰ δὲ μή, τί δεῖ στυγεῖν;
   ἡμᾶς δ᾽ ἔδωκε Τυνδάρεως τῷ σῷ πατρὶ
οὐχ ὥστε θνῄσκειν οὐδ᾽ ἃ γειναίμην ἐγώ.
1020  κεῖνος δὲ παῖδα τὴν ἐμὴν Ἀχιλλέως
λέκτροισι πείσας ᾤχετ᾽ ἐκ δόμων ἄγων
πρυμνοῦχον Αὖλιν, ἔνθ᾽ ὑπερτείνας πυρᾶς
λευκὴν διήμησ᾽ Ἰφιγόνης παρηίδα.
κεἰ μὲν πόλεως ἄλωσιν ἐξιώμενος
1025  ἢ δῶμ᾽ ὀνήσων τἆλλα τ᾽ ἐκσῴζων τέκνα
ἔκτεινε πολλῶν μίαν ὕπερ, συγγνώστ᾽ ἂν ἦν·
νῦν δ᾽ οὕνεχ᾽ Ἑλένη μάργος ἦν ὅ τ᾽ αὖ λαβὼν
ἄλοχον κολάζειν προδότιν οὐκ ἠπίστατο,
τούτων ἕκατι παῖδ᾽ ἐμὴν διώλεσεν.
1030     ἐπὶ τοῖσδε τοίνυν καίπερ ἠδικημένη
οὐκ ἠγριώμην οὐδ᾽ ἂν ἔκτανον πόσιν.
ἀλλ᾽ ἦλθ᾽ ἔχων μοι μαινάδ᾽ ἔνθεον κόρην
λέκτροις τ᾽ ἐπεισέφρησε, καὶ νύμφα δύο
ἐν τοῖσιν αὐτοῖς δώμασιν κατεῖχ᾽ ὁμοῦ.
1035  μῶρον μὲν οὖν γυναῖκες, οὐκ ἄλλως λέγω·
ὅταν δ᾽, ὑπόντος τοῦδ᾽, ἁμαρτάνῃ πόσις
τἄνδον παρώσας λέκτρα, μιμεῖσθαι θέλει
γυνὴ τὸν ἄνδρα χἄτερον κτᾶσθαι φίλον.

of his kin he ought least to have plotted against. Still, I shall speak. Yet when evil repute takes a woman as its prey, her words have an unwelcome character to them: most unfairly, in my judgment, for though it is proper to hate when one has learned the facts and hating is justified, when that is not the case, why should one hate?

My father Tyndareus did not give me to your father so that I or the children I bore should be killed. Yet that man, enticing my child with a marriage to Achilles, went off with her to the harbor at Aulis, and there, stretching Iphigenia out above an altar, he slit her pale white throat. If he had killed one child for the sake of many, trying to avert the sack of our city or to benefit our house and save our other children, it would be forgivable. But as it is, he killed her only because Helen was a whore and the man who married her did not know how to chastise the wife who betrayed him.

Well, even though I was wronged, it was not this that made me savage, and not for this would I have killed him. But he came home with the god-possessed seer girl[29] and installed her in his bed and meant to keep two women at the same time in the same house. Woman, to be sure, is a thing of folly, I do not deny it. Yet, with this fact as given, when a husband errs by rejecting the woman in his house, the wife desires to imitate her husband and acquire a new

[29] The Trojan princess Cassandra, who was given prophetic powers by Apollo.

1016 ἔχῃ Seidler: ἔχῃς L    1025 ἐκσώσων Nauck
1033 εἰσέφρησε Dawes: -κε L
1034 κατεῖχ᾿ ὁμοῦ Dawes: κατείχομεν L

κἄπειτ᾽ ἐν ἡμῖν ὁ ψόγος λαμπρύνεται,
1040 οἱ δ᾽ αἴτιοι τῶνδ᾽ οὐ κλύουσ᾽ ἄνδρες κακῶς.
   [εἰ δ᾽ ἐκ δόμων ἥρπαστο Μενέλεως λάθρᾳ,
κτανεῖν μ᾽ Ὀρέστην χρῆν, κασιγνήτης πόσιν
Μενέλαον ὡς σώσαιμι; σὸς δὲ πῶς πατὴρ
ἠνέσχετ᾽ ἂν ταῦτ᾽; εἶτα τὸν μὲν οὐ θανεῖν
1045 κτείνοντα χρῆν τἄμ᾽, ἐμὲ δὲ πρὸς κείνου παθεῖν;]
   ⟨τάχ᾽ οὖν ἂν εἴποις ὡς σὺν ἀνδρὶ δυσμενεῖ⟩
ἔκτειν᾽. ἐτρέφθην ἥπερ ἦν πορεύσιμον
πρὸς τοὺς ἐκείνῳ πολεμίους. φίλων γὰρ ἂν
τίς ἂν φόνου σοῦ πατρὸς ἐκοινώνησέ μοι;
λέγ᾽ εἴ τι χρῄζεις κἀντίθες παρρησίᾳ,
1050 ὅπως τέθνηκε σὸς πατὴρ οὐκ ἐνδίκως.

ΧΟΡΟΣ

δίκαι᾽ ἔλεξας· ἡ δίκη δ᾽ αἰσχρῶς ἔχει.
γυναῖκα γὰρ χρὴ πάντα συγχωρεῖν πόσει,
ἥτις φρενήρης· ᾗ δὲ μὴ δοκεῖ τάδε,
οὐδ᾽ εἰς ἀριθμὸν τῶν ἐμῶν ἥκει λόγων.

⟨ΗΛΕΚΤΡΑ⟩

1055 μέμνησο, μῆτερ, οὓς ἔλεξας ὑστάτους
λόγους, διδοῦσα πρός σέ μοι παρρησίαν.

ΚΛΥΤΑΙΜΗΣΤΡΑ

καὶ νῦν γέ φημι κοὐκ ἀπαρνοῦμαι, τέκνον.

1041–5 del. Wilamowitz
1046 ante h. v. lac. indic. Diggle      v. distinxit Kovacs
1048 φόνου σοῦ πατρὸς Denniston: π- σ- φόνον L
1051n Χο. Camper: Ηλ. L

lover. And after this it is we who are loudly blamed, while men, the authors of this situation, hear no criticism!

[If Menelaus had been abducted from his house in secret, would I have been right to kill Orestes in order to preserve Menelaus, my sister's husband? How would your father have put up with that? So can you claim it would have been wrong for him to be killed for killing my child, yet right for me to suffer at his hands?]

⟨Perhaps you will say that it was with the help of his enemy that⟩ I did the killing. I turned down the only path I could travel, to those who were his foes. For who that loved him would have shared in your father's murder with me?

If you so desire, speak and tell me in perfect liberty how it was unjust that your father was killed.

CHORUS LEADER

You plead justice, but the justice you plead is shameful. A woman, one who is sound in mind, ought to accede in all things to her husband's wishes. Anyone who disagrees with this does not even enter into consideration with me.

⟨ELECTRA⟩

Remember, mother, the last words you said, giving me liberty to speak to you.

CLYTAEMESTRA

That is what I say now, and I do not unsay it, my child.

---

1052 χρὴ Matthiae: χρῆν L
1053 ᾗ Reiske: εἰ L
1054 λόγων] φίλων Blaydes
1055n ⟨Ἠλ.⟩ Camper

ΗΛΕΚΤΡΑ

ἆρ' ἂν κλυοῦσα, μῆτερ, εἶτ' ἔρξαις κακῶς;

ΚΛΥΤΑΙΜΗΣΤΡΑ

οὐκ ἔστι, τῇ σῇ δ' ἡδὺ προσθέσθαι φρενί.

ΗΛΕΚΤΡΑ

1060 λέγοιμ' ἄν, εὐχὴ δ' ἥδε μοι προοίμιον·
εἴθ' εἶχες, ὦ τεκοῦσα, βελτίους φρένας.
τὸ μὲν γὰρ εἶδος αἶνον ἄξιον φέρειν
Ἑλένης τε καὶ σοῦ, δύο δ' ἔφυτε συγγόνω,
ἄμφω ματαίω Κάστορός τ' οὐκ ἀξίω.
1065 ἡ μὲν γὰρ ἁρπασθεῖσ' ἑκοῦσ' ἀπώλετο,
σὺ δ' ἄνδρ' ἄριστον Ἑλλάδος διώλεσας,
σκῆψιν προτείνουσ' ὡς ὑπὲρ τέκνου πόσιν
ἔκτεινας· οὐ γάρ <σ'> ὡς ἔγωγ' ἴσασιν εὖ.
ἥτις, θυγατρὸς πρὶν κεκυρῶσθαι σφαγάς,
1070 νέον τ' ἀπ' οἴκων ἀνδρὸς ἐξωρμημένου,
ξανθὸν κατόπτρῳ πλόκαμον ἐξήσκεις κόμης.
γυνὴ δ' ἀπόντος ἀνδρὸς ἥτις ἐκ δόμων
ἐς κάλλος ἀσκεῖ, διάγραφ' ὡς οὖσαν κακήν.
οὐδὲν γὰρ αὐτὴν δεῖ θύρασιν εὐπρεπὲς
1075 φαίνειν πρόσωπον, ἤν τι μὴ ζητῇ κακόν.
μόνην δὲ πασῶν οἶδ' ἐγὼ σ' Ἑλληνίδων,
εἰ μὲν τὰ Τρώων εὐτυχοῖ, κεχαρμένην,
εἰ δ' ἧσσον' εἴη, συννεφοῦσαν ὄμματα,
Ἀγαμέμνον' οὐ χρῄζουσαν ἐκ Τροίας μολεῖν.

1058 ἆρ' ἂν ... ἔρξαις Broadhead: ἆρα ... ἔρξεις L

**ELECTRA**

Will you hear me, mother, and then do me harm?

**CLYTAEMESTRA**

No: it is a pleasure to accommodate myself to your mind.

**ELECTRA**

I shall speak, and this wish shall be the beginning of my speech: how I wish, mother, that you had better sense! For while your beauty and Helen's deserve praise, the two of you are sisters, both foolish women and unworthy of Castor. She was willingly abducted and went to ruin, while you killed the noblest man in Greece and gave as your excuse that you were killing your husband in recompense for your child. People do not know you as well as I do.

When your husband had just left the house and before the murder of your daughter had been ordered, you began to primp your golden tresses before a mirror. Any woman who preens while her husband is away from home you may scratch off your list as a whore. She has no need to show a lovely face to those outside the house unless she is looking for mischief. I know that you alone of all Greek women rejoiced when the Trojans were enjoying good fortune, but if they were being defeated, you wore a gloomy expression since you did not wish Agamemnon to return from Troy.

---

1059 προσθέσθαι Weil: -θήσω L

1060 εὐχὴ Vitelli: ἀρχὴ L      προοίμιον Weil: -οιμίου L

1062 φέρειν Porson: φέρει L

1068 ⟨σ'⟩ Dobree      1072 post h. v. lac. indic. et suppl. Diggle, e.g. ⟨θύραζε φοιτήσουσα πέπλοισιν δέμας⟩

1077 τὰ Τρώων εὐτυχοῖ Musgrave: πατρῷ' ἦν εὐτυχῇ L

1080 καίτοι καλῶς γε σωφρονεῖν παρεῖχέ σοι·
ἄνδρ᾽ εἶχες οὐ κακίον᾽ Αἰγίσθου πόσιν,
ὃν Ἑλλὰς αὑτῆς εἵλετο στρατηλάτην·
Ἑλένης δ᾽ ἀδελφῆς τοιάδ᾽ ἐξειργασμένης
ἐξῆν κλέος σοι μέγα λαβεῖν· τὰ γὰρ κακὰ
1085 παράδειγμα τοῖς ἐσθλοῖσιν εἴσοψίν τ᾽ ἔχει.
     εἰ δ᾽, ὡς λέγεις, σὴν θυγατέρ᾽ ἔκτεινεν πατήρ,
ἐγὼ τί σ᾽ ἠδίκησ᾽ ἐμός τε σύγγονος;
πῶς οὐ πόσιν κτείνασα πατρῴους δόμους
ἡμῖν προσῆψας, ἀλλ᾽ ἐπηνέγκω λέχει
1090 τἀλλότρια, μισθοῦ τοὺς γάμους ὠνουμένη,
κοὔτ᾽ ἀντιφεύγει παιδὸς ἀντὶ σοῦ πόσις
οὔτ᾽ ἀντ᾽ ἐμοῦ τέθνηκε, δὶς τόσως ἐμὲ
κτείνας ἀδελφῆς ζῶσαν; εἰ δ᾽ ἀμείψεται
φόνον δικάζων φόνος, ἀποκτενῶ σ᾽ ἐγὼ
1095 καὶ παῖς Ὀρέστης πατρὶ τιμωρούμενοι.
εἰ γὰρ δίκαι᾽ ἐκεῖνα, καὶ τάδ᾽ ἔνδικα.
[ὅστις δὲ πλοῦτον ἢ εὐγένειαν εἰσιδὼν
γαμεῖ πονηράν, μῶρός ἐστι· μικρὰ γὰρ
μεγάλων ἀμείνω σώφρον᾽ ἐν δόμοις λέχη.

ΧΟΡΟΣ

1100 τύχη γυναικῶν ἐς γάμους. τὰ μὲν γὰρ εὖ,
τὰ δ᾽ οὐ καλῶς πίπτοντα δέρκομαι βροτῶν.]

ΚΛΥΤΑΙΜΗΣΤΡΑ

ὦ παῖ, πέφυκας πατέρα σὸν στέργειν ἀεί·
ἔστιν δὲ καὶ τόδ᾽· οἱ μέν εἰσιν ἀρσένων,

1089 ἐπηνέγκω λέχει Camper: ἀπ- λέχῃ L

And yet you had every inducement to be virtuous: you had
a man as your husband who was superior to Aegisthus, a
man Hellas chose as its command in chief; and when your
sister Helen had behaved so badly, you could have won
great glory for yourself. For bad conduct serves to high-
light what is good and makes it shine out.

But if, as you say, my father killed your daughter, what
wrong did my brother and I do you? Why, when you had
killed your husband, did you not give us our ancestral
home but instead brought, as dowry to your marriage,
property that belongs to someone else, buying a husband
for a price? Why is not your husband now in exile in re-
quital for Orestes' exile, why is he not dead in requital for
me since he has inflicted on me in life twice the death my
sister suffered? But if one deed of murder decrees another
in requital, I shall kill you, I and your son Orestes, in
vengeance for our father. For if what you have done is just,
this too is right. [Whoever marries a bad woman because
he looks at wealth or high birth is a fool: for it is better to
have in the house a wife of low rank who is chaste than one
who is high-born.

CHORUS

Chance rules over marriage with women. I see that some
mortals have good luck, others bad.]

CLYTAEMESTRA

My child, you have always been inclined to love your father.
This is a fact of life: some children belong to the male side,

---

1097–9 del. Hartung    1100–1 del. Nauck
1103–4 del. Kirchhoff

οἱ δ' αὖ φιλοῦσι μητέρας μᾶλλον πατρός.
1105 συγγνώσομαί σοι· καὶ γὰρ οὐχ οὕτως ἄγαν
1106 χαίρω τι, τέκνον, τοῖς δεδραμένοις ἐμοί.
1109 οἴμοι τάλαινα τῶν ἐμῶν βουλευμάτων·
1110 ὡς μᾶλλον ἢ χρῆν ἤλασ' εἰς ὀργὴν πόσει.

ΗΛΕΚΤΡΑ
ὀψὲ στενάζεις, ἡνίκ' οὐκ ἔχεις ἄκη.
πατὴρ μὲν οὖν τέθνηκε· τὸν δ' ἔξω χθονὸς
πῶς οὐ κομίζῃ παῖδ' ἀλητεύοντα σόν;

ΚΛΥΤΑΙΜΗΣΤΡΑ
δέδοικα· τοὐμὸν δ', οὐχὶ τοὐκείνου σκοπῶ.
1115 πατρὸς γάρ, ὡς λέγουσι, θυμοῦται φόνῳ.

ΗΛΕΚΤΡΑ
τί δ' αὖ πόσιν σὸν ἄγριον εἰς ἡμᾶς ἔχεις;

ΚΛΥΤΑΙΜΗΣΤΡΑ
τρόποι τοιοῦτοι· καὶ σὺ δ' αὐθάδης ἔφυς.

ΗΛΕΚΤΡΑ
ἀλγῶ γάρ· ἀλλὰ παύσομαι θυμουμένη.

ΚΛΥΤΑΙΜΗΣΤΡΑ
καὶ μὴν ἐκεῖνος οὐκέτ' ἔσται σοι βαρύς.

ΗΛΕΚΤΡΑ
1120 φρονεῖ μέγ'· ἐν γὰρ τοῖς ἐμοῖς ναίει δόμοις.

ΚΛΥΤΑΙΜΗΣΤΡΑ
ὁρᾷς; ἀν' αὖ σὺ ζωπυρεῖς νείκη νέα.

1107–8 vide post 1131

others love their mothers more than their fathers. I shall
forgive you: for in fact, my child, I do not feel such great
joy at the deeds I have done. Ah, how wretched my plotting
has made me! How excessively I raged against my husband!

ELECTRA

Your groaning comes too late: you can do nothing to mend
matters. Well, my father is dead. But why do you not bring
back your son who is wandering abroad?

CLYTAEMESTRA

I am afraid: I look to my interest, not his. They say he is
angry at his father's murder.

ELECTRA

Why then do you keep your husband in a rage against me?

CLYTAEMESTRA

That is just his character. And you too are self-willed.

ELECTRA

Yes, for I am in pain. But I shall stop being angry.

CLYTAEMESTRA

Then he will no longer be resentful toward you.

ELECTRA

He is proud: he dwells in my house.[30]

CLYTAEMESTRA

See? You rekindle old quarrels again and make them new.

---

[30] There is a *double-entendre* in that Aegisthus' body now
dwells in Electra's cottage.

1110 πόσει Gomperz: πόσιν L      1116 δ' αὖ Nauck: δαὶ L

ΗΛΕΚΤΡΑ

σιγῶ· δέδοικα γάρ νιν ὡς δέδοικ' ἐγώ.

ΚΛΥΤΑΙΜΗΣΤΡΑ

παῦσαι λόγων τῶνδε. ἀλλὰ τί μ' ἐκάλεις, τέκνον;

ΗΛΕΚΤΡΑ

ἤκουσας, οἶμαι, τῶν ἐμῶν λοχευμάτων·
1125  τούτων ὕπερ μοι θῦσον (οὐ γὰρ οἶδ' ἐγώ)
δεκάτην σελήνην παιδὸς ὡς νομίζεται.
τρίβων γὰρ οὐκ εἴμ', ἄτοκος οὖσ' ἐν τῷ πάρος.

ΚΛΥΤΑΙΜΗΣΤΡΑ

ἄλλης τόδ' ἔργον, ἥ σ' ἔλυσεν ἐκ τόκων.

ΗΛΕΚΤΡΑ

αὐτὴ 'λόχευον κἄτεκον μόνη βρέφος.

ΚΛΥΤΑΙΜΗΣΤΡΑ

1130  οὕτως ἀγείτων οἶκος ἵδρυται φίλων;

ΗΛΕΚΤΡΑ

1131  πένητας οὐδεὶς βούλεται κτᾶσθαι φίλους.

ΚΛΥΤΑΙΜΗΣΤΡΑ

1107  σὺ δ' ὧδ' ἄλουτος καὶ δυσείματος χρόα
1108  λεχὼ νεογνῶν ἐκ τόκων πεπαυμένη;
1132  ἀλλ' εἶμι, παιδὸς ἀριθμὸν ὡς τελεσφόρον
θύσω θεοῖσι· σοὶ δ' ὅταν πράξω χάριν
τήνδ', εἶμ' ἐπ' ἀγρὸν οὗ πόσις θυηπολεῖ
1135  Νύμφαισιν. ἀλλὰ τούσδ' ὄχους, ὀπάονες,

───────────────

1126 δεκάτην σελήνην Musgrave: -η -η L

ELECTRA

I will be silent. My fear of him is as it is.

CLYTAEMESTRA

Enough of this subject. Why did you summon me, my child?

ELECTRA

You have heard, I suppose, that I have given birth. In thanks for this (since I know not how to do it) perform the sacrifice for the child's tenth night, as custom ordains.[31] I am inexperienced, for I have never been a mother before.

CLYTAEMESTRA

This is a job for someone else, the woman who delivered your baby.

ELECTRA

I was my own midwife and bore my child alone.

CLYTAEMESTRA

Is your house so lonely and so friendless?

ELECTRA

No one wants to make friends with paupers.

CLYTAEMESTRA

But you—so unwashed and your body so ill-clad when you have just given birth? Well, I shall go in to make sacrifice to the gods in thanks that for the completion of these days. But when I have done you this favor, I will go to the field where my husband is sacrificing to the Nymphs. Slaves,

[31] See above on line 654

---

1107–8 huc trai. Weil

φάτναις ἄγοντες πρόσθεθ'· ἡνίκ' ἂν δέ με
δοκῆτε θυσίας τῆσδ' ἀπηλλάχθαι θεοῖς,
πάρεστε· δεῖ γὰρ καὶ πόσει δοῦναι χάριν.

ΗΛΕΚΤΡΑ

χώρει πένητας ἐς δόμους· φρούρει δέ μοι
1140 μή σ' αἰθαλώσῃ πολύκαπνον στέγος πέπλους.
θύσεις γὰρ οἷα χρή σε δαίμοσιν θύη.
κανοῦν δ' ἐνῆρκται καὶ τεθηγμένη σφαγίς,
ἥπερ καθεῖλε ταῦρον, οὗ πέλας πεσῇ
πληγεῖσα· νυμφεύσῃ δὲ κἀν Ἅιδου δόμοις
1145 ᾧπερ ξυνηῦδες ἐν φάει. τοσήνδ' ἐγὼ
δώσω χάριν σοι, σὺ δὲ δίκην ἐμοὶ πατρός.

ΧΟΡΟΣ

στρ.

ἀμοιβαὶ κακῶν· μετάτροποι πνέου-
σιν αὖραι δόμων. τότε μὲν ⟨ἐν⟩ λουτροῖς
ἔπεσεν ἐμὸς ἐμὸς ἀρχέτας,
1150 ἰάχησε δὲ στέγα λάινοί τε θριγκοὶ δόμων,
τάδ' ἐνέποντος· Ὦ σχέτλιε, τί με, γύναι, φονεύεις
φίλαν
πατρίδα δεκέτεσι σποραῖ-
σιν ἐλθόντ' ἐμάν;
⟨. . . . . . . . . . . . . . . . . . . . . . .
. . . . . . . . . . . . . . . . . . . . . . .⟩.

---

1146 δὲ δίκην ἐμοὶ Bothe: δ' ἐμοὶ δ- L        1148 ⟨ἐν⟩ Seidler
1152 σχέτλιε Diggle cl. *IT* 651: -ία L        φονεύεις Victorius:
-σεις L        1154 post h. v. lac. indic. Tr²

take this carriage and put the horses to feed. When you judge that I am through with this sacrifice to the gods, come back. For I must do a service to my husband as well.

*Exit* CLYTAEMESTRA *into the house, the servants by Eisodos A.*

### ELECTRA

Go, enter this poor house! But please take care that the sooty chamber not stain your clothes! You shall make such sacrifice as is right to the gods. The sacrificial basket has been prepared and the knife sharpened which killed the bull, and at his side you will fall stricken. In the world below you shall be bride to the man you slept with in life. That will be my favor to you, but you shall give me satisfaction for my father.

*Exit* ELECTRA *into the house.*

### CHORUS

There is requital for wrong: the winds of this house
are veering round. Once my lord and king
fell slain in his bath,
and the roof and stone cornice of the palace
resounded as he cried, "Why, cruel woman, do you kill me
   when I have returned
after ten harvests
to my beloved native land?"
<. . . . . . . . . . . . . . . . . .
. . . . . . . . . . . . . . . . . . .>.

# EURIPIDES

ἀντ.

1155 παλίρρους δὲ τάνδ᾿ ὑπάγεται δίκα
διαδρόμου λέχους, μέλεον ἃ πόσιν
χρόνιον ἱκόμενον ἑστίαν
Κυκλώπειά τ᾿ οὐράνια τείχε᾿ ὀξυθήκτῳ βέλει
1160 κατέκαν᾿ αὐτόχειρ, πέλεκυν ἐν χεροῖν λαβοῦσ᾿. ὧ
τλάμων
πόσις, ὅ τι ποτε τὰν τάλαι-
ναν ἔσχεν κακόν.
ὀρεία τις ὡς λέαιν᾿ ὀργάδων
δρύοχα νεμομένα, τάδε κατήνυσεν.

ΚΛΥΤΑΙΜΗΣΤΡΑ

(ἔσωθεν)
1165 ὧ τέκνα, πρὸς θεῶν, μὴ κτάνητε μητέρα.

ΧΟΡΟΣ

κλύεις ὑπώροφον βοάν;

ΚΛΥΤΑΙΜΗΣΤΡΑ

ἰώ μοί μοι.

ΧΟΡΟΣ

ᾤμωξα κἀγὼ πρὸς τέκνων χειρουμένης.
νέμει τοι δίκαν θεός, ὅταν τύχῃ·
1170 σχέτλια μὲν ἔπαθες, ἀνόσια δ᾿ εἰργάσω,
τάλαιν᾿, εὐνέταν.

1155 δίκα Victorius: -αν L
1157 ἑστίαν Page: εἰς οἴκους L: ἐς δόμους Heimsoeth
1159 βέλει κατέκαν᾿ Seidler: βέλους ἔκανεν L

Justice, in its backward ebb, indicts her for the faithless-
ness of her bed:
her poor husband,
returned at long last to his hearth
and the heaven-high walls the Cyclopes built, with sharp
weapon
she killed with her own hand, seizing the ax herself! How
unfortunate
the husband, whatever the bane was
that seized the cruel wife.
Like some lioness of the mountain,
prowling the wooded glens, she wrought this deed.

CLYTAEMESTRA

(*within*) My children, in the gods' name, do not kill your
mother!

CHORUS

Do you hear a cry within the house?

CLYTAEMESTRA

Ah me, ah me!

CHORUS

I too utter a cry of pity as she is overcome by her children.
Truly the god dispenses retribution, late or soon.
Miserable was your suffering, but unholy your deeds,
cruel woman, against your husband!

*Enter* ELECTRA, ORESTES, *and Pylades from the house.*

---

1160 λαβοῦσ'. ὦ Fix: λαβοῦσα L

—ἀλλ᾽ οἵδε μητρὸς νεοφόνοις ἐν αἵμασιν
πεφυρμένοι βαίνουσιν ἐξ οἴκων πόδα.
⟨καὶ μὴν ἐν αὐταῖς δὴ πυλαῖς νεκροὺς ὁρῶ
τῶν πρὶν τυράννων, δυσφιλεστάτης μάχης⟩
τρόπαια δεῖγμά τ᾽ ἀθλίων προσφθεγμάτων.
1175 οὐκ ἔστιν οὐδεὶς οἶκος ἀθλιώτερος
τῶν Τανταλείων οὐδ᾽ ἔφυ ποτ᾽ ἐκγόνων.

στρ. α

ΟΡΕΣΤΗΣ

ἰὼ Γᾶ ⟨τε⟩ καὶ Ζεῦ πανδερκέτα
βροτῶν, ἴδετε τάδ᾽ ἔργα φόνι-
α μυσαρά, δίγονα σώματ᾽ ἐν
1180 χθονὶ κεχυμένα πλαγᾷ ⟨διπλᾷ⟩
χερὸς ὑπ᾽ ἐμᾶς, ἄποιν᾽ ἐμῶν
πημάτων ⟨. . . . . . . . . . . . . .
. . . . . . . . . . . . . . . . . . . . . .
. . . . . . . . . . . . . . . . . . . . . . ⟩.

ΗΛΕΚΤΡΑ

δακρύτ᾽ ἄγαν, ὦ σύγγον᾽, αἰτία δ᾽ ἐγώ.
διὰ πυρὸς ἔμολον ἁ τάλαινα ματρὶ τᾷδ᾽,
ἅ μ᾽ ἔτικτε κούραν.

ΧΟΡΟΣ

1185 ἰὼ τύχας, σ⟨τερρ⟩ᾶς τύχας,

---

1173 post h. v. lac. indic. Paley
1174 δεῖγμά τ᾽ Kovacs: δείγματ᾽ L     1177 ⟨τε⟩ Elmsley
1180 κεχυμένα . . . ⟨διπλᾷ⟩ Diggle: κείμενα L

### CHORUS LEADER

But here they are: stained with their mother's newly shed
blood, they are coming out of the house!

*The bodies of Clytaemestra and Aegisthus are wheeled out
on the* eccyclema.

‹And look, within the doors I see the bodies of those
who once ruled,› trophies ‹of a hateful struggle› and clear
proof of what those piteous cries meant. There is not—nor
has there ever been—a house more wretched than the
offspring of Tantalus.

### ORESTES

O Earth and Zeus who sees
all mortal affairs, look upon these deeds of blood
and defilement, two bodies laid out
upon the earth by a ‹double› blow,
by my hand, in payment
for my woes ‹. . . . . . .
. . . . . . . . . . . . . . . .
. . . . . . . . . . . . . . . .›!

### ELECTRA

Pitiable indeed, my brother, is this sight, yet I am the one
 to blame.
For I burned with hatred against the mother
who bore me as her daughter!

### CHORUS

O what a cruel fate was yours!

---

1181 post πημάτων lac. indic. Seidler
1185 σ‹τερρ›ᾶς Diggle

μᾶτερ τεκοῦσ᾽ ⟨ἄλαστα⟩,
ἄλαστα μέλεα καὶ πέρα
παθοῦσα σῶν τέκνων ὑπαί.
πατρὸς δ᾽ ἔτεισας φόνον δικαίως.

ἀντ. α

ΟΡΕΣΤΗΣ

1190  ἰὼ Φοῖβ᾽, ⟨ἄγ⟩αν ὕμνησας δίκαι᾽
ἄφαντα, φανερὰ δ᾽ ἐξέπρα-
ξας ἄχεα, φόνια δ᾽ ὥπασας
λάχε᾽ ἀπὸ γᾶς Ἑλλανίδος.
τίνα δ᾽ ἑτέραν μόλω πόλιν;
1195  τίς ξένος, τίς εὐσεβὴς
ἐμὸν κάρα προσόψεται
ματέρα κτανόντος;

ΗΛΕΚΤΡΑ

ἰὼ ἰώ μοι. ποῖ δ᾽ ἐγώ, τίν᾽ ἐς χορόν,
τίνα γάμον εἶμι; τίς πόσις με δέξεται
1200  νυμφικὰς ἐς εὐνάς;

ΧΟΡΟΣ

πάλιν πάλιν φρόνημα σὸν
μετεστάθη πρὸς αὔραν·
φρονεῖς γὰρ ὅσια νῦν, τότ᾽ οὐ
φρονοῦσα, δεινὰ δ᾽ εἰργάσω,
1205  φίλα, κασίγνητον οὐ θέλοντα.

στρ. β

ΟΡΕΣΤΗΣ

κατεῖδες οἷον ἁ τάλαιν᾽ ἔξω πέπλων

You bore children none shall forget,
and unforgettable and more
were the sufferings brought on you by your children!
Yet it was right that you paid for their father's murder.

ORESTES

Ah Phoebus, the justice your song spoke of
is all too obscure, but all too plain to see
are the woes you have wrought, and the lot you gave me
was that of murderer banished from Greece!
What other city shall I go to?
What friend, what godly man
shall look upon me
now that I have killed my mother?

ELECTRA

Ah me, ah me! Where shall I go, to what dance
or to what marriage? What husband will receive me
into a bridal bed?

CHORUS

Again, again your mind
veers round with the changing breeze.
Your mind is now god-fearing, though before
it was not so, and you have done a terrible thing,
my friend, to your reluctant brother.

ORESTES

Did you see how the poor woman stripped off her clothing

---

1186 ⟨ἄλαστα⟩ Grotefend    1190 ⟨ἄγ⟩αν ὕμνησας Willink:
ἀνύμνησας L    δίκαι᾽ Murray: δίκαν L
1193 λάχε᾽ Weil: λέχε᾽ L
1206 ἔξω Seidler: ἐῶν L

ἔβαλεν ἔδειξε μαστὸν ἐν φοναῖσιν,
ἰώ μοι, πρὸς πέδῳ
τιθεῖσα γόνιμα μέλεα; τακόμαν δ' ἐγώ.

ΧΟΡΟΣ

1210 σάφ' οἶδα, δι' ὀδύνας ἔβας,
ἰήιον κλύων γόον
ματρὸς ἅ σ' ἔτικτε.

ἀντ. β

ΟΡΕΣΤΗΣ

βοὰν δ' ἔλασκε τάνδε, πρὸς γένυν ἐμὰν
1215 τιθεῖσα χεῖρα· Τέκος ἐμόν, λιταίνω.
παρήδων τ' ἐξ ἐμᾶν
ἐκρίμναθ', ὥστε χέρας ἐμὰς λιπεῖν βέλος.

ΧΟΡΟΣ

τάλαινα. πῶς ⟨δ'⟩ ἔτλας φόνον
δι' ὀμμάτων ἰδεῖν σέθεν
1220 ματρὸς ἐκπνεούσας;

στρ. γ

ΟΡΕΣΤΗΣ

ἐγὼ μὲν ἐπιβαλὼν φάρη κόραις ἐμαῖς
φασγάνῳ κατηρξάμαν
ματέρος ἔσω δέρας μεθείς.

ΗΛΕΚΤΡΑ

ἐγὼ δέ γ' ἐπεκέλευσά σοι
1225 ξίφους τ' ἐφηψάμαν ἅμα.
δεινότατον παθέων ἔρεξα.

and exposed her breast as we killed her?
Ah, did you see how on the ground
she laid the limbs that gave me birth? It caused me to melt!

CHORUS

I know well: what agony you felt
to hear the piteous wail
of the mother who bore you!

ORESTES

This was the cry she uttered as against my chin
she put her hand: "My child, I beg you!"
From my cheek
she hung, so that my hands let go of the weapon!

CHORUS

Unhappy woman! But how did you have the courage
to look with open eyes on the slaughter
as your mother breathed her last?

ORESTES

As for me, I veiled my eyes with my garments
as I sacrificed my mother, thrusting
my sword through her neck.

ELECTRA

And I, I urged you on
and, as I did so, put my hand to the sword!
It was the most terrible of sufferings that I brought to pass!

---

1209 τακόμαν Seidler: τὰν κόμαν L
1218 ⟨δ'⟩ Weil
1226 Electrae contin. Seidler: choro trib. L    ἔρεξα Seidler:
-ξας L

ἀντ. γ

ΟΡΕΣΤΗΣ

λαβοῦ, κάλυπτε μέλεα ματέρος πέπλοις
⟨καὶ⟩ καθάρμοσον σφαγάς.
φονέας ἔτικτες ἆρά σοι.

ΗΛΕΚΤΡΑ

1230 ἰδού, φίλᾳ τε κοὐ φίλᾳ
φάρεα τάδ᾽ ἀμφιβάλλομεν,
τέρμα κακῶν μεγάλων δόμοισιν.

ΧΟΡΟΣ

ἀλλ᾽ οἵδε δόμων ὑπὲρ ἀκροτάτων
βαίνουσί τινες δαίμονες ἢ θεῶν
1235 τῶν οὐρανίων· οὐ γὰρ θνητῶν γ᾽
ἥδε κέλευθος. τί ποτ᾽ ἐς φανερὰν
ὄψιν βαίνουσι βροτοῖσιν;

ΚΑΣΤΩΡ

Ἀγαμέμνονος παῖ, κλῦθι· δίπτυχοι δέ σε
καλοῦσι μητρὸς σύγγονοι Διόσκοροι,
1240 Κάστωρ κασίγνητός τε Πολυδεύκης ὅδε.
δεινὸν δὲ ναυσὶν ἀρτίως πόντου σάλον
παύσαντ᾽ ἀφίγμεθ᾽ Ἄργος, ὡς ἐσείδομεν
σφαγὰς ἀδελφῆς τῆσδε, μητέρος δὲ σῆς.
δίκαια μέν νυν ἥδ᾽ ἔχει, σὺ δ᾽ οὐχὶ δρᾷς.
1245 Φοῖβος δέ, Φοῖβος—ἀλλ᾽ ἄναξ γάρ ἐστ᾽ ἐμός,

1228 ⟨καὶ⟩ Seidler
1231 τάδ᾽ Kirchhoff: γ᾽ L

**ORESTES**

Take hold, and with her robe cover our mother's limbs
and close her wounds.
It was your own murderers, then, that you gave birth to.

*Electra covers her mother's body.*

**ELECTRA**

There, upon her who is dear and yet not dear
I put these garments,
the last and greatest of our house's great woes.

*Enter* CASTOR *and Polydeuces through the air on the*
mechane.

**CHORUS LEADER**

But see, above the housetops mighty spirits or heavenly
gods are approaching: for that is no place for mortal feet
to tread. Why do they show themselves plainly to mortal
eyes?

**CASTOR**

Son of Agamemnon, hear us: the twin brothers of your
mother, the Dioscuri, are calling you, I, Castor, and my
brother Polydeuces here. We have just calmed a ship-
threatening tempest and have come to Argos, since we
have seen the slaughter of our sister and your mother. The
treatment she received was just, but the act that you did
was not. And Phoebus, Phoebus—but no, since he is my

---

1234 βαίνουσι Hartung: φαίν-L
1241 ναυσὶν Barnes: ναὸς L

σιγῶ· σοφὸς δ' ὢν οὐκ ἔχρησέ σοι σοφά.
αἰνεῖν δ' ἀνάγκη ταῦτα, τἀντεῦθεν δὲ χρὴ
πράσσειν ἃ Μοῖρα Ζεύς τ' ἔκρανε σοῦ πέρι.

Πυλάδῃ μὲν Ἠλέκτραν δὸς ἄλοχον ἐς δόμους,
1250 σὺ δ' Ἄργος ἔκλιπ'· οὐ γὰρ ἔστι σοι πόλιν
τήνδ' ἐμβατεύειν, μητέρα κτείναντα σήν.
δειναὶ δὲ Κῆρές <σ'> αἱ κυνώπιδες θεαὶ
τροχηλατήσουσ' ἐμμανῆ πλανώμενον.

ἐλθὼν δ' Ἀθήνας Παλλάδος σεμνὸν βρέτας
1255 πρόσπτυξον· εἴρξει γάρ νιν ἐπτοημένας
δεινοῖς δράκουσιν ὥστε μὴ ψαύειν σέθεν,
γοργῶφ' ὑπερτείνουσα σῷ κάρᾳ κύκλον.
ἔστιν δ' Ἄρεώς τις ὄχθος, οὗ πρῶτον θεοὶ
ἕζοντ' ἐπὶ ψήφοισιν αἵματος πέρι,
1260 Ἁλιρρόθιον ὅτ' ἔκταν' ὠμόφρων Ἄρης,
μῆνιν θυγατρὸς ἀνοσίων νυμφευμάτων,
πόντου κρέοντος παῖδ', ἵν' εὐσεβεστάτη
ψήφου βεβαία τ' ἐστὶν ἐκ τούτου θέσις.

ἐνταῦθα καὶ σὲ δεῖ δραμεῖν φόνου πέρι.
1265 ἴσαι δέ σ' ἐκσώσουσι μὴ θανεῖν δίκῃ
ψῆφοι τεθεῖσαι· Λοξίας γὰρ αἰτίαν
ἐς αὑτὸν οἴσει, μητέρος χρήσας φόνον.
καὶ τοῖσι λοιποῖς ὅδε νόμος τεθήσεται,
νικᾶν ἴσαις ψήφοισι τὸν φεύγοντ' ἀεί.
1270 δειναὶ μὲν οὖν θεαὶ τῷδ' ἄχει πεπληγμέναι
πάγον παρ' αὐτὸν χάσμα δύσονται χθονός,

1252 <σ'> L. Dindorf

288

lord, I hold my peace. Still, wise god though he is, his oracle to you was not wise. Yet you must acquiesce in these things, and for the future you must carry out what fate and Zeus have ordained for you.

Give Electra to Pylades to take home as his wife. You yourself leave Argos behind. It is not possible for you to tread this city's ground since you have killed your mother. The dread Death Spirits, hound-faced goddesses, will send you running pell-mell in a wandering madness.

But go to Athens and embrace the holy statue of Pallas. Though they flutter with serpents, she will prevent these creatures from touching you by holding over your head her Gorgon shield.[32] There is a place called Ares' Hill where the gods first sat in judgment in a case of murder, when cruel Ares killed Poseidon's son, Halirrhothius, in anger for his daughter's rape. Here, ever since then, votes are cast in a god-fearing and incorruptible manner.

You too must here run your course on a charge of murder. But votes justly cast in equal numbers shall prevent your being killed. For Apollo, god of prophecy, will take the responsibility on himself since he commanded you to kill your mother. And for all generations to come this law will be established: when the votes are equal the defendant always gains the verdict. And so these dread goddesses, hard-struck by grief at this, will sink into a cleft in the earth

---

[32] Athena is represented as having a shield with a Gorgon's head on it.

---

1263 ψήφου . . . θέσις Tucker: ψῆφος . . . θεοῖς L    ἐκ τούτου Pierson: ἔκ τε τοῦ L
1265 ἐκσώσουσι Porson: ἐκσώζ- L

σεμνὸν βροτοῖσιν εὐσεβέσι χρηστήριον.
σὲ δ' Ἀρκάδων χρὴ πόλιν ἐπ' Ἀλφειοῦ ῥοαῖς
οἰκεῖν Λυκαίου πλησίον σηκώματος·
1275 ἐπώνυμος δὲ σοῦ πόλις κεκλήσεται.
  σοὶ μὲν τάδ' εἶπον· τόνδε δ' Αἰγίσθου νέκυν
Ἄργους πολῖται γῆς καλύψουσιν τάφῳ.
μητέρα δὲ τὴν σὴν ἄρτι Ναυπλίαν παρὼν
Μενέλαος, ἐξ οὗ Τρωικὴν εἷλε χθόνα,
1280 Ἑλένη τε θάψει· Πρωτέως γὰρ ἐκ δόμων
ἥκει λιποῦσ' Αἴγυπτον οὐδ' ἦλθεν Φρύγας·
Ζεὺς δ', ὡς ἔρις γένοιτο καὶ φόνος βροτῶν,
εἴδωλον Ἑλένης ἐξέπεμψ' ἐς Ἴλιον.
  Πυλάδης μὲν οὖν κόρην τε καὶ δάμαρτ' ἔχων
1285 Ἀχαιίδος γῆς οἴκαδ' ἐκπορευέτω,
καὶ τὸν λόγῳ σὸν πενθερὸν κομιζέτω
Φωκέων ἐς αἶαν καὶ δότω πλούτου βάρος·
σὺ δ' Ἰσθμίας γῆς αὐχέν' ἐμβαίνων ποδὶ
χώρει πρὸς ὄχθον Κεκροπίας εὐδαίμονα.
1290 πεπρωμένην γὰρ μοῖραν ἐκπλήσας φόνου
εὐδαιμονήσεις τῶνδ' ἀπαλλαχθεὶς πόνων.

ΟΡΕΣΤΗΣ
ὦ παῖδε Διός, θέμις ἐς φθογγὰς
τὰς ὑμετέρας ἡμῖν πελάθειν;

1272 εὐσεβέσι Clarke: -βὲς L: ἀστιβὲς Reiske    μυστή-
ριον Hartung    1285 ἐκπορευέτω Reiske: εἰσ- L
1287 βάθος Herwerden
1289 ὄχθον Valckenaer: οἶκον L

290

near the hill, an oracle revered by god-fearing mortals. But you must found a city in Arcadia by the streams of the Alpheus river near the grove of Zeus Lycaeus: the city will be called by your name.[33]

These are my words to you. The body of Aegisthus will be buried in its grave of earth by the citizens of Argos. As for your mother, she will be buried by Menelaus, just arrived at Nauplia after the sack of Troy, and by Helen. For Helen has left Egypt and the house of Proteus behind and come home. She never went to Troy.[34] Rather, in order to cause strife and the slaying of mortals, Zeus sent an image of Helen to Troy.

So let Pylades leave the country of Achaea and go home with Electra, who is both virgin and wife. Let him take your supposed brother-in-law to the land of Phocis and there bestow on him great wealth. But you must tread the Isthmus and go to the blessed hill of Cecropia.[35] For when you have fulfilled the fated course that the murder requires, you will be freed from these troubles and find happiness.

ORESTES

Sons of Zeus, is it allowed for us to converse with you?

[33] This gives the etymology of a city in Arcadia called Orestheion.

[34] This is the version of the story Euripides later put in his *Helen*, though there were precedents for it in the work of Stesichorus and in Herodotus. Zeus's plan to rid the world of excess population recalls the post-Homeric epic poem *Cypria*.

[35] The Acropolis of Athens.

ΚΑΣΤΩΡ

θέμις, οὐ μυσαροῖς τοῖσδε σφαγίοις.

ΗΛΕΚΤΡΑ

1295  κἀμοὶ μύθου μέτα, Τυνδαρίδαι;

ΚΑΣΤΩΡ

καὶ σοί· Φοίβῳ τήνδ᾽ ἀναθήσω
πρᾶξιν φονίαν.

ΟΡΕΣΤΗΣ

πῶς ὄντε θεὼ τῆσδέ τ᾽ ἀδελφὼ
τῆς καπφθιμένης
1300  οὐκ ἠρκέσατον Κῆρας μελάθροις;

ΚΑΣΤΩΡ

μοῖρά τ᾽ ἀνάγκη τ᾽ ἦγ᾽ ἐς τὸ χρεὼν
Φοίβου τ᾽ ἄσοφοι γλώσσης ἐνοπαί.

ΗΛΕΚΤΡΑ

τίς δ᾽ ἔμ᾽ Ἀπόλλων, ποῖοι χρησμοὶ
φονίαν ἔδοσαν μητρὶ γενέσθαι;

ΚΑΣΤΩΡ

1305  κοιναὶ πράξεις, κοινοὶ δὲ πότμοι,
μία δ᾽ ἀμφοτέρους
ἄτη πατέρων διέκναισεν.

ΟΡΕΣΤΗΣ

ὦ σύγγονέ μοι, χρονίαν σ᾽ ἐσιδὼν

1301 μοῖρά τ᾽ Bothe: μοίρας L    ἀνάγκη τ᾽ Diggle:
ἀνάγκης L    ἦγ᾽ ἐς τὸ Tucker: ἡγεῖτο L
1303 τίς δ᾽ ἔμ᾽ Bothe: τί δαί μ᾽ L

## ELECTRA

**CASTOR**

Yes, for you are not polluted with this murder.[36]

**ELECTRA**

May I also address you, sons of Tyndareus?

**CASTOR**

You also may do so. For I shall ascribe this bloody deed to Apollo.

**ORESTES**

Why did you, being gods and brothers to the dead woman here, not ward off the Death Spirits from this house?

**CASTOR**

Fate and Necessity and the unwise words of Phoebus' tongue were directing events toward their destined goal.

**ELECTRA**

Yet what Apollo and what oracles made me become the murderer of my mother?

**CASTOR**

Just as your acts were in common, so too were your fates, and it was a single ruin derived from your ancestors[37] that has crushed you both.

**ORESTES**

My sister, I see you now after such a long separation, yet I

---

[36] Apollo is responsible, as Castor makes explicit in 1296-7. Normally the fact of bloodshed, irrespective of circumstance, was thought to carry pollution, but a similarly "moral" view of pollution (i.e. one that takes motive into account) is found at *Orestes* 75-6. [37] Tantalus, Pelops, and Atreus were all great sinners (*Orestes* 1-15), and the descendants' troubles are caused by their ancestors' wrongdoing.

τῶν σῶν εὐθὺς φίλτρων στέρομαι
1310 καὶ σ' ἀπολείψω σοῦ λειπόμενος.

ΚΑΣΤΩΡ
πόσις ἔστ' αὐτῇ καὶ δόμος· οὐχ ἥδ'
οἰκτρὰ πέπονθεν, πλὴν ὅτι λείπει
πόλιν Ἀργείων.

ΗΛΕΚΤΡΑ
καὶ τίνες ἄλλαι στοναχαὶ μείζους
1315 ἢ γῆς πατρίας ὅρον ἐκλείπειν;

ΟΡΕΣΤΗΣ
ἀλλ' ἐγὼ οἴκων ἔξειμι πατρὸς
καὶ ἐπ' ἀλλοτρίαις ψήφοισι φόνον
μητρὸς ὑφέξω.

ΚΑΣΤΩΡ
ὁσίαν, θάρσει, Παλλάδος ἥξεις
1320 πόλιν· ἀλλ' ἀνέχου.

ΗΛΕΚΤΡΑ
περί μοι στέρνοις στέρνα πρόσαψον,
σύγγονε φίλτατε·
διὰ γὰρ ζευγνῦσ' ἡμᾶς πατρίων
μελάθρων μητρὸς φόνιοι κατάραι.

ΟΡΕΣΤΗΣ
1325 βάλε, πρόσπτυξον σῶμα· θανόντος δ'
ὡς ἐπὶ τύμβῳ καταθρήνησον.

ΚΑΣΤΩΡ
φεῦ φεῦ· δεινὸν τόδ' ἐγηρύσω

am robbed at once of your love and must leave you and be
left by you!

CASTOR

She has a husband and a home. She has not suffered things
deserving of pity, except that she leaves the city of Argos.

ELECTRA

Yet what greater grief is there than to leave one's native
land?

ORESTES

But I must leave my father's house and be tried by the votes
of strangers for my mother's murder.

CASTOR

Be of good cheer: you are going to the city of Pallas, a
god-fearing city. Bear up!

ELECTRA

Clasp your breast to mine, dearest brother! The curse of
our mother's murder is separating us from the house of our
fathers!

ORESTES

Come, embrace me! And utter a dirge for me like that over
a dead man's tomb!

CASTOR

Ah me! The cry you have uttered is a terrible one even for

---

1314n Ἠλ. Bothe: Ὀρ. L
1319 ὀ- θ- Π- ἤ- Weil: θ- Π- ὀ- ἤ- L

καὶ θεοῖσι κλυεῖν.
ἔνι γὰρ κἀμοὶ τοῖς τ' οὐρανίδαις
1330 οἶκτος θνητῶν πολυμόχθων.

ΟΡΕΣΤΗΣ
οὐκέτι σ' ὄψομαι.

ΗΛΕΚΤΡΑ
οὐδ' ἐγὼ ἐς σὸν βλέφαρον πελάσω.

ΟΡΕΣΤΗΣ
τάδε λοίσθιά μοι προσφθέγματά σου.

ΗΛΕΚΤΡΑ
ὦ χαῖρε, πόλις·
1335 χαίρετε δ' ὑμεῖς πολλά, πολίτιδες.

ΟΡΕΣΤΗΣ
ὦ πιστοτάτη, στείχεις ἤδη;

ΗΛΕΚΤΡΑ
στείχω βλέφαρον τέγγουσ' ἁπαλόν.

ΟΡΕΣΤΗΣ
1340 Πυλάδη, χαίρων ἴθι, νυμφεύου
δέμας Ἠλέκτρας.

ΚΑΣΤΩΡ
τοῖσδε μελήσει γάμος· ἀλλὰ κύνας
τάσδ' ὑποφεύγων στεῖχ' ἐπ' Ἀθηνῶν·
δεινὸν γὰρ ἴχνος βάλλουσ' ἐπὶ σοὶ
1345 χειροδράκοντες χρῶτα κελαιναί,
δεινῶν ὀδυνῶν καρπὸν ἔχουσαι·
νὼ δ' ἐπὶ πόντον Σικελὸν σπουδῇ

# ELECTRA

the gods to hear! For even the gods and I feel pity for struggling mortals.

### ORESTES
No more shall I see you!

### ELECTRA
Nor shall I draw near your gaze!

### ORESTES
This is the last greeting I shall have from you!

### ELECTRA
City, farewell! A fond farewell to you, women of my city!

### ORESTES
Sister most loyal, are you going already?

### ELECTRA
I am going and in the going wet my tender eyes.

### ORESTES
Pylades, go in joy and be husband to Electra!

### CASTOR
These two shall make marriage their care. But look, the hounds approach: you must flee from them toward Athens. They are pursuing you on their dread feet, these creatures with snakes for arms and black skin, and the yield they bring forth is terrible woe. We shall go in haste to the Sicilian sea in order to rescue the ships that ply the deep.

---

1330 οἶκτος Diggle: -οι L

σώσοντε νεῶν πρώρας ἐνάλους.
διὰ δ' αἰθερίας στείχοντε πλακὸς
1350 τοῖς μὲν μυσαροῖς οὐκ ἐπαρήγομεν,
οἷσιν δ' ὅσιον καὶ τὸ δίκαιον
φίλον ἐν βιότῳ, τούτους χαλεπῶν
ἐκλύοντες μόχθων σῴζομεν.
οὕτως ἀδικεῖν μηδεὶς θελέτω
1355 μηδ' ἐπιόρκων μέτα συμπλείτω·
θεὸς ὢν θνητοῖς ἀγορεύω.

ΧΟΡΟΣ
χαίρετε· χαίρειν δ' ὅστις δύναται
καὶ ξυντυχίᾳ μή τινι κάμνει
θνητῶν εὐδαίμονα πράσσει.

1348 post h. v. (vel post 1347) lac. indic. Denniston

As we pass along the plain of heaven we do not lend aid to those who are defiled, but we rescue from hard toils and save all those who in their lives love piety and justice. So let no one willingly do wrong or sail with those who break their oaths. I am a god, and this is my warning to mortals.

*Exit* CASTOR *and Polydeuces by the* mechane.

### CHORUS LEADER
Farewell! The mortal man who can fare well and suffers no misfortune is indeed blessed.

*Exit by Eisodos B* ELECTRA, ORESTES, *Pylades, and the* CHORUS.

# HERACLES

# INTRODUCTION

Like several of Euripides' plays, *Heracles*, put on ca. 416 B.C., portrays more than one reversal in the fortunes of its characters. The play has two sequences of action, both resulting in a sudden change, the first from bad to good fortune, the second from good to bad. The suddenness of these reversals and their divine causation make a powerful statement of the archaic Greek theme of the fragility of human happiness and the unforseeability of the future. Greek myth is full of stories demonstrating that not even the greatest of men (an Achilles, a Heracles) or the most fortunate (a Cadmus, a Peleus) is exempt from the general fragility of the mortal condition. Euripides' play, though adding reflections of other kinds, makes much the same point as the myth on which it is based.

Heracles is the son of Zeus and Alcmene, wife of Amphitryon: Zeus disguised himself as Amphitryon in order to lie with Amphitryon's wife. (Though in actual paternity, Heracles is the son of Zeus, Amphitryon is also spoken of throughout the play as his father.) Just as his father is the mightiest of gods, so Heracles is the mightiest of heroes, but he has a powerful enemy, from whom his name is actually derived, Zeus's wife Hera, who persecutes the hero because he is her husband's bastard son.

In most versions of the Labors of Heracles, the hero

murders his wife and children in a fit of madness sent by
Hera and must perform the Labors for Eurystheus in ex-
piation. Euripides reverses the order of events, putting the
death of Heracles' family after the Labors. This means that
the Labors must be given another motivation: Heracles
offers to work for Eurystheus so that he and his father,
Amphitryon, may return to Argos, from which Amphitryon
has been banished. In this way the killing of his family can
be left as the final reversal of the hero's good fortune.

The play is set in Thebes, where Heracles has settled.
He is married to Megara, the daughter of the king of The-
bes, but is away on his Labors, having been sent to the
Underworld to fetch Cerberus. In the first half of the play,
he is presumed to be dead, and his wife, their children, and
his father are being threatened with death by a usurper
named Lycus. (This part of the plot may well be Euripides'
own invention.) They have taken refuge at the altar of Zeus
the Savior, but the threat of being burned alive has per-
suaded them to abandon their sanctuary and submit to
death at the hands of Lycus. Heracles returns in the nick
of time, rescues his family, and kills Lycus. The Chorus of
old men of Thebes, who are loyal to Heracles but power-
less to help him, react to the death of the usurper with a
choral ode affirming the justice of the gods and the divine
paternity of Heracles.

No sooner have the notes of this ode died out than the
minor divinities Iris and Lyssa (Madness) descend on Her-
acles' house, sent there by Hera. Iris, who is acting as
Hera's second-in-command, orders Lyssa to bring a fit of
madness on Heracles so that he will kill his own children.
Lyssa disappears into the house; cries are heard within; and
a messenger comes out to tell how Heracles went mad,

killed his three sons and his wife, and almost killed his father. Amphitryon, to prevent further murder, has tied him to a fallen pillar.

By the use of the *eccyclema*, a wheeled platform for bringing an indoor scene out of doors, Euripides allows the audience to see Heracles, tied to the pillar and lying unconscious. At last he stirs, and the Chorus and Amphitryon bravely prepare to deal with the erstwhile madman. When he awakes, however, his fit has passed. Like Agave in *Bacchae*, he is gradually brought face to face with the enormity of what he did when out of his mind. He determines to kill himself.

Before he can carry out this intention, however, Theseus, king of Athens, arrives. Coming with an army to rescue Thebes from the usurper, he finds Heracles amid the corpses of his family. When Heracles is induced to speak, he explains that his life is now in ruins and that he cannot go on living. But Theseus persuades him to give up his intention to kill himself. As they depart for Athens, Heracles likens himself to a small boat being towed by another boat (1423-4). The very same image, expressed with the same rare word (*epholkis*) had been used at the end of the rescue scene (631), where the children cling to Heracles as their savior. The repeated image emphasizes the completeness of the reversal: where previously Heracles had towed his children along, now he is the one being towed.

The justice of the gods is explicitly and implicitly raised as a serious problem in this play. On the one hand, the gods are explicitly credited with the destruction of the cruel and tyrannical Lycus, and it is suggested that they had a hand in rescuing the family of Heracles at the last moment. (Compare the way in which the death of Ion and Creusa in *Ion* are narrowly averted by divine intervention.) On the other hand, Hera's persecution of Heracles is utterly unjust. It is merely because he is the fruit of her husband's adultery that she hates him, and the most natural interpretation of Iris' words at 841-2 is that failure to ruin Heracles would be proof of Hera's impotence. Greek polytheism, however, was not wedded to the doctrine of divine moral perfection. The Greeks noted the fall of great wrongdoers with satisfaction as showing that the gods rule in heaven and punish the wicked. But this in no way compelled them to see the gods' justice in everything, and when one of the good met with undeserved disaster, they did not feel obliged to say, as a monotheist might, that this was divine beneficence heavily disguised. Instead, the sufferer may be paying for the sins of his ancestors, or, though otherwise decent, may have incurred the wrath of a god and be suffering out of proportion to his guilt. Alternatively, undeserved suffering simply proves the truth of the view (see Achilles' speech to Priam in *Iliad* 24) that mortals are born to trouble and not even the greatest and the best can be exempt. Unmerited suffering is a fact of life. Greeks of the archaic and classical periods, ever realists, did not try to pretend that the gods' dealings are manifestly just.

There is one short passage in *Heracles* where a rather different note seems to be struck, one discordant with the archaic theme of the gods and their dispensing of good and evil. Near the end of the play, Theseus argues that the gods too have to put up with the knowledge of their evil deeds (adultery, putting their fathers in chains), and that for Heracles to kill himself would show that he expects a better lot than theirs. In his reply to this argument, Heracles says (1341-6) that he does not believe in gods who do such things: no true god commits adultery or is another's master, since a god, if he is truly a god, needs nothing. A similar argument was made more than half a century earlier by the Ionian philosopher Xenophanes of Colophon. Xenophanes reasoned that the anthropomorphic idea of divinity was false, and that the true god was a mind free of human passion. Just how far Euripides himself agreed with the argument he puts in Heracles' mouth cannot be determined. It is tempting to think that he saw the force of it. For the purposes of the play, however, such an idea cannot be the dramatic truth about Heracles' situation. He is the product of the adulterous union of Zeus and Alcmene, and Hera is his jealous persecutor. In the world of the play the gods do feel passions, both erotic and vengeful, and the world is the way it is in part because that is so.

## SELECT BIBLIOGRAPHY

### Editions

U. von Wilamowitz-Moellendorff², 3 vols. (Berlin, 1895, rpt. Darmstadt, 1959).

G. W. Bond (Oxford, 1981).

K. H. Lee (Leipzig, 1988).

S. A. Barlow (Warminster, 1996).

### Literary Criticism

A. W. H. Adkins, "Basic Greek Values in Euripides' *Hecuba* and *Hercules Furens*," *CQ* 16 (1966), 193-219.

W. Arrowsmith, Introduction to *Heracles* in *The Complete*

*Greek Tragedies*, ed. D. Grene and R. Lattimore, *Euripides* vol. 2 (Chicago, 1956).

A. P. Burnett, *Catastrophe Survived: Euripides' Plays of Mixed Reversal* (Oxford, 1971), pp. 157-82.

H. H. O. Chalk, "Ἀρετή and βία in Euripides' *Heracles*," *JHS* 82 (1962), 7-18.

M. Cropp, "*Heracles, Electra* and the *Odyssey*," in M. Cropp, E. Fantham, S. E. Scully, edd., *Greek Tragedy and Its Legacy: Essays Presented to D. J. Conacher* (Calgary, 1986), pp. 187-99.

G. K. Galinsky, *The Heracles Theme* (Oxford, 1972).

J. Gregory, "Euripides' *Heracles*," *YCS* 25 (1977), 259-75.

M. R. Halleran, "Rhetoric, Irony, and the Ending of Euripides' *Heracles*," *CA* 5 (1986), 171-81.

—— *The Heracles of Euripides* (Cambridge, Mass., 1988), pp. 71-86.

K. H. Lee, "The Iris-Lyssa Scene in Euripides' *Heracles*," *Antichthon* 16 (1982), 44-53.

—— "Human and Divine in Euripides' *Heracles*," in *Vindex Humanitatis: Essays in Honour of J. H. Bishop* (Armidale, 1980), pp. 34-45.

J. D. Mikalson, "Zeus the Father and Heracles the Son in Tragedy," *TAPA* 116 (1986), 89-98.

## Dramatis Personae

| | |
|---|---|
| ΑΜΦΙΤΡΥΩΝ | AMPHITRYON, husband of Alcmene, mortal father of Heracles |
| ΜΕΓΑΡΑ | MEGARA, wife of Heracles |
| ΧΟΡΟΣ | CHORUS of old men of Thebes |
| ΛΥΚΟΣ | LYCUS, usurper of the throne of Thebes |
| ΗΡΑΚΛΗΣ | HERACLES, son of Zeus |
| ΙΡΙΣ | IRIS, minor divinity serving Hera |
| ΛΥΣΣΑ | LYSSA, goddess of madness |
| ΕΞΑΓΓΕΛΟΣ | MESSENGER from within the house |
| ΘΗΣΕΥΣ | THESEUS, King of Athens |
| Nonspeaking roles: | Heracles' three young sons |

## A Note on Staging

The *skene* represents the house of Heracles in Thebes. Eisodos A leads to other places in Thebes, Eisodos B to places outside the city.

# ΗΡΑΚΛΗΣ

ΑΜΦΙΤΡΥΩΝ

Τίς τὸν Διὸς σύλλεκτρον οὐκ οἶδεν βροτῶν,
Ἀργεῖον Ἀμφιτρύων', ὃν Ἀλκαῖός ποτε
ἔτιχθ' ὁ Περσέως, πατέρα τόνδ' Ἡρακλέους;
ὃς τάσδε Θήβας ἔσχον, ἔνθ' ὁ γηγενὴς
5 Σπαρτῶν στάχυς ἔβλαστεν, ὧν γένους Ἄρης
ἔσωσ' ἀριθμὸν ὀλίγον, οἳ Κάδμου πόλιν
τεκνοῦσι παίδων παισίν· ἔνθεν ἐξέφυ
Κρέων Μενοικέως παῖς, ἄναξ τῆσδε χθονός.
Κρέων δὲ Μεγάρας τῆσδε γίγνεται πατήρ,
10 ἣν πάντες ὑμεναίοισι Καδμεῖοί ποτε
λωτῷ συνηλάλαξαν ἡνίκ' εἰς ἐμοὺς
δόμους ὁ κλεινὸς Ἡρακλῆς νιν ἤγετο.
    λιπὼν δὲ Θήβας, οὗ κατῳκίσθην ἐγώ,
Μεγάραν τε τήνδε πενθερούς τε παῖς ἐμὸς
15 Ἀργεῖα τείχη καὶ Κυκλωπίαν πόλιν

4 ἔσχον Naber: -εν L

---

1 The teeth of the serpent of Ares, sown in the ground, sprang
up as armed men. They fought each other and most were killed.

# HERACLES

*Before the house of Heracles is the altar of Zeus the Savior,*
*at which* AMPHITRYON, MEGARA, *and Heracles' three sons*
*sit as suppliants.*

### AMPHITYRON

What mortal does not know me, Amphitryon of Argos, the
man who shared his wife with Zeus? My father was Al-
caeus, son of Perseus, and I am the father of Heracles. I
took this city of Thebes as my home, the place where the
earthborn harvest, the Sown Men, once sprang up.[1] Only
a small number of their race were spared by Ares, but they
begot in their posterity the city of Cadmus. It was from
them that this land's king, Creon, son of Menoeceus, was
descended, and Creon was the father of Megara here. All
the people of Thebes once sang her wedding song to the
music of the pipe on the day when the illustrious Heracles
brought her to my house as his bride.

But my son, quitting Thebes, where I had settled, and
leaving behind Megara and his family by marriage, yearned
to make Argos, the city built by the Cyclopes, his home,

The survivors were the ancestors of the Theban nobility. In the
usual version of the story, Cadmus, founder of Thebes, kills the
serpent and sows its teeth. In this play (see lines 252-3 below) the
sower is Ares.

ὠρέξατ᾽ οἰκεῖν, ἣν ἐγὼ φεύγω κτανὼν
Ἠλεκτρύωνα. συμφορὰς δὲ τὰς ἐμὰς
ἐξευμαρίζων καὶ πάτραν οἰκεῖν θέλων
καθόδου δίδωσι μισθὸν Εὐρυσθεῖ μέγαν,
20 ἐξημερῶσαι γαῖαν, εἴθ᾽ Ἥρας ὕπο
κέντροις δαμασθεὶς εἴτε τοῦ χρεὼν μέτα.
καὶ τοὺς μὲν ἄλλους ἐξεμόχθησεν πόνους,
τὸ λοίσθιον δὲ Ταινάρου διὰ στόμα
βέβηκ᾽ ἐς Ἅιδου τὸν τρισώματον κύνα
25 ἐς φῶς ἀνάξων, ἔνθεν οὐχ ἥκει πάλιν.
γέρων δὲ δή τις ἔστι Καδμείων λόγος
ὡς ἦν πάρος Δίρκης τις εὐνήτωρ Λύκος
τὴν ἑπτάπυργον τήνδε δεσπόζων πόλιν,
τὼ λευκοπώλω πρὶν τυραννῆσαι χθονὸς
30 Ἀμφίον᾽ ἠδὲ Ζῆθον, ἐκγόνω Διός.
οὗ ταὐτὸν ὄνομα παῖς πατρὸς κεκλημένος,
Καδμεῖος οὐκ ὢν ἀλλ᾽ ἀπ᾽ Εὐβοίας μολών,
κτείνει Κρέοντα καὶ κτανὼν ἄρχει χθονός,
στάσει νοσοῦσαν τήνδ᾽ ἐπεσπεσὼν πόλιν.
35 ἡμῖν δὲ κῆδος ἐς Κρέοντ᾽ ἀνημμένον
κακὸν μέγιστον, ὡς ἔοικε, γίγνεται.
τοὐμοῦ γὰρ ὄντος παιδὸς ἐν μυχοῖς χθονὸς
ὁ καινὸς οὗτος τῆσδε γῆς ἄρχων Λύκος
τοὺς Ἡρακλείους παῖδας ἐξελεῖν θέλει
40 κτανὼν δάμαρτά ⟨θ᾽⟩, ὡς φόνῳ σβέσῃ φόνον,
κἄμ᾽ (εἴ τι δὴ χρὴ κἄμ᾽ ἐν ἀνδράσιν λέγειν,
γέροντ᾽ ἀχρεῖον), μή ποθ᾽ οἵδ᾽ ἠνδρωμένοι
μήτρωσιν ἐκπράξωσιν αἵματος δίκην.

the city from which I am exiled for killing Electryon.[2] He wanted to dwell in our homeland and thereby lighten my troubles, and so—either goaded on by Hera's compulsion or because it was his fate—he offered Eurystheus a huge price for our return, the taming of the earth. After completing all his other labors, he has gone down, as his last labor, through the mouth of Taenarum to Hades in order to bring up to the daylight Cerberus, the dog with three bodies. From there he has not returned.

For a long time now the Thebans have been telling the story that a certain Lycus, husband to Dirce, was once master over this seven-gated city before Zeus's sons Amphion and Zethus, they of the white horses, became the land's rulers. The son of this Lycus, bearing his father's name, no Cadmean but an immigrant from Euboea, killed Creon and having killed him rules the land: he attacked the city when it was suffering from civil discord. Our marriage tie with Creon is proving, it seems, a great curse. For while my son is in the depths of the earth, this Lycus, the land's new king, intends to murder Heracles' sons and wife, wiping away old blood with new, and to kill me as well, if you can count me, a useless graybeard, among men. He is afraid that these sons, grown to manhood, may some day punish him for the death of their mother's kin. And since

---

[2] Electryon was the father of Alcmene, Amphitryon's wife. In some versions the killing is accidental, in others deliberate.

---

18 ⟨μ'⟩ οἰκεῖν Herwerden     21 fort. ἀασθείς
38 καινὸς Elmsley: κλεινὸς L
40 ⟨θ'⟩ Canter

# EURIPIDES

ἐγὼ δέ (λείπει γάρ με τοῖσδ᾽ ἐν δώμασιν
45 τροφὸν τέκνων οἰκουρόν, ἡνίκα χθονὸς
μέλαιναν ὄρφνην εἰσέβαινε, παῖς ἐμός)
σὺν μητρὶ τέκνα, μὴ θάνωσ᾽, Ἡρακλέους
βωμὸν καθίζω τόνδε σωτῆρος Διός,
ὃν καλλινίκου δορὸς ἄγαλμ᾽ ἱδρύσατο
50 Μινύας κρατήσας οὑμὸς εὐγενὴς τόκος.

πάντων δὲ χρεῖοι τάσδ᾽ ἕδρας φυλάσσομεν,
σίτων ποτῶν ἐσθῆτος, ἀστρώτῳ πέδῳ
πλευρὰς τιθέντες· ἐκ γὰρ ἐσφραγισμένοι
δόμων καθήμεθ᾽ ἀπορίᾳ σωτηρίας.
55 φίλων δὲ τοὺς μὲν οὐ σαφεῖς ὁρῶ φίλους,
οἱ δ᾽ ὄντες ὀρθῶς ἀδύνατοι προσωφελεῖν.
τοιοῦτον ἀνθρώποισιν ἡ δυσπραξία
ἧς μήποθ᾽ ὅστις καὶ μέσως εὔνους ἐμοὶ
τύχοι, φίλων ἔλεγχον ἀψευδέστατον.

## ΜΕΓΑΡΑ

60 ὦ πρέσβυ, Ταφίων ὅς ποτ᾽ ἐξεῖλες πόλιν
στρατηλατήσας κλεινὰ Καδμείων δορός,
ὡς οὐδὲν ἀνθρώποισι τῶν θείων σαφές.
ἐγὼ γὰρ οὔτ᾽ ἐς πατέρ᾽ ἀπηλάθην τύχης,
ὃς οὕνεκ᾽ ὄλβου μέγας ἐκομπάσθη ποτὲ
65 ἔχων τυραννίδ᾽, ἧς μακραὶ λόγχαι πέρι
πηδῶσ᾽ ἔρωτι δώματ᾽ εἰς εὐδαίμονα,

48 fort. ⟨᾽ς⟩ τόνδε: sed cf. Ion 1314
63 fort. οὖν . . . ἐπειράθην

314

my son left me here to tend the home as his children's nurse when he entered the gloomy depths of the earth, to prevent their death I have set Heracles' children and their mother as suppliants at the altar of Zeus the Savior here. This was a monument to his victorious spear set up by my nobly born son after his victory over the Minyans.[3]

We lack all necessities as we keep our station here: we have no food, drink, or clothing, and we lie upon the bare ground. We have been locked out of the house, and we sit here without any means of saving our lives. Some of our friends, I now see, are not friends in deed, while those who truly are so are powerless to help us. That is what misfortune brings to mortals. May no one of even moderate good will toward me have to endure this, the truest test of friends!

### MEGARA

Old sir, who once captured the city of the Taphians,[4] gloriously leading the army of Thebes, how little of what the gods send can be known by mortal men! Where my father was concerned I was not deprived of good fortune. He was extolled as a man of great blessedness, because he possessed a throne, for whose sake long spears leap in eager desire against the houses of the blessed, and because of his

[3] The Minyans of Orchomenus were Thebes' chief rival in Boeotia.

[4] The Taphians lived in northwest Greece. They killed Alcmene's brothers in a cattle raid, and she demanded that Amphitryon avenge their killing if he was to marry her.

---

65–6 in suspicionem voc. Diggle, qui etiam 67 τε pro δέ scribit
66 δώματ' Mekler: σώματ' L

ἔχων δὲ τέκνα· κἄμ᾽ ἔδωκε παιδὶ σῷ
ἐπίσημον εὐνήν, Ἡρακλεῖ συνοικίσας.
καὶ νῦν ἐκεῖνα μὲν θανόντ᾽ ἀνέπτατο,
70  ἐγὼ δὲ καὶ σὺ μέλλομεν θνῄσκειν, γέρον,
οἵ θ᾽ Ἡράκλειοι παῖδες, οὓς ὑπὸ πτεροῖς
σῴζω νεοσσοὺς ὄρνις ὣς ὑφειμένους.
οἱ δ᾽ εἰς ἔλεγχον ἄλλος ἄλλοθεν πίτνων
Ὦ μῆτερ, αὐδᾷ, ποῖ πατὴρ ἄπεστι γῆς;
75  τί δρᾷ, πόθ᾽ ἥξει; τῷ νέῳ δ᾽ ἐσφαλμένοι
ζητοῦσι τὸν τεκόντ᾽· ἐγὼ δὲ διαφέρω
λόγοισι μυθεύουσα. θαυμάζων δ᾽ ὅταν
πύλαι ψοφῶσι πᾶς ἀνίστησιν πόδα,
ὡς πρὸς πατρῷον προσπεσούμενοι γόνυ.
80   νῦν οὖν τίν᾽ ἐλπίδ᾽ ἢ πόρον σωτηρίας
ἐξευμαρίζῃ, πρέσβυ; πρὸς σὲ γὰρ βλέπω.
ὡς οὔτε γαίας ὅρι᾽ ἂν ἐκβαῖμεν λάθρα
(φυλακαὶ γὰρ ἡμῶν κρείσσονες κατ᾽ ἐξόδους)
οὔτ᾽ ἐν φίλοισιν ἐλπίδες σωτηρίας
85  ἔτ᾽ εἰσὶν ἡμῖν. ἥντιν᾽ οὖν γνώμην ἔχεις
λέγ᾽ ἐς τὸ κοινόν, μὴ θανεῖν ἕτοιμον ᾖ,
χρόνον δὲ μηκύνωμεν ὄντες ἀσθενεῖς.

ΑΜΦΙΤΡΥΩΝ

ὦ θύγατερ, οὔτοι ῥᾴδιον τὰ τοιάδε
φαύλως παραινεῖν, σπουδάσαντ᾽ ἄνευ πόνου.

ΜΕΓΑΡΑ

90  λύπης τι προσδεῖς ἢ φιλεῖς οὕτω φάος;

children. And he made a brilliant marriage for me by giving me as a bride to your son Heracles. Now, however, all that good fortune has taken wing and gone, and you and I, sir, will soon be killed, and Heracles' children as well, children I shelter like a bird her brood, nestling under my wings. They fall to questioning me, one from this direction, another from that, saying, "Mother, where in the world has father gone off to, what is he doing, when will he come back?" In their youthful confusion they look for their father. I tell them stories to put them off. Whenever the door creaks, they all in wonder jump up in order to hurl themselves at their father's knees.

So now what hope or what means of survival can you provide, sir? For it is to you that I look. We cannot secretly cross the borders of Thebes (the guards stationed at the gates are too powerful for us), and we have no hope of rescue from friends. Say openly what you think, so that we may not out of weakness, with our death already fixed, be drawing out the time it takes to die.

AMPHITRYON

Daughter, it goes against the grain to give such advice rashly, showing zeal without labor.

MEGARA

Do you need still more pain? Are you so in love with the sun's light?

---

72 ὑφειμένους Kirchhoff: -μένη L
77 θαυμάζων Kirchhoff: -ζω L
80 πόρον Musgrave: πέδον L

# EURIPIDES

### ΑΜΦΙΤΡΥΩΝ

καὶ τῷδε χαίρω καὶ φιλῶ τὰς ἐλπίδας.

### ΜΕΓΑΡΑ

κἀγώ· δοκεῖν δὲ τἀδόκητ᾽ οὐ χρή, γέρον.

### ΑΜΦΙΤΡΥΩΝ

ἐν ταῖς ἀναβολαῖς τῶν κακῶν ἔνεστ᾽ ἄκη.

### ΜΕΓΑΡΑ

ὁ δ᾽ ἐν μέσῳ γε λυπρὸς ὢν δάκνει χρόνος.

### ΑΜΦΙΤΡΥΩΝ

95   ⟨χρόνῳ⟩ γένοιτ᾽ ἄν, θύγατερ, οὔριος δρόμος
ἐκ τῶν παρόντων τῶνδ᾽ ἐμοὶ καὶ σοὶ κακῶν
ἔλθοι τ᾽ ἔτ᾽ ἂν παῖς οὑμός, εὐνήτωρ δὲ σός.
ἀλλ᾽ ἡσύχαζε καὶ δακρυρρόους τέκνων
πηγὰς ἀφαίρει καὶ παρευκήλει λόγοις,
100  κλέπτουσα μύθοις ἀθλίους κλοπὰς ὅμως.
κάμνουσι γάρ τοι καὶ βροτῶν αἱ συμφοραί,
καὶ πνεύματ᾽ ἀνέμων οὐκ ἀεὶ ῥώμην ἔχει,
οἵ τ᾽ εὐτυχοῦντες διὰ τέλους οὐκ εὐτυχεῖς·
ἐξίσταται γὰρ πάντ᾽ ἀπ᾽ ἀλλήλων δίχα.
105  οὗτος δ᾽ ἀνὴρ ἄριστος ὅστις ἐλπίσιν
πέποιθεν αἰεί· τὸ δ᾽ ἀπορεῖν ἀνδρὸς κακοῦ.

94 γε Dobree: με L
95 ⟨χρόνῳ⟩ γένοιτ᾽ ἄν, θύγατερ M. Schmidt: γένοιτ᾽ ἄν, ὢ
θύγατερ L
103 om. t, del. Nauck

**AMPHITRYON**

I enjoy the sunlight, and I hold hope dear.

**MEGARA**

So do I. Yet one must not hope, sir, for what is beyond hoping.

**AMPHITRYON**

Yet in postponing disaster there is some healing of it.

**MEGARA**

Still, the time in between gnaws cruelly.

**AMPHITRYON**

‹In time›, my daughter, there may come a favoring breeze to succeed the troubles that now beset you and me, and my son, your husband, may yet return. So keep calm and with the charm of speech still your sons' tears, and though it is but a pitiful deception, yet deceive them with your stories. Just as the winds do not always keep the same force, so too, you know, the disasters that beset mortals abate, and those who enjoy good fortune are not fortunate to the end. Everything in the world retires and separates from each other. The bravest man is he who always puts his trust in hope. To surrender to helplessness is the mark of a coward.

*Enter old men of Thebes as* CHORUS *by Eisodos A. They have staves in their hands to steady their tottering gait.*

319

ΧΟΡΟΣ

στρ.

    ὑψόροφα μέλαθρα καὶ γεραι-
    ὰ δέμνι᾿ ἀμφὶ βάκτροις
    ἔρεισμα θέμενος ἐστάλην
110  ἰηλέμων γέρων ἀοι-
    δὸς ὥστε πολιὸς ὄρνις,
    ἔπεα μόνον καὶ δόκημα νυκτερω-
    πὸν ἐννύχων ὀνείρων,
    τρομερὰ μέν, ἀλλ᾿ ὅμως πρόθυμ᾿,
115  ὦ τέκεα τέκεα πατρὸς ἀπάτορ᾿,
    ὦ γεραιὲ σύ τε τάλαινα μᾶ-
    τερ, ἃ τὸν ⟨ἐν⟩ Ἀΐδα δόμοις
    πόσιν ἀναστενάζεις.

ἀντ.

    μὴ πόδα πρόκαμνε βαρύ τε κῶ-
120  λον ὥστε πρὸς πετραῖον
    λέπας ζυγηφόρος πονῶν
    ἄναντα βάρος ⟨ὄχου⟩ φέρων
    τροχηλάτοιο πῶλος.
    λαβοῦ χερῶν καὶ πέπλων, ὅτου λέλοι-
125  πε ποδὸς ἀμαυρὸν ἴχνος·
    γέρων γέροντα παρακόμιζ᾿,
128  ᾧ ξύνοπλα δόρατα νέα νέῳ

107 ὑψόροφα Musgrave: ὑπώροφα L    110 γέρων Nauck:
γόων L, quam lect. def. Renehan, *CP* 80 (1985), 147–9
114 μὲν Tyrwhitt: μόνον L    117 ⟨ἐν⟩ Hermann

HERACLES

CHORUS

For this high-roofed house and the old man's
bed, easing my weight
about my staff, I have set out,
an aged singer of lament
like some bird of white plumage.
Mere words am I now and an insubstantial
vision seen at night,
trembling, but full of eagerness,
children, children, of father bereft,
and you, old man, and you, unhappy mother,
who mourn your husband
in the house of Hades.

Do not let your feet and your heavy legs
grow weary like a burdened horse
laboring up the rocky hill
trying to carry
the weight of the wheel-borne chariot.
Grasp the hands and garments
of anyone whose footstep is unsteady!
Help an old man along, though you yourself are old.
His brother in arms were you

---

119 πόδα πρόκαμνε Diggle: προκάμητε πόδα L

121-3 sic post Hartung (ζυγηφόρος . . . βάρος φέρων
τροχηλάτοιο πῶλος, etiam ‹ὄχου› ante τρ-) et Wecklein (ἄναν-
τες) Willink: ζυγηφόρον πῶλον ἀνέντες ὡς βάρος φέρον
τροχηλάτοιο πώλου L

124 χερὸς Wilamowitz
127 et 128 inter se trai. Musgrave

321

127 τὸ πάρος ἐν ἡλίκων πόνοι-
σιν ἦν ποτ’, εὐκλεεστάτας
130 πατρίδος οὐκ ὀνείδη.

ἐπῳδ.

ἴδετε, πατέρος ὡς γορ-
γῶπες αἵδε προσφερεῖς
ὀμμάτων αὐγαί,
τὸ δὲ κακοτυχὲς οὐ λέλοιπεν ἐκ τέκνων
οὐδ’ ἀποίχεται χάρις.
135 Ἑλλὰς ὦ ξυμμάχους
οἵους οἵους ὀλέσασα
τούσδ’ ἀποστερήσῃ.

—ἀλλ’ εἰσορῶ γὰρ τῆσδε κοίρανον χθονὸς
Λύκον περῶντα τῶνδε δωμάτων πέλας.

ΛΥΚΟΣ

140 τὸν Ἡράκλειον πατέρα καὶ ξυνάορον,
εἰ χρή μ’, ἐρωτῶ· χρὴ δ’, ἐπεί γε δεσπότης
ὑμῶν καθέστηχ’, ἱστορεῖν ἃ βούλομαι.
τίν’ ἐς χρόνον ζητεῖτε μηκῦναι βίον;
τίν’ ἐλπίδ’ ἀλκήν τ’ εἰσορᾶτε μὴ θανεῖν;
145 ἦ τὸν παρ’ Ἅιδῃ πατέρα τῶνδε κείμενον
πιστεύεθ’ ἥξειν; ὡς ὑπὲρ τὴν ἀξίαν
τὸ πένθος αἴρεσθ’ εἰ θανεῖν ὑμᾶς χρεών,
σὺ μὲν καθ’ Ἑλλάδ’ ἐκβαλὼν κόμπους κενοὺς
ὡς σύγγαμός σοι Ζεὺς τέκνου τε κοινεῶν,
150 σὺ δ’ ὡς ἀρίστου φωτὸς ἐκλήθης δάμαρ.

when you were both young and grasped the spear
in the battles of your youth:
you did not disgrace your glorious country.

See how the fierce glance
in these children's eyes
resembles their father's!
The ill luck that dogged him has not abandoned his sons,
nor yet has his loveliness vanished.
O Greece, what allies,
what allies you will have lost
when these are taken from you!

*Enter LYCUS with retinue by Eisodos A.*

CHORUS LEADER

But I see the country's ruler, Lycus, approaching this
house.

LYCUS

Heracles' father and wife, here is a question for you, if I
may ask it—and since I have become your master, I may
ask you what I wish: how long are you planning to prolong
your life? What hope, what defense against death do you
see? Do you believe that the father of these children, who
lies dead in Hades, will return? How excessively you grieve
that you must die, one of you uttering throughout Greece
the foolish boast that Zeus shared your wife with you and
was partner in the begetting of your son, the other that you
are called the wife of the noblest of heroes!

---

127–9 πόνοισιν ἦν Willink: πόνοις ξυνῆν L
146 ὡς Matthiae: ὥσθ᾽ L
149 τέκνου τε κοινεών Heath: τέκοι νέον L

τί δὴ τὸ σεμνὸν σῷ κατείργασται πόσει,
ὕδραν ἕλειον εἰ διώλεσε κτανὼν
ἢ τὸν Νέμειον θῆρ᾽, ὃν ἐν βρόχοις ἑλὼν
βραχίονός φησ᾽ ἀγχόναισιν ἐξελεῖν;
155 τοῖσδ᾽ ἐξαγωνίζεσθε; τῶνδ᾽ ἄρ᾽ οὕνεκα
τοὺς Ἡρακλείους παῖδας οὐ θνῄσκειν χρεών;
ὁ δ᾽ ἔσχε δόξαν οὐδὲν ὢν εὐψυχίας
θηρῶν ἐν αἰχμῇ, τἄλλα δ᾽ οὐδὲν ἄλκιμος,
ὃς οὔποτ᾽ ἀσπίδ᾽ ἔσχε πρὸς λαιᾷ χερὶ
160 οὐδ᾽ ἦλθε λόγχης ἐγγὺς ἀλλὰ τόξ᾽ ἔχων,
κάκιστον ὅπλων, τῇ φυγῇ πρόχειρος ἦν.
ἀνδρὸς δ᾽ ἔλεγχος οὐχὶ τόξ᾽ εὐψυχίας
ἀλλ᾽ ὃς μένων βλέπει τε κἀντιδέρκεται
δορὸς ταχεῖαν ἄλοκα τάξιν ἐμβεβώς.
165 ἔχει δὲ τοὐμὸν οὐκ ἀναίδειαν, γέρον,
ἀλλ᾽ εὐλάβειαν· οἶδα γὰρ κατακτανὼν
Κρέοντα πατέρα τῆσδε καὶ θρόνους ἔχων.
οὔκουν τραφέντων τῶνδε τιμωροὺς ἐμοὶ
χρῄζω λιπέσθαι, τῶν δεδραμένων δίκην.

ΑΜΦΙΤΡΥΩΝ

170 τῷ τοῦ Διὸς μὲν Ζεὺς ἀμυνέτω μέρει
παιδός· τὸ δ᾽ εἰς ἔμ᾽, Ἡράκλεις, ἐμοὶ μέλει
λόγοισι τὴν τοῦδ᾽ ἀμαθίαν ὑπὲρ σέθεν
δεῖξαι· κακῶς γάρ σ᾽ οὐκ ἐατέον κλύειν.
πρῶτον μὲν οὖν τἄρρητ᾽ (ἐν ἀρρήτοισι γὰρ
175 τὴν σὴν νομίζω δειλίαν, Ἡράκλεες)
σὺν μάρτυσιν θεοῖς δεῖ μ᾽ ἀπαλλάξαι σέθεν.

What impressive deed was it that your husband performed in killing a marsh snake or that Nemean creature? He caught it in a snare and claimed he killed it barehanded! On claims like these will you struggle to the end? Is it because of these deeds that Heracles' children ought not to be put to death?

Heracles, though worthless, has acquired a reputation for courage by fighting with beasts, though in other things he is not brave at all. He has never strapped a shield on his left arm, never faced the spear point. He had a bow, basest of weapons, in his hand and was ready to run away! A bow does not show a man's courage: that is done by standing your ground, looking straight at the swift swathe cut by enemy spears, and holding ranks.

What I am doing, old man, is not ruthlessness but prudent caution. I know that it is because I killed Creon, this woman's father, that I have the throne. So I do not wish to raise these children to manhood and leave for myself avengers to punish me for my deeds.

#### AMPHITRYON

As regards Zeus's part in his son, let Zeus himself defend it. As for my own part, Heracles, my care is to show by argument how senseless this man is where you are concerned: I cannot allow you to be reviled.

First I must free you from an unspeakable slander (for I regard cowardice in you, Heracles, as an unspeakable idea) with the gods as my witnesses. I call on the thunder-

---

157 ὁ δ᾽ Wilamowitz: ὃς L      161 ὅπλων Elmsley: -ον L
167 καὶ] τοὺς Luppe
168 ἐμοὶ Π sicut coni. Camper: ἐμοὺς L

Διὸς κεραυνὸν ἠρόμην τέθριππά τε
ἐν οἷς βεβηκὼς τοῖσι γῆς βλαστήμασιν
Γίγασι πλευροῖς πτήν' ἐναρμόσας βέλη
180 τὸν καλλίνικον μετὰ θεῶν ἐκώμασεν·
τετρασκελές θ' ὕβρισμα, Κενταύρων γένος,
Φολόην ἐπελθών, ὦ κάκιστε βασιλέων,
ἐροῦ τίν' ἄνδρ' ἄριστον ἐκκρίνειαν ἄν·
ἢ οὐ παῖδα τὸν ἐμόν, ὃν σὺ φὴς εἰκῆ δοκεῖν;
185 Δίρφυν τ' ἐρωτῶν ἤ σ' ἔθρεψ' Ἀβαντίδα—
οὐκ ἄν σέ γ' αἰνέσειεν· οὐ γὰρ ἔσθ' ὅπου
ἐσθλόν τι δράσας μάρτυρ' ἂν λάβοις πάτραν.
    τὸ πάνσοφον δ' εὕρημα, τοξήρη σαγήν,
μέμφῃ· κλυών νυν τἀπ' ἐμοῦ σοφὸς γενοῦ.
190 ἀνὴρ ὁπλίτης δοῦλός ἐστι τῶν ὅπλων
193 θραύσας τε λόγχην οὐκ ἔχει τῷ σώματι
194 θάνατον ἀμῦναι, μίαν ἔχων ἀλκὴν μόνον·
191 καὶ τοῖσι συνταχθεῖσιν οὖσι μὴ ἀγαθοῖς
192 αὐτὸς τέθνηκε, δειλίᾳ τῇ τῶν πέλας.
195 ὅσοι δὲ τόξοις χεῖρ' ἔχουσιν εὔστοχον,
ἓν μὲν τὸ λῷστον, μυρίους οἰστοὺς ἀφεὶς
ἄλλοις τὸ σῶμα ῥύεται μὴ κατθανεῖν,
ἑκὰς δ' ἀφεστὼς πολεμίους ἀμύνεται
τυφλοῖς ὁρῶντας οὐτάσας τοξεύμασιν
200 τὸ σῶμά τ' οὐ δίδωσι τοῖς ἐναντίοις,

177 κεραυνὸν Wilamowitz: -ὸν δ' L
183 ἐκκρίνειαν Dobree: cf. S. Phil. 1425: ἐγκρίν- L
184 εἰκῆ Reiske: εἶναι L: εἶναι κακόν Wilamowitz
185 ἐρωτῶνθ' A. S. Henry

bolt of Zeus, I call on the chariot in which he stood when
he shot his winged arrows into the flanks of the earthborn
Giants[5] and then celebrated his victory in the company of
the gods! Go to Pholoë, you most cowardly of rulers, and
ask the Centaurs,[6] those violent four-legged creatures,
what man they would consider to be the bravest. Is it not
my son, who you say is falsely reputed brave? And if you
asked Mt. Dirphys in Abantid Euboea, which raised you
up, it is not you it would praise. Never did you do any brave
deed that your homeland could attest to!

You find fault with that cleverest of inventions, the bow.
Hear then what I have to say and learn wisdom! The infan-
tryman is the slave of his arms, and if he breaks his spear,
he cannot ward off death from himself since that is his only
defense. And because the men who are with him in the
ranks are not brave, he is killed, and the cause is the cow-
ardice of his neighbors. But the man who is skilled with the
bow has this one great advantage: when he has shot count-
less arrows, he still has others to defend himself from
death. He stands far off and avenges himself on his ene-
mies by wounding them with arrows they cannot see even
though their eyes are open. He does not expose his body

---

[5] Heracles helped Zeus and the Olympians to defeat an attack
by the Giants, offspring of Earth. See Pindar, *Nemean* 1.67-9 and
M. L. West's commentary on Hesiod, *Theogony* 954.

[6] On Heracles' fight with the Centaurs see lines 364-74 below.
Pholoë is in Arcadia.

---

186 σέ γ᾽ αἰνέσειεν Wilamowitz: ἐπαινέσειεν L
187 δρᾶσαι Musgrave
191-2 post 194 trai. Wilamowitz

327

# EURIPIDES

ἐν εὐφυλάκτῳ δ᾽ ἐστί. τοῦτο δ᾽ ἐν μάχῃ
σοφὸν μάλιστα, δρῶντα πολεμίους κακῶς
σῴζειν τὸ σῶμα, μὴ ᾽κ τύχης ὡρμισμένον.
    λόγοι μὲν οἵδε τοῖσι σοῖς ἐναντίαν
205 γνώμην ἔχουσι τῶν καθεστώτων πέρι.
παῖδας δὲ δὴ τί τούσδ᾽ ἀποκτεῖναι θέλεις;
τί σ᾽ οἵδ᾽ ἔδρασαν; ἕν τί σ᾽ ἡγοῦμαι σοφόν,
εἰ τῶν ἀρίστων τἄκγον᾽ αὐτὸς ὢν κακὸς
δέδοικας. ἀλλὰ τοῦθ᾽ ὅμως ἡμῖν βαρύ,
210 εἰ δειλίας σῆς κατθανούμεθ᾽ οὕνεκα,
ὃ χρῆν σ᾽ ὑφ᾽ ἡμῶν τῶν ἀμεινόνων παθεῖν,
εἰ Ζεὺς δικαίας εἶχεν εἰς ἡμᾶς φρένας.
εἰ δ᾽ οὖν ἔχειν γῆς σκῆπτρα τῆσδ᾽ αὐτὸς θέλεις,
ἔασον ἡμᾶς φυγάδας ἐξελθεῖν χθονός·
215 βίᾳ δὲ δράσῃς μηδὲν ἢ πείσῃ βίαν
ὅταν θεοῦ σοι πνεῦμα μεταβαλὸν τύχῃ.
    φεῦ·
ὦ γαῖα Κάδμου (καὶ γὰρ ἐς σ᾽ ἀφίξομαι
λόγους ὀνειδιστῆρας ἐνδατούμενος),
τοιαῦτ᾽ ἀμύνεθ᾽ Ἡρακλεῖ τέκνοισί τε,
220 Μινύαις ὃς εἷς ἅπασι διὰ μάχης μολὼν
Θήβας ἔθηκεν ὄμμ᾽ ἐλεύθερον βλέπειν;
οὐδ᾽ Ἑλλάδ᾽ ᾔνεσ᾽ (οὐδ᾽ ἀνέξομαί ποτε
σιγῶν) κακίστην λαμβάνων ἐς παῖδ᾽ ἐμόν,
ἣν χρῆν νεοσσοῖς τοῖσδε πῦρ λόγχας ὅπλα
225 φέρουσαν ἐλθεῖν, ποντίων καθαρμάτων
χέρσου τ᾽ ἀμοιβὰς ὧν ἐμόχθησεν χερί.
    τὰ δ᾽, ὦ τέκν᾽, ὑμῖν οὔτε Θηβαίων πόλις

to the enemy but keeps it well protected. This is the
shrewdest thing in battle, to hurt the enemy and save your
own life, being independent of fortune.

These words of mine give the opposite view to yours on
a subject of conventional opinion. But tell me, why do you
want to kill these children? What have they done to you?
It is only on one point, I think, that you are wise: being a
coward yourself you are scared of the sons of heroes. Still,
being put to death because of your cowardice is hard for
us to take. This is what should have been done to you by
us, who are your betters, if Zeus were just toward us. Well
then, if you want to keep the scepter of this land yourself,
let us depart as exiles. But do not act with violence, or
violence is what you will suffer when the winds sent by
Heaven change.

Ah me! Land of Cadmus (for I shall come to you too as
I distribute my words of reproach), is this the help you
offer Heracles and his children, the man who battled all
the Minyans single-handed and caused Thebes to look
once more with freedom in her glance? I have no word of
praise for Greece either (I shall never keep silent on this
point), since I have found her disloyal toward my son. She
should have come bringing fire, spears, and shields to these
children in payment for the cleansing of land and sea
wrought by his hand. This protection, children, neither

---

[203] ὡρμισμένον Reiske: -μένους L    [205] παρεστώτων
Wilamowitz cl. *Pho.* 1309    [215] βίᾳ . . . βίαν Reiske: βίαν
. . . λίαν L    [220] Μινύαις ὃς εἷς ἅπασι Elmsley: ὃς εἷς
Μινύαισι πᾶσι L    [221] Θήβας Heiland: -αις L
[226] ἐμόχθησεν χερί Diggle: -σας χάριν L

οὔθ᾽ Ἑλλὰς ἀρκεῖ· πρὸς δ᾽ ἔμ᾽ ἀσθενῆ φίλον
δεδόρκατ᾽, οὐδὲν ὄντα πλὴν γλώσσης ψόφον.
230 ῥώμη γὰρ ἐκλέλοιπεν ἣν πρὶν εἴχομεν,
γήρᾳ δὲ τρομερὰ γυῖα κἀμαυρὸν σθένος.
εἰ δ᾽ ἦ νέος τε κἄτι σώματος κρατῶν,
λαβὼν ἂν ἔγχος τοῦδε τοὺς ξανθοὺς πλόκους
καθῃμάτωσ᾽ ἄν, ὥστ᾽ Ἀτλαντικῶν πέραν
235 φεύγειν ὅρων ἂν δειλίᾳ τοὐμὸν δόρυ.

ΧΟΡΟΣ

ἆρ᾽ οὐκ ἀφορμὰς τοῖς λόγοισιν ἀγαθοὶ
θνητῶν ἔχουσι, κἂν βραδύς τις ᾖ λέγειν;

ΛΥΚΟΣ

σὺ μὲν λέγ᾽ ἡμᾶς οἷς πεπύργωσαι λόγοις,
ἐγὼ δὲ δράσω σ᾽ ἀντὶ τῶν λόγων κακῶς.
240 ἄγ᾽, οἱ μὲν Ἑλικῶν᾽, οἱ δὲ Παρνασοῦ πτυχὰς
τέμνειν ἄνωχθ᾽ ἐλθόντες ὑλουργοὺς δρυὸς
κορμούς· ἐπειδὰν δ᾽ ἐσκομισθῶσιν πόλει,
βωμὸν πέριξ νήσαντες ἀμφήρη ξύλα
ἐμπίμπρατ᾽ αὐτῶν κἀκπυροῦτε σώματα
245 πάντων, ἵν᾽ εἰδῶσ᾽ οὕνεκ᾽ οὐχ ὁ κατθανὼν
κρατεῖ χθονὸς τῆσδ᾽ ἀλλ᾽ ἐγὼ τὰ νῦν τάδε.
ὑμεῖς δέ, πρέσβεις, ταῖς ἐμαῖς ἐναντίοι
γνώμαισιν ὄντες, οὐ μόνον στενάξετε
τοὺς Ἡρακλείους παῖδας ἀλλὰ καὶ δόμου
250 τύχας, ὅταν πάσχῃ τι, μεμνήσεσθε δὲ
δοῦλοι γεγῶτες τῆς ἐμῆς τυραννίδος.

Thebes nor Greece is offering you. You must look to me,
a friend who is weak, nothing but a noise of the tongue.
The vigor I once had has left me, my limbs tremble with
age, and my strength is faint. If I were a young man and
still had power over my body, I would have taken a spear
and bloodied those golden locks of his, so that he would
run away in cowardice beyond the pillars of Atlas.

CHORUS LEADER

Do not brave men, even when they lack a ready tongue,
find good things to say?

LYCUS

Go on reviling me with the words you are so proud of! I
shall pay you back for words with deeds!

Come, some of you go to Helicon, others to the glens
of Parnassus, and order the woodsmen to cut logs of oak!
When these have been brought into the city, pile the wood
close about the altar and set alight and burn the bodies of
them all! Then they will know that it is not the dead man
but I who now rule this land!

*Two of Lycus' retinue depart by Eisodos B.*

And you, old men, who oppose my decisions, you will
weep not only for the sons of Heracles but for the misfor-
tunes of your own houses when they suffer disaster: you
will remember that you are slaves subject to my rule!

---

235 ἂν] νιν Elmsley
241 ἐλθόντες Dobree: -τας L
244 κἀκπυροῦτε Wecklein: καὶ πυρ- L

ΧΟΡΟΣ

ὦ γῆς λοχεύμαθ᾽, οὓς Ἄρης σπείρει ποτὲ
λάβρον δράκοντος ἐξερημώσας γένυν,
οὐ σκῆπτρα, χειρὸς δεξιᾶς ἐρείσματα,
255  ἀρεῖτε καὶ τοῦδ᾽ ἀνδρὸς ἀνόσιον κάρα
καθαιματώσεθ᾽, ὅστις οὐ Καδμεῖος ὢν
ἄρχει κάκιστα τῶν ἐτῶν ἔπηλυς ὤν;
ἀλλ᾽ οὐκ ἐμοῦ γε δεσπόσεις χαίρων ποτὲ
οὐδ᾽ ἀπόνησα πόλλ᾽ ἐγὼ καμὼν χερὶ
260  ἕξεις. ἀπέρρων δ᾽ ἔνθεν ἦλθες ἐνθάδε
ὕβριζ᾽. ἐμοῦ γὰρ ζῶντος οὐ κτενεῖς ποτε
τοὺς Ἡρακλείους παῖδας. οὐ τοσόνδε γῆς
263  ἔνερθ᾽ ἐκεῖνος κρύπτεται λιπὼν τέκνα.
268    ὦ δεξιὰ χείρ, ὡς ποθεῖς λαβεῖν δόρυ,
ἐν δ᾽ ἀσθενείᾳ τὸν πόθον διώλεσας·
270  ἐπεί σ᾽ ἔπαυσ᾽ ἂν δοῦλον ἐννέποντά με
καὶ τάσδε Θήβας εὐκλεῶς ὠνήσαμεν,
ἐν αἷς σὺ χαίρεις· οὐ γὰρ εὖ φρονεῖ πόλις
στάσει νοσοῦσα καὶ κακοῖς βουλεύμασιν.
274  οὐ γάρ ποτ᾽ ἂν σὲ δεσπότην ἐκτήσατο·
264  ἐπεὶ σὺ μὲν γῆν τήνδε διολέσας ἔχεις,
265  ὁ δ᾽ ὠφελήσας ἀξίων οὐ τυγχάνει.
266  κἄπειτα πράσσω πόλλ᾽ ἐγώ, φίλους ἐμοὺς
267  θανόντας εὖ δρῶν, οὗ φίλων μάλιστα δεῖ;

254 ἐρείσματα Stephanus: ὁρίσματα L
257 κάκιστα Kovacs: -ος L     ἐτῶν Reiske: νέων L
264–7 vide post 274

### CHORUS LEADER

Offspring of earth that Ares once sowed when he had despoiled the fierce jaw of the dragon,[7] will you not take up the staves that prop your right hands and bloody this man's godless head? He is no true Theban, and rules most wrongfully over the citizens since he is an immigrant. But you will never get away with lording it over me, nor take from me what I have worked so hard to get. Go back to where you came from and be high-handed there! While I live you will never kill the children of Heracles: not so deep as that is he buried in the ground, leaving his children behind!

O right arm of mine, how you long to take up the spear! Yet because of your weakness your longing has come to naught. Otherwise I would have put a stop to your calling me "slave" and would have done a glorious service to Thebes, in which you are now reveling. Thebes is not in its right mind, it suffers from civil strife and bad counsel. Otherwise it would never have taken you for a master. You have destroyed this country and you now rule it, but Heracles, who did it great service, does not get his due reward. Am I a meddler, then, if I do good to my friends when they are dead, the time when friends are most needed?

[7] See note on line 5 above.

---

269 τὸν πόθον] fort. τοὔντονον
271 ὠνήσαμεν Hermann: ᾠκήσ- L
264–7 post 274 trai. West

333

ΜΕΓΑΡΑ

275 γέροντες, αἰνῶ· τῶν φίλων γὰρ οὕνεκα
ὀργὰς δικαίας τοὺς φίλους ἔχειν χρεών.
ἡμῶν δ᾽ ἕκατι δεσπόταις θυμούμενοι
πάθητε μηδέν. τῆς δ᾽ ἐμῆς, Ἀμφιτρύων,
γνώμης ἄκουσον, ἤν τί σοι δοκῶ λέγειν.
280 ἐγὼ φιλῶ μὲν τέκνα· πῶς γὰρ οὐ φιλῶ
ἄτικτον, ἁμόχθησα; καὶ τὸ κατθανεῖν
δεινὸν νομίζω· τῷ δ᾽ ἀναγκαίῳ τρόπῳ
ὃς ἀντιτείνει σκαιὸν ἡγοῦμαι βροτῶν.
ἡμᾶς δ᾽, ἐπειδὴ δεῖ θανεῖν, θνήσκειν χρεὼν
285 μὴ πυρὶ καταξανθέντας, ἐχθροῖσιν γέλων
διδόντας, οὑμοὶ τοῦ θανεῖν μεῖζον κακόν.
ὀφείλομεν γὰρ πολλὰ δώμασιν καλά·
σὲ μὲν δόκησις ἔλαβεν εὐκλεὴς δορός,
ὥστ᾽ οὐκ ἀνεκτὸν δειλίας θανεῖν σ᾽ ὕπο·
290 οὑμὸς δ᾽ ἀμαρτύρητος εὐκλεὴς πόσις;
ὃς τούσδε παῖδας οὐκ ἂν ἐκσῶσαι θέλοι
δόξαν κακὴν λαβόντας· οἱ γὰρ εὐγενεῖς
κάμνουσι τοῖς αἰσχροῖσι τῶν τέκνων ὕπερ·
ἐμοί τε μίμημ᾽ ἀνδρὸς οὐκ ἀπωστέον.
295   σκέψαι δὲ τὴν σὴν ἐλπίδ᾽ ᾗ λογίζομαι·
ἥξειν νομίζεις παῖδα σὸν γαίας ὕπο;
καὶ τίς θανόντων ἦλθεν ἐξ Ἅιδου πάλιν;
ἀλλ᾽ ὡς λόγοισι τόνδε μαλθάξαιμεν ἄν;
ἥκιστα· φεύγειν σκαιὸν ἄνδρ᾽ ἐχθρὸν χρεών,
300 σοφοῖσι δ᾽ εἴκειν καὶ τεθραμμένοις καλῶς·
ῥᾷον γὰρ αἰδοῖ σ᾽ ὑποβαλὼν φίλ᾽ ἂν τέμοις.

### MEGARA

Old sirs, I thank you. It is good that friends should make a just display of anger on behalf of their friends. Yet please do not come to grief because you are angry with your master in our cause. Amphitryon, listen to me and see if you think what I say makes sense. I love my children: how can I not love the ones I bore and labored over? And I think it a terrible thing to be put to death. But any man, I believe, who struggles against the course of fate is a fool. Since we must die, it is wrong for us to die by the torture of the fire, allowing our enemies to laugh at us: this, in my eyes, is a greater calamity than death. We must act nobly—this house deserves no less of us. You have great fame as a warrior, and therefore it is intolerable for you to be killed in coward's fashion. And is my glorious husband without witnesses to his valor? He would not wish to save these children's lives if it meant they would be thought cowards. Noble parents are troubled by disgrace in their children. And I must not reject my husband's example.

Consider how I view this hope of yours. Do you think your son will return from beneath the earth? Which of the dead ever came back from Hades? Well, then, will you claim that we can soften this man with our words? Impossible. If someone who has no sense is your enemy, you should stay away from him, and make concessions only to those who are wise and have had a good upbringing: you will more easily be able to cast yourself on their sense of

---

283 βροτῶν Porson: -όν L

293 αἰσχροῖσι Stephanus: ἐχθρ- L   301 αἰδοῖ σ᾽ ὑπο-
βαλὼν Brunck (ὑποβαλών) et Cropp: αἰδοῦς ὑπολαβὼν L

ἤδη δ' ἐσῆλθέ μ' εἰ παραιτησαίμεθα
φυγὰς τέκνων τῶνδ'· ἀλλὰ καὶ τόδ' ἄθλιον,
πενίᾳ σὺν οἰκτρᾷ περιβαλεῖν σωτηρίαν·
305  ὡς τὰ ξένων πρόσωπα φεύγουσιν φίλοις
ἐν ἦμαρ ἡδὺ βλέμμ' ἔχειν φασὶν μόνον.
  τόλμα μεθ' ἡμῶν θάνατον, ὃς μένει σ' ὅμως·
προκαλούμεθ' εὐγένειαν, ὦ γέρον, σέθεν.
τὰς τῶν θεῶν γὰρ ὅστις ἐκμοχθεῖ τύχας,
310  πρόθυμός ἐστιν, ἡ προθυμία δ' ἄφρων.
ὃ χρὴ γὰρ οὐδεὶς μὴ χρεὼν θήσει ποτέ.

ΧΟΡΟΣ

εἰ μὲν σθενόντων τῶν ἐμῶν βραχιόνων
ἦν τίς σ' ὑβρίζων, ῥᾳδίως ἔπαυσά τἄν·
νῦν δ' οὐδέν ἐσμεν. σὸν δὲ τοὐντεῦθεν σκοπεῖν
315  ὅπως διώσῃ τὰς τύχας, Ἀμφιτρύων.

ΑΜΦΙΤΡΥΩΝ

οὔτοι τὸ δειλὸν οὐδὲ τοῦ βίου πόθος
θανεῖν ἐρύκει μ', ἀλλὰ παιδὶ βούλομαι
σῶσαι τέκν'· ἄλλως δ' ἀδυνάτων ἔοικ' ἐρᾶν.
  ἰδού, πάρεστιν ἥδε φασγάνῳ δέρη,
  ⟨πάρεστι μήτηρ σὺν τέκνοισιν ἀθλία⟩
320  κεντεῖν φονεύειν ἱέναι πέτρας ἄπο.
μίαν δὲ νῷν δὸς χάριν, ἄναξ, ἱκνούμεθα·
κτεῖνόν με καὶ τήνδ' ἀθλίαν παίδων πάρος,
ὡς μὴ τέκν' εἰσίδωμεν, ἀνόσιον θέαν,

305 φίλοις Matthiae: -οι L
311 χρεὼν Porson: θεῶν L

decency and reach an understanding. I have thought of asking for exile for the children. But this too is a wretched fate, to save their lives at the cost of a miserable poverty: hosts' faces, they say, smile only for a single day upon exiled friends.

Join me in enduring bravely the death that awaits you in any case: I appeal to your noble blood, old sir. Whoever struggles against what the gods ordain shows, to be sure, an ardor, but an ardor that is foolish. No one can ever make unfated what fate has ordained.

### CHORUS LEADER

If someone were committing violence against you while my arm had its strength, I would easily have stopped him. As it is, I am of no account. From now on it is up to you, Amphitryon, to consider how you will thrust a way through your fate.

### AMPHITRYON

It is not cowardice or a clinging to life that prevents me from dying, but the desire to save the lives of my son's children. Yet it seems I am foolishly in love with the impossible.

*Amphitryon comes down from the altar.*

See, my neck stands ready for your sword, ⟨and here is the unlucky mother with her children, ready⟩ to be stabbed, murdered, thrown from a cliff! But, my lord, grant us this one favor, we beg of you: kill the poor woman and me before you kill the children so that we may not see the

---

319 post h. v. lac. indic. et suppl. Wilamowitz

ψυχορραγοῦντα καὶ καλοῦντα μητέρα
325 πατρός τε πατέρα. τἄλλα δ᾽ ἢ πρόθυμος εἶ
πρᾶσσ᾽· οὐ γὰρ ἀλκὴν ἔχομεν ὥστε μὴ θανεῖν.

ΜΕΓΑΡΑ

κἀγώ σ᾽ ἱκνοῦμαι χάριτι προσθεῖναι χάριν,
ἡμῖν ἵν᾽ ἀμφοῖν εἷς ὑπουργήσῃς διπλᾶ·
κόσμον πάρες μοι παισὶ προσθεῖναι νεκρῶν,
330 δόμους ἀνοίξας (νῦν γὰρ ἐκκεκλήμεθα),
ὡς ἀλλὰ ταῦτά γ᾽ ἀπολάχωσ᾽ οἴκων πατρός.

ΛΥΚΟΣ

ἔσται τάδ᾽· οἴγειν κλῆθρα προσπόλοις λέγω.
κοσμεῖσθ᾽ ἔσω μολόντες· οὐ φθονῶ πέπλων.
ὅταν δὲ κόσμον περιβάλησθε σώμασιν
335 ἥξω πρὸς ὑμᾶς νερτέρᾳ δώσων χθονί.

ΜΕΓΑΡΑ

ὦ τέκν᾽, ὁμαρτεῖτ᾽ ἀθλίῳ μητρὸς ποδὶ
πατρῷον ἐς μέλαθρον, οὗ τῆς οὐσίας
ἄλλοι κρατοῦσι, τὸ δ᾽ ὄνομ᾽ ἔσθ᾽ ἡμῶν ἔτι.

ΑΜΦΙΤΡΥΩΝ

ὦ Ζεῦ, μάτην ἄρ᾽ ὁμόγαμόν σ᾽ ἐκτησάμην,
340 μάτην δὲ παιδὸς κοινεῶν᾽ ἐκλῄζομεν·
σὺ δ᾽ ἦσθ᾽ ἄρ᾽ ἧσσον ἢ 'δόκεις εἶναι φίλος.
ἀρετῇ σε νικῶ θνητὸς ὢν θεὸν μέγαν·
παῖδας γὰρ οὐ προύδωκα τοὺς Ἡρακλέους.

325 ἢ Elmsley: εἰ L    340 κοινεῶν᾽ post Scaliger (κοινεῶν
ἐκλῃζόμην) Murray: τὸν νεῶν L

338

ghastly sight of children gasping out their lives and calling out to their mother and grandfather. The rest do as you desire. We have no way to defend ourselves against death.

MEGARA

And I beg you to add a second favor to the first, so that you, who are but one man, may do us two a double service: open the house (we are locked out) and let me put funeral adornments on the children, so that they may receive this at least as patrimony from their father's house.

LYCUS

It shall be so. Servants, unlock the doors!

*Lycus' servants open the doors.*

Go inside and put on your adornment! I do not begrudge you the clothes. But when you have put on the finery, I shall return to send you to the world below.

*Exit LYCUS and retinue by Eisodos A.*

MEGARA

Children, follow your unhappy mother as she goes into your father's house! The house is ours in name, but the substance is in the hands of others.

*Exit MEGARA and the children into the house.*

AMPHITRYON

Zeus, it does no good that you were my wife's lover, no good that I have called you sharer in my son's begetting. You were, it now appears, not as near a friend as I thought. In goodness I, though mortal, surpass you, a mighty god. I have not abandoned the children of Heracles. But you,

339

σὺ δ' ἐς μὲν εὐνὰς κρύφιος ἠπίστω μολεῖν,
345 τἀλλότρια λέκτρα δόντος οὐδενὸς λαβών,
σῴζειν δὲ τοὺς σοὺς οὐκ ἐπίστασαι φίλους.
ἀμαθής τις εἶ θεὸς ἢ δίκαιος οὐκ ἔφυς.

ΧΟΡΟΣ

στρ. α

αἴλινον μὲν ἐπ' εὐτυχεῖ
μολπᾷ Φοῖβος ἰαχεῖ
350 τὸν καλλίφθογγον κιθάραν
ἐλαύνων πλήκτρῳ χρυσέῳ·
ἐγὼ δὲ τὸν γᾶς ἐνέρων τ' ἐς ὄρφναν
μολόντα παῖδ', εἴτε Διός νιν εἴπω
εἴτ' Ἀμφιτρύωνος ἶνιν,
355 ὑμνῆσαι στεφάνωμα μό-
χθων δι' εὐλογίας θέλω.
γενναίων δ' ἀρεταὶ πόνων
τοῖς θανοῦσιν ἄγαλμα.

μεσῳδ. α

πρῶτον μὲν Διὸς ἄλσος
360 ἠρήμωσε λέοντος,
πυρσῷ δ' ἀμφεκαλύφθη

---

350 καλλίφθογγον Stephanus: -φθιτον L

---

8 The rest of this ode is a catalogue, in highly decorative style,
of twelve of the Labors of Heracles. (The number was to become
canonical, though there is considerable variation in the list.) The
usual names for those in Euripides' catalogue are: the Nemean

though you know well enough how to slip secretly into bed
and take other men's wives when no one has given you
permission, do not know how to save the lives of your
nearest and dearest. Either you are a fool of a god or there
is no justice in your nature.

*Exit* AMPHITRYON *into the house.*

CHORUS
"Chant sorrow, sorrow," Phoebus sings
after a song of good fortune
as he plies his sweet-voiced lyre
with a plectrum of gold.
In like fashion the man gone into the dark of earth, the
realm of the dead
(son of Zeus shall I call him,
or of Amphitryon?)
I wish to praise
as a coronal to his labors.
For high deeds of noble toil
are a glory to those who have perished.[8]

First Zeus's grove
he cleared of the lion
and covered his blond head

lion (359-63), the Centauromachy (364-74), the hind of Arte-
mis (375-9), the Thracian mares of Diomedes (380-8; cf. *Alcestis*
481-506), Cycnus (389-93), the apples of the Hesperides (394-
400), the clearing of the sea (400-2), Atlas (403-7), the girdle of
Hippolyta, queen of the Amazons (408-18), the Lernaean hydra
(419-22), the cattle of Geryon (423-4), and the fetching of Cer-
berus (425-9).

ξανθὸν κρᾶτ᾽ ἐπινωτίσας
δεινῷ χάσματι θηρός.

ἀντ. α

τάν τ᾽ ὀρεινόμον ἀγρίων
365 Κενταύρων ποτὲ γένναν
ἔστρωσεν τόξοις φονίοις,
ἐναίρων πτανοῖς βέλεσιν.
ξύνοιδε Πηνειὸς ὁ καλλιδίνας
μακραί τ᾽ ἄρουραι πεδίων ἄκαρποι
370 καὶ Πηλιάδες θεράπναι
σύγχορτοί θ᾽ Ὁμόλας ἔναυ-
λοι, πεύκαισιν ὅθεν χέρας
πληροῦντες χθόνα Θεσσαλῶν
ἱππείαις ἐδάμαζον.

ἐπῳδ. α

375 τάν τε χρυσοκάρανον
δόρκα ποικιλόνωτον
συλήτειραν ἀγρωστᾶν
κτείνας θηροφόνον θεὰν
Οἰνῶτιν ἀγάλλει.

στρ. β

380 τεθρίππων τ᾽ ἐπέβα
καὶ ψαλίοις ἐδάμασσε πώλους
Διομήδεος, αἳ φονίαισι φάτναις
ἀχάλιν᾽ ἐθόαζον
κάθαιμα σῖτα γένυσι, χαρ-
385 μοναῖσιν ἀνδροβρῶσι δυστράπεζοι·
πέραν δ᾽ ἀργυρορρύταν

with the tawny thing, drawing it over his back,
the beast's dread gaping jaws.

Then the mountain-dwelling tribe
of fierce Centaurs
with his deadly arrows he laid low,
killing them with his winged shafts.
The Peneus river with its lovely eddies is witness,
and the far-flung lands of its plain made barren,
the steadings of Mount Pelion
and the settlements that neighbor Mount Homole,
from which the Centaurs filled
their hands with pine-tree trunks and lorded it
over Thessaly with their horsemanship.

The golden-headed hind
with dappled back,
who plundered the farmers,
he killed and gave joy
to the huntress goddess of Oenoë.[9]

The chariot and four he mounted as well
and broke to the bit the horses
of Diomedes. These from troughs soaked in blood
moved nimbly with unbridled zest
their bloody food to their jaws,
unseemly diners rejoicing
in the flesh of men. He crossed

[9] Artemis.

---

363 δεινοῦ Diggle

Ἕβρον διεπέρασε, μό-
χθον Μυκηναίῳ πονῶν τυράννῳ.

μεσῳδ. β

ἄν τε Πηλιάδ' ἀκτὰν
390  Ἀναύρου παρὰ παγὰς
Κύκνον ξεινοδαΐκταν
τόξοις ὤλεσεν, Ἀμφαναί-
ας οἰκήτορ' ἄμεικτον.

ἀντ. β

ὑμνῳδούς τε κόρας
395  ἤλυθεν ἑσπέριόν ⟨τ'⟩ ἐς αὐλὰν
χρύσεον πετάλων ἀπὸ μηλοφόρων
χερὶ καρπὸν ἀμέρξων,
δράκοντα πυρσόνωτον, ὅς ⟨σφ'⟩
ἄπλατον ἀμφελικτὸς ἕλικ' ἐφρούρει,
400  κτανών· ποντίας θ' ἁλὸς
μυχοὺς εἰσέβαινε, θνα-
τοῖς γαλανείας τιθεὶς ἐρετμοῖς.

ἐπῳδ. β

οὐρανοῦ θ' ὑπὸ μέσσαν
ἐλαύνει χέρας ἕδραν,
405  Ἄτλαντος δόμον ἐλθών,
ἀστρωποὺς τε κατέσχεν οἴ-

---

387–8 διεπέρασε, μόχθον Musgrave: διεπέρασ' ὄχθον L
389 ἄν Musgrave: τάν L      Μηλιάδ' Hermann
391 ξεινοδαΐκταν Pflugk: δὲ ξενοδαΐκταν L
394 ὑμῳδῶν τε κορᾶν Nauck (omisso τ' 395)
395 ⟨τ'⟩ Fix

over the silver-flowing Hebrus, performing
his task for the king of Mycenae.

On the shore hard by Mount Pelion,
near the waters of the Anaurus,
Cycnus, the cleaver of travelers,[10]
he slew with his arrows, the unsociable settler
in the land of Amphanae.

The maiden singers he visited
and their dwelling in the West[11]
to pluck the golden fruit
from the leaves that bore them,
slaying the dragon with tawny back
who guarded it with his fearsome
coils twisted about it. He entered thereby
the far recesses of the sea
and made calm sailing for the ships of mortal men.

He went to the house of Atlas
and thrust his hands beneath the middle
of the heavens' resting place,
holding aloft by his manstrength

[10] Cycnus cut off the heads of visitors (to Delphi in most versions, here near Pelion) to build a temple of their skulls.
[11] The Hesperides were divine singers in whose garden grew golden apples guarded by a dragon.

---

396 χρύσεον Wakefield: -έων L
398 ⟨σφ'⟩ Hermann

κους εὐανορίᾳ θεῶν.

στρ. γ

τὸν ἱππευτάν τ' Ἀμαζόνων στρατὸν
Μαιῶτιν ἀμφὶ πολυπόταμον
410 ἔβα δι' ἄξεινον οἶδμα λίμνας,
τίν' οὐκ ἀφ' Ἑλλανίας
ἄγορον ἁλίσας φίλων,
κόρας Ἀρείας πλέων
χρυσεοστόλου φάρους
415 ζωστῆρος ὀλεθρίους ἄγρας·
τὰ κλεινὰ δ' Ἑλλὰς ἔλαβε βαρβάρου κόρας
λάφυρα καὶ σῴζεται Μυκήναις.

μεσῳδ. γ

τάν τε μυριόκρανον
420 πολύφονον κύνα Λέρνας
ὕδραν ἐξεπύρωσεν,
βέλεσί τ' ἀμφέβαλ' ⟨ἰόν⟩,
τὸν τρισώματον οἶσιν ἔ-
κτα βοτῆρ' Ἐρυθείας.

ἀντ. γ

425 δρόμων τ' ἄλλων ἀγάλματ' εὐτυχῆ
διῆλθε τόν ⟨τε⟩ πολυδάκρυον
ἔπλευσ' ἐς Ἅιδαν, πόνων τελευτάν,

410 ἄξεινον Markland: εὔξεινον L
413 πλέων Murray: πέπλων L
414 χρυσεοστόλου φάρους Schenkl: -όστολον φάρος L
422 ⟨ἰόν⟩ Wilamowitz
426 ⟨τε⟩ πολυδάκρυον Wakefield: πολυδάκρυτον L

the starry homes of the gods.[12]

Sailing against the mounted throng of the Amazons,
in Maiotis of the many rivers,
he went through the swell of the Sea Inhospitable[13]
taking from all of Greece
assemblies of his friends,
sailing to fetch the cinch that girded
the warrior maiden's gold-bedecked
garments, a deadly quest.
Greece took the famous spoils from the barbarian maid
and they are kept safe in Mycenae.

The myriad-headed
murderous hound of Lerna,
the hydra, he destroyed by fire
and smeared its poison on his arrows.
With these the beast of three bodies
he slew, the herdsman of Erytheia.[14]

The glorious successes of his other quests
he completed and also sailed to the land of lamentation,
to Hades, the last of his labors.

[12] In most versions Heracles takes Atlas' place so that Atlas can
bring him the apples of the Hesperides. Here it seems to be a
separate exploit.

[13] The Black Sea was called *Euxeinos*, "hospitable," either
ironically or in an attempt to placate its actual inhospitableness.
Here it is called *Axeinos*, "inhospitable."

[14] Geryon, three-bodied monster whose cattle Heracles had
to take from him.

ἵν᾽ ἐκπεραίνει τάλας
βίοτον οὐδ᾽ ἔβα πάλιν.
430  στέγαι δ᾽ ἔρημοι φίλων,
τὰν δ᾽ ἀνόστιμον τέκνων
Χάρωνος ἐπιμένει πλάτα
βίου κέλευθον ἄθεον ἄδικον· ἐς δὲ σὰς
435  χέρας βλέπει δώματ᾽ οὐ παρόντος.
ἐπῳδ. γ

εἰ δ᾽ ἐγὼ σθένος ἥβων
δόρυ τ᾽ ἔπαλλον ἐν αἰχμᾷ
Καδμείων τε σύνηβοι,
τέκεσιν ἂν προπαρέσταν
440  ἄλκαρ· νῦν δ᾽ ἀπολείπομαι
τᾶς εὐδαίμονος ἥβας.

—ἀλλ᾽ ἐσορῶ γὰρ τούσδε φθιμένων
ἔνδυτ᾽ ἔχοντας,
τοὺς τοῦ μεγάλου δή ποτε παῖδας
445  τὸ πρὶν Ἡρακλέους, ἄλοχόν τε φίλην
ὑπὸ σειραίοις ποσὶν ἕλκουσαν
τέκνα καὶ γεραιὸν πατέρ᾽ Ἡρακλέους.
δύστηνος ἐγώ,
δακρύων ὡς οὐ δύναμαι κατέχειν
450  γραίας ὄσσων ἔτι πηγάς.

ΜΕΓΑΡΑ
εἶέν· τίς ἱερεύς, τίς σφαγεὺς τῶν δυσπότμων;

435 δώματ᾽ οὐ Musgrave: σῶμα τοῦ L

348

There the luckless man reached
the end of his life and did not return.
His house is bereft of friends,
and the oar of the boatman Charon lies in prospect
for the path the children's lives take, a path that has no
    return
and is forsaken of the gods and of justice. To your
strong arm, Heracles, the house looks, though you are not
    with us.

If I were young in strength
and able to brandish my spear in battle
and my agemates in Thebes with me,
I would have stood before the children
as shield. But now I have lost
the blessed vigor of youth.

*Enter from the house* MEGARA, AMPHITRYON, *and the chil-
dren, dressed for burial in ankle-length white robes.*

### CHORUS LEADER
But look, I see the children here with the finery of the dead
upon them, children of Heracles once mighty, I see his
dear wife moving the children forward, as they cling to her
legs that draw them like a trace horse, and the old father
of Heracles. Ah unhappy me, I cannot check the tears
flowing from my old eyes!

### MEGARA
Come, where is the priest, the sacrificer, to slay the unfor-

---

440 ἄλκαρ Nauck: ἀλκᾷ L

[ἢ τῆς ταλαίνης τῆς ἐμῆς ψυχῆς φονεύς;]
ἕτοιμ᾽ ἄγειν τὰ θύματ᾽ εἰς Ἅιδου τάδε.
  ὦ τέκν᾽, ἀγόμεθα ζεῦγος οὐ καλὸν νεκρῶν,
455  ὁμοῦ γέροντες καὶ νέοι καὶ μητέρες.
ὦ μοῖρα δυστάλαιν᾽ ἐμή τε καὶ τέκνων
τῶνδ᾽, οὓς πανύστατ᾽ ὄμμασιν προσδέρκομαι.
ἐτέκομεν ὑμᾶς, πολεμίοις δ᾽ ἐθρεψάμην
ὕβρισμα κἀπίχαρμα καὶ διαφθοράν.
  φεῦ·
460  ἦ πολύ γε δόξης ἐξέπεσον εὐέλπιδος,
ἣν πατρὸς ὑμῶν ἐκ λόγων ποτ᾽ ἤλπισα.
σοὶ μὲν γὰρ Ἄργος ἔνεμ᾽ ὁ κατθανὼν πατήρ,
Εὐρυσθέως δ᾽ ἔμελλες οἰκήσειν δόμους
τῆς καλλικάρπου κράτος ἔχων Πελασγίας,
465  στολήν τε θηρὸς ἀμφέβαλλε σῷ κάρᾳ
λέοντος, ἧπερ αὐτὸς ἐξωπλίζετο.
σὺ δ᾽ ἦσθα Θηβῶν τῶν φιλαρμάτων ἄναξ,
ἔγκληρα πεδία τἀμὰ γῆς κεκτημένος,
ὡς ἐξέπειθες τὸν κατασπείραντά σε,
470  ἐς δεξιάν τε σὴν ἀλεξητήριον
ξύλον καθίει δαίδαλον, ψευδῆ δόσιν.
σοὶ δ᾽ ἦν ἔπερσε τοῖς ἑκηβόλοις ποτὲ
τόξοισι δώσειν Οἰχαλίαν ὑπέσχετο.
τρεῖς δ᾽ ὄντας ⟨ὑμᾶς⟩ τριπτύχοις τυραννίσιν
475  πατὴρ ἐπύργου, μέγα φρονῶν εὐανδρίᾳ.
ἐγὼ δὲ νύμφας ἠκροθινιαζόμην
κήδη συνάψους᾽ ἔκ τ᾽ Ἀθηναίων χθονὸς
Σπάρτης τε Θηβῶν θ᾽, ὡς ἀνημμένοι κάλως

350

tunate? [Where is the murderer of my poor life?] These
victims are ready to be taken to the Underworld!

Children, we are led away as an inglorious yoked team
of corpses, old men and children and mothers all together!
O luckless fate, mine and my children's here! My eyes look
on you now for the last time! I gave you birth, but in raising
you I raised only something for my enemies to insult, treat
with malicious glee, and kill.

Ah me, how far I have been cast down from the san-
guine hopes your father's words once raised in me! To you,
my son, your dead father used to assign Argos, and you
were going to dwell in the palace of Eurystheus and hold
sway over fertile Pelasgia. He used to put about your head
the lion skin which was his armor. And you, child, were the
ruler of Thebes that delights in chariots, and you took the
plains of my country for your inheritance—such was the
persuasion you worked upon your father—and he lowered
into your hand the finely wrought club that warded off
danger, a gift in pretense only. And to you, my son, he
promised to give Oechalia, which he once sacked with his
far-flying arrows. The three ⟨of you⟩ your father fortified
with three thrones, proud of his martial valor. And I was
choosing the finest of brides for you and was making mar-
riage alliances with Athens, Sparta, and Thebes so that

---

452 del. Paley

456 ἐμή Kirchhoff: ἐμῶν L

458 ἐτέκομεν Wilamowitz: ἔτεκον μὲν L

460 γε . . . ἐξέπεσον εὐέλπιδος Hirzel: με . . . ἐξέπαισαν
ἐλπίδες L        469 ἐξέπειθες Hermann: -θε L

470 τε Musgrave: δὲ L        474 ⟨ὑμᾶς⟩ Canter

πρυμνησίοισι βίον ἔχοιτ᾽ εὐδαίμονα.
480 καὶ ταῦτα φροῦδα· μεταβαλοῦσα δ᾽ ἡ τύχη
νύμφας μὲν ὑμῖν Κῆρας ἀντέδωκ᾽ ἔχειν,
ἐμοὶ δὲ δάκρυα λουτρὰ δυστήνῳ φέρειν.
πατὴρ δὲ πατρὸς ἑστιᾷ γάμους ὅδε,
Ἅιδην νομίζων πενθερόν, κῆδος πικρόν.
485 ὤμοι, τίν᾽ ὑμῶν πρῶτον ἢ τίν᾽ ὕστατον
πρὸς στέρνα θῶμαι; τῷ προσαρμόσω στόμα;
τίνος λάβωμαι; πῶς ἂν ὡς ξουθόπτερος
μέλισσα συνενέγκαιμ᾽ ἂν ἐκ πάντων γόους,
ἐς ἓν δ᾽ ἐνεγκοῦσ᾽ ἀθρόον ἀποδοίην δάκρυ;
490 ὦ φίλτατ᾽, εἴ τις φθόγγος εἰσακούεται
θνητῶν παρ᾽ Ἅιδη, σοὶ τάδ᾽, Ἡράκλεις, λέγω·
θνήσκει πατὴρ σὸς καὶ τέκν᾽, ὄλλυμαι δ᾽ ἐγώ,
ἣ πρὶν μακαρία διὰ σ᾽ ἐκληζόμην βροτοῖς.
ἄρηξον, ἐλθέ· καὶ σκιὰ φάνηθί μοι·
495 ἅλις γὰρ ἐλθὼν κἂν ὄναρ γένοιο σύ·
κακοὶ γάρ εἰσιν οἳ τέκνα κτείνουσι σά.

ΑΜΦΙΤΡΥΩΝ

σὺ μὲν τὰ νέρθεν εὐτρεπῆ ποιοῦ, γύναι·
ἐγὼ δὲ σ᾽, ὦ Ζεῦ, χεῖρ᾽ ἐς οὐρανὸν δικὼν
αὐδῶ, τέκνοισιν εἴ τι τοισίδ᾽ ὠφελεῖν
500 μέλλεις, ἀμύνειν, ὡς τάχ᾽ οὐδὲν ἀρκέσεις.
καίτοι κέκλησαι πολλάκις· μάτην πονῶ·

482 δυστήνῳ Fix: -ος L    φέρειν Bothe: φρενῶν L
484 πικρόν Reiske: πατρός L
490 φθόγγος εἰσακούεται Nauck: φθόγγον εἰσακούσεται L

with your stern cables fastened to firm anchorage you
might have a happy life. These hopes are all gone: your
fortune changed and instead gave to you as your brides
death spirits, and to unlucky me as the bath I should have
brought you she gave tears.[15] Your grandfather is the host
for the wedding banquet, and he acknowledges Hades as
the father-in-law, a marriage tie most unwelcome. Ah me,
which of you shall I clasp first to my breast, which last? On
whose cheek shall I plant my kisses? Whom shall I cling
to? How I wish that like a bee with tawny wings I might
gather your lamentations from you all and then combining
them give them all back as a single tear!

Dearest Heracles, if any mortal words are heard in the
house of Hades, I say this to you: your father and children
are being killed and I as well, I whom mortals once called
happy because of you! Come rescue us! Appear to me even
as a ghost! Even if you came as a dream vision it would
suffice! For the men who are killing your children are cow-
ards.

### AMPHITRYON

You, dear woman, continue trying to win over the realm
below. For my part, Zeus, I address you and cast my hands
heavenward: if you mean to lend any aid to these children,
defend them, since soon aid from you will be in vain. And
yet you have been called upon many times. My labor is

---

[15] Before the wedding both bride and groom were given a
ritual bath, which it was the mother's job to provide: see *Iphigenia
among the Taurians* 818 and *Phoenician Women* 344-9.

---

495 κἂν ὄναρ Wilamowitz: ἱκανὸν ἂν L

θανεῖν γάρ, ὡς ἔοικ᾽, ἀναγκαίως ἔχει.
   ἀλλ᾽, ὦ γέροντες, σμικρὰ μὲν τὰ τοῦ βίου,
τοῦτον δ᾽ ὅπως ἥδιστα διαπεράσατε
505 ἐξ ἡμέρας ἐς νύκτα μὴ λυπούμενοι.
ὡς ἐλπίδας μὲν ὁ χρόνος οὐκ ἐπίσταται
σῴζειν, τὸ δ᾽ αὑτοῦ σπουδάσας διέπτατο.
ὁρᾶτ᾽ ἔμ᾽ ὅσπερ ἦ περίβλεπτος βροτοῖς
ὀνομαστὰ πράσσων, καί μ᾽ ἀφείλεθ᾽ ἡ τύχη
510 ὥσπερ πτερὸν πρὸς αἰθέρ᾽ ἡμέρᾳ μιᾷ.
ὁ δ᾽ ὄλβος ὁ μέγας ἥ τε δόξ᾽ οὐκ οἶδ᾽ ὅτῳ
βέβαιός ἐστι. χαίρετ᾽· ἄνδρα γὰρ φίλον
πανύστατον νῦν, ἥλικες, δεδόρκατε.

ΜΕΓΑΡΑ

ἔα·
ὦ πρέσβυ, λεύσσω τἀμὰ φίλτατ᾽, ἢ τί φῶ;

ΑΜΦΙΤΡΥΩΝ

515 οὐκ οἶδα, θύγατερ· ἀφασία δὲ κἄμ᾽ ἔχει.

ΜΕΓΑΡΑ

ὅδ᾽ ἐστὶν ὃν γῆς νέρθεν εἰσηκούομεν,
εἰ μή γ᾽ ὄνειρον ἐν φάει τι λεύσσομεν.
τί φημί, ποῖ᾽ ὄνειρα κηραίνουσ᾽ ὁρᾶν;
οὐκ ἔσθ᾽ ὅδ᾽ ἄλλος ἀντὶ σοῦ παιδός, γέρον.
520    δεῦρ᾽, ὦ τέκν᾽, ἐκκρίμασθε πατρῴων πέπλων,
ἴτ᾽ ἐγκονεῖτε, μὴ μεθῆτ᾽, ἐπεὶ Διὸς
σωτῆρος ὑμῖν οὐδέν ἐσθ᾽ ὅδ᾽ ὕστερος.

518 ὁρᾶν Musgrave: ὁρῶ L

fruitless: our death, it seems, is fated.

Well then, old sirs, our life is but a trifle: pass through it as pleasantly as you can, feeling no distress as day gives way to night. Time does not know how to preserve our hopes intact but worries about its own affairs and flies on. Look at me, who once did glorious deeds and was the object of mortal gaze! And now fortune has robbed me of all this, like a feather is carried off into the air, in a single day! I do not know any mortal who has great wealth and reputation as his secure possession. Farewell! My age-mates, you are now looking for the last time on your friend!

*Enter* HERACLES *by Eisodos B.*

#### MEGARA

But what is this sight, sir? Do I see the one I love best, or what am I to say?

#### AMPHITRYON

I do not know, my child. I too am struck speechless.

#### MEGARA

This is the man we heard was in the Underworld, unless it is a dream by daylight that we are looking at! What shall I say I see, what delirious visions? This man is none other than your son, old sir!

Come, children, cling to your father's clothing, go, hurry, do not let him go, since he is no less your rescuer than Zeus the Savior is![16]

---

[16] At whose altar they sit as suppliants. The action "freezes" for a few seconds (Megara's order is probably carried out at 530) to allow Heracles to react separately.

ΗΡΑΚΛΗΣ

ὦ χαῖρε, μέλαθρον πρόπυλά θ᾽ ἑστίας ἐμῆς,
ὡς ἄσμενός σ᾽ ἐσεῖδον ἐς φάος μολών.
525 ἔα· τί χρῆμα; τέκν᾽ ὁρῶ πρὸ δωμάτων
στολμοῖσι νεκρῶν κρᾶτας ἐξεστεμμένα
ὄχλῳ τ᾽ ἐν ἀνδρῶν τὴν ἐμὴν ξυνάορον
πατέρα τε δακρύοντα· συμφορὰς τίνας;
φέρ᾽ ἐκπύθωμαι τῶνδε, πλησίον σταθείς,
530 τί καινὸν ⟨ἡμῖν⟩ ἦλθε δώμασιν χρέος.

ΑΜΦΙΤΡΥΩΝ

ὦ φίλτατ᾽ ἀνδρῶν, ὦ φάος μολὼν πατρί,
ἥκεις, ἐσώθης εἰς ἀκμὴν ἐλθὼν φίλοις;

ΗΡΑΚΛΗΣ

τί φής; τίν᾽ ἐς ταραγμὸν ἥκομεν, πάτερ;

ΜΕΓΑΡΑ

διωλλύμεσθα· σὺ δέ, γέρον, σύγγνωθί μοι,
535 εἰ πρόσθεν ἥρπασ᾽ ἃ σὲ λέγειν πρὸς τόνδ᾽ ἐχρῆν·
τὸ θῆλυ γάρ πως μᾶλλον οἰκτρὸν ἀρσένων,
καὶ τἄμ᾽ ἔθνῃσκε τέκν᾽, ἀπωλλύμην δ᾽ ἐγώ.

ΗΡΑΚΛΗΣ

Ἄπολλον, οἵοις φροιμίοις ἄρχῃ λόγου.

ΜΕΓΑΡΑ

τεθνᾶσ᾽ ἀδελφοὶ καὶ πατὴρ οὑμὸς γέρων.

530 τί Elmsley: γύναι τι L    ⟨ἡμῖν⟩ Wilamowitz (ἦλθε
⟨τοῖσδε⟩ Elmsley)
531n Ἀμ. Elmsley: Με. L

356

### HERACLES

House, doors, and hearth, I bid you greeting! How glad I am to return to the light and see you!

But what is this? I see my children in front of the house, their heads covered with the clothing of the dead, my wife standing amid a crowd of men, and my father weeping: at what woes? Come, let me draw nearer and ask them what new mischance has come upon my house.

*He approaches the house. The children run to him.*

### AMPHITRYON

Dearest of men, light of rescue shining on your father, have you really come, have you safely reached your family in their hour of utmost danger?

### HERACLES

What do you mean? What is the trouble we are in, father?

### MEGARA

We were being killed. Forgive me, old sir, for snatching from you the words that were your right to speak to him. For women are somehow more full of pity than men, and it was my children who were being killed, and I with them.

### HERACLES

Apollo! What a beginning this is for your story!

### MEGARA

My brothers and my old father are dead.

ΗΡΑΚΛΗΣ

540 πῶς φής; τί δράσας ἢ μόρου ποίου τυχών;

ΜΕΓΑΡΑ

Λύκος σφ' ὁ καινὸς γῆς ἄναξ διώλεσεν.

ΗΡΑΚΛΗΣ

ὅπλοις ἀπαντῶν ἢ νοσησάσης χθονός;

ΜΕΓΑΡΑ

στάσει· τὸ Κάδμου δ' ἑπτάπυλον ἔχει κράτος.

ΗΡΑΚΛΗΣ

τί δῆτα πρὸς σὲ καὶ γέροντ' ἦλθεν φόβος;

ΜΕΓΑΡΑ

545 κτείνειν ἔμελλε πατέρα κἀμὲ καὶ τέκνα.

ΗΡΑΚΛΗΣ

τί φής; τί ταρβῶν ὀρφάνευμ' ἐμῶν τέκνων;

ΜΕΓΑΡΑ

μή ποτε Κρέοντος θάνατον ἐκτεισαίατο.

ΗΡΑΚΛΗΣ

κόσμος δὲ παίδων τίς ὅδε νερτέροις πρέπων;

ΜΕΓΑΡΑ

θανάτου τάδ' ἤδη περιβόλαι' ἐνήμμεθα.

ΗΡΑΚΛΗΣ

550 καὶ πρὸς βίαν ἐθνήσκετ'; ὦ τλήμων ἐγώ.

540 μόρου Purgold cl. *Hec.* 773: δορὸς L
541 καινὸς Elmsley: κλεινὸς L

**HERACLES**

What is this? What did he do or what was the fate he met?

**MEGARA**

Lycus, the new ruler of the land, killed him.

**HERACLES**

Did he meet them in battle? Or was it because of faction in the city?

**MEGARA**

It was faction. He now rules over seven-gated Thebes.

**HERACLES**

Why then did danger come to you and my old father?

**MEGARA**

He was about to kill your father, me, and the children.

**HERACLES**

What do you mean? Why was he afraid of my orphaned children?

**MEGARA**

He feared they might make him pay for Creon's death.

**HERACLES**

What is the meaning of the children's being dressed as befits the dead?

**MEGARA**

Death's garments—we have already put them on.

**HERACLES**

Were you really being violently put to death? O what woe is mine!

ΜΕΓΑΡΑ

φίλων ⟨γ᾽⟩ ἔρημοι· σὲ δὲ θανόντ᾽ ἠκούομεν.

ΗΡΑΚΛΗΣ

πόθεν δ᾽ ἐς ὑμᾶς ἥδ᾽ ἐσῆλθ᾽ ἀθυμία;

ΜΕΓΑΡΑ

Εὐρυσθέως κήρυκες ἤγγελλον τάδε.

ΗΡΑΚΛΗΣ

τί δ᾽ ἐξελείπετ᾽ οἶκον ἑστίαν τ᾽ ἐμήν;

ΜΕΓΑΡΑ

555 βίᾳ, πατὴρ μὲν ἐκπεσὼν στρωτοῦ λέχους . . .

ΗΡΑΚΛΗΣ

κοὐκ ἔσχεν αἰδὼς τὸν γέροντ᾽ ἀτιμάσαι;

ΜΕΓΑΡΑ

αἰδώς; ἀποικεῖ τῆσδε τῆς θεοῦ πρόσω.

ΗΡΑΚΛΗΣ

οὕτω δ᾽ ἀπόντες ἐσπανίζομεν φίλων;

ΜΕΓΑΡΑ

φίλοι γάρ εἰσιν ἀνδρὶ δυστυχεῖ τίνες;

ΗΡΑΚΛΗΣ

560 μάχας δὲ Μινυῶν ἃς ἔτλην ἀπέπτυσαν;

ΜΕΓΑΡΑ

ἄφιλον, ἵν᾽ αὖθίς σοι λέγω, τὸ δυστυχές.

551 ⟨γ᾽⟩ Hermann
556 αἰδὼς Pearson: αἰδῶ L
557 αἰδώς; Badham: αἰδώς γ᾽ L

MEGARA

Yes: we were bereft of friends. And we were told that you
had died.

HERACLES

How did this discouragement come into your hearts?

MEGARA

It was Eurystheus' heralds who brought this news.

HERACLES

But why did you leave my house and hearth?

MEGARA

Under compulsion: your father was thrown from his
bed . . .

HERACLES

Did decency not prevent him from doing dishonor to an
old man?

MEGARA

Decency? Lycus lives far off from *that* goddess.

HERACLES

Was I so lacking in friends when I was absent?

MEGARA

What friends does a man in misfortune have?

HERACLES

Did they think so little of the battles I fought with the
Minyans?

MEGARA

Once more I say: misfortune has no friends.

ΗΡΑΚΛΗΣ

οὐ ῥίψεθ᾽ Ἅιδου τάσδε περιβολὰς κόμης
καὶ φῶς ἀναβλέψεσθε, τοῦ κάτω σκότου
φίλας ἀμοιβὰς ὄμμασιν δεδορκότες;
565 ἐγὼ δέ—νῦν γὰρ τῆς ἐμῆς ἔργον χερός—
πρῶτον μὲν εἶμι καὶ κατασκάψω δόμους
καινῶν τυράννων, κρᾶτα δ᾽ ἀνόσιον τεμὼν
ῥίψω κυνῶν ἕλκημα· Καδμείων δ᾽ ὅσους
κακοὺς ἐφηῦρον εὖ παθόντας ἐξ ἐμοῦ
570 τῷ καλλινίκῳ τῷδ᾽ ὅπλῳ χειρώσομαι,
τοὺς δὲ πτερωτοῖς διαφορῶν τοξεύμασιν
νεκρῶν ἅπανθ᾽ Ἰσμηνὸν ἐμπλήσω φόνου,
Δίρκης τε νᾶμα λευκὸν αἱμαχθήσεται.
τῷ γάρ μ᾽ ἀμύνειν μᾶλλον ἢ δάμαρτι χρὴ
575 καὶ παισὶ καὶ γέροντι; χαιρόντων πόνοι·
μάτην γὰρ αὐτοὺς τῶνδε μᾶλλον ἤνυσα.
καὶ δεῖ μ᾽ ὑπὲρ τῶνδ᾽, εἴπερ οἵδ᾽ ὑπὲρ πατρός,
θνῄσκειν ἀμύνοντ᾽· ἢ τί φήσομεν καλὸν
ὕδρᾳ μὲν ἐλθεῖν ἐς μάχην λέοντί τε
580 Εὐρυσθέως πομπαῖσι, τῶν δ᾽ ἐμῶν τέκνων
οὐκ ἐκπονήσω θάνατον; οὐκ ἄρ᾽ Ἡρακλῆς
ὁ καλλίνικος ὡς πάροιθε λέξομαι.

ΧΟΡΟΣ

δίκαιά τοι τεκόντα σ᾽ ὠφελεῖν τέκνα
πατέρα τε πρέσβυν τήν τε κοινωνὸν γάμων.

ΑΜΦΙΤΡΥΩΝ

585 πρὸς σοῦ μέν, ὦ παῖ, τοῖς φίλοις ⟨τ᾽⟩ εἶναι φίλον

### HERACLES

Tear these trappings of death from your hair! Look at the light once more, gaze on this sweet exchange for the darkness below! But now there is work for my arm to do. First I shall go and raze to the ground the house of this new king, cut off his godless head and throw it to the dogs to tear at. And all the Thebans I find ungrateful for my good treatment of them I shall vanquish with this victorious club of mine. Others I shall shoot with my feathered arrows, fill the whole of the Ismenus River with the gore of dead bodies, and redden the clear spring of Dirce with blood. Whom shall I defend rather than my wife and my children and my old father? Farewell to my labors! It was to no purpose that I accomplished them rather than the tasks to be done here. Since these children were being put to death for their father, I must risk death in their defense. What fine deed shall we call it to do battle with a hydra and a lion at Eurystheus' behest if I do not prevent the death of my children? In that case, I shall not be called, as I once was, Heracles glorious in victory.

### CHORUS LEADER

It is right for you, their father, to help the children and also your aged father and your wife.

### AMPHITRYON

It is in your nature, my son, to be loving to your friends

---

583 δίκαιά τοι τεκόντα σ᾽ Herwerden: δίκαια τοὺς τεκόντας L

585 ⟨τ᾽⟩ Pflugk

τά τ᾽ ἐχθρὰ μισεῖν· ἀλλὰ μὴ ᾽πείγου λίαν.

ΗΡΑΚΛΗΣ

τί δ᾽ ἐστὶ τῶνδε θᾶσσον ἢ χρεών, πάτερ;

ΑΜΦΙΤΡΥΩΝ

[πολλοὺς πένητας, ὀλβίους δὲ τῷ λόγῳ
δοκοῦντας εἶναι, συμμάχους ἄναξ ἔχει,
590 οἳ στάσιν ἔθηκαν καὶ διώλεσαν πόλιν
ἐφ᾽ ἁρπαγαῖσι τῶν πέλας, τὰ δ᾽ ἐν δόμοις
δαπάναισι φροῦδα διαφυγόνθ᾽ ὑπ᾽ ἀργίας.]
ὤφθης ἐσελθὼν πόλιν· ἐπεὶ δ᾽ ὤφθης, ὅρα
ἐχθροὺς ἀθροίσας μὴ παρὰ γνώμην πέσῃς.

ΗΡΑΚΛΗΣ

595 μέλει μὲν οὐδὲν εἴ με πᾶσ᾽ εἶδεν πόλις·
ὄρνιν δ᾽ ἰδών τιν᾽ οὐκ ἐν αἰσίοις ἕδραις
ἔγνων πόνον τιν᾽ ἐς δόμους πεπτωκότα,
ὥστ᾽ ἐκ προνοίας κρύφιος εἰσῆλθον χθόνα.

ΑΜΦΙΤΡΥΩΝ

καλῶς· παρελθὼν νῦν πρόσειπέ θ᾽ Ἑστίαν
600 καὶ δὸς πατρῴοις δώμασιν σὸν ὄμμ᾽ ἰδεῖν.
ἥξει γὰρ αὐτὸς σὴν δάμαρτα καὶ τέκνα
ἕλξων φονεύσων κἄμ᾽ ἐπισφάξων ἄναξ.
μένοντι δ᾽ αὐτοῦ πάντα σοι γενήσεται
τῇ τ᾽ ἀσφαλείᾳ κερδανεῖς· πόλιν δὲ σὴν
605 μὴ πρὶν ταράξῃς πρὶν τόδ᾽ εὖ θέσθαι, τέκνον.

ΗΡΑΚΛΗΣ

δράσω τάδ᾽, εὖ γὰρ εἶπας· εἶμ᾽ ἔσω δόμων.

and to hate your enemies. But do not be too hasty.

### HERACLES
Which of my actions is hastier than is right, father?

### AMPHITRYON
[The king has as allies many men, poor but reputed to be rich, who have formed a faction and destroyed the city in order to plunder their neighbors' possessions since through extravagance and laziness their own property is dissipated.] You were seen entering the city. And since you were seen, take care that you do not cause your enemies to unite and yourself take an unexpected fall.

### HERACLES
I care not if the whole city has seen me. But I saw a bird sitting in a perch of bad omen, and I realized that some trouble had fallen on my house, and therefore as a precaution I came into the country secretly.

### AMPHITRYON
Good. Go inside then and greet the hearth goddess and show your face to your ancestral home. The king will come himself to drag off and slaughter your wife and children and to cut my throat over them. If you stay here everything you want will be yours, and you profit by the safety of this plan. Do not throw the city into confusion until you have set things here to rights, my son.

### HERACLES
Your advice is good, and I shall take it: I shall go into the

---

588–92 del. Wilamowitz     593 ἐσελθών Kirchhoff: ἐπ- L
599 παρελθών Wecklein: προσ- L

χρόνῳ δ᾽ ἀνελθὼν ἐξ ἀνηλίων μυχῶν
Ἅιδου Κόρης ⟨τ᾽⟩ ἔνερθεν οὐκ ἀτιμάσω
θεοὺς προσειπεῖν πρῶτα τοὺς κατὰ στέγας.

ΑΜΦΙΤΡΥΩΝ

610 ἦλθες γὰρ ὄντως δώματ᾽ εἰς Ἅιδου, τέκνον;

ΗΡΑΚΛΗΣ

καὶ θῆρά γ᾽ ἐς φῶς τὸν τρίκρανον ἤγαγον.

ΑΜΦΙΤΡΥΩΝ

μάχῃ κρατήσας ἢ θεᾶς δωρήμασιν;

ΗΡΑΚΛΗΣ

μάχῃ· τὰ μυστῶν δ᾽ ὄργι᾽ ηὐτύχησ᾽ ἰδών.

ΑΜΦΙΤΡΥΩΝ

ἦ καὶ κατ᾽ οἴκους ἐστὶν Εὐρυσθέως ὁ θήρ;

ΗΡΑΚΛΗΣ

615 Χθονίας νιν ἄλσος Ἑρμιών τ᾽ ἔχει πόλις.

ΑΜΦΙΤΡΥΩΝ

οὐδ᾽ οἶδεν Εὐρυσθεύς σε γῆς ἥκοντ᾽ ἄνω;

ΗΡΑΚΛΗΣ

οὐκ οἶδ᾽, ἵν᾽ ἐλθὼν τἀνθάδ᾽ εἰδείην πάρος.

608 ⟨τ᾽⟩ Reiske
617 οἶδ᾽, ἵν᾽ Matthiae: οἶδεν L

---

17 According to mythographical sources possibly reflecting a
lost poem of the sixth century, Heracles prepared for his Under-

house. Since I have come up at long last from the sunless realms of Hades and Persephone, I shall not refuse to give my first greeting to the gods within the house.

AMPHITRYON
Did you really go down to the house of Hades, my son?

HERACLES
Yes, and I brought the three-headed beast up to the light.

AMPHITRYON
Did you master him in a fight, or did the goddess give him to you?

HERACLES
In a fight: my luck was good since I had seen the Mysteries.[17]

AMPHITRYON
Is the creature in the house of Eurystheus?

HERACLES
The grove of the Underworld Goddess and the city of Hermion[18] are keeping him.

AMPHITRYON
And does Eurystheus not know that you have returned to the upper world?

HERACLES
No: I came here first to learn how things stand.

world journey by initiation into the Eleusinian Mysteries. Those so initiated were thought to enjoy special favor from the gods.

[18] Hermion or Hermione was a city in the Peloponnesus near Trozen. According to Pausanias 2.35.7, there was a ravine here thought to be Heracles' route from the Underworld.

# EURIPIDES

ΑΜΦΙΤΡΥΩΝ

χρόνον δὲ πῶς τοσοῦτον ἦσθ᾽ ὑπὸ χθονί;

ΗΡΑΚΛΗΣ

Θησέα κομίζων ἐχρόνισ᾽ ἐξ Ἅιδου, πάτερ.

ΑΜΦΙΤΡΥΩΝ

620    καὶ ποῦ ᾽στιν; ἢ γῆς πατρίδος οἴχεται πέδον;

ΗΡΑΚΛΗΣ

βέβηκ᾽ Ἀθήνας νέρθεν ἄσμενος φυγών.
   ἀλλ᾽ εἶ᾽ ὁμαρτεῖτ᾽, ὦ τέκν᾽, ἐς δόμους πατρί·
καλλίονές τἄρ᾽ εἴσοδοι τῶν ἐξόδων
πάρεισιν ὑμῖν. ἀλλὰ θάρσος ἴσχετε
625    καὶ νάματ᾽ ὄσσων μηκέτ᾽ ἐξανίετε,
σύ τ᾽, ὦ γύναι μοι, σύλλογον ψυχῆς λαβὲ
τρόμου τε παῦσαι, καὶ μέθεσθ᾽ ἐμῶν πέπλων·
οὐ γὰρ πτερωτὸς οὐδὲ φευξείω φίλους.
ἆ,
οἵδ᾽ οὐκ ἀφιᾶσ᾽ ἀλλ᾽ ἀνάπτονται πέπλων
630    τοσῷδε μᾶλλον· ὧδ᾽ ἔβητ᾽ ἐπὶ ξυροῦ;
ἄξω λαβών γε τούσδ᾽ ἐφολκίδας χεροῖν,
ναῦς δ᾽ ὡς ἐφέλξω· καὶ γὰρ οὐκ ἀναίνομαι
θεράπευμα τέκνων. πάντα τἀνθρώπων ἴσα·
φιλοῦσι παῖδας οἵ τ᾽ ἀμείνονες βροτῶν
635    οἵ τ᾽ οὐδὲν ὄντες· χρήμασιν δὲ διάφοροι·
ἔχουσιν, οἱ δ᾽ οὔ· πᾶν δὲ φιλότεκνον γένος.

ΧΟΡΟΣ

στρ. α

ἁ νεότας μοι φίλον· ἄ-

368

**AMPHITRYON**

Why were you so long beneath the earth?

**HERACLES**

I brought Theseus back from Hades, father: hence my delay.

**AMPHITYRON**

Where is he? Has he gone off to his native land?

**HERACLES**

He has gone back to Athens, glad to have escaped from the Underworld.

But come, children, accompany your father into the house. It seems your going in will be better than your coming out. Take courage and dry your tears! And you, wife, pull your spirit together and stop trembling! Let go of my clothing, all of you! I have no wings and will not run from my family! Ah me, these children do not let me go but grasp my garments all the harder! Were you in such great danger as that? Well, I will take these tow boats in by the hand and like a ship drag them after me. I do not refuse to tend my children. Men's lot is everywhere the same. High and low alike love their children; they differ in wealth, and some are rich, others poor, but the whole human race is fond of its young.

*Exit HERACLES, MEGARA, AMPHITRYON, and children into the house.*

**CHORUS**

Youth is the thing I love.

χθος δὲ τὸ γῆρας αἰεὶ
βαρύτερον Αἴτνας σκοπέλων
640 ἐπὶ κρατὶ κεῖται, βλεφάρῳ
σκοτεινὸν φάρος ἐπικαλύψαν.
μή μοι μήτ' Ἀσιήτιδος
τυραννίδος ὄλβος εἴη,
645 μὴ χρυσοῦ δώματα πλήρη
τᾶς ἥβας ἀντιλαβεῖν,
ἃ καλλίστα μὲν ἐν ὄλβῳ,
καλλίστα δ' ἐν πενίᾳ.
τὸ δὲ λυγρὸν φόνιόν τε γῆ-
650 ρας μισῶ· κατὰ κυμάτων δ'
ἔρροι· μηδέποτ' ὤφελεν
θνατῶν δώματα καὶ πόλεις
ἐλθεῖν, ἀλλὰ κατ' αἰθέρ' αἰ-
εὶ πτεροῖσι φορεῖσθαι.

ἀντ. α
655 εἰ δὲ θεοῖς ἦν ξύνεσις
καὶ σοφία κατ' ἄνδρας,
δίδυμον ἂν ἥβαν ἔφερον,
φανερὸν χαρακτῆρ' ἀρετᾶς
660 ὅσοισιν μέτα, καὶ θανόντες
εἰς αὐγὰς πάλιν ἁλίου
δισσοὺς ἂν ἔβαν διαύλους
ἁ δυσγένεια δ' ἁπλοῦν ἂν

638 δὲ τὸ Musgrave: τὸ δὲ L
640 βλεφάρῳ Reiske: -ων L

But age is a burden that always
lies heavier than the crags of Aetna
upon the head, and over my eye
it casts a veil of darkness.
May I not have the wealth
of Asian potentates,
nor houses filled with gold
to take in the place of youth!
Youth is the fairest thing in the midst of riches,
fairest too in poverty.
But grim and deadly
old age I hate. Beneath the waves
may it vanish! Would that it had never
come to visit the houses and cities of mortal men
but were always being
whirled along on the upper air!

If the gods had understanding
and wisdom where men are concerned,
a double youth would they win
as a clear mark of goodness,
they who were good, and when they died,
they would run back to the light of the sun
on the return leg of the course.
But the ignoble would have

---

643 fort. ὄλβον
649 φθονερόν Wilamowitz
650 κυμάτων δ'] κυμάτων Willink
654 φορεῖσθαι Musgrave: -είσθω L
660 καὶ θανόντες Reiske: καὶ θνατοὶ L

εἶχε ζόας βίοτον,
665 καὶ τῷδ' ἂν τούς τε κακοὺς ἦν
γνῶναι καὶ τοὺς ἀγαθούς,
ἴσον ἅτ' ἐν νεφέλαισιν ἄ-
στρων ναύταις ἀριθμὸς πέλει.
νῦν δ' οὐδεὶς ὅρος ἐκ θεῶν
670 χρηστοῖς οὐδὲ κακοῖς σαφής,
ἀλλ' εἱλισσόμενός τις αἰ-
ὼν πλοῦτον μόνον αὔξει.

στρ. β

οὐ παύσομαι τὰς Χάριτας
ταῖς Μούσαισιν συγκαταμει-
675 γνύς, ἡδίσταν συζυγίαν.
μὴ ζῴην μετ' ἀμουσίας,
αἰεὶ δ' ἐν στεφάνοισιν εἴην·
ἔτι τοι γέρων ἀοιδὸς
κελαδῶ Μναμοσύναν,
680 ἔτι τὰν Ἡρακλέους
καλλίνικον ἀείδω
παρά τε Βρόμιον οἰνοδόταν
παρά τε χέλυος ἑπτατόνου
μολπὰν καὶ Λίβυν αὐλόν.
685 οὔπω καταπαύσομεν
Μούσας αἵ μ' ἐχόρευσαν.

664 βίοτον Kirchhoff: βιοτάν L: στάδιον Reiske
665 τῷδ' ἂν . . . ἦν Hermann: τῷδε . . . ἂν L

372

but a single life's course to run,
and by this means one could tell
the bad from the good,
just as through the clouds
the sailor sees the throng of stars.
But as things stand, there is no reliable fixed mark
from the gods to judge the good and the bad,
but the course of a man's life as it whirls along
serves only to glorify his wealth.

I shall not cease mingling
the Graces and the Muses,
a union most sweet.
May I never live a Muse-less life!
Ever may I go garlanded!
Old singer that I am I still
sing the praise of Mnemosyne,[19]
still hymn Heracles'
glorious victory
in company with Bacchus giver of wine,
in company with the song
of the seven-stringed tortoise shell and the Libyan pipe.
Never shall I check
the Muses who have made me dance!

[19] Mother of the Muses.

---

679 κελαδῶ Stephanus: -εῖ L
681 ἀείδω Elmsley: ἀείσω L

ἀντ. β

παιᾶνα μὲν Δηλιάδες
⟨ναῶν⟩ ὑμνοῦσ' ἀμφὶ πύλας
τὸν Λατοῦς εὔπαιδα γόνον,
690 εἰλίσσουσαι καλλίχοροι·
παιᾶνας δ' ἐπὶ σοῖς μελάθροις
κύκνος ὡς γέρων ἀοιδὸς
πολιᾶν ἐκ γενύων
κελαδήσω· τὸ γὰρ εὖ
695 τοῖς ὕμνοισιν ὑπάρχει.
Διὸς ὁ παῖς· τᾶς δ' εὐγενίας
πλέον ὑπερβάλλων ⟨ἀρετᾷ⟩
μοχθήσας τὸν ἄκυμον
θῆκεν βίοτον βροτοῖς
700 πέρσας δείματα θηρῶν.

ΛΥΚΟΣ

ἐς καιρὸν οἴκων Ἀμφιτρύων ἔξω περᾷς·
χρόνος γὰρ ἤδη δαρὸς ἐξ ὅτου πέπλοις
κοσμεῖσθε σῶμα καὶ νεκρῶν ἀγάλμασιν.
ἀλλ' εἶα, παῖδας καὶ δάμαρθ' Ἡρακλέους
705 ἔξω κέλευε τῶνδε φαίνεσθαι δόμων,
ἐφ' οἷς ὑπέστητ' αὐτεπάγγελτοι θανεῖν.

ΑΜΦΙΤΡΥΩΝ

ἄναξ, διώκεις μ' ἀθλίως πεπραγότα
ὕβριν θ' ὑβρίζεις ἐπὶ θανοῦσι τοῖς ἐμοῖς·

688 ⟨ναῶν⟩ Diggle    690 καλλίχοροι Hermann: -ον L
691 παιᾶν' αὖτ' West    697 ⟨ἀρετᾷ⟩ Nauck

374

A paean about their temple gates
the maidens of Delos sing
to the fair son of Leto,
weaving their lovely dance steps.
And paeans about your house
I, an aged singer, swan-like[20]
from my hoary throat
shall pour forth. For the power of right
is in my hymns.
He is the son of Zeus. But surpassing even this high birth
with his deeds of valor,
he has made peaceful by his struggles
the life of mortals
and overcome dread monsters.

*Enter* AMPHITRYON *from the house and* LYCUS *with atten-
dants by Eisodos A.*

LYCUS

It is high time, Amphitryon, for you to be coming out of
the house. You have spent a long time adorning yourselves
with the finery of death.

But come, bid the children and wife of Heracles show
themselves outside the house in accordance with your
promise to die voluntarily.

AMPHITRYON

My lord, you press me hard in my distress and commit
outrage upon me in my bereavement. You should temper

---

[20] Swans were thought to sing when about to die: cf. Aeschy-
lus, *Agamemnon* 1444-5.

ἃ χρῆν σε μετρίως, κεἰ κρατεῖς, σπουδὴν ἔχειν.
710 ἐπεὶ δ᾽ ἀνάγκην προστίθης ἡμῖν θανεῖν,
στέργειν ἀνάγκη, δραστέον θ᾽ ἅ σοὶ δοκεῖ.

ΛΥΚΟΣ
ποῦ δῆτα Μεγάρα; ποῦ τέκν᾽ Ἀλκμήνης γόνου;

ΑΜΦΙΤΡΥΩΝ
δοκῶ μὲν αὐτήν, ὡς θύραθεν εἰκάσαι . . .

ΛΥΚΟΣ
τί χρῆμα; δόξης τίνος ἔχεις τεκμήριον;

ΑΜΦΙΤΡΥΩΝ
715 . . . ἱκέτιν πρὸς ἁγνοῖς Ἑστίας θάσσειν
βάθροις . . .

ΛΥΚΟΣ
ἀνόνητά γ᾽ ἱκετεύουσαν ἐκσῶσαι βίον.

ΑΜΦΙΤΡΥΩΝ
. . . καὶ τὸν θανόντα γ᾽ ἀνακαλεῖν μάτην πόσιν.

ΛΥΚΟΣ
ὁ δ᾽ οὐ πάρεστιν οὐδὲ μὴ μόλῃ ποτέ.

ΑΜΦΙΤΡΥΩΝ
οὔκ, εἴ γε μή τις θεῶν ἀναστήσειέ νιν.

ΛΥΚΟΣ
720 χώρει πρὸς αὐτὴν κἀκκόμιζε δωμάτων.

ΑΜΦΙΤΡΥΩΝ
μέτοχος ἂν εἴην τοῦ φόνου δράσας τόδε.

your zeal, even if you are the ruler. But since you force us
to die, we must put up with it and do as you decree.

LYCUS

Where is Megara? Where are the children of Alcmene's
son?

AMPHITRYON

I suppose, as far as I can guess from out here . . .

LYCUS

What is it? To what conclusion does your evidence point?

AMPHITRYON

. . . that she is sitting as a suppliant at the holy altar of
Hestia . . .

LYCUS

Yes, making a useless supplication to save her life.

AMPHITRYON

. . . and fruitlessly trying to summon her dead husband.

LYCUS

He is not here and will never return.

AMPHITRYON

No, unless some god raises him from the dead.

LYCUS

Go to her and bring her out of the house.

AMPHITRYON

But that would make me party to her murder.

---

711 θ᾽ Nauck: δ᾽ L      714 τίνος Boissonade: τῆσδ᾽ L
717 ἀνακαλεῖν Hermann: -εῖ L
720 κἀκκόμιζε Elmsley: καὶ κόμ- L

ΛΥΚΟΣ

ἡμεῖς ⟨δ᾽⟩, ἐπειδὴ σοὶ τόδ᾽ ἔστ᾽ ἐνθύμιον,
οἱ δειμάτων ἔξωθεν ἐκπορεύσομεν
σὺν μητρὶ παῖδας. δεῦρ᾽ ἔπεσθε, πρόσπολοι,
725 ὡς ἂν σχολὴν λεύσσωμεν ἄσμενοι πόνων.

ΑΜΦΙΤΡΥΩΝ

σὺ δ᾽ οὖν ἴθ᾽, ἔρχῃ δ᾽ οἷ χρεών· τὰ δ᾽ ἄλλ᾽ ἴσως
ἄλλῳ μελήσει. προσδόκα δὲ δρῶν κακῶς
κακόν τι πράξειν. ὦ γέροντες, ἐς καλὸν
στείχει, βρόχοισι δ᾽ ἀρκύων κεκλήσεται
730 ξιφηφόροισι, τοὺς πέλας δοκῶν κτενεῖν
ὁ παγκάκιστος. εἶμι δ᾽, ὡς ἴδω νεκρὸν
πίπτοντ᾽· ἔχει γὰρ ἡδονὰς θνῄσκων ἀνὴρ
ἐχθρὸς τίνων τε τῶν δεδραμένων δίκην.

ΧΟΡΟΣ

στρ. α

735—μεταβολὰ κακῶν· μέγας ὁ πρόσθ᾽ ἄναξ
πάλιν ὑποστρέφει βίοτον ἐξ Ἅιδα.
ἰὼ δίκα καὶ θεῶν
παλίρρους πότμος.
740—ἦλθες χρόνῳ μὲν οὗ δίκην δώσεις θανών,
ὕβρεις ὑβρίζων εἰς ἀμείνονας σέθεν.
—χαρμοναὶ δακρύων
ἔδοσαν ἐκβολάς·

722 ⟨δ᾽⟩ Bothe    723 οἰκημάτων vel τῶν δωμάτων F. W.
Schmidt    729 κεκλήσεται Elmsley: γενήσεται L
736 ἐξ Ἅιδα Wilamowitz: ἐς Ἀίδαν L    738 ἴτω Diggle

378

**LYCUS**

Since you feel this scruple, I, who stand outside fear, shall
bring mother and children out. Come with me, attendants,
so that we may win a welcome rest from our labors.

*Exit LYCUS with retinue into the house.*

**AMPHITRYON**

Go, then! You are going where destiny leads! Someone
else, no doubt, will concern himself with the rest. You are
doing ill, and you must expect to fare ill. Old friends, his
going is most opportune, and he will be caught fast in the
trap, a trap of cold steel, the knave who thought he would
kill others. I shall go in to see him being killed. There is
pleasure when an enemy is killed and pays the penalty for
his misdeeds.

*Exit AMPHITRYON into the house.*

**CHORUS**

Our woes depart! Mighty is our former lord
as he returns alive from Hades!
Hail, justice and the tide-turning
fate of the gods!

**CHORUS LEADER**

You have come at long last to the place where you will pay
with your life for the outrages you commit against better
men than yourself.

**CHORUS**

Joy brings the tear
from my eye.

745 πάλιν ἔμολεν ⟨ἔμολεν⟩, ἃ πάρος οὔποτε δι-
ὰ φρενὸς ἤλπισ' ⟨ἂν⟩ παθεῖν, γᾶς ἄναξ.
—ἀλλ', ὦ γεραιοί, καὶ τὰ δωμάτων ἔσω
σκοπῶμεν, εἰ πράσσει τις ὡς ἐγὼ θέλω.

ΛΥΚΟΣ

(ἔσωθεν)
ἰώ μοί μοι.

ἀντ. α
750—τόδε κατάρχεται μέλος ἐμοὶ κλύειν
φίλιον ἐν δόμοις· θάνατος οὐ πόρσω.
βοᾷ φόνου φροίμιον
στενάζων ἄναξ.

ΛΥΚΟΣ

(ἔσωθεν)
ὦ πᾶσα Κάδμου γαῖ', ἀπόλλυμαι δόλῳ.

ΧΟΡΟΣ
755—καὶ γὰρ διώλλυς· ἀντίποινα δ' ἐκτίνων
τόλμα, διδούς γε τῶν δεδραμένων δίκην.
—τίς ὁ θεοὺς ἀνομίᾳ
χραίνων, θνατὸς ὤν,
οὐρανίων ⟨ὃς⟩ ἄφρονα μακάρων κατέβα-
λε λόγον ὡς ἄρ' οὐ σθένουσιν θεοί;
760—γέροντες, οὐκέτ' ἔστι δυσσεβὴς ἀνήρ.
σιγᾷ μέλαθρα· πρὸς χοροὺς τραπώμεθα.

744 ⟨ἔμολεν⟩ Diggle    746 ⟨ἂν⟩ Pflugk
747 γεραιοί Kirchhoff: -αιέ L

He has returned, ‹returned,› this country's king,
a thing I never thought would befall me!

CHORUS LEADER

Well, old friends, let us see how things stand indoors,
whether a certain person is faring as I would like.

LYCUS

(*within*) O misery!

CHORUS

In the house begins the song
I love to hear! His death is not far off!
They prelude his murder,
the king's shouts and groans!

LYCUS

You citizens of Thebes, I am being treacherously slain!

CHORUS LEADER

Yes, for treacherously you slew! You must steel yourself to
pay in full for your misdeeds.

CHORUS

Who was it, mortal though he was,
that tainted the gods with lawlessness
and put forth the senseless tale about the blessed powers
  above
that they have no strength?

CHORUS LEADER

Old friends, the godless man is no more: the house is silent.
Let us turn ourselves to dancing. [For my friends, as I

---

<sup>757</sup> θεούς] fort. νόμους     <sup>758–9</sup> sic post Diggle (‹ὃς›)
Willink: ἄφρονα λόγον οὐρανίων μακάρων κατέβαλ᾽ L

381

## EURIPIDES

[φίλοι γὰρ εὐτυχοῦσιν οὓς ἐγὼ θέλω.]

στρ. β

    χοροὶ χοροὶ καὶ θαλίαι
    μέλουσι Θήβας ἱερὸν κατ᾽ ἄστυ.
765  μεταλλαγαὶ γὰρ δακρύων,
    μεταλλαγαὶ συντυχίας
    ἔτεκον ⟨ἔτεκον⟩ ἀοιδάς.
    βέβακ᾽ ἄναξ ὁ καινός, ὁ δὲ παλαίτερος
770  κρατεῖ, λιμένα λιπών γε τὸν Ἀχερόντιον.
    δοκημάτων ἐκτὸς ἦλθεν ἐλπίς.

ἀντ. β

    θεοὶ θεοὶ τῶν ἀδίκων
    μέλουσι καὶ τῶν ὁσίων ἐπάειν.
    ὁ χρυσὸς ἅ τ᾽ εὐτυχία
775  φρενῶν βροτοὺς ἐξάγεται
    δύνασιν ἄδικον ἐφέλκων.
    Χρόνου γὰρ οὔτις τὸ πάλιν εἰσορᾶν ἔτλα,
    νόμον παρέμενος, ἀνομίᾳ χάριν διδούς·
780  ἔθραυσεν ὄλβου κελαινὸν ἅρμα.

στρ. γ

    Ἰσμήν᾽ ὦ στεφαναφόρει
    ξεσταί θ᾽ ἑπταπύλου πόλεως
    ἀναχορεύσατ᾽ ἀγυιαὶ
    Δίρκα θ᾽ ἁ καλλιρρέεθρος,
785  σύν τ᾽ Ἀσωπιάδες κόραι

762 del. Nauck    767 ⟨ἔτεκον⟩ Bothe
768 καινός Pierson: κλεινός L

hoped, are successful.]

### CHORUS

Dance, dance and feasting,
shall fill our thoughts in the holy city of Thebes!
The changing of our tears to joy,
the changing of our fortunes,
have brought forth new song!
The usurper has gone, and the old king
reigns: he has left behind the harbor of Acheron.
Beyond all expectation my hope has come!

The gods, the gods take care
to mark the wicked and the righteous.
Golden good fortune
tempts mortal men from their senses
as it brings in its train unjust power.
For no one can bring himself to consider Time's future
    course
as he transgresses law and gratifies his lawlessness.
Thus he wrecks wealth's dark chariot.

Go gaily in garlands, River Ismenus,
and O ye smooth-worn streets
of the city of seven gates, strike up the dance,
and Dirce too with your lovely streams!
Come as well, daughters of Asopus,

---

<sup>775</sup> φρενῶν L. Dindorf: φρονεῖν L
<sup>777</sup> τὸ πάλιν εἰσορᾶν ἔτλα Hermann: ἔτλα τ. π. εἰσορᾶν L
<sup>781</sup> στεφαναφόρει Tyrwhitt: στεφαναφορία L

πατρὸς ὕδωρ βᾶτε λιποῦ-
σαί ⟨μοι⟩ συναοιδοὶ
Νύμφαι τὸν Ἡρακλέους
καλλίνικον ἀγῶνα.
790 Πυθίου δενδρῶτι πέτρα
Μουσᾶν θ' Ἑλικωνίδων
δώματ', ⟨ὦ⟩
αὔξετ' εὐγαθεῖ κελάδῳ
ἐμὰν πόλιν, ἐμὰ τείχη,
Σπαρτῶν ἵνα γένος ἔφανθη,
795 χαλκασπίδων λόχος, ὃς γᾶν
τέκνων τέκνοις μεταμείβει,
Θήβαις ἱερὸν φῶς.

ἀντ. γ

ὦ λέκτρων δύο συγγενεῖς
εὐναί, θνατογενοῦς τε καὶ
800 Διός, ὃς ἦλθεν ἐς εὐνὰν
νύμφας τᾶς Περσηίδος· ὡς
πιστόν μοι τὸ παλαιὸν ἤ-
δη λέχος, ὦ Ζεῦ, τὸ σὸν οὐκ
εὐέλπιδι φάνθη
805 λαμπρὰν δ' ἔδειξ' ὁ χρόνος
σάν, Ἡράκλεες, ἀλκάν,

787 ⟨μοι⟩ Hermann      788 Νύμφαι] ὑμνεῖν Bond
789 ἀγῶνα Wilamowitz: ἀγῶν' ὦ L
791 ⟨ὦ⟩ Verrall      792 αὔξετ' Fix: ἤξετ' L
794 ἐφάνθη Pflugk: ἔφανε L
800 εὐνὰν Wecklein: -ὰς L

leave your father's waters
and join me in singing,
Nymphs, of Heracles'
glorious victory!
O tree-clad cliff of Apollo,[21]
and the home of the Muses
of Helicon, O
glorify with your glad shout
my city and its walls,
where the Sown Men appeared,
the company clad in brazen shields. These
as they pass the land in turn to their children's children
are a holy light shining upon Thebes.

O double marriage
of one woman with a mortal
and with Zeus, who came to the bed
of Perseus' granddaughter![22] How
the truth of this ancient
siring by you, Zeus,
shone forth to me when my hopes were gone!
Time has revealed as glorious
your strength, Heracles:

[21] Presumably the double peak of Parnassus.
[22] Alcmene's father, Electryon, was the son of Perseus and
Andromeda.

---

801 ὡς Musgrave: καὶ L
804 εὐέλπιδι Bond: ἐπ' ἐλπίδι L
806 σάν, Ἡράκλεες Willink: τὰν Ἡρακλέος L

ὃς γᾶς ἐξέβας θαλάμων
Πλούτωνος δῶμα λιπὼν
νέρτερον.
κρείσσων μοι τύραννος ἔφυς
810    ἢ δυσγένει᾽ ἀνάκτων,
ἃ νῦν ἐσορῶντι φαίνει
ξιφηφόρων ἐς ἀγώνων
ἄμιλλαν εἰ τὸ δίκαιον
θεοῖς ἔτ᾽ ἀρέσκει.

815    —ἔα ἔα·
ἆρ᾽ ἐς τὸν αὐτὸν πίτυλον ἥκομεν φόβου,
γέροντες, οἷον φάσμ᾽ ὑπὲρ δόμων ὁρῶ;
—φυγῇ φυγῇ
νωθὲς πέδαιρε κῶλον, ἐκποδὼν ἔλα.
820    ὦναξ Παιάν,
ἀπότροπος γένοιό μοι πημάτων.

IPIΣ

θαρσεῖτε Νυκτὸς τήνδ᾽ ὁρῶντες ἔκγονον
Λύσσαν, γέροντες, κἀμὲ τὴν θεῶν λάτριν
Ἶριν· πόλει γὰρ οὐδὲν ἥκομεν βλάβος,
825    ἑνὸς δ᾽ ἐπ᾽ ἀνδρὸς δώματα στρατεύομεν,
ὅν φασιν εἶναι Ζηνὸς Ἀλκμήνης τ᾽ ἄπο.
πρὶν μὲν γὰρ ἄθλους ἐκτελευτῆσαι πικρούς,

807 ἐξέβας Diggle: -έβα L
811 ἐσορῶντι Wecklein olim: -ορᾶν L

23 A title of Apollo as healer god.

you came forth from the recesses of earth
and left behind Pluto's
home below.
You are more kingly in my eyes
than the ignoble tyrant.
His fate makes plain, to anyone who looks
at this sword-bearing
contest of arms, whether the gods
still take pleasure in righteous conduct.

*On the* mechane *two goddesses,* LYSSA, *snaky-haired goddess of madness, and* IRIS, *messenger of the gods, fly through the air and alight on the roof of the palace.*

#### CHORUS LEADER
But what is this? Has the old fluttering of fear returned, my friends, with such an apparition visible above the house?

#### CHORUS
Take flight, take flight!
Lift your sluggish limbs, get away from here!
O lord Paean,[23]
avert this woe from me!

*The Chorus begin to flee but stop when addressed by Iris.*

#### IRIS
Old sirs, take heart! You are looking at Lyssa, daughter of Night, and me, Iris, the gods' servant. We have not come to hurt the city: our expedition is aimed at a single man's house, the man reported to be the son of Zeus and Alcmene. Before he finished his difficult labors, Fate pre-

387

τὸ χρή νιν ἐξέσῳζεν οὐδ' εἴα πατὴρ
Ζεύς νιν κακῶς δρᾶν οὔτ' ἔμ' οὔθ' Ἥραν ποτέ·
830    ἐπεὶ δὲ μόχθους διεπέρασ' Εὐρυσθέως,
Ἥρα προσάψαι κοινὸν αἷμ' αὐτῷ θέλει
παῖδας κατακτείναντι, συνθέλω δ' ἐγώ.
    ἀλλ' εἴ' ἄτεγκτον συλλαβοῦσα καρδίαν,
Νυκτὸς κελαινῆς ἀνυμέναιε παρθένε,
835    μανίας τ' ἐπ' ἀνδρὶ τῷδε καὶ παιδοκτόνους
φρενῶν ταραγμοὺς καὶ ποδῶν σκιρτήματα
ἔλαυνε κίνει, φόνιον ἐξίει κάλων,
ὡς ἂν πορεύσας δι' Ἀχερούσιον πόρον
τὸν καλλίπαιδα στέφανον αὐθέντῃ φόνῳ
840    γνῷ μὲν τὸν Ἥρας οἷός ἐστ' αὐτῷ χόλος,
μάθῃ δὲ τὸν ἐμόν· ἢ θεοὶ μὲν οὐδαμοῦ,
τὰ θνητὰ δ' ἔσται μεγάλα, μὴ δόντος δίκην.

ΛΥΣΣΑ

ἐξ εὐγενοῦς μὲν πατρὸς ἔκ τε μητέρος
πέφυκα, Νυκτὸς Οὐρανοῦ τ' ἀφ' αἵματος,
845    †τιμάς τ' ἔχω τάσδ' οὐκ ἀγασθῆναι φίλοις†
οὐδ' ἥδομαι φοιτῶσ' ἐπ' ἀνθρώπων φίλους.
παραινέσαι δέ, πρὶν σφαλεῖσαν εἰσιδεῖν,
Ἥρᾳ θέλω σοί τ', ἢν πίθησθ' ἐμοῖς λόγοις.
ἀνὴρ ὅδ' οὐκ ἄσημος οὔτ' ἐπὶ χθονὶ
850    οὔτ' ἐν θεοῖσιν, οὗ σύ μ' ἐσπέμπεις δόμους·
ἄβατον δὲ χώραν καὶ θάλασσαν ἀγρίαν

831 κοινὸν Wakefield: καινὸν L
845 v. conclamatus: post τάσδ' aliquid excidisse suspicatus est

served his life, and Zeus his father forbade Hera and me to harm him at any time. But now that he has finished Eurystheus' tasks, Hera wishes to stain him with kindred bloodshed, the blood of his own children, and that is my will too.

But come now, maiden daughter of black Night, pull together your implacable heart and send upon this man madness and child-killing derangement of mind, cause his feet to dance, go against him in deadly full sail so that when he has by his own murderous hand sent his sons, fair glory of his life, across the strait of Acheron, he may know the nature of Hera's wrath against him and may know mine. Else—if he be not punished—the gods will be of no account and it is mortals who will be great.

## LYSSA

It is from a noble father and mother that I was begotten, from the lineage of Night and Heaven,[24] and from them I possess this office of mine, and I am not accustomed to feel ill will[25] nor do I take pleasure in visiting those mortals I hold dear. I wish to give advice to Hera, before I see her trip up, and to you, if you will take it. The man into whose house you are sending me is of great renown both on earth and in heaven. He tamed the pathless wilderness and the

---

[24] In Hesiod's *Theogony* Lyssa, like the Erinyes, is the offspring of Night.

[25] Text uncertain.

---

Murray, e.g. ⟨ἐχθροδαίμονας κακοῦν. / τοῖς δ' εὐσεβοῦσιν⟩ οὐκ ἀγασθῆναι φιλῶ (φιλῶ Murray)

846 δόμους Baumann: φρένας Kayser

850 σύ Hartung: γε L

ἐξημερώσας θεῶν ἀνέστησεν μόνος
τιμὰς πιτνούσας ἀνοσίων ἀνδρῶν ὕπο·
⟨οὔτ' οὖν ἐς αὐτὸν ἔχθρ' ἐμοὶ ποιεῖν φίλον⟩
σοί τ' οὐ παραινῶ μεγάλα βουλεῦσαι κακά.

ΙΡΙΣ

855 μὴ σὺ νουθέτει τά θ' Ἥρας κἀμὰ μηχανήματα.

ΛΥΣΣΑ

ἐς τὸ λῷον ἐμβιβάζω σ' ἴχνος ἀντὶ τοῦ κακοῦ.

ΙΡΙΣ

οὐχὶ σωφρονεῖν γ' ἔπεμψε δεῦρό σ' ἡ Διὸς δάμαρ.

ΛΥΣΣΑ

Ἥλιον μαρτυρόμεσθα δρῶσ' ἃ δρᾶν οὐ βούλομαι.
εἰ δὲ δή μ' Ἥρᾳ θ' ὑπουργεῖν σοί τ' ἀναγκαίως ἔχει
860 τάχος ἐπιρροίβδην θ' ὁμαρτεῖν ὡς κυνηγέτῃ κύνας,
εἶμί γ'· οὔτε πόντος οὕτω κύμασι στένων λάβρος
οὔτε γῆς σεισμὸς κεραυνοῦ τ' οἶστρος ὠδῖνας πνέων,
οἷ' ἐγὼ στάδια δραμοῦμαι στέρνον εἰς Ἡρακλέους·
καὶ καταρρήξω μέλαθρα καὶ δόμους ἐπεμβαλῶ,
865 τέκν' ἀποκτείνασα πρῶτον· ὁ δὲ κανὼν οὐκ εἴσεται
παῖδας οὓς ἔτικτεν ἐναρών, πρὶν ἂν ἐμὰς λύσσας
ἀφῇ.
ἢν ἰδού· καὶ δὴ τινάσσει κρᾶτα βαλβίδων ἄπο
καὶ διαστρόφους ἑλίσσει σῖγα γοργωποὺς κόρας,
ἀμπνοὰς δ' οὐ σωφρονίζει, ταῦρος ὣς ἐς ἐμβολήν,

<hr/>

853 post h.v. lac. ind. Wilamowitz
854 βουλεῦσαι Camper: βούλεσθαι L

sea's wild waves, and he alone has restored the worship of
the gods when it was being cast into oblivion by godless
men. ⟨And so, just as I am loath to attack him,⟩ so I advise
you not to plot great mischief against him.

IRIS

Don't try to correct Hera's plans and mine.

LYSSA

I am trying to set you on the better path, not the worse.

IRIS

Zeus's wife did not send you here to show good sense.

LYSSA

I call the Sun to witness that what I am doing I do against
my will! But if I must perform this service for Hera and am
obliged to follow on your heels with all speed like a hunts-
man's pack of dogs, I shall go. The sea with its roaring
waves is not so violent, not so violent the earthquake or the
sting of the lightning bolt that fills the air with pain, as will
be my dash into the breast of Heracles. I shall break down
his roof and cast his house upon his head, but first I'll kill
his children. And their slayer will not know that he has
killed the sons he begot until he gets clear of my madness.

See! He has left the starting gate. He shakes his head
about, saying not a word but rolling his fierce eyes out of
their sockets; his breathing is disquieted, like a bull about
to charge, and he bellows frightfully, calling forth the death

---

855 κἀμὰ Reiske: κακὰ L    860 fort. κύνα (noluit Jackson)
862 οἰστὸς Wakefield
866 ἔτικτεν ἐναρών Wilamowitz: ἔτικτ' ἐναίρων Lγρ
869 οὐ σωφρονίζει fort. corrupta

EURIPIDES

870  δεινὰ μυκᾶται δὲ Κῆρας ἀνακαλῶν τὰς Ταρτάρου.
     τάχα σ᾽ ἐγὼ μᾶλλον χορεύσω καὶ καταυλήσω
        φόβῳ.
     στεῖχ᾽ ἐς Οὔλυμπον πεδαίρουσ᾽, Ἶρι, γενναῖον πόδα·
     ἐς δόμους δ᾽ ἡμεῖς ἄφαντοι δυσόμεσθ᾽ Ἡρακλέους.

ΧΟΡΟΣ

875  ὀτοτοτοῖ, στέναξον· ἀποκείρεται
     σὸν ἄνθος πόλεος, ὁ Διὸς ἔκγονος·
     μέλεος Ἑλλάς, ἃ τὸν εὐεργέταν
     ἀποβαλεῖς ὀλεῖς μανιάσιν λύσσαις
     χορευθέντ᾽ ἐναύλοις.
880  βέβακεν ἐν δίφροισιν ἁ πολύστονος,
     ἅρμασι δ᾽ ἐνδίδωσι
     κέντρον ὡς ἐπὶ λώβᾳ
     Νυκτὸς Γοργὼν ἑκατογκεφάλοις
     ὄφεων ἰαχήμασι Λύσσα μαρμαρωπός.
     ταχὺ τὸν εὐτυχῆ μετέβαλεν δαίμων,
885  ταχὺ δὲ πρὸς πατρὸς τέκν᾽ ἐκπνεύσεται.

ΑΜΦΙΤΡΥΩΝ

(ἔσωθεν)
ἰώ μοι μέλεος.

ΧΟΡΟΣ

ἰὼ Ζεῦ, σὸν ἄγονον αὐτίκα γένος

882 post h.v. forsitan exciderit aliquid, e.g. ⟨κακὰ δ᾽ ὡς
ῥέξουσ᾽ εἴσω φροῦδα⟩
886 σὸν ἄγονον αὐτίκα γένος Diggle: τὸ σὸν γ. ἄ. αὐτ. L

392

spirits from Tartarus. Soon I shall make you dance still
more and charm your ears with the pipe of panic! Lift your
noble feet, Iris, and make your way up to Olympus! I shall
go down invisible into the house of Heracles.

*Exit* IRIS *by the* mechane, LYSSA *by a stairway into the*
skene.

CHORUS

Ah! Ah! Groan aloud! Cut off
is the fair flower of the city, Zeus's son!
Desolate are you, Hellas, your great benefactor
you shall let slip, shall lose, who with the shrill pipe
of madness in his ears is made to dance!
She of the many groans is mounted on her chariot,
and lays the lash hard
on the horses to hurt them,[26]
Night's Gorgon daughter, Lyssa,
whose head gleams with the open mouths of a hundred
    snakes.
Swiftly fate has overthrown the fortunate,
and swiftly the children will be destroyed by their father's
    hand!

AMPHITRYON

(*within*) Ah, woe is me!

CHORUS

Ah, Zeus! Your son will be laid out in ruin,

---

[26] If this refers to Lyssa, the chariot is metaphorical, for she
does not leave by the *mechane*. It is possible, however, that Iris is
meant and that a line has dropped out, e.g. "‹But the other is gone
within to do harm,› Night's Gorgon daughter, Lyssa."

λυσσάδες ὠμοβρῶτες ἄδικοι Ποιναὶ
κακοῖσιν ἐκπετάσουσιν.

ΑΜΦΙΤΡΥΩΝ

ἰὼ στέγαι.

ΧΟΡΟΣ

κατάρχεται χορεύματ᾽ ἄτερ τυπάνων
890 Βρομίου κεχαρισμένων θύρσῳ . . .

ΑΜΦΙΤΡΥΩΝ

ἰὼ δόμοι.

ΧΟΡΟΣ

πρὸς αἵματ᾽, οὐχὶ τᾶς Διονυσιάδος
βοτρύων ἐπὶ χεύμασιν λοιβᾶς.

ΑΜΦΙΤΡΥΩΝ

φυγῇ, τέκν᾽, ἐξορμᾶτε.

ΧΟΡΟΣ

δάιον τόδε
895 δάιον μέλος ἐπαυλεῖται.
κυναγετεῖ τέκνων διωγμόν· οὔποτ᾽ ἄκραντα δόμοισι
Λύσσα βακχεύσει.

ΑΜΦΙΤΡΥΩΝ

αἰαῖ κακῶν.

ΧΟΡΟΣ

900 αἰαῖ δῆτα· τὸν γεραιὸν ὡς στένω

---

887 ὠμοβρῶτες Wakefield: ὠμόβροτος L    ἄδικοι Ποι-
ναὶ Wilamowitz: ἀποινόδικοι δίκαι L

his sons gone, by spirits of madness,
bloodthirsty and unjust spirits of punishment!

#### AMPHITRYON

Alas for the house!

#### CHORUS

The dance begins, a dance without the drums
that add pleasure to the thyrsus of Dionysus . . .

#### AMPHITRYON

Alas for my home!

#### CHORUS

. . . a dance that ends in death, not in the pressing out
of Dionysus' grapes!

#### AMPHITRYON

Run, children, run!

#### CHORUS

        This is a murderous,
murderous song that is piped!
He hunts down his children, pursues them! Lyssa's bac-
   chant frenzy
in the house shall not be in vain!

#### AMPHITRYON

Alas for the ruin!

#### CHORUS

Yes, alas! How I groan for his aged father

---

889 χορεύματ' ἄτερ τυπάνων Hermann: χόρευμα τυμπάνων
ἄτερ L      890 Βρομίου κεχαρισμένων post Hartung (Βρο-
μίου) Willink: οὐ Βρομίῳ κεχαρισμένα L

πατέρα τάν τε παιδοτρόφον, ⟨ᾇ⟩ μάταν
τέκεα γεννᾶται.
ἰδοὺ ἰδού,
905  θύελλα σείει δῶμα, συμπίπτει στέγη.
ἢ ἤ·
τί δρᾷς, ὦ Διὸς παῖ, μελάθρῳ;
τάραγμα ταρτάρειον, ὡς ἐπ' Ἐγκελάδῳ ποτὲ
    Παλλάς,
ἐς δόμους πέμπεις.

ΕΞΑΓΓΕΛΟΣ
910  ὦ λευκὰ γήρᾳ σώματ' . . .

ΧΟΡΟΣ
                              ἀνακαλεῖς με τίνα
βοάν;

ΕΞΑΓΓΕΛΟΣ
    . . . ἄλαστα τὰν δόμοισι.

ΧΟΡΟΣ
                              μάντιν οὐχ
ἕτερον ἄξομαι.

ΕΞΑΓΓΕΛΟΣ
τεθνᾶσι παῖδες.

ΧΟΡΟΣ
        αἰαῖ.

ΕΞΑΓΓΕΛΟΣ
στενάζεθ' ὡς στενακτά.

901 ⟨ᾇ⟩ Musgrave

and for her who raised his children,
children she bore in vain!
Look, look!
A mighty wind is shaking the house, the roof is falling in!
Ah, ah!
Son of Zeus, what are you doing in the house?
It is hellish confusion you send against it,
as of old Athena did to Enceladus![27]

*A servant comes out of the skene as* MESSENGER.

MESSENGER
Aged and white-haired sirs . . .

CHORUS
                    What is this shout
you make to me?

MESSENGER
        . . . dreadful is all within!

CHORUS
                                No prophet
do I need to tell me this!

MESSENGER
The children are dead.

CHORUS
        Alas!

MESSENGER
Groan aloud, for groans this well deserves.

[27] Enceladus was a Giant, defeated by Athena in the Gigan-
tomachy.

ΧΟΡΟΣ

δάιοι φόνοι,
915 δάιοι δὲ τοκέων χέρες.

ΕΞΑΓΓΕΛΟΣ

οὐκ ἄν τις εἴποι μᾶλλον ἢ πεπόνθαμεν.

ΧΟΡΟΣ

πῶς πᾶσι στενακτὸν ἄταν ἄταν
πατέρος ἀμφαίνεις;
920 λέγε τίνα τρόπον ἔσυτο θεόθεν ἐπὶ μέλα-
θρα τάδε τλάμονάς τε παίδων ψυχάς.

ΕΞΑΓΓΕΛΟΣ

ἱερὰ μὲν ἦν πάροιθεν ἐσχάρας Διὸς
καθάρσι᾽ οἴκων, γῆς ἄνακτ᾽ ἐπεὶ κτανὼν
ἐξέβαλε τῶνδε δωμάτων Ἡρακλέης·
925 χορὸς δὲ καλλίμορφος εἱστήκει τέκνων
πατήρ τε Μεγάρα τ᾽, ἐν κύκλῳ δ᾽ ἤδη κανοῦν
εἵλικτο βωμοῦ, φθέγμα δ᾽ ὅσιον εἴχομεν.
μέλλων δὲ δαλὸν χειρὶ δεξιᾷ φέρειν,
ἐς χέρνιβ᾽ ὡς βάψειεν, Ἀλκμήνης τόκος
930 ἔστη σιωπῇ. καὶ χρονίζοντος πατρὸς
παῖδες προσέσχον ὄμμ᾽· ὁ δ᾽ οὐκέθ᾽ αὑτὸς ἦν,
ἀλλ᾽ ἐν στροφαῖσιν ὀμμάτων ἐφθαρμένος
ῥίζας τ᾽ ἐν ὄσσοις αἱματῶπας ἐκβαλὼν
ἀφρὸν κατέσταζ᾽ εὐτρίχος γενειάδος.
935 ἔλεξε δ᾽ ἅμα γέλωτι παραπεπληγμένῳ·
Πάτερ, τί θύω πρὶν κτανεῖν Εὐρυσθέα
καθάρσιον πῦρ καὶ πόνους διπλοῦς ἔχω;

CHORUS

       Murderous was the slaughter,
murderous the father's hands!

MESSENGER

No words can describe our misfortune.

CHORUS

How can you make clear to us the father's ruin,
a ruin to make all groan aloud?
Say how it was that from high heaven
it rushed upon this house and the poor lives of his children.

MESSENGER

Sacrificial victims were standing before Zeus's altar to pu-
rify the house, since Heracles had killed the land's ruler
and flung him out of doors. His children stood by as a lovely
chorus, and his father and Megara too, and the sacred
basket had made its circular course about the altar: we
were all keeping a reverent silence. When he was about to
bring a torch in his right hand to dip in the holy water,
Alcmene's son stood stock still in silence. The children
turned their faces toward him in wonder at their father's
tarrying. His looks were utterly changed: his face was dis-
torted with the agitation of his eyes, and in these blood-red
streaks appeared, while foam dripped onto his handsome
beard. With a maniacal laugh he said, "Father, why am I
kindling the flame for purification before killing Eurys-

---

916 fort. lac. post h. v. indicanda, e.g. ⟨ἀπροσδόκητα καὶ
στενακτὰ πήματα⟩
917 πᾶσι στενακτὸν Willink: παισὶ στενακτὰν L
921 τάδε Willink: κακὰ τ- L    ψυχάς Wilamowitz: τύχας
L

ἔργον μιᾶς μοι χειρὸς εὖ θέσθαι τάδε.
ὅταν δ' ἐνέγκω δεῦρο κρᾶτ' Εὐρυσθέως,
940 ἐπὶ τοῖσι νῦν θανοῦσιν ἁγνιῶ χέρας.
ἐκχεῖτε πηγάς, ῥίπτετ' ἐκ χειρῶν κανᾶ.
τίς μοι δίδωσι τόξα; τίς δ' ὅπλον χερός;
πρὸς τὰς Μυκήνας εἶμι· λάζυσθαι χρεὼν
μοχλοὺς δικέλλας θ' ὥστε Κυκλώπων βάθρα
945 φοίνικι κανόνι καὶ τύκοις ἡρμοσμένα
στρεπτῷ σιδήρῳ συντριαινῶσαι πάλιν.
κἀκ τοῦδε βαίνων ἅρματ' οὐκ ἔχων ἔχειν
ἔφασκε δίφρου τ' εἰσέβαινεν ἄντυγα
κἄθεινε, κέντρῳ δῆθεν ὡς θείνων, χερί.
950 διπλοῦς δ' ὀπαδοῖς ἦν γέλως φόβος θ' ὁμοῦ,
καί τις τόδ' εἶπεν, ἄλλος εἰς ἄλλον δρακών·
Παίζει πρὸς ἡμᾶς δεσπότης ἢ μαίνεται;
ὁ δ' εἷρπ' ἄνω τε καὶ κάτω κατὰ στέγας,
μέσον δ' ἐς ἀνδρῶν' ἐσπεσὼν Νίσου πόλιν
955 ἥκειν ἔφασκε, δωμάτων τ' ἔσω βεβὼς
κλιθεὶς ἐς οὖδας, ὡς ἔχει, σκευάζεται
θοίνην. διελθὼν δ' ἐπὶ βραχὺν χρόνον †μονῆς†
Ἰσθμοῦ ναπαίας ἔλεγε προσβαίνειν πλάκας.
κἀνταῦθα γυμνὸν σῶμα θεὶς πορπαμάτων
960 πρὸς οὐδέν' ἡμιλλᾶτο κἀκηρύσσετο
αὐτὸς πρὸς αὑτοῦ καλλίνικος, οὐδενὸς
ἀκοὴν ὑπειπών. δεινὰ δ' Εὐρυσθεῖ βρέμων

938 ἔργον Matthiae: ἐξὸν L
947 κἀκ Diggle: ἐκ L

400

theus? I am making twice the labor for myself! I can put
this right single-handedly. When I bring back Eurystheus'
head to Thebes, then I shall purify my hands for those just
killed. Pour out the lustral water, drop the baskets from
your hands! Who will give me my bow, who my club? I am
off to Mycenae! I must take crowbars and pickaxes to pry
up with the twisted iron the Cyclopean foundations fitted
snug with red plumbline and mason's hammer!" At this he
strode off saying he had a chariot, though he had none, and
made as if to step behind a chariot rail and struck with his
hand as though striking his horses with a goad.

The servants' feelings were torn between mirth and
fear, and one of them, looking at his fellows, would say, "Is
our master playing a game with us, or is he insane?" Her-
acles moved back and forth through the house, and charg-
ing into the middle of the men's quarters he said he had
come to the city of Nisus.[28] Then, coming to a halt in the
bedchamber, he reclined upon the floor, just as he was, and
prepared his dinner. Then, having marched for a short time
through the house he said that he was approaching the
wooded plains of the Isthmus. Here he stripped himself of
his garments, wrestled without an opponent, had himself
proclaimed victor with himself as herald, and called for
silence from a nonexistent throng.[29] Then uttering fierce

---

[28] Megara, just north of the Isthmus of Corinth.

[29] Heracles imagines he is taking part in the Isthmian Games.

---

955–6 δωμάτων τ' . . . κλιθεὶς Wilamowitz: δωμάτων . . .
κλιθεὶς δ' L

957 ἐπὶ Kovacs cl. *Med.* 355, *El.* 425: εἰς L    μονῆς] fort.
στέγη: ἐν μονῇ βραχὺν χρόνον Wilamowitz

ἦν ἐν Μυκήναις τῷ λόγῳ. πατὴρ δέ νιν
θιγὼν κραταιᾶς χειρὸς ἐννέπει τάδε·
965 Ὦ παῖ, τί πάσχεις; τίς ὁ τρόπος ξενώσεως
τῆσδ'; οὔ τί που φόνος σ' ἐβάκχευσεν νεκρῶν
οὓς ἄρτι καίνεις; ὁ δέ νιν Εὐρυσθέως δοκῶν
πατέρα προταρβοῦνθ' ἱκέσιον ψαύειν χερὸς
ὠθεῖ, φαρέτραν δ' εὐτρεπῆ σκευάζεται
970 καὶ τόξ' ἑαυτοῦ παισί, τοὺς Εὐρυσθέως
δοκῶν φονεύειν. οἱ δὲ ταρβοῦντες φόβῳ
ὤρουον ἄλλος ἄλλοσ', ἐς πέπλους ὁ μὲν
μητρὸς ταλαίνης, ὁ δ' ὑπὸ κίονος σκιάν,
ἄλλος δὲ βωμὸν ὄρνις ὡς ἔπτηξ' ὕπο.
975 βοᾷ δὲ μήτηρ· Ὦ τεκών, τί δρᾷς; τέκνα
κτείνεις; βοᾷ δὲ πρέσβυς οἰκετῶν τ' ὄχλος.
    ὁ δ' ἐξελίσσων κίονος κύκλῳ πόδα
τόρνευμα δεινὸν παῖδ' ἐναντίον σταθεὶς
βάλλει πρὸς ἧπαρ· ὕπτιος δὲ λαΐνους
980 ὀρθοστάτας ἔδευσεν ἐκπνέων βίον.
ὁ δ' ἠλάλαξε κἀπεκόμπασεν τάδε·
Εἷς μὲν νεοσσὸς ὅδε θανὼν Εὐρυσθέως
ἔχθραν πατρῴαν ἐκτίνων πέπτωκέ μοι.
ἄλλῳ δ' ἐπεῖχε τόξ', ὃς ἀμφὶ βωμίαν
985 ἔπτηξε κρηπῖδ' ὡς λεληθέναι δοκῶν.
φθάνει δ' ὁ τλήμων γόνασι προσπεσὼν πατρὸς
καὶ πρὸς γένειον χεῖρα καὶ δέρην βαλὼν
Ὦ φίλτατ', αὐδᾷ, μή μ' ἀποκτείνῃς, πάτερ·
σός εἰμι· σὸν παῖδ', οὐ τὸν Εὐρυσθέως, ὀλεῖς.

threats against Eurystheus he was, by his own account, in
Mycenae. But his father, grasping him by his mighty hand,
said, "My son, what has come over you? What is this change
you have undergone? Surely it was not the blood of the
men you just killed that has made you mad?" But thinking
that Eurystheus' father was grasping his hand in fear as a
suppliant, Heracles pushed him away and prepared arrows
and bow against his own children, believing that he was
killing Eurystheus' children. These in fear rushed in dif-
ferent directions, one to his poor mother's skirts, another
to the shelter of a column, another cowering like a bird
under the protection of the altar. Their mother cried out,
"Ah, what are you doing? You are their father: will you kill
the children?" Old Amphitryon and the throng of servants
shouted too.

But he, circling a grim turn around the column, stood
facing the boy and shot him through the heart. The boy fell
on his back, and as he breathed out his life he drenched
the stone pillars with his blood. Heracles shouted in tri-
umph and uttered this boast: "Here's one fledgling of Eu-
rystheus dead: his death is payment to me for his father's
hostility!" He aimed his bow at a second, who was cower-
ing near the base of the altar, thinking he escaped notice.
But before Heracles could shoot, the poor boy fell at his
father's knees and thrust his hand at his chin and his neck;
"Dearest father," he said, "do not kill me. I am yours! It
is *your* son, not Eurystheus' child, you are going to slay!"

---

975 ῏Ω τί δρᾷς; τεκὼν τέκνα West

977–8 κίονος κύκλῳ πόδα / τόρνευμα δεινόν, παῖδ᾽ Dobree:
παῖδα κίονος κύκλῳ / τόρνευμα δεινὸν ποδός L

989 σὸν παῖδ Elmsley: σὸς παῖς L

990 ὁ δ' ἀγριωπὸν ὄμμα Γοργόνος στρέφων,
ὡς ἐντὸς ἔστη παῖς λυγροῦ τοξεύματος
μυδροκτύπον μίμημ' ὑπὲρ κάρα βαλὼν
ξύλον καθῆκε παιδὸς ἐς ξανθὸν κάρα
ἔρρηξε δ' ὀστᾶ. δεύτερον δὲ παῖδ' ἑλὼν
995 χωρεῖ τρίτον θῦμ' ὡς ἐπισφάξων δυοῖν.
ἀλλὰ φθάνει νιν ἡ τάλαιν' ἔσω δόμων
μήτηρ ὑπεκλαβοῦσα καὶ κλήει πύλας.
ὁ δ' ὡς ἐπ' αὐτοῖς δὴ Κυκλωπίοισιν ὢν
σκάπτει μοχλεύει θύρετρα κἀκβαλὼν σταθμὰ
1000 δάμαρτα καὶ παῖδ' ἑνὶ κατέστρωσεν βέλει.
      κἀνθένδε πρὸς γέροντος ἱππεύει φόνον·
ἀλλ' ἦλθεν, εἰκὼν ⟨δ'⟩ ὡς ὁρᾶν ἐφαίνετο,
Παλλάς, κραδαίνουσ' ἔγχος ἐπίλογχον χερί,
κἄρριψε πέτρον στέρνον εἰς Ἡρακλέους,
1005 ὅς νιν πόνου μαργῶντος ἔσχε κὰς ὕπνον
καθῆκε· πίτνει δ' ἐς πέδον, πρὸς κίονα
νῶτον πατάξας, ὃς πεσήμασι στέγης
διχορραγὴς ἔκειτο κρηπίδων ἔπι.
1010    ἡμεῖς δ' ἐλευθεροῦντες ἐκ δρασμῶν πόδα
1009 σὺν τῷ γέροντι δεσμὰ σειραίων βρόχων
ἀνήπτομεν πρὸς κίον', ὡς λήξας ὕπνου
μηδὲν προσεργάσαιτο τοῖς δεδραμένοις.
εὕδει δ' ὁ τλήμων ὕπνον οὐκ εὐδαίμονα
παῖδας φονεύσας καὶ δάμαρτ'. ἐγὼ μὲν οὖν
1015 οὐκ οἶδα θνητῶν ὅστις ἀθλιώτερος.

1002 ⟨δ'⟩ Robertson

404

But he merely turned his fierce Gorgon gaze upon him and, since the boy stood too close for the deadly bow shot, lifted his club above his head and—just like a smith forging iron—brought it down on the boy's blond head and smashed his skull. Having killed his second son, he went off to sacrifice a third victim on top of the other two. But before he could do so the boy's mother snatched him up, took him inside the chamber, and barred the door. Heracles, just as if he were besieging Mycenae, dug under the door, pried it up, pulled out the doorposts, and with a single arrow felled both wife and child.

Then he raced off to murder his old father. But now there came into the house—and she was like a statue to look upon—Pallas Athena, brandishing her sharp-pointed spear in her hand. She hurled a stone at the chest of Heracles, which checked him from his mad labor and cast him into a sleep. He fell to the ground, striking his back against a pillar that in the collapse of the house lay broken in two upon the foundations.

Freeing ourselves from our panic flight, we helped the old man bind Heracles to the pillar with a bond of twisted rope to prevent him when he woke up from doing still more harm. The poor man sleeps an unenviable sleep, having murdered his children and his wife. I know of no mortal more unfortunate than he.

*Exit* MESSENGER *into the house.*

---

1003 ἐπίλογχον χερί Canter: ἐπὶ λόφω κέαρ L
1005 πόνου Willink: φόνου L     1007 μαλάξας West
1009 et 1010 inter se trai. Pierson

ΧΟΡΟΣ

ὁ φόνος ἦν ὃν Ἀργολὶς ἔχει πέτρα
τότε μὲν περισαμότατος καὶ ἄπιστος
Ἑλλάδι τῶν Δαναοῦ παίδων·
τάδε δὲ παρέδραμεν τὰ τότε κακὰ τάλανι
1020 διογενεῖ κόρῳ.
μονότεκνον Πρόκνας φόνον ἔχω λέξαι
†θυόμενον† Μούσαις·
σὺ δὲ τέκνα τρίγονα τεκόμενος,
ὦ δάιε, λυσσάδι συγκατειργάσω μοίρᾳ.
1025 αἰαῖ, τίνα στεναγμὸν
ἢ γόον ἢ φθιτῶν ᾠδὰν ἢ τίν᾽ Ἅι-
δα χορὸν ἀχήσω;
φεῦ φεῦ·
ἴδεσθε, διάνδιχα κλῇθρα
1030 κλίνεται ὑψιπύλων δόμων.
ἰώ μοι·
ἴδεσθε δὲ τέκνα πρὸ πατρὸς
ἄθλια κείμενα δυστάνου,
εὕδοντος ὕπνον δεινὸν ἐκ παίδων φόνου,
1035 περὶ δὲ δεσμὰ καὶ πολύβροχ᾽ ἀμμάτων

1017 ἄπιστος Reiske: ἄριστος L
1019 τάδε δὲ Wunder: τάδ᾽ L    παρέδραμεν Bothe: ὑπερ-
έβαλεν π- L
1022 θρεόμενον Heath: κλεόμενον Willink
1025 αἰαῖ Hartung: ἐς L
1032 δὲ Elmsley: τάδε L
1034 ἐκ παίδων Burges: ἐκποδὼν L

406

CHORUS

The murder done by Danaus' daughters,
murder remembered by rocky Argos,[30]
was renowned in its day and found disbelief in Greece.
But those deeds are surpassed by these terrible events
afflicting the son of Zeus.
I can tell of Procne's murder of her only child,[31]
a theme of song for the Muses.
But you sired three children,
murderous man, and killed them by the mad fate that was
    yours!
Alas, what groan,
what wail, what song for the dead,
what chorus of Hades shall I raise?

*The doors of the skene open and* HERACLES *is wheeled out
on the eccyclema, tied to a pillar and with his slaughtered
sons and wife around him.*

Ah, ah!
See, they part, the doors
of the high-gated palace!
Woe is me!
See the poor children lying
before their unhappy father,
who after his children's murder sleeps a dreadful sleep!
Around him is the binding, the prop of many ropes

[30] The fifty daughters of Danaus were compelled to marry
their fifty cousins, the sons of Aegyptus. They conspired to murder
their bridegrooms on the wedding night.

[31] Procne, wife of Tereus, killed her son Itys to punish her
husband's infidelity. She was transformed into a nightingale.

ἐρείσμαθ᾽ Ἡράκλειον
ἀμφὶ δέμας τάδε λαΐνοις
ἀνημμένα κίοσιν ἀμφ᾽ οἴκων.

—ὁ δ᾽ ὥς τις ὄρνις ἄπτερον καταστένων
1040 ὠδῖνα τέκνων πρέσβυς ὑστέρῳ ποδὶ
πικρὰν διώκων ἤλυσιν πάρεσθ᾽ ὅδε.

ΑΜΦΙΤΡΥΩΝ

Καδμεῖοι γέροντες, οὐ σῖγα σῖ-
γα τὸν ὕπνῳ παρειμένον ἐάσετ᾽ ἐκ-
λαθέσθαι κακῶν;

ΧΟΡΟΣ

1045 κατά σε δακρύοις στένω, πρέσβυ, καὶ
τέκεα καὶ τὸ καλλίνικον κάρα.

ΑΜΦΙΤΡΥΩΝ

ἑκαστέρω πρόβατε, μὴ
κτυπεῖτε, μὴ βοᾶτε, μὴ
1050 τὸν εὐδιά τ᾽ ἄγονθ᾽ ὑπνώδεά τ᾽ ἐγεί-
ρετ᾽ εὐνᾶς.

ΧΟΡΟΣ

οἴμοι. φόνος ὅσος ὅδ᾽ . . .

ΑΜΦΙΤΡΥΩΝ

ἆ ἆ,

διά μ᾽ ὀλεῖτε.

1038 κίοσιν ἀμφ᾽ Willink: ἀμφὶ κίοσιν L
1049 εὐδιά τ᾽ ἄγονθ᾽ Willink: εὖ διαύοντα L

wound about the body
of Heracles, bound to the marble
pillars of his house.

*Enter* AMPHITRYON *from the skene.*

### CHORUS LEADER
And here, like a bird in mourning for the unfledged young
it has given birth to, comes old Amphitryon on a joyless
journey.

### AMPHITRYON
Old men of Thebes, won't you in silence, silence,
allow the man relaxed in sleep
to forget his woes?

### CHORUS
I weep for you, old sir,
and the children, and the man once glorious in victory.

### AMPHITRYON
Come further away, make
no sound, do not shout, do not
awaken from his bed
one in the peace of sleep!

### CHORUS
       Alas! What pools of blood . . .

### AMPHITRYON
                             Stop!

you will destroy me!

---

1050–1 ἐγείρετ᾿ εὐνᾶς Conradt: εὐ- ἐγ- L

ΧΟΡΟΣ

. . . κεχυμένος ἐπαντέλλει.

ΑΜΦΙΤΡΥΩΝ

οὐκ ἀτρεμαῖα θρῆνον αἰ-
άξετ᾽, ὦ γέροντες;
1055  ἢ δέσμ᾽ ἀνεγειρόμενος χαλάσας ἀπολεῖ πόλιν,
ἀπὸ δὲ πατέρα, μέλαθρά τε καταρρήξει.

ΧΟΡΟΣ

ἀδύνατ᾽ ἀδύνατ᾽· οἴμοι.

ΑΜΦΙΤΡΥΩΝ

1060  σῖγα, πνοὰς μάθω· φέρε πρὸς οὖς βάλω.

ΧΟΡΟΣ

εὕδει;

ΑΜΦΙΤΡΥΩΝ

ναί, εὕδει,
†ὕπνον ὕπνον† ὀλόμενον ὃς ἔκανεν ἄλο-
χον, ἔκανε δὲ τέκεα τοξήρει ψαλμῷ.

ΧΟΡΟΣ

στέναζέ νυν . . .

ΑΜΦΙΤΡΥΩΝ

στενάζω.

ΧΟΡΟΣ

1065  . . . τέκνων ὄλεθρον . . .

1058 οἴμοι Diggle: μοι L
1062 πόνον ἀπόπονον vel ὀλόμενον e.g. Willink

# HERACLES

**CHORUS**
. . . spilt upon the ground rise up to meet me!

**AMPHITRYON**
Make your lament
softly, old sirs!
Or he will waken, slip his bonds, and destroy the city,
destroy his father, smash the whole house in pieces!

**CHORUS**
I cannot do it, cannot, alas!

**AMPHITRYON**
Hush! Let me hear his breathing! Come, let me put my ear
to him!

**CHORUS**
Is he sleeping?

**AMPHITRYON**
Yes, he is sleeping,
a sleep of wretchedness, this man who killed his wife,
killed his children with his bow's whirring tune.

**CHORUS**
Lament then . . .

**AMPHITRYON**
I lament.

**CHORUS**
. . . the children's destruction . . .

---

1063 ψαλμῷ Madvig: ψ- τοξεύσας L

411

ΑΜΦΙΤΡΥΩΝ

ὤμοι.

ΧΟΡΟΣ

. . . σέθεν τε παιδός.

ΑΜΦΙΤΡΥΩΝ

αἰαῖ.

ΧΟΡΟΣ

ὦ πρέσβυ . . .

ΑΜΦΙΤΡΥΩΝ

σῖγα σῖγα· παλίντροπος ἐξε-
γειρόμενος στρέφεται·
1070 φέρ’, ἀπόκρυφα δέμας ὑπὸ μέλαθρον κρύψω.

ΧΟΡΟΣ

θάρσει· νὺξ ἔχει βλέφαρα παιδὶ σῷ.

ΑΜΦΙΤΡΥΩΝ

ὁρᾶθ’ ὁρᾶτε. τὸ φάος ἐκ-
λιπεῖν μὲν ἐπὶ κακοῖσιν οὐ
1075 φεύγω τάλας, ἀλλ’ εἴ με κανεῖ πατέρ’ ὄντα,
πρὸς δὲ κακοῖς κακὰ μήσε-
ται πρὸς Ἐρινύσι θ’ αἷμα
σύγγονον ἕξει.

ΧΟΡΟΣ

τότε θανεῖν σ’ ἐχρῆν ὅτε δάμαρτι σᾷ
φόνον ὁμοσπόρων ἔμολες ἐκπράξας,

<sup>1070</sup> ἀπόκρυφα Willink: -φον L

412

AMPHITRYON

Ah me!

CHORUS

. . . and that of your son.

AMPHITRYON

Alas!

CHORUS

Old sir . . .

AMPHITRYON

Hush, hush! He turns about
and stirs to wakefulness!
Come, let me conceal myself in the shelter of the house!

CHORUS

Have no fear! Night still shrouds your son's eyes.

AMPHITRYON

Look out, look out! It is not from death
in my misery that I shrink,
but I fear he will kill me, his father,
and commit woe on woe,
adding to the Furies' curse
the stain of kindred blood!

CHORUS

You should have died on the day when for your wife
you returned from avenging her brothers' death

---

1073-4 τὸ φάος ἐκλιπεῖν μὲν Wilamowitz: τὸ μὲν φ- ἐ- L
1079 ἔμολες Bothe: ἔμελλες L    ἐκπράξας Hartung:
ἐκπράξειν L

1080 Ταφίων περίκλυστον ἄστυ πέρσας.

ΑΜΦΙΤΡΥΩΝ
φυγὰν φυγάν, γέροντες, ἀποπρὸ δωμάτων
διώκετε· φεύγετε μάργον ἄνδρ᾽ ἐπεγειρόμενον.
1085 ⟨ἢ⟩ τάχα φόνον ἕτερον ἐπὶ φόνῳ βαλὼν
ἀν᾽ αὖ βακχεύσει Καδμείων πόλιν.

ΧΟΡΟΣ
ὦ Ζεῦ, τί παῖδ᾽ ἤχθηρας ὧδ᾽ ὑπερκότως
τὸν σόν, κακῶν δὲ πέλαγος ἐς τόδ᾽ ἤγαγες;

ΗΡΑΚΛΗΣ
ἔα·
ἔμπνους μέν εἰμι καὶ δέδορχ᾽ ἅπερ με δεῖ,
1090 αἰθέρα τε καὶ γῆν τόξα θ᾽ Ἡλίου τάδε.
ὡς ⟨δ᾽⟩ ἐν κλύδωνι καὶ φρενῶν ταράγματι
πέπτωκα δεινῷ καὶ πνοὰς θερμὰς πνέω
μετάρσι᾽, οὐ βέβαια πλευμόνων ἄπο.
ἰδού, τί δεσμοῖς ναῦς ὅπως ὡρμισμένος
1095 νεανίαν θώρακα καὶ βραχίονα
πρὸς ἡμιθραύστῳ λαΐνῳ τυκίσματι
ἧμαι, νεκροῖσι γείτονας θάκους ἔχων;

1085 ⟨ἢ⟩ Wilamowitz
1086 ἀν᾽ αὖ βακχεύει Nauck: ἀναβ- L
1089 ἔννους Wecklein cl. *Ba.* 1270
1091 ⟨δ᾽⟩ Reiske: sed fort. lac. ante h. v. indicanda, e.g. ⟨ἐπησθόμην δὲ πῦρ ἔχων ἐν δεξιᾷ⟩
1096 τυκίσματι Fix: τειχ- L
1097 ἧμαι . . . ἔχων Musgrave: ἢ μὲν . . . ἔχω L

by sacking the Taphians' seagirt city.[32]

### AMPHITRYON

Run from the house, run, old sirs!
Flee from the madman awakened!
Or soon adding new murders on top of old
he will throw the whole city of Thebes into confusion!

### CHORUS LEADER

Zeus, why do you so hate your own son? Why have you
brought him into this sea of woes?

### HERACLES

(*Stirring to wakefulness*) Ah, what does this mean? I am
alive, and I see what I ought to see, the bright air, the earth,
the shafts of sunlight.[33] <But> I am fallen as if into a wave
and into dread confusion of mind, and my breath comes
hot and in shallow panting, not steadily from my lungs.

Look, why am I sitting here, my vigorous chest and
arms moored like a ship to this half-defaced stonework,
with corpses for neighbors? Scattered on the ground are

---

[32] See note on line 60 above.

[33] It is possible that Heracles first observes not that he is alive
(ἔμπνους), but that he is now in his right mind (Wecklein's ἔν-
νους): see *Bacchae* 1264-70, where Agave's ability to see the
brightness of the heaven is evidence that her madness has passed
and that she is once more sane. In that case instead of supplying
a connective in 1091, we could mark a lacuna before it with a verb
of noticing in a past tense. This would give easier employment for
ὡς and make both πέπτωκα (I am fallen) and πνέω (I breathe)
refer to past time, as, e.g., at 1167-8.

# EURIPIDES

πτερωτὰ δ' ἔγχη τόξα τ' ἔσπαρται πέδῳ,
ἃ πρὶν παρασπίζοντ' ἐμοῖς βραχίοσιν
1100 ἔσῳζε πλευρὰς ἐξ ἐμοῦ τ' ἐσῴζετο.
οὔ που κατῆλθον αὖθις εἰς Ἅιδου πάλιν,
Εὐρυσθέως δίαυλον ἐξ Ἅιδου μολών;
ἀλλ' οὔτε Σισύφειον εἰσορῶ πέτρον
Πλούτωνά τ' οὐδὲ σκῆπτρα Δήμητρος κόρης.
1105 ἔκ τοι πέπληγμαι· ποῦ ποτ' ὢν ἀμηχανῶ;
    ὠή, τίς ἐγγὺς ἢ πρόσω φίλων ἐμῶν,
δύσγνοιαν ὅστις τὴν ἐμὴν ἰάσεται;
σαφῶς γὰρ οὐδὲν οἶδα τῶν εἰωθότων.

ΑΜΦΙΤΡΥΩΝ
γέροντες, ἔλθω τῶν ἐμῶν κακῶν πέλας;

ΧΟΡΟΣ
1110 κἀγώ γε σὺν σοί, μὴ προδῶ σὰς συμφοράς.

ΗΡΑΚΛΗΣ
πάτερ, τί κλαίεις καὶ συναμπίσχῃ κόρας,
τοῦ φιλτάτου σοι τηλόθεν παιδὸς βεβώς;

ΑΜΦΙΤΡΥΩΝ
ὦ τέκνον· εἶ γὰρ καὶ κακῶς πράσσων ἐμός.

ΗΡΑΚΛΗΣ
πράσσω δ' ἐγὼ τί λυπρὸν οὗ δακρυρροεῖς;

ΑΜΦΙΤΡΥΩΝ
1115 ἃ κἂν θεῶν τις, εἰ μάθοι, καταστένοι.

1098 δ' Hermann: τ' L

416

## HERACLES

my bow and feathered arrows, stout allies ere now to these arms of mine, allies who saved my skin while I took care of them. Surely I have not gone down to Hades again after coming back from there on the return leg of Eurystheus' errand? No, I do not see Sisyphus' rock nor Pluto nor yet the scepter of Persephone. I am utterly astonished. Where can I be that I am so perplexed?

Ho there! Who of my friends, nearby or at a distance, can cure my ignorance? For I do not recognize clearly any of my usual circumstances.

### AMPHITRYON

Sirs, shall I approach my own calamity?

### CHORUS LEADER

Yes, and I will go with you so as not to abandon you in misfortune.

### HERACLES

Father, why do you weep and veil your eyes, standing far off from the son you love?

### AMPHITRYON

My son: for even in misfortune you are mine!

### HERACLES

What misfortune is mine, misfortune to make you weep?

### AMPHITRYON

Things even a god, if he learned of them, would weep at.

---

1102 ἐξ Bothe: εἰς L
1104 Πλούτωνά τ'] οὐ δώματ' Wilamowitz
1110 προδῶ σὰς Lenting: προδῶς τὰς L
1115 εἰ μάθοι Paley: εἴπαθ οἱ L: εἰ πάθοι Scaliger

417

ΗΡΑΚΛΗΣ

μέγας γ' ὁ κόμπος, τὴν τύχην δ' οὔπω λέγεις.

ΑΜΦΙΤΡΥΩΝ

1117  ὁρᾷς γὰρ αὐτός, εἰ φρονῶν ἤδη κυρεῖς.

ΗΡΑΚΛΗΣ

1120  παπαῖ, τόδ' ὡς ὕποπτον ἠνίξω πάλιν.

ΑΜΦΙΤΡΥΩΝ

1121  καί σ' εἰ βεβαίως εὖ φρονεῖς ἤδη σκοπῶ.

ΗΡΑΚΛΗΣ

1118  εἴπ' εἴ τι καινὸν ὑπογράφῃ τὠμῷ βίῳ.

ΑΜΦΙΤΡΥΩΝ

1119  εἰ μηκέθ' Ἅιδου βάκχος εἶ, φράσαιμεν ἄν.

ΗΡΑΚΛΗΣ

1122  οὐ γάρ τι βακχεύσας γε μέμνημαι φρένας.

ΑΜΦΙΤΡΥΩΝ

λύσω, γέροντες, δεσμὰ παιδός; ἢ τί δρῶ;

ΗΡΑΚΛΗΣ

καὶ τόν γε δήσαντ' εἴπ'· ἀναινόμεσθα γάρ.

ΑΜΦΙΤΡΥΩΝ

1125  τοσοῦτον ἴσθι σῶν κακῶν, τὰ δ' ἄλλ' ἔα.

ΗΡΑΚΛΗΣ

ἀρκεῖ σιωπῇ γὰρ μαθεῖν ὃ βούλομαι;

1118–9 post 1121 trai. Nauck    1121 fort. βεβαίως ⟨γ'⟩
1125 σῶν Diggle: τῶν L    1126 ὃ Heath: οὐ L

418

### HERACLES

These are big words: but you have not yet said what is wrong.

### AMPHITRYON

No, for you yourself see it, if you are now in your right mind.

### HERACLES

Ah me! Yet another riddling response!

### AMPHITRYON

I am examining you to see if you are now quite sane.

### HERACLES

Tell me if you are hinting at some disastrous change in my life.

### AMPHITRYON

I will tell you if you are no longer an infernal Bacchant.

### HERACLES

I have no memory that my mind was crazed.

### AMPHITRYON

Sirs, shall I loose my son's bonds? What shall I do?

### HERACLES

Yes, and tell me who put them on me: I feel disgust at them.

### AMPHITRYON

This much of your misfortunes should you know. The rest let be.

### HERACLES

What? Is silence good enough to tell me what I would learn?

# EURIPIDES

### ΑΜΦΙΤΡΥΩΝ

ὦ Ζεῦ, παρ᾽ Ἥρας ἆρ᾽ ὁρᾷς θρόνων τάδε;

### ΗΡΑΚΛΗΣ

ἀλλ᾽ ἦ τι κεῖθεν πολέμιον πεπόνθαμεν;

### ΑΜΦΙΤΡΥΩΝ

τὴν θεὸν ἐάσας τὰ σὰ περιστέλλου κακά.

### ΗΡΑΚΛΗΣ

1130 ἀπωλόμεσθα· συμφορὰν λέξεις τινά.

### ΑΜΦΙΤΡΥΩΝ

ἰδού, θέασαι τάδε τέκνων πεσήματα.

### ΗΡΑΚΛΗΣ

οἴμοι· τίν᾽ ὄψιν τήνδε δέρκομαι τάλας;

### ΑΜΦΙΤΡΥΩΝ

ἀπόλεμον, ὦ παῖ, πόλεμον ἔσπευσας τέκνοις.

### ΗΡΑΚΛΗΣ

τί πόλεμον εἶπας; τούσδε τίς διώλεσεν;

### ΑΜΦΙΤΡΥΩΝ

1135 σὺ καὶ σὰ τόξα καὶ θεῶν ὃς αἴτιος.

### ΗΡΑΚΛΗΣ

τί φής; τί δράσας; ὦ κάκ᾽ ἀγγέλλων πάτερ.

### ΑΜΦΙΤΡΥΩΝ

μανείς· ἐρωτᾷς δ᾽ ἄθλι᾽ ἑρμηνεύματα.

### ΗΡΑΚΛΗΣ

ἦ καὶ δάμαρτός εἰμ᾽ ἐγὼ φονεὺς ἐμῆς;

1130 λέξεις Brodaeus: ἕξεις L

420

# HERACLES

**AMPHITRYON**
O Zeus, seated by the throne of Hera, do you see this?

**HERACLES**
Is it from that quarter then that I have been attacked?

**AMPHITRYON**
Let the goddess be and see to your own misfortune.

**HERACLES**
My life is over! It is some disaster you are going to tell
me of!

**AMPHITRYON**
Look there and see the bodies of these children.

**HERACLES**
Alas! What is this sight that greets my unhappy eyes?

**AMPHITRYON**
A war that is no war have you waged against your children.

**HERACLES**
What do you mean "war"? Who killed them?

**AMPHITRYON**
You and your arrows and whatever god is responsible.

**HERACLES**
What do you mean? How? These are dread tidings you
bring, father!

**AMPHITRYON**
In a fit of madness: the answers to your questions are full
of woe.

**HERACLES**
Am I also the murderer of my wife?

ΑΜΦΙΤΡΥΩΝ

μιᾶς ἅπαντα χειρὸς ἔργα σῆς τάδε.

ΗΡΑΚΛΗΣ

1140 αἰαῖ· στεναγμῶν γάρ με περιβάλλει νέφος.

ΑΜΦΙΤΡΥΩΝ

1141 τούτων ἕκατι σὰς καταστένω τύχας.

ΗΡΑΚΛΗΣ

1144 ποῦ δ᾽ οἶστρος ἡμᾶς ἔλαβε; ποῦ διώλεσεν;

ΑΜΦΙΤΡΥΩΝ

1145 ὅτ᾽ ἀμφὶ βωμὸν χεῖρας ἡγνίζου πυρί.

ΗΡΑΚΛΗΣ

1142 ἦ γὰρ συνήραξ᾽ οἶκον ἀβάκχευσ᾽ ἐμόν;

ΑΜΦΙΤΡΥΩΝ

1143 οὐκ οἶδα πλὴν ἕν· πάντα δυστυχεῖ τὰ σά.

ΗΡΑΚΛΗΣ

1146 οἴμοι· τί δῆτα φείδομαι ψυχῆς ἐμῆς
τῶν φιλτάτων μοι γενόμενος παίδων φονεύς;
οὐκ εἶμι πέτρας λισσάδος πρὸς ἅλματα
ἢ φάσγανον πρὸς ἧπαρ ἐξακοντίσας
1150 τέκνοις δικαστὴς αἵματος γενήσομαι,
ἢ σάρκα τὴν πατρῷον ἐμπρήσας πυρὶ
δύσκλειαν ἢ μένει μ᾽ ἀπώσομαι βίου;
ἀλλ᾽ ἐμποδών μοι θανασίμων βουλευμάτων

1144-5 ante 1142 trai. Wilamowitz
1142 ἀβάκχευσ᾽ Bond: ἢ βάκχευσ᾽ L
1148 οὐκ Elmsley: κοὐκ L    1151 πατρῷον Allen: ἐμὴν L

422

**AMPHITRYON**

All this is the work of your single hand.

**HERACLES**

Ah, ah! What a cloud of lamentation now surrounds me!

**AMPHITRYON**

It is for this reason that I lament your fate.

**HERACLES**

When did madness' sting attack me? When did it destroy my life?

**AMPHITRYON**

When you were next to the altar purifying your hands with the fire.

**HERACLES**

And did my Bacchic insanity destroy my house?

**AMPHITRYON**

I know only one thing: all your fortunes are in ruins.

**HERACLES**

Woe is me! Why then do I spare my life when I have become the murderer of my dear children? Shall I not go and leap from a sheer cliff or stab myself with my sword and thus give my children justice for their murder? Shall I not burn their father's flesh with fire and thrust from myself the ignominy that awaits me in my life?

*Enter* THESEUS *by Eisodos B.*

But here's an impediment to my plan of death, the

Θησεὺς ὅδ᾽ ἕρπει συγγενὴς φίλος τ᾽ ἐμός·
1155 ὀφθησόμεσθα, καὶ τεκνοκτόνον μύσος
ἐς ὄμμαθ᾽ ἥξει φιλτάτῳ ξένων ἐμῶν.
οἴμοι, τί δράσω; ποῖ κακῶν ἐρημίαν
εὕρω, πτερωτὸς ἢ κατὰ χθονὸς μολών;
φέρ᾽, ἀμφὶ κρατὶ περιβάλω <πέπλων> σκότον.
1160 αἰσχύνομαι γὰρ τοῖς δεδραμένοις κακοῖς,
καὶ τῷδε προστρόπαιον αἷμα προσβαλὼν
οὐδὲν κακῶσαι τοὺς ἀναιτίους θέλω.

ΘΗΣΕΥΣ
ἥκω σὺν ἄλλοις, οἳ παρ᾽ Ἀσωποῦ ῥοὰς
μένουσιν, ἔνοπλοι γῆς Ἀθηναίων κόροι,
1165 σῷ παιδί, πρέσβυ, σύμμαχον φέρων δόρυ.
κληδὼν γὰρ ἦλθεν εἰς Ἐρεχθειδῶν πόλιν
ὡς σκῆπτρα χώρας τῆσδ᾽ ἀναρπάσας Λύκος
ἐς πόλεμον ὑμῖν καὶ μάχην καθίσταται.
τίνων δ᾽ ἀμοιβὰς ὧν ὑπῆρξεν Ἡρακλῆς
1170 σώσας με νέρθεν ἦλθον, εἴ τι δεῖ, γέρον,
ἢ χειρὸς ὑμᾶς τῆς ἐμῆς ἢ συμμάχων.
ἔα· τί νεκρῶν τῶνδε πληθύει πέδον;
οὔ που λέλειμμαι καὶ νεωτέρων κακῶν
ὕστερος ἀφῖγμαι; τίς τάδ᾽ ἔκτεινεν τέκνα;
1175 τίνος γεγῶσαν τήνδ᾽ ὁρῶ ξυνάορον;
οὐ γὰρ δορός γε παῖδες ἵστανται πέλας,
ἀλλ᾽ ἄλλο πού τι καινὸν εὑρίσκω κακόν.

1156 φιλτάτῳ Reiske: -των L

424

arrival of Theseus, my friend and kinsman. He will see me, and the pollution for children murdered will taint the eyes of my dearest friend![34] Ah, what am I to do? Where must I go to escape misfortune? Soar to high heaven or sink beneath the earth? Come, let me cast about my head the darkness ⟨of my garments⟩! For I feel shame at the harm I have done, and I do not want to wrong an innocent man by putting on him the stain of bloodshed!

*Heracles veils his head in his garments.*

I have come to bring military might to help your son, old sir: my companions, young men of Athens under arms, are waiting by the banks of the Asopus. A report came to the city of the Erechtheids that Lycus has seized power in this city and was making war against you. I have come here to repay the good deed Heracles did to me when he rescued me from the Underworld, in case he has any need of my right hand or of allies.

But what is this? Why is the ground strewed with these corpses? Can it be that I have been outstripped and have come too late to prevent fresh disasters? Who killed these children? Whose wife is this I see here? Children do not stand in the line of battle. Rather it is some other new trouble I find here.

[34] It was thought that someone guilty of murder communicated a taint (*miasma*) to others who had contact with him.

---

1159 ἀμφὶ Faust: ἄν τι L  ⟨πέπλων⟩ σκότον post Pflugk
(σκότον ⟨πέπλων⟩) Diggle   1175 σφαγεῖσαν Broadhead
1177 πού τι Wilamowitz: τι που L

# EURIPIDES

ΑΜΦΙΤΡΥΩΝ

ὦ τὸν ἐλαιοφόρον ὄχθον ἔχων ⟨ἄναξ⟩ . . .

ΘΗΣΕΥΣ

τί χρῆμά μ᾽ οἰκτροῖς ἐκάλεσας προοιμίοις;

ΑΜΦΙΤΡΥΩΝ

1180 . . . ἐπάθομεν πάθεα μέλεα πρὸς θεῶν.

ΘΗΣΕΥΣ

οἱ παῖδες οἵδε τίνος ἐφ᾽ οἷς δακρυρροεῖς;

ΑΜΦΙΤΡΥΩΝ

1182 ἔτεκε μέν ⟨νιν⟩ οὑμὸς ἶνις τάλας,
1184 τεκόμενος δ᾽ ἔκανε, φόνιον αἷμα τλάς.

ΘΗΣΕΥΣ

1187 τί φῄς; τί δράσας;

ΑΜΦΙΤΡΥΩΝ

μαινομένῳ πιτύλῳ πλαγχθεὶς
1188 ἑκατογκεφάλου βαφαῖς ὕδρας.

ΘΗΣΕΥΣ

1185 εὔφημα φώνει.

ΑΜΦΙΤΡΥΩΝ

βουλομένοισιν ἐπαγγέλλῃ.

1178 ⟨ἄναξ⟩ Hermann
1181 τίνος Wecklein: τίνες L
1182 ⟨νιν⟩ Elmsley
1187-8 post 1184 trai. Dobree

426

# HERACLES

**AMPHITRYON**[35]

O \<lord\> of the hill that bears the olive . . .

**THESEUS**

Why do you address me in pitiable accents?

**AMPHITRYON**

. . . terrible are our sufferings at the hands of the gods!

**THESEUS**

Whose children are these for whom you weep?

**AMPHITRYON**

Their begetter was my ill-fated son,
and when he had begotten them he killed them and suf-
fered the taint of their blood.

**THESEUS**

What are you saying? How?

**AMPHITRYON**

In his madness,
with arrows dipped in the hundred-headed hydra's blood.

**THESEUS**

Hush, say not such words of evil omen!

**AMPHITRYON**

How I wish I could
do what you ask!

---

[35] From here until line 1213 Amphitryon's words are sung.

ΘΗΣΕΥΣ

1186  ὦ δεινὰ λέξας.

ΑΜΦΙΤΡΥΩΝ
οἰχόμεθ᾽ οἰχόμεθα πτανοί.

ΘΗΣΕΥΣ

1189  Ἥρας ὅδ᾽ ἀγών· τίς δ᾽ ὅδ᾽ οὖν νεκροῖς, γέρον;

ΑΜΦΙΤΡΥΩΝ

1190  ἐμὸς ἐμὸς ὅδε γόνος ὁ πολύπονος, ὃς ἐπὶ
δόρυ γιγαντοφόνον ἦλθεν σὺν θεοῖ-
σι Φλεγραῖον ἐς πεδίον ἀσπιστάς.

ΘΗΣΕΥΣ

1195  φεῦ φεῦ· τίς ἀνδρῶν ὧδε δυσδαίμων ἔφυ;

ΑΜΦΙΤΡΥΩΝ
οὐκ ἂν εἰδείης ἕτερον
πολυμοχθότερον πολυπλαγκτότερόν τε θνατῶν.

ΘΗΣΕΥΣ
τί γὰρ πέπλοισιν ἄθλιον κρύπτει κάρα;

ΑΜΦΙΤΡΥΩΝ

1200  αἰδόμενος τὸ σὸν ὄμμα καὶ φιλίαν ὁμόφυλον
αἷμά τε παιδοφόνον.

ΘΗΣΕΥΣ
ἀλλ᾽ εἰ συναλγῶν γ᾽ ἦλθον; ἐκκάλυπτέ νιν.

1189 δ᾽ ὅδ᾽ οὖν Reiske: δόλου L
1202 εἰ συναλγῶν γ᾽ Wakefield (ὡς συναλγῶν γ᾽) et Seidler:
εἰς συναλγοῦντ᾽ L

# HERACLES

**THESEUS**
What dreadful things you have said!

**AMPHITRYON**
We are lost and gone
our happiness has taken wing!

**THESEUS**
This is Hera's work. But who is this lying among the corpses?

**AMPHITRYON**
This is my son, the man of many woes, who came
with the gods as a warrior to fight in the plain
of Phlegra where the Giants were killed.

**THESEUS**
Ah me! Who of mortal men was ever born to such wretchedness?

**AMPHITRYON**
You will never learn of another
among mortals more labored and driven than he.

**THESEUS**
But why does he cover his poor head with his garments?

**AMPHITRYON**
In shame before your face and the kinship he has to you
and the blood of his children slain.

**THESEUS**
But what if I have come to share his grief? Uncover his head!

# EURIPIDES

## ΑΜΦΙΤΡΥΩΝ

ὦ τέκνον,
πάρες ἀπ᾽ ὀμμάτων πέπλον, ἀπόδικε, ῥέθος
ἀελίῳ δεῖξον.
1205 βάρος ἀντίπαλον δακρύοις συναμιλλᾶται·
ἱκετεύομεν ἀμφὶ γενειάδα καὶ
γόνυ καὶ χέρα σὰν προπίτνων, πολιὸν
1210 δάκρυον ἐκβάλλων· ἰὼ παῖ, κατά-
σχεθε λέοντος ἀγρίου θυμόν, ᾧ
δρόμον ἐπὶ φόνιον ἀνόσιον ἐξάγῃ
κακὰ θέλων κακοῖς συνάψαι, τέκνον.

## ΘΗΣΕΥΣ

εἶέν· σὲ τὸν θάσσοντα δυστήνους ἕδρας
1215 αὐδῶ φίλοισιν ὄμμα δεικνύναι τὸ σόν.
οὐδεὶς σκότος γὰρ ὧδ᾽ ἔχει μέλαν νέφος
ὅστις κακῶν σῶν συμφορὰν κρύψειεν ἄν.
τί μοι προσείων χεῖρα σημαίνεις φόβον;
ὡς μὴ μύσος με σῶν βάλῃ προσφθεγμάτων;
1220 οὐδὲν μέλει μοι σύν γε σοὶ πράσσειν κακῶς·
κεὶ γάρ ποτ᾽ ηὐτύχησ᾽, ἐκεῖσ᾽ ἀνοιστέον
ὅτ᾽ ἐξέσωσάς μ᾽ ἐς φάος νεκρῶν πάρα.
χάριν δὲ γηράσκουσαν ἐχθαίρω φίλων

1207–8 γενειάδα . . . χέρα σὰν Wilamowitz: σὰν γ- . . . . χ-
L     1209 πολιὸν Hartung: πολιόν τε L
1210 ἐκβάλλων Wilamowitz: -βαλών L
1210–1 κατάσχεθε Elmsley: κάτασχε L
1211 ᾧ Schenkl: ὅπως L
1212 δρόμον Reiske: βρόμον L

### AMPHITRYON

My son,
cast from your eyes your garment, throw it off, show
   your face to the sun!

*Amphitryon kneels before Heracles as a suppliant.*

The weight of my body joins with my tears in contention:
I fall about your chin,
your knees, your hands, weeping dark
tears and entreating you: my son,
check the wild lion's proud spirit in your breast, the spirit
   by which
you are carried on a course of bloodshed and impiety,
wishing to add new griefs to old.

*Heracles keeps an obdurate silence.*

### THESEUS

Well, then. You, sitting in the seat of wretchedness, I bid
you show your face to your friends! No night can envelop
you in darkness so black that it could hide the blow of this
disaster. *(Heracles makes a sign for him to depart.)* Why do
you wave your hand at me to signify danger? For fear that
I may be tainted by words from your lips? It does not
matter to me if I join you in misfortune. For any good
fortune I have enjoyed must be traced back to the day
when you brought me up from the Underworld into the
light. I hate it when the gratitude owed to a friend grows

---

1218 φόβον Blomfield: φόνον L
1221 κεἰ Kirchhoff: καὶ L

# EURIPIDES

καὶ τῶν καλῶν μὲν ὅστις ἀπολαύειν θέλει,
1225 συμπλεῖν δὲ τοῖς φίλοισι δυστυχοῦσιν οὔ.
ἀνίστασ᾽, ἐκκάλυψον ἄθλιον κάρα,
βλέψον πρὸς ἡμᾶς. ὅστις εὐγενὴς βροτῶν,
φέρει †τὰ τῶν θεῶν γε† πτώματ᾽ οὐδ᾽ ἀναίνεται.

ΗΡΑΚΛΗΣ
Θησεῦ, δέδορκας τόνδ᾽ ἀγῶν᾽ ἐμῶν τέκνων;

ΘΗΣΕΥΣ
1230 ἤκουσα, καὶ βλέποντι σημαίνεις κακά.

ΗΡΑΚΛΗΣ
τί δῆτά μου κρᾶτ᾽ ἀνεκάλυψας ἡλίῳ;

ΘΗΣΕΥΣ
τί δ᾽; οὐ μιαίνεις θνητὸς ὢν τὰ τῶν θεῶν.

ΗΡΑΚΛΗΣ
φεῦγ᾽, ὦ ταλαίπωρ᾽, ἀνόσιον μίασμ᾽ ἐμόν.

ΘΗΣΕΥΣ
οὐδεὶς ἀλάστωρ τοῖς φίλοις ἐκ τῶν φίλων.

ΗΡΑΚΛΗΣ
1235 ἐπήνεσ᾽· εὖ δράσας δέ σ᾽ οὐκ ἀναίνομαι.

ΘΗΣΕΥΣ
ἐγὼ δὲ πάσχων εὖ τότ᾽ οἰκτίρω σε νῦν.

ΗΡΑΚΛΗΣ
οἰκτρὸς γάρ εἰμι τἄμ᾽ ἀποκτείνας τέκνα;

1228 τά γ᾽ ἐκ θεῶν Headlam: e contextu autem vv. 1220–6
φίλων γε vel συνηθέων expectares: τὰ θνητῶν West

432

old and weak, hate it when a man is willing to share in happy moments but not to voyage with friends in misfortune. Stand up, uncover your luckless head, look at me! Any mortal who is noble bears his friends' misfortunes and does not reject them.

*Heracles unveils his face.*

#### HERACLES
Theseus, do you see the struggle my children have undergone?

#### THESEUS
I have heard the report, and now you reveal the disaster to my eyes.

#### HERACLES
Why then did you unveil my head to the sun?

#### THESEUS
Why? You, a mortal, cannot pollute the divine realm.

#### HERACLES
Flee, poor man, from this unholy taint of mine!

#### THESEUS
No spirit of divine vengeance attacks a friend because of those he befriends.

#### HERACLES
I thank you: since I am your benefactor I do not refuse your aid.

#### THESEUS
And I give you my pity now, I whom you once helped.

#### HERACLES
Is it pity I deserve for killing my sons?

433

ΘΗΣΕΥΣ

κλαίω χάριν σὴν ἐφ᾽ ἑτέραισι συμφοραῖς.

ΗΡΑΚΛΗΣ

ηὗρες δέ γ᾽ ἄλλους ἐν κακοῖσι μείζοσιν;

ΘΗΣΕΥΣ

1240 ἅπτῃ κάτωθεν οὐρανοῦ δυσπραξίᾳ.

ΗΡΑΚΛΗΣ

τοιγὰρ παρεσκευάσμεθ᾽ ὥστε κατθανεῖν.

⟨ΘΗΣΕΥΣ

τί δῆτ᾽ ἔχοις ἄν, εἰ τόδ᾽ ἔρξειας, πλέον;

ΗΡΑΚΛΗΣ

τοῖς θεῶν ἀθίκτοις ἐμβαλῶ βωμοῖς μύσος.⟩

ΘΗΣΕΥΣ

δοκεῖς ἀπειλῶν σῶν μέλειν τι δαίμοσιν;

ΗΡΑΚΛΗΣ

αὔθαδες ὁ θεός, πρὸς δὲ τοὺς θεοὺς ἐγώ.

ΘΗΣΕΥΣ

ἴσχε στόμ᾽, ὡς μὴ μέγα λέγων μεῖζον πάθῃς.

ΗΡΑΚΛΗΣ

1245 γέμω κακῶν δὴ κοὐκέτ᾽ ἔσθ᾽ ὅπῃ τεθῇ.

ΘΗΣΕΥΣ

δράσεις δὲ δὴ τί; ποῖ φέρῃ θυμούμενος;

1241 lac. post h. v. indic. W. Schmid: nulla lac. indicata καὶ
θενεῖν pro κατθανεῖν Harry

**THESEUS**

I weep that your goodness is so ill repaid.

**HERACLES**

Have you seen others in greater misfortune than mine?

**THESEUS**

In your misfortune you reach from earth all the way to heaven.

**HERACLES**

And therefore I have prepared myself to die.

**‹THESEUS**

What advantage will you get if you do that?

**HERACLES**

I will defile with my blood the hallowed altars of the gods.›[36]

**THESEUS**

Do you think the powers above care for your threats?

**HERACLES**

Heaven pleases itself: in the teeth of heaven I do the same.

**THESEUS**

Hush! Your proud words could bring you worse disaster!

**HERACLES**

With disaster I am freighted full: there is no place to put more.

**THESEUS**

But what do you mean to do? Where will your wrath carry you?

[36] If there is a lacuna here, only some such threat would explain Theseus' next line.

ΗΡΑΚΛΗΣ

θανών, ὅθενπερ ἦλθον, εἶμι γῆς ὕπο.

ΘΗΣΕΥΣ

εἴρηκας ἐπιτυχόντος ἀνθρώπου λόγους.

ΗΡΑΚΛΗΣ

σὺ δ᾽ ἐκτὸς ὤν γε συμφορᾶς με νουθετεῖς.

ΘΗΣΕΥΣ

1250 ὁ πολλὰ δὴ τλὰς Ἡρακλῆς λέγει τάδε;

ΗΡΑΚΛΗΣ

οὔκουν τοσαῦτά γ᾽· ἐν μέτρῳ μοχθητέον.

ΘΗΣΕΥΣ

εὐεργέτης βροτοῖσι καὶ μέγας φίλος;

ΗΡΑΚΛΗΣ

οἱ δ᾽ οὐδὲν ὠφελοῦσί μ᾽, ἀλλ᾽ Ἥρα κρατεῖ.

ΘΗΣΕΥΣ

οὐκ ἄν σ᾽ ἀνάσχοιθ᾽ Ἑλλὰς ἀμαθίᾳ θανεῖν.

ΗΡΑΚΛΗΣ

1255 ἄκουε δή νυν, ὡς ἁμιλληθῶ λόγοις
πρὸς νουθετήσεις σάς· ἀναπτύξω δέ σοι
ἀβίωτον ἡμῖν νῦν τε καὶ πάροιθεν ὄν.
    πρῶτον μὲν ἐκ τοῦδ᾽ ἐγενόμην, ὅστις κτανὼν
μητρὸς γεραιὸν πατέρα προστρόπαιος ὢν
1260 ἔγημε τὴν τεκοῦσαν Ἀλκμήνην ἐμέ.
ὅταν δὲ κρηπὶς μὴ καταβληθῇ γένους

1251 ἐν Hermann: εἰ L

**HERACLES**

I mean to die and to return to the Underworld from which
I have just come.

**THESEUS**

This is spoken like some ordinary person.

**HERACLES**

You give me advice, untouched by grief yourself.

**THESEUS**

Is this Heracles the all-enduring who speaks?

**HERACLES**

This much I have *not* endured: there must be a limit to
suffering.

**THESEUS**

Is this humanity's great benefactor and friend?

**HERACLES**

Humanity can do nothing for me: Hera is in control.

**THESEUS**

Greece will not put up with your dying in folly.

**HERACLES**

Listen then so that I may reply to your admonitions. I shall
demonstrate to you that my life, both now and of old, is not
worth living.

First my origins: my father had killed the old father of
my mother, Alcmene, and was guilty of bloodshed at the
time he married her. When the foundation of a family is

---

1256 νουθετήσεις Pierson: νουθεσίας L

ὀρθῶς, ἀνάγκη δυστυχεῖν τοὺς ἐκγόνους.
Ζεὺς δ', ὅστις ὁ Ζεύς, πολέμιόν μ' ἐγείνατο
Ἥρᾳ (σὺ μέντοι μηδὲν ἀχθεσθῇς, γέρον·
1265 πατέρα γὰρ ἀντὶ Ζηνὸς ἡγοῦμαι σ' ἐγώ),
ἔτ' ἐν γάλακτί τ' ὄντι γοργωποὺς ὄφεις
ἐπεισέφρησε σπαργάνοισι τοῖς ἐμοῖς
ἡ τοῦ Διὸς σύλλεκτρος, ὡς ὀλοίμεθα.
ἐπεὶ δὲ σαρκὸς περιβόλαι' ἐκτησάμην
1270 ἡβῶντα, μόχθους οὓς ἔτλην τί δεῖ λέγειν;
ποίους ποτ' ἢ λέοντας ἢ τρισωμάτους
Τυφῶνας ἢ Γίγαντας ἢ τετρασκελῆ
κενταυροπληθῆ πόλεμον οὐκ ἐξήνυσα;
τήν τ' ἀμφίκρανον καὶ παλιμβλαστῆ κύνα
1275 ὕδραν φονεύσας μυρίων τ' ἄλλων πόνων
διῆλθον ἀγέλας κἀς νεκροὺς ἀφικόμην,
Ἅιδου πυλωρὸν κύνα τρίκρανον ἐς φάος
ὅπως πορεύσαιμ' ἐντολαῖς Εὐρυσθέως.
    τὸν λοίσθιον δὲ τόνδ' ἔτλην τάλας πόνον,
1280 παιδοκτονήσας δῶμα θριγκῶσαι κακοῖς.
ἥκω δ' ἀνάγκης ἐς τόδ'· οὔτ' ἐμαῖς φίλαις
Θήβαις ἐνοικεῖν ὅσιον· ἢν δὲ καὶ μένω,
ἐς ποῖον ἱερὸν ἢ πανήγυριν φίλων
εἶμ'; οὐ γὰρ ἄτας εὐπροσηγόρους ἔχω.
1285 ἀλλ' Ἄργος ἔλθω; πῶς, ἐπεὶ φεύγω πάτραν;
φέρ' ἀλλ' ἐς ἄλλην δή τιν' ὁρμήσω πόλιν,
κἄπειθ' ὑποβλεπώμεθ' ὡς ἐγνωσμένοι,
γλώσσης πικροῖς κέντροισι †κλῃδουχούμενοι†·
Οὐχ οὗτος ὁ Διός, ὃς τέκν' ἔκτεινέν ποτε

not laid straight, the descendants are fated to suffer ill fortune. Then Zeus—whoever Zeus is—begot me as an object of Hera's hatred (no, old sir, do not take offense: I regard you, not Zeus, as my father), and while I was still a suckling babe in swaddling clothes Zeus's wife sent fierce serpents to destroy me. But what need to mention all the labors I endured once the firm muscles of youth had clothed my young body? What lions, what three-bodied Typhons, what Giants did I not slay, what throngs of four-legged Centaurs did I not make war against? I killed the beast whose many heads on all sides grow back again, the hydra, and when I had undergone throngs of countless other labors I went down to the dead to fetch Hades' gatekeeper, the three-headed dog, up to the light in obedience to the commands of Eurystheus.

But the last labor I endured was this, to kill my children and put the capstone of disaster upon my house. This is the hard compulsion into which I have come: I cannot live in my beloved Thebes without committing impiety; and if I do stay, what temple can I enter, what gathering of friends may I join? For the ruin I have about me is one with no lovely name. Shall I then go to Argos? It cannot be: I am in exile from my country. But shall I then set off for some other city? And after this shall I be looked at askance as infamous, kept in check by the painful barbs of people's tongues? "Is this not the son of Zeus, who once killed his

---

1272 τετρασκελῆ Reiske: -εῖς L
1279 πόνον Reiske: φόνον L
1283 φίλων] θεῶν F. W. Schmidt
1287 κεχρωσμένοι Herwerden
1288 κηλιδούμενοι Hermann: v. delere paene malit West

1290 δάμαρτά τ᾽; οὐ γῆς τῆσδ᾽ ἀποφθαρήσεται;
[κεκλημένῳ δὲ φωτὶ μακαρίῳ ποτὲ
αἱ μεταβολαὶ λυπηρόν· ᾧ δ᾽ ἀεὶ κακῶς
ἔστ᾽, οὐδὲν ἀλγεῖ συγγενῶς δύστηνος ὤν.]
    ἐς τοῦτο δ᾽ ἥξειν συμφορᾶς οἶμαί ποτε·
1295 φωνὴν γὰρ ἥσει χθὼν ἀπεννέπουσά με
μὴ θιγγάνειν γῆς καὶ θάλασσα μὴ περᾶν
πηγαί τε ποταμῶν, καὶ τὸν ἁρματήλατον
Ἰξίον᾽ ἐν δεσμοῖσιν ἐκμιμήσομαι.
[καὶ ταῦτ᾽ ἄριστα, μηδέν᾽ Ἑλλήνων μ᾽ ὁρᾶν,
1300 ἐν οἷσιν εὐτυχοῦντες ἦμεν ὄλβιοι.]
τί δῆτά με ζῆν δεῖ; τί κέρδος ἕξομεν
βίον γ᾽ ἀχρεῖον ἀνόσιον κεκτημένοι;
χορευέτω δὴ Ζηνὸς ἡ κλεινὴ δάμαρ
κρούους᾽ Ὀλύμπου δῖον ἀρβύλῃ πέδον.
1305 ἔπραξε γὰρ βούλησιν ἣν ἐβούλετο
ἄνδρ᾽ Ἑλλάδος τὸν πρῶτον αὐτοῖσιν βάθροις
ἄνω κάτω στρέψασα. τοιαύτῃ θεῷ
τίς ἂν προσεύχοιθ᾽; ἣ γυναικὸς οὕνεκα
λέκτρων φθονοῦσα Ζηνὶ τοὺς εὐεργέτας
1310 Ἑλλάδος ἀπώλεσ᾽ οὐδὲν ὄντας αἰτίους.

ΘΗΣΕΥΣ
οὐκ ἔστιν ἄλλου δαιμόνων ἀγὼν ὅδε
ἢ τῆς Διὸς δάμαρτος· εὖ τόδ᾽ αἰσθάνῃ.
<ἀλλ᾽ εἰ θανεῖν δεῖ τῶνδ᾽ ἕκατι χρὴ σκοπεῖν·

1291-3 del. Wilamowitz
1299-1300 del. Wilamowitz

440

wife and his children? Will he not clear off from this coun-
try?" [For a man who has once borne the name of fortu-
nate, change is painful. The man whose life has been al-
ways bad feels no pain since he is innately wretched.]

I think that one day my misfortunes will reach this
point: the earth will break into speech forbidding me to
touch the ground, and the sea and the streams of rivers will
forbid me to cross them, and I shall be like Ixion in chains,
turned upon his wheel.[37] [It is best that none of the Greeks
see me where I once enjoyed good fortune.] Why then
should I live? What advantage shall I have if I possess an
accursed and useless life? So let Zeus's glorious wife dance
for joy, striking the bright floor of Olympus with her slip-
per! She has brought to fulfilment the desire she conceived
and has utterly overturned, foundations and all, the best
man in Greece! To such a goddess what man would offer
prayer? Because she felt grudging ill will toward Zeus for
his love of a mortal woman, she destroyed a man who had
benefited Greece, though he was guiltless.

### THESEUS

The contest we see here was with no other power than
Hera, Zeus's wife. You have marked this well. ⟨But you
should consider whether you must die on this account.

---

[37] Ixion was the first to shed kindred blood and also attempted
to rape Hera. His punishment in the Underworld is to be bound
upon a wheel.

---

1304 Ὀλύμπου Heath: Ὀλυμπίου L    δῖον Nauck: Ζηνὸς
L    πέδον Brodaeus: πόδα L
1313 ante h. v. lac. indic. Victorius

ἀκήρατον γὰρ εἰ βροτοῖς ἄγειν βίον
θεοὶ διδοῖεν, σοὶ μόνῳ δ' ἐφθαρμένον,
διεργάσασθαι σαυτὸν οὐκ ἐς ἀμβολὰς›
παραινέσαιμ' ἂν μᾶλλον ἢ πάσχειν κακῶς.
οὐδεὶς δὲ θνητῶν ταῖς τύχαις ἀκήρατος,
1315  οὐ θεῶν, ἀοιδῶν εἴπερ οὐ ψευδεῖς λόγοι.
οὐ λέκτρ' ἐν ἀλλήλοισιν, ὧν οὐδεὶς νόμος,
συνῆψαν; οὐ δεσμοῖσι διὰ τυραννίδα
πατέρας ἐκηλίδωσαν; ἀλλ' οἰκοῦσ' ὅμως
Ὄλυμπον ἠνέσχοντό θ' ἡμαρτηκότες.
1320  καίτοι τί φήσεις, εἰ σὺ μὲν θνητὸς γεγὼς
φέρεις ὑπέρφευ τὰς τύχας, θεοὶ δὲ μή;

Θήβας μὲν οὖν ἔκλειπε τοῦ νόμου χάριν,
ἕπου δ' ἅμ' ἡμῖν πρὸς πόλισμα Παλλάδος.
ἐκεῖ χέρας σὰς ἁγνίσας μιάσματος
1325  δόμους τε δώσω χρημάτων τ' ἐμῶν μέρος.
ἃ δ' ἐκ πολιτῶν δῶρ' ἔχω σώσας κόρους
δὶς ἑπτά, ταῦρον Κνώσιον κατακτανών,
σοὶ ταῦτα δώσω. πανταχοῦ δέ μοι χθονὸς
τεμένη δέδασται· ταῦτ' ἐπωνομασμένα
1330  σέθεν τὸ λοιπὸν ἐκ βροτῶν κεκλήσεται
ζῶντος· θανόντα δ', εὖτ' ἂν εἰς Ἅιδου μόλῃς,
θυσίαισι λαΐνοισί τ' ἐξογκώμασιν
τίμιον ἀνάξει πᾶσ' Ἀθηναίων πόλις.
καλὸς γὰρ ἀστοῖς στέφανος Ἑλλήνων ὕπο

1316 λέκτρ' ἐν Lobeck: λέκτρα τ' L    1317 τυραννίδα Dobree: -ίδας L    1321 στένεις Musgrave: fort. ψέγεις
1331 θανόντα Dobree: -τος L

Now if the gods allowed mortals to live lives untouched
and to you alone they gave a tainted existence, ⟩ I would
advise you ⟨to die at once⟩ rather than to suffer ill treat-
ment. But no mortal is untainted by fortune, and no god
either, if the poets' stories are true. Have they not lain with
each other in unlawful unions?[38] Have they not dishonored
their fathers with chains in order to become king?[39] But
for all that they continue to live on Olympus and endure
their sinful state. But what will your defense be if you, a
mortal, find fault so excessively with your fortune while the
gods do not?

For the law's sake, then, leave Thebes and come with
me to the citadel of Pallas Athena. There I shall cleanse
your hands from this taint and give you a home and a
portion of my wealth. I shall give you the gifts I received
from my fellow citizens for killing the bull of Knossos and
saving the lives of the fourteen children.[40] All about the
country allotments of land have been given to me. Mortals
will henceforth call these yours for as long as you live. And
when you die and go to the Underworld, the whole city of
Athens will honor you with sacrifices and with massive
temples of stone. For it will be a glorious achievement for

[38] Most divine amours involve mortals, and in these the gods
do not commit adultery "with each other." But Theseus may have
in mind Ares' adultery with Aphrodite (*Odyssey* 8.266-366).

[39] Kronos, Zeus's father, was dethroned by him and put in
chains.

[40] Minos had demanded a yearly tribute of seven boys and
seven girls to be given to the Minotaur. One of Theseus' first
exploits was to volunteer to be one of the seven boys in order to
kill the monster.

EURIPIDES

1335 ἄνδρ' ἐσθλὸν ὠφελοῦντας εὐκλείας τυχεῖν.
κἀγὼ χάριν σοι τῆς ἐμῆς σωτηρίας
τήνδ' ἀντιδώσω· νῦν γὰρ εἶ χρεῖος φίλων.
[θεοὶ δ' ὅταν τιμῶσιν, οὐδὲν δεῖ φίλων·
ἅλις γὰρ ὁ θεὸς ὠφελῶν, ὅταν θέλῃ.]

ΗΡΑΚΛΗΣ

1340 οἴμοι· πάρεργα ⟨μὲν⟩ τάδ' ἔστ' ἐμῶν κακῶν,
ἐγὼ δὲ τοὺς θεοὺς οὔτε λέκτρ' ἃ μὴ θέμις
στέργειν νομίζω δεσμά τ' ἐξάπτειν χεροῖν
οὔτ' ἠξίωσα πώποτ' οὔτε πείσομαι
οὐδ' ἄλλον ἄλλου δεσπότην πεφυκέναι.

1345 δεῖται γὰρ ὁ θεός, εἴπερ ἔστ' ὀρθῶς θεός,
οὐδενός· ἀοιδῶν οἵδε δύστηνοι λόγοι.

ἐσκεψάμην δὲ καίπερ ἐν κακοῖσιν ὤν,
μὴ δειλίαν ὄφλω τιν' ἐκλιπὼν φάος·
ταῖς συμφοραῖς γὰρ ὅστις οὐχ ὑφίσταται

1350 οὐδ' ἀνδρὸς ἂν δύναιθ' ὑποστῆναι βέλος
ἐγκαρτερήσας θάνατον· εἶμι δ' ἐς πόλιν
τὴν σήν, χάριν τε μυρίαν δώρων ἔχω.
ἀτὰρ πόνων δὴ μυρίων ἐγευσάμην,
ὧν οὔτ' ἀπεῖπον οὐδέν οὔτ' ἀπ' ὀμμάτων

1355 ἔσταξα πηγάς, οὐδ' ἂν ᾠόμην ποτὲ
ἐς τοῦθ' ἱκέσθαι, δάκρυ' ἀπ' ὀμμάτων βαλεῖν.
νῦν δ', ὡς ἔοικε, τῇ τύχῃ δουλευτέον.

1338–9 del. Nauck    1340 ⟨μὲν⟩ ed. Brubach.
1346 δυστήνων Naber
1351 ἐγκαρτερήσας Kirchhoff: -ήσω L, quo accepto βίοτον
pro θάνατον Wecklein, πότμον Heimsoeth
1352 μυρίαν Wakefield: μυρίων L
444

the citizens in the eyes of Greece to win fair renown by doing good service to a noble hero. And this will also be my repayment to you for saving my life: for at present you stand in need of friends. [When the gods honor us, we do not need friends. The help of a god, when he wants to give it, is enough.]

## HERACLES

Ah me! This is, to be sure, a diversion from my misfortunes, but I do not think, have never believed, and will never be convinced that the gods have illicit love affairs or bind each other with chains or that one is master of another. A god, if he is truly a god, needs nothing. These are the wretched tales of the poets.[41]

But in my misfortune I have taken thought that I may not deserve the name of coward by dying. The man who does not withstand misfortune could not withstand the weapon of a human foe, braving death. I will go to your city, and I feel immense gratitude for your gifts. Yet countless were the labors I have had. Not a single one have I shirked, nor did my eyes weep. I did not think it would ever come to this, that I should shed tears. But now, it seems, I must be the slave of circumstance.

[41] Heracles' words seem to echo the radical critique of Olympian polytheism made by the Ionian philosopher Xenophanes, who criticized the anthropomorphic conception of the gods and recommended a purely spiritual one. Such a view, however, contradicts the premises of the play, for it is Hera's jealousy that destroys Heracles. Indeed Heracles reverts to the mythical view of his fate at the end of the speech (1392-3; cf. 1263-8, 1303-10).

εἶέν· γεραιέ, τὰς ἐμὰς φυγὰς ὁρᾷς,
ὁρᾷς δὲ παίδων ὄντα μ' αὐθέντην ἐμῶν·
1360 δὸς τούσδε τύμβῳ καὶ περίστειλον νεκροὺς
δακρύοισι τιμῶν (ἐμὲ γὰρ οὐκ ἐᾷ νόμος)
πρὸς στέρν' ἐρείσας μητρὶ δούς τ' ἐς ἀγκάλας,
κοινωνίαν δύστηνον, ἣν ἐγὼ τάλας
διώλεσ' ἄκων. γῇ δ' ἐπὴν κρύψῃς νεκρούς,
1365 οἴκει πόλιν τήνδ' ἀθλίως μὲν ἀλλ' ὅμως
[ψυχὴν βιάζου τἀμὰ συμφέρειν κακά].
    ὦ τέκν', ὁ φύσας καὶ τεκὼν ὑμᾶς πατὴρ
ἀπώλεσ', οὐδ' ὤνασθε τῶν ἐμῶν καλῶν,
ἁγὼ παρεσκεύαζον ἐκμοχθῶν βίου
1370 εὔκλειαν ὑμῖν, πατρὸς ἀπόλαυσιν καλήν.
σέ τ' οὐχ ὁμοίως, ὦ τάλαιν', ἀπώλεσα
ὥσπερ σὺ τἀμὰ λέκτρ' ἔσῳζες ἀσφαλῶς,
μακρὰς διαντλοῦσ' ἐν δόμοις οἰκουρίας.
    οἴμοι δάμαρτος καὶ τέκνων, οἴμοι δ' ἐμοῦ,
1375 ὡς ἀθλίως πέπραγα κἀποζεύγνυμαι
τέκνων γυναικός τ'· ὦ λυγραὶ φιλημάτων
τέρψεις, λυγραὶ δὲ τῶνδ' ὅπλων κοινωνίαι.
ἀμηχανῶ γὰρ πότερ' ἔχω τάδ' ἢ μεθῶ,
ἃ πλευρὰ τἀμὰ προσπίτνοντ' ἐρεῖ τάδε·
1380 Ἡμῖν τέκν' εἷλες καὶ δάμαρθ'· ἡμᾶς ἔχεις
παιδοκτόνους σούς. εἶτ' ἐγὼ τάδ' ὠλέναις
οἴσω; τί φάσκων; ἀλλὰ γυμνωθεὶς ὅπλων
ξὺν οἷς τὰ κάλλιστ' ἐξέπραξ' ἐν Ἑλλάδι

So. Old father, you see that I am in exile, and that I am my own children's murderer. Give them a burial and the proper clothes, honor them with your tears (for by law I may not do so) and put them in their mother's embrace against her breast in a fellowship of misfortune, the mother I killed, unhappy man that I am, unwittingly. When you have buried them, continue to live in this city: it will be unhappy for you but do it still. [Force your soul to bear my misfortunes.]

My children, the father who begot you has killed you. You did not reap the benefit—a lovely reaping it would have been from a father—of my glorious deeds, deeds meant to work a life of glory for you. And you, dear wife, how different was my destruction of you from your faithful keeping of my marriage bed as you watched over the house in my long absence!

Alas for my wife and my children, but alas for myself, for my unhappy state, my wretched separation from my children and my wife! How painful the pleasure of kissing you, how painful that I still have about me these weapons! I do not know whether I should keep them or let them go, since they will hang at my flanks and say to me, "By means of us you killed your children and your wife: us, the slayers of your children, you still keep." Shall I then carry them on my arm? What will be my plea? Or shall I strip myself of the weapons with whose aid I performed my glorious exploits in Greece, put myself at the mercy of my enemies,

---

1363 fort. οὖς      1366 del. Nauck
1367 καὶ Nauck: χὠ L
1369 βίου Dobree: βίᾳ L

447

ἐχθροῖς ἐμαυτὸν ὑποβαλὼν αἰσχρῶς θάνω;
1385 οὐ λειπτέον τάδ', ἀθλίως δὲ σωστέον.

ἔν μοί τι, Θησεῦ, σύγκαμ'· ἀγρίου κυνὸς
κόμιστρ' ἐς Ἄργος συγκατάστησον μολών,
λύπῃ τι παίδων μὴ πάθω μονούμενος.

ὦ γαῖα Κάδμου πᾶς τε Θηβαῖος λεώς,
1390 κείρασθε, συμπενθήσατ', ἔλθετ' ἐς τάφον
παίδων· ἅπαντας δ' ἐνὶ λόγῳ πενθήσετε
νεκρούς τε κἀμέ· πάντες ἐξολώλαμεν
Ἥρας μιᾷ πληγέντες ἄθλιοι τύχῃ.

ΘΗΣΕΥΣ

ἀνίστασ', ὦ δύστηνε· δακρύων ἅλις.

ΗΡΑΚΛΗΣ

1395 οὐκ ἂν δυναίμην· ἄρθρα γὰρ πέπηγέ μου.

ΘΗΣΕΥΣ

καὶ τοὺς σθένοντας γὰρ καθαιροῦσιν τύχαι.

ΗΡΑΚΛΗΣ

φεῦ·
αὑτοῦ γενοίμην πέτρος ἀμνήμων κακῶν.

ΘΗΣΕΥΣ

παῦσαι· δίδου δὲ χεῖρ' ὑπηρέτῃ φίλῳ.

ΗΡΑΚΛΗΣ

ἀλλ' αἷμα μὴ σοῖς ἐξομόρξωμαι πέπλοις.

1386 ἀγρίου Wakefield: ἀθλίου L
1391 ἅπαντας Hermann: -ες L     πενθήσετε Murray: -
σατε L

448

and thus meet a disgraceful death? I must not let them go
but must in misery keep them.

Do me one service, Theseus: come and help me to
bring the savage dog back to Argos so that I may not, in
grief for the children, suffer some misfortune in my lone-
liness.

O land of Cadmus and all you people of Thebes, cut
your hair in mourning with me, attend the burial of my
children! For all of us at once will you mourn, for the dead
and for me! We have all been miserably destroyed struck
down by a single blow from Hera.

THESEUS
Get up, unhappy man: enough of weeping!

HERACLES
I cannot: my joints are frozen fast.

THESEUS
Yes, for even the mighty are brought low by misfortune.

HERACLES
Ah! How I wish I might here and now become a rock,
insensible of calamity!

THESEUS
No more! Give your hand to your friend who would serve
you.

HERACLES
But let me not wipe blood off upon your garments.

---

1393 ἄθλιοι Nauck: ἀθλίῳ L
1394 δακρύων Nauck: δ- δ' L

ΘΗΣΕΥΣ

1400 ἔκμασσε, φείδου μηδέν· οὐκ ἀναίνομαι.

ΗΡΑΚΛΗΣ

παίδων στερηθεὶς παῖδ᾽ ὅπως ἔχω σ᾽ ἐμόν.

ΘΗΣΕΥΣ

δίδου δέρῃ σὴν χεῖρ᾽, ὁδηγήσω δ᾽ ἐγώ.

ΗΡΑΚΛΗΣ

ζεῦγός γε φίλιον· ἄτερος δὲ δυστυχής.
ὦ πρέσβυ, τοιόνδ᾽ ἄνδρα χρὴ κτᾶσθαι φίλον.

ΑΜΦΙΤΡΥΩΝ

1405 ἡ γὰρ τεκοῦσα τόνδε πατρὶς εὔτεκνος.

ΗΡΑΚΛΗΣ

Θησεῦ, πάλιν με στρέψον ὡς ἴδω τέκνα.

ΘΗΣΕΥΣ

ὡς δὴ τί; φίλτρον τοῦτ᾽ ἔχων ῥᾴων ἔσῃ;

ΗΡΑΚΛΗΣ

ποθῶ, πατρός τε στέρνα προσθέσθαι θέλω.

ΑΜΦΙΤΡΥΩΝ

ἰδοὺ τάδ᾽, ὦ παῖ· τἀμὰ γὰρ σπεύδεις φίλα.

ΘΗΣΕΥΣ

1410 οὕτω πόνων σῶν οὐκέτι μνήμην ἔχεις;

ΗΡΑΚΛΗΣ

ἅπαντ᾽ ἐλάσσω κεῖνα τῶνδ᾽ ἔτλην κακά.

1403 post h. v. lac. unius v. indic. Wilamowitz

## HERACLES

**THESEUS**

Wipe it off, do not spare me! I feel no disgust.

**HERACLES**

Having lost my sons, I regard you as my son.

**THESEUS**

Put your arm about my neck and I shall lead the way.

**HERACLES**

Two friends in harness, one of them in ruin. Old father, such is the friend one ought to make.

**AMPHITRYON**

Yes: the land that bore him breeds good offspring.

**HERACLES**

Turn me about again, Theseus, so that I may see my children.

**THESEUS**

What for? Will having this token of love make you easier?

**HERACLES**

That is what I long for. I also want to embrace my father.

**AMPHITRYON**

(*embracing him*) Here is what you ask for. What you wish I wish too.

**THESEUS**

Are you so forgetful of your labors?

**HERACLES**

All their misery is less than my present woe.

1408 τε Musgrave: γε L
1410–7 suspectos habet Diggle, post 1253 trai. Bond

# EURIPIDES

ΘΗΣΕΥΣ

εἴ σ' ὄψεταί τις θῆλυν ὄντ' οὐκ αἰνέσει.

ΗΡΑΚΛΗΣ

ζῶ σοι ταπεινός; ἀλλὰ πρόσθεν οὐ δοκῶ.

ΘΗΣΕΥΣ

ἄγαν γ'· ὁ κλεινὸς Ἡρακλῆς οὐκ εἶ νοσῶν.

ΗΡΑΚΛΗΣ

1415   σὺ ποῖος ἦσθα νέρθεν ἐν κακοῖσιν ὤν;

ΘΗΣΕΥΣ

ὡς ἐς τὸ λῆμα παντὸς ἦν ἥσσων ἀνήρ.

ΗΡΑΚΛΗΣ

πῶς οὖν †ἔτ' εἴπῃς† ὅτι συνέσταλμαι κακοῖς;

ΘΗΣΕΥΣ

πρόβαινε.

ΗΡΑΚΛΗΣ

χαῖρ', ὦ πρέσβυ.

ΑΜΦΙΤΡΥΩΝ

καὶ σύ μοι, τέκνον.

ΗΡΑΚΛΗΣ

θάφθ' ὥσπερ εἶπον παῖδας.

ΑΜΦΙΤΡΥΩΝ

ἐμὲ δὲ τίς, τέκνον;

1413 πρόσθεν οὐ Jacobs: προσθεῖναι L
1414 οὐκ εἶ νοσῶν Wilamowitz: ποῦ κεῖνος ὤν L

452

# HERACLES

**THESEUS**

If someone sees you being womanish, he will disapprove.

**HERACLES**

Is my life a lowly one in your eyes? It was not so before, I think.

**THESEUS**

Lowly indeed. In your trouble you are not the famous Heracles.

**HERACLES**

And what was your behavior when you were in trouble in the Underworld?

**THESEUS**

In pride I was every man's inferior.

**HERACLES**

How then can you say that I am humbled by misfortune?

**THESEUS**

March on!

**HERACLES**

Farewell, old father!

**AMPHITRYON**

Farewell to you, my son!

**HERACLES**

Bury my children, as I asked you.

**AMPHITRYON**

But who will bury me?

---

1417 ἔμ᾽ εἶπας Paley

# EURIPIDES

### ΗΡΑΚΛΗΣ

1420 ἐγώ.

### ΑΜΦΙΤΡΥΩΝ

πότ᾽ ἐλθών;

### ΗΡΑΚΛΗΣ

ἡνίκ᾽ ἂν θάνῃς, πάτερ.

### [ΑΜΦΙΤΡΥΩΝ

πῶς;

### ΗΡΑΚΛΗΣ

εἰς Ἀθήνας πέμψομαι Θηβῶν ἄπο.]
ἀλλ᾽ ἐσκόμιζε τέκνα δυσκόμιστ᾽ ἄχη·
ἡμεῖς δ᾽ ἀναλώσαντες αἰσχύναις δόμον
Θησεῖ πανώλεις ἑψόμεσθ᾽ ἐφολκίδες.
1425 ὅστις δὲ πλοῦτον ἢ σθένος μᾶλλον φίλων
ἀγαθῶν πεπᾶσθαι βούλεται, κακῶς φρονεῖ.

### ΧΟΡΟΣ

στείχομεν οἰκτροὶ καὶ πολύκλαυτοι,
τὰ μέγιστα φίλων ὀλέσαντες.

1420 θάνῃς, πάτερ Bond (θάνῃς) et Diggle: θάψῃς τέκνα L
1421 del. Diggle (1419-21 iam del. Conradt, fort. recte)
1422 δυσκόμιστ᾽ ἄχη Wilamowitz: δυσκόμιστα γῇ L

HERACLES
I will.

AMPHITRYON
When will you return?

HERACLES
After your death.

[AMPHITRYON
How?

HERACLES
I shall have your remains brought from Thebes to Athens.]
Convey the children indoors, then, though they are a grief
hard to convey. I, who have destroyed my house in shame,
will in my utter misery follow Theseus like a boat under
tow. Whoever desires to get wealth or strength rather than
good friends is a fool.

*The* eccyclema *wheels the bodies of Megara and the chil-
dren back into the house. Exit* HERACLES *and* THESEUS *by
Eisodos B and* AMPHITRYON *into the house.*

CHORUS LEADER
We go now with pity and in tears: we have lost our greatest
friend.

*Exit* CHORUS *by Eisodos A.*

*Composed in ZephGreek and ZephText by*
*Technologies 'N Typography, Merrimac, Massachusetts.*
*Printed in Great Britain by St Edmundsbury Press Ltd,*
*Bury St Edmunds, Suffolk, on acid-free paper.*
*Bound by Hunter & Foulis Ltd, Edinburgh, Scotland.*